Discordant Comrades

Identities and Loyalties
on the South African Left

Allison Drew

Ashgate

Aldershot • Burlington USA • Singapore • Sydney

Published by

Ashgate Publishing Ltd
Gower House, Croft Road,
Aldershot, Hampshire GU11 3HR
England

Ashgate Publishing Company
131 Main Road
Burlington, Vermont 05401–5600
USA

Ashgate website: http://www.ashgate.com

ISBN 0 7546 0195 1

100213776 X

British Library Cataloguing-in-Publication Data
Drew, Allison
  Discordant Comrades: Identities and Loyalties on the South African Left
  1. Socialism—South Africa—History—20th century. 2. Labour
  movement—South Africa—History—20th century. 3. South Africa—
  Politics and government—20th century. I. Title.
  320.5'31'0968

US Library of Congress Cataloging-in-Publication Data
The Library of Congress Catalog Card Number is pre-assigned as: 00–102169

T

This volume is printed on acid-free paper.

Typeset by Book Production Services, London
Printed and bound in Great Britain by MPG Books Ltd, Bodmin, Cornwall

Contents

Acknowledgements

Many people have helped me over the years in the preparation of this long manuscript. Research for this book has been carried out at libraries and universities in South Africa, Britain, the United States and Russia, and I would like to thank the staff of the following institutions: in South Africa, the Historical Papers Library at the University of the Witwatersrand, the Manuscripts and Archives Department of the University of Cape Town Libraries, the Mayibuye Centre Historical Papers Archive at the University of the Western Cape, and the South African Reference Library in Cape Town; in Britain, the Borthwick Institute of Historical Research at the University of York, the British Library in London, the Brynmor Jones Library at the University of Hull, the Institute of Commonwealth Studies Library and the School of Oriental and African Studies Library at the University of London, the Kingston upon Hull Local Studies Library, the Modern Records Centre at the University of Warwick Library, the National Museum of Labour History in Manchester, the Public Records Office at Kew, and the Working Class Movement Library in Salford; and in the United States, the Hoover Institution Archives at Stanford University, the Houghton Library at Harvard University, the Prometheus Research Library in New York City, the Special Collections at the University Research Library, University of California, Los Angeles, and the Manuscripts and Archives office at Yale University Library.

My research in Moscow was possible thanks to grants from the British Academy and the Lipman-Miliband Trust. The latter, and the Barry Amiel and Norman Melburn Trust, also provided grants to help with the manuscript's production. I am very grateful to a number of Russian colleagues for their help. Professor Vladimir Shubin and the staff at the Institute for African Studies helped me to find my way around Moscow. Dr Kirill Anderson and the staff at the Russian Centre for the Conservation and Study of Modern History Records provided a congenial working environment and patiently assisted me with my queries. Professor A. B. Davidson of Moscow State University and Professor Valentin Gorodnov of the Institute of Universal History discussed various aspects of this research with me. Dennis Pennington assisted me as translator and interpreter during my sojourns in Moscow.

Ned Alpers has shown continuing encouragement over the years, and Charlie van Gelderen has engaged me in many stimulating conversations about South African socialist history. Neville Alexander, Alex Callinicos, Ron Kieve, Lungisile Ntsebeza and John Saville read the entire draft and gave me many insightful comments. Ralph Saville prepared the index. Alec McAulay at Ashgate Publishing has been a very supportive editor. Most importantly, David Howell read endless drafts, engaged in endless discussions with me about the histories of the South African and British socialist movements and has helped me to appreciate the role of contingency in history – and in life. Any errors are, of course, my own responsibility.

List of abbreviations

AAC	All African Convention
AFTU	African Federation of Trade Unions
AMWU	African Mine Workers' Union
ANC	African National Congress
Anti-CAD	Anti-Coloured Affairs Department
APO	African People's (formerly Political) Organisation
CLSA	Communist League of South Africa
CNETU	Council of Non-European Trade Unions
Comintern	Communist International
CPGB	Communist Party of Great Britain
CPSA	Communist Party of South Africa
DPC	District Party Committee
ECCI	Executive Committee of the Communist International
FNETU	Federation of Non-European Trade Unions
GWU	Garment Workers' Union
Gezerd	*Gezelshaft far Erd*
IFTU	International Federation of Trade Unions
ICU	Industrial and Commercial Workers' Union
ILP	Independent Labour Party
ISCOR	Iron and Steel Corporation
IWA	Industrial Workers of Africa
IWW	Industrial Workers of the World
KUTVU	Eastern Workers Communist University
NEC	National Executive Committee
NEUF	Non-European United Front
NEUM	Non-European Unity Movement
NLL	National Liberation League
NRC	Natives Representative Council
PB	Political Bureau or Politburo
PTU	Progressive Trade Union group
RILU	Red International of Labour Unions
SAAEO	South African Association of Employees' Organisation
SAIF	South African Industrial Federation
SAMWU	South African Mine Workers' Union
SANNC	South African Native National Congress
SDF	Social Democratic Federation
SDP	Social Democratic Party
SLP	Socialist Labour Party
TARC	Train Apartheid Resistance Campaign
TUC	Trades Union Congress

Writing South African socialist history

South Africa's socialist movement has attracted little interest from scholars despite its prominence in the country's liberation struggle and in present-day politics. The dominant body of historical writing about the South African left has been by South African Communists or former Communists.[1] This Party historiography portrays the early years of South African socialism as a brief period of socialist experimentation in which the International Socialist League, a radical offshoot of the white South African Labour Party, took the initiative in forming a centralized socialist body that affiliated to the Communist International (Comintern) in 1921. The transition that led to the formation of the Communist Party of South Africa (CPSA) is seen as unproblematic. Jack and Ray Simons describe the CPSA as 'virtually a continuation of' the International Socialist League, a view reflected in Yusuf Dadoo's introduction to *South African Communists Speak*, a documentary history edited by Brian Bunting. Similarly, the disbanding of the CPSA in 1950, far from signalling the collapse of socialism as an autonomous political movement, is depicted by the Simonses as heralding the merger of the class and the national liberation struggles.[2]

Such teleological perspectives have been the bane of many socialist writings about socialist movements. This tendency stems, at least in part, from socialism's origins as a nineteenth-century progressive movement. Socialism has always been envisioned by its advocates as a transcendence of capitalism, whether by evolutionary or revolutionary means. As such, it bears the stigma of the nineteenth-century concept of linear historical progress.

This belief in the inevitability of progress, which infused the socialist movement, contained both scientific and ethical components. Along with teleological views went a quest for – if not an obsession with – the ideal of scientific truth. The scientific methods of the nineteenth century – methods of production and of analysis – made the discovery of truth seem feasible. Armed with a self-consciously scientific method, many nineteenth-century socialists set out in search of the socialist utopia; in the twentieth century, they tried to engineer social revolutions.

But science did not have a monopoly in its search for the truth or for the good life. Nineteenth-century socialism had an ethical component as well, arising out of moral repugnance for the excesses or evils of capitalism; socialism became intertwined with religion, as well as science. Like science, religion also aims at the truth, although its methods and conclusions differ fundamentally from those of science.

Interpreters of religion divine the future; interpreters of science make calculations and estimations about it. The influence of religion on socialism took different forms. In nineteenth-century Britain, a culture of ethical socialism was built on a Protestant tradition; ethical socialism held that understanding was available on an individual basis to all who made the appropriate moral choice. Even before the First World War many British socialists criticized continental European Marxism for having 'turned Marx's writings into liturgy' and for its 'various dogmatic tendencies'.[3] But it was through the Comintern, which existed from 1919 to 1943, that the interpretation of Marxism became ritualized in an elaborate hierarchical style reminiscent of Catholicism.[4]

Socialism, especially Marxist socialism, sees itself as an international movement in opposition to the international capitalist system. This self-image reached its apogee during the heyday of the Comintern, in the late 1920s and 1930s. Not only were socialists around the world bedazzled by the Russian Revolution of 1917 that led to the Comintern's formation. The failure of the revolution to spread to other countries enhanced the status and the power of Russian Communists in the Comintern. The vulnerability of many Communist Parties in the face of setbacks made them susceptible to the imposition of doctrine from above.[5]

The Comintern set itself up as the supreme authority on and interpreter of Marxism. Ironically, although scientific socialists generally saw themselves as opponents of religion, officials of the Comintern's Executive Committee styled themselves as Marxism's high priests – interpreters of doctrine that would guarantee the salvation of socialism in life after capitalism. Truth was confirmed not through individual conscience but by reference to the text – the word became paramount over the feeling. Moscow became the 'Socialist Vatican', one British socialist complained, 'issuing Bulls and Pronunciamentos on the Gospel according to St Lenin'.[6]

As the Comintern's policies oscillated, especially in the late 1920s and the 1930s, its officials strove to ensure that the leadership of the local Communist Parties accepted its ultimate authority. For historical reasons, South African socialism has been particularly porous to international influences. In part this reflected the predominantly foreign origins of the first generation of socialists, many of whom were Eastern European immigrants. But it also reflected the lack of a social-democratic tradition in South Africa, not to mention any other established socialist perspective. Given this absence, the Comintern inevitably became the measure by which South African socialists judged themselves and each other. South African Communists were awed by the Comintern's apparent theoretical mastery and political accomplishments. They identified Moscow as the headquarters of their international movement. This was not peculiar to the CPSA, even if their acceptance of Moscow's authority took, at times, a more extreme form than in many other countries. The reification of imported doctrine and the lack of confidence in their own theoretical ability reflected the particularly difficult conditions under which South African Communists and other socialists worked.[7]

While the opening of the Comintern Archives has provoked stimulating debates and reassessments by historians of socialist movements around the world, the CPSA has so far escaped such scrutiny. The two main works dealing with the relationship of the Comintern and its South African affiliate are *S. P. Bunting* by Eddie Roux and *Class and Colour in South Africa* by Jack and Ray Simons. Roux had already withdrawn from the CPSA by the time he picked up his pen to write his biography of Sidney Bunting, one of the Party's founding members. Disillusioned by the experiences of the CPSA in the late 1920s and 1930s and ashamed of his own role in betraying Sidney Bunting, his comrade and political mentor, Roux portrayed the CPSA as the puppet of the Comintern. In this respect, his work falls within a school of thought that sees the Comintern as the dominating force over its national affiliates.

Jack and Ray Simons's work, by contrast, was written in part as a critique of Roux, whom, they felt, overestimated the role of the Comintern while underestimating the responsibility of South African Communists for their own choices. Concerned with Communist activity on the ground, the Simonses took a bottom-up approach characteristic of an influential tradition of labour historiography.[8] Their perspective reflected both their generation and their location in Cape Town. Jack and Ray Simons were young adults in the late 1930s. They came of political age as the Second World War loomed on the horizon. This was a period when the Comintern began to lose contact with many of its affiliates, including the CPSA. It also coincided with the shift of the CPSA's headquarters from the troubled locale of Johannesburg to the more tranquil zone of Cape Town – a move that ruptured the established lines of contact between Moscow and Johannesburg. Thus, the Simonses missed the heyday of Comintern intervention in South Africa, and their perspective necessarily differed sharply from that of Roux. Nonetheless, their conclusion that through its affiliation to the Comintern the CPSA 'acquired the ideological equipment it needed to cope with the complexities of a society divided into antagonistic classes, races and nationalities', is remarkably naive.[9] There has been, subsequently, very little attempt to reassess the relationship between the Comintern and the CPSA or the Comintern's broader impact on the South African socialist movement.

There is little doubt that the Comintern had a destructive impact on the CPSA through its interventions. Most critically, it distorted the way South African socialists perceived and related to each other, both inside and outside the CPSA. Local Communists suffered from a divided loyalty, as rival individuals and factions appealed to the Comintern to buttress their own arguments against each other. They adopted the Comintern's demonization of socialists who criticized Moscow's attempt to control its affiliates and the political repression within the Soviet Union. South African socialism became rigidly bifurcated between Third International Communism and Trotskyism – a division that, because of the influence of socialist activists and of socialist ideas, came to permeate the entire national liberation movement. Moreover, both socialist tendencies saw themselves as the bearers of the true socialist ideal and the correct interpreters of Marxist doctrine.[10]

Contingency is the antithesis of teleology. When we look back at the earliest years of South African socialism without the distorting lens that prioritizes a particular type of organizational politics, this enables us to ask new questions about the trajectory and development of South African socialism. For instance, we can consider the questions of whether the marginalization of many of the various strands composing the early socialist movement was inevitable and, if not, why some strands became dominant. We can also speculate about the possibilities that may have been lost through their marginalization. Most importantly, history, rather than being seen in evolutionary terms as the inevitable progression to the best of all possible outcomes – the revolutionary party – can be seen as the product both of structural parameters, including the weight of the past, and of contingency. And it is only by recognizing the significance of historical contingency – that events did not have to unfold as they did – that we can envision the possibility of our role in changing history.

Notes

1. R. K. Cope, *Comrade Bill: The Life and Times of W. H. Andrews, Workers' Leader*, Cape Town: Stewart, 1944; Edward Roux, *S. P. Bunting: A Political Biography* [1944], Bellville: Mayibuye, 1993; Edward Roux, *Time Longer than Rope* [1948], 2nd edition, Wisconsin: University of Wisconsin, 1964; Eddie and Win Roux, *Rebel Pity: The Life of Eddie Roux*, London: Rex Collings, 1970; Jack and Ray Simons, *Class and Colour in South Africa 1850–1950* [1968], International Defence and Aid Fund for Southern Africa, 1983; A. Lerumo [Michael Harmel], *Fifty Fighting Years: The Communist Party of South Africa 1921–1971*, London: Inkululeko, 1971; Brian Bunting, *Moses Kotane: South African Revolutionary*, London: Inkululeko, 1975; Brian Bunting, ed., *South African Communists Speak: Documents from the History of the South African Communist Party 1915–1980*, London: Inkululeko, 1981. Other memoirs and biographical accounts of Communists or former Communists include, *inter alia*, Wilfred H. Harrison, *Memoirs of a Socialist in South Africa 1903–1947*, Cape Town, 1948; Sadie Forman and André Odendaal, eds, *A Trumpet from the Housetops: the Selected Writings of Lionel Forman*, London: Zed, Athens, OH: Ohio University, and Cape Town: David Philip and Bellville: Mayibuye, 1992; Pauline Podbrey, *White Girl in Search of the Party*, Pietermaritzburg: Hadeda, 1993; Joe Slovo, *Slovo: The Unfinished Autobiography*, Randburg: Ravan, 1995 and London: Hodder & Stoughton, 1996; Gillian Slovo, *Every Secret Thing: My Family, My Country*, London: Little, Brown, 1997; Alex La Guma, *Jimmy La Guma: A Biography*, ed. by Mohamed Adhikari, Cape Town: Friends of the South African Library, 1997. Baruch Hirson, *Revolutions in My Life*, Johannesburg: Witwatersrand University Press, 1995, recounts the political memoirs of a Trotskyist. See also Jonathan Grossman, 'Class Relations and the Policies of the Communist Party of South Africa, 1921–1950', PhD, University of Warwick, 1985; Baruch Hirson, *Yours for the Union: Class and Community Struggles in South Africa*, London: Zed and Johannesburg: Witwatersrand University, 1989; Robert Fine with Dennis Davis, *Beyond Apartheid: Labour and Liberation in South Africa*, London and Concord, MA: Pluto, 1991; and Sheridan Johns, *Raising the Red Flag: The International Socialist League and the Communist Party of South Africa, 1914–1932*, Bellville: Mayibuye, 1995.
2. Simons and Simons, *Class and Colour*, 261, 10; Bunting, ed., *South African Communists*

Speak, xv.

3. Stuart Macintyre, *A Proletarian Science: Marxism in Britain, 1917–1933*, Cambridge: Cambridge University, 1980, 220.

4. For accounts of the Comintern see, *inter alia*, Leon Trotsky, *The Third International After Lenin*, London: New Park, 1974; Fernando Claudin, *The Communist Movement: From Comintern to Cominform*, part 1, New York and London: Monthly Review, 1975; E. H. Carr, *The Twilight of Comintern, 1930–1935*, London and Basingstoke: Macmillan, 1982; and Kevin McDermott and Jeremy Agnew, *The Comintern: A History of International Communism from Lenin to Stalin*, Basingstoke and London: Macmillan, 1996.

5. Macintyre, *Proletarian Science*, 236.

6. Quoted in Macintyre, *Proletarian Science*, 222.

7. Macintyre, *Proletarian Science*, 233.

8. For an overview of these two perspectives see Andrew Thorpe, 'Comintern "Control" of the Communist Party of Great Britain, 1920–43', *English Historical Review*, June 1998, 637–62, 637–8.

9. Simons and Simons, *Class and Colour*, 620.

10. The Communist International was also known as the Third International. Leon Trotsky and his followers formed the Fourth International in September 1938.

Chapter 1

The international and national origins of South African socialism

South African socialists have faced a particularly arduous task. By comparison with most European countries, the socialist movement in South Africa developed relatively late, emerging in fits and starts in the early years of the twentieth century. Its development paralleled that of the urban working class, which, with the significant exception of the Western Cape, had only begun to emerge in the late nineteenth century. Moreover, unlike several European countries, South Africa lacked an indigenous socialist tradition. Its first socialists were foreign-born and its socialism, as a movement to transcend capitalism, was an imported doctrine. Its late development and its foreign roots left South African socialists particularly open to international influences as guides or models.

They were also confronted by the problems of a unique political economy for which there were no readily apparent international solutions. For South Africa has had a distinctively national pattern of development – a racial capitalist path – in which the ideology of race and a racial division of the working class played a central role in the development and stabilization of capitalism – arguably to a far greater extent than in any other country. In the first two decades of this century, following an orthodox interpretation of Marxism, socialists focused their efforts on organizing urban workers. But these were white workers who were overwhelmingly racist and protectionist in their outlook. Socialists gradually lost their belief in the revolutionary potential of white workers and turned their attention to the organization of black workers and to the issues of racial oppression and national liberation.*

The international roots of South African socialism

The dynamic between the national and the international in the development of South African socialism is best illustrated by the role of immigrants in the movement. Several distinctive socialist traditions were carried to South Africa, one by Eastern European exiles, generally Yiddish-speaking Jews; a second, by English-speaking immigrants or sojourners, generally British. A third and weaker tradition, in which syndicalism played an important role, traced its origins to the United

States. These diverse traditions did not mix easily. Yet each one had a resonance with certain aspects of South African society.

The Eastern European Jews who emigrated to South Africa brought to their understanding of socialism their long history of severe repression in the Russian Empire. In the late eighteenth century Jews were expelled from many villages and cities, forced to live in the Pale of Settlement and to obtain special permits to travel outside it. They were subjected to numerous restraints and restrictions regarding employment and trade, and were forbidden to use 'the Hebrew language' for business. 1881 and 1882 saw mass pogroms against Jews and increased restrictions on the acquisition of property and access to education and the professions. More pogroms took place in the context of the 1905 Russian revolution, and further restrictions on Jewish access to education were enacted in 1905 and 1907.[1]

Not surprisingly, Jews were disproportionately attracted to radical and revolutionary politics. Socialism in the Russian Empire began as an ideology of the radical intelligentsia before the development of an urban working class and under the shadow of an authoritarian state that ruled a multinational empire. 'What began as a philosophy of life and personal ethics for a generation of rebellious individuals, and then became a popular movement founded on an idealization of the peasantry and countryside', writes Stephen Kotkin, 'by the end of the nineteenth century had become an ideology of development centred on the working class and industry.'[2] In the repressive conditions of Tsarist Russia, a premium came to be placed on secret organization and clandestine activity. In the 1870s many Jews were attracted to Populism and, subsequently, in the late 1880s and 1890s, to Marxism. The General Union of Jewish Workers in Russia and Poland – the *Bund* – was formed in 1897. The following year, the *Bund* joined the newly-formed Russian Democratic Labour Party and played an important role in the revolutionary movement until it dissolved after the 1917 revolution.[3]

The 1881 pogroms precipitated a mass exodus of Jews from Eastern Europe. 1880–1910 was the peak period of Jewish immigration to South Africa – about 40,000 Jews entered the country during those decades. In comparison, fewer than 30,000 Jews came to South Africa during the next four decades, although 1924–30 saw a rise in Jewish immigration. By 1946, Jews constituted about 4.39 per cent of the white population.[4]

The South African Jewish community has been called a colony of Lithuanian or *Litvak* Jewry. Although it is impossible to trace their precise origins, probably three-quarters of the Eastern European Jews who emigrated to South Africa were *Litvaks*. By 1910, this group comprised a majority of South African Jews, even though prominent English-born or Anglicized Jews were influential.[5] Yiddish was the language of Jewish workers and of radicals. By contrast, middle-class Zionist Jews used Hebrew, while the middle- and upper-class Jews who sought acculturation into the dominant society spoke English. Corresponding with the first major wave of Jewish immigration from Eastern Europe, the 1890s saw the formation of several small Jewish workers' initiatives in Johannesburg and Cape Town, and the early 1900s saw the establishment of local branches of the *Bund*.[6]

The British socialist experience was profoundly different. In this birthplace of many first-generation South African socialists, the socialist movement developed after the formation of an urban working class, under a liberal state whose populace became enfranchised gradually over many decades.[7] Britain experienced the world's first industrial revolution and with it, the problems of industrial capitalism: proletarianization, exodus from countryside to cities, urban overcrowding, unemployment and poverty, and pollution. The earliest manifestations of urban working-class radicalism culminated in the Chartist movement of the 1840s – a mass movement that was defeated. Thereafter some more secure sections of the male working class organized through trade unions, cooperatives and friendly societies. Radical liberalism became an influential expression of this working-class political outlook. By the late nineteenth century, as socialism began to revive, British economic hegemony had already passed its peak. The first explicitly socialist organization of this revival, the Social Democratic Federation (SDF), founded in 1883, presented itself as a mainstream Marxist Second International party, while nonetheless encompassing a range of views. Broadly, it advocated a Co-operative Commonwealth and was committed to reform through parliamentary and municipal politics as a stepping stone to revolution.[8]

The 1880s saw a rapid diffusion of socialist ideas in Britain. At the end of the decade new unions of the so-called unskilled were formed, often by socialists. Older, craft unions faced the challenges of new technology and more robust managerial policies. By the 1890s these craft unions faced internal challenges to traditional policies from socialist activists. New social movements – cultural, feminist and ecological movements – formed and, in some cases, interacted with socialist groups. There was no socialist orthodoxy nor any socialist organizational monopoly. A Socialist League was founded in 1884, when William Morris and Eleanor Marx, amongst others, broke from the SDF. The Independent Labour Party (ILP), espousing an ethical socialism, was formed in 1893. Building on local initiatives, this contrasted itself with the Marxist SDF, although the distinction at the grass-roots level was less clear-cut. The ILP was more open to alliances than the SDF. In 1900 it formed an alliance with trade unions to form the Labour Representation Committee, precursor to the British Labour Party. The SDF was an initial participant but soon left. The Fabians rejected class struggle and adopted the idea of a state-led socialism at both national and municipal levels in which intellectuals and administrators were to be the vanguard. But people moved from one organization to another, and different groups banded together in common struggles.[9] British emigrants to South Africa founded local branches of the SDF, the ILP and the Fabian movement.

In those years, writes Stephen Yeo, socialism 'involved a whole change in way of life. It was not just a question of being entered on a party's membership list. ... A separation from older jobs, friends, places and habits was succeeded by acquisition of new ones.'[10] Socialism as a way of life meant bridging the gap between the public and the private, the political and the personal, which had developed in bourgeois society and had become the hallmark of the Victorian age. Since its advocates believed that socialism was developing in all spheres of life, there was no premium placed on having the vote – which British women only achieved in two instalments in 1918 and 1928 – or on being an industrial worker and trade union member. This was reflected in the striking social diversity of the converts to this movement.[11] The ethical socialist tradition that developed in those years has been described as 'a religion of socialism'.

South Africa had its own link to this tradition through the person of Olive Schreiner – socialist, pacifist, feminist and renowned novelist. She lived in Britain during the 1880s and mingled with British socialists – counting Eleanor Marx, Havelock Ellis and Edward Carpenter amongst her closest friends – and was probably the first South African socialist to publicize the brutalities of British imperial policy. Her life and writings epitomized the values of the organizationally eclectic socialism of late nineteenth-century Britain – most importantly, a profound concern with moral dilemmas and with the relationship between the personal and the political.[12]

The American socialist tradition, developing in an immigrant society that had conquered and marginalized the indigenous population, differed from both the Russian and British experiences. While many accounts stress the limited influence of American socialism, before the First World War it had a significant impact on socialist activity in other parts of the world. The Socialist Labour Party was founded in Chicago in the late 1870s, its growth spurred by waves of immigrants. In 1890 the Caribbean-born Daniel De Leon took over its leadership. Sceptical of electoral politics, De Leon sought to Americanize the Socialist Labour Party, both by publishing literature in English and by requiring socialists to work in trade unions, using American ideas and methods. For De Leon, socialism and nationalism were not inherently incompatible. 'Socialism is that idea that alone can raise patriotism to its completest development', he claimed. But he also promoted a rigid conception of socialist organization. Eschewing the notion of a broad and eclectic party, which could only be 'an ash-barrel for the refuse of others', he tried to build 'a party of cast-iron revolutionary principles'. While many socialists were alienated by his political sectarianism, others found the idea of revolutionary purity appealing. In 1903 the Socialist Labour Party developed a base in Scotland, reflecting local dissatisfaction with the SDF's perceived lack of rigour and principle.[13]

Syndicalism became an important current in American socialism in the early twentieth century. Rooted in the experiences of migrant and unskilled workers in the American west, syndicalism emphasized the organization of all workers in a common union, in contrast to the prevailing ethnic stratification within existing American labour organizations. It found organizational expression in the Industrial Workers of the World (IWW), founded in 1905 as a radical alternative to the American Federation of Labor, which refused to accept those whom it defined as 'foreigners'. The IWW was part of a broader current of direct action that could be seen as a response to modernizing managerial strategies that attempted to erode the power of craft workers, and initially it had a strong miners' constituency. Its ideal was 'one big union'. Until 1908 the IWW attempted to reconcile and hold together diverse socialist positions, including that of the Socialist Labour Party. However, De Leon saw trade union work primarily as a means to promote the party, while many other IWW activists saw militant trade unionism as a priority and to some degree as an alternative to specifically political activity. This was not surprising, given that many IWW supporters – including migrant workers unable to establish voting residency, disenfranchised African-Americans, women and new immigrants – lacked the vote. Syndicalism developed within the shadow of, and was eventually smashed by, the repressive American state. Nevertheless, the IWW's style found a resonance in many English-speaking societies before the First World War, including western Canada, South Wales, Ireland, Australia and South Africa.[14]

Racial capitalism and the South African political economy

These varied traditions met in South Africa in the early years of the twentieth century. Each contained elements that linked with aspects of South African society. The Eastern European socialist tradition brought a recognition of national oppression and of the difficulties of clandestine work. The eclectic British socialist tradition found greatest resonance in the Cape Province, the most liberal region of South Africa. The syndicalist tradition resonated with the Witwatersrand's frontier society.

But the society they encountered was one in which a distinctively racial form of capitalism was developing as a response to the extremely rapid British imperialist penetration that had followed European colonial conquest and settlement. The first European settlement in this part of Africa was established at the Cape in 1652 by Jan van Riebeeck of the Dutch East India Company, leading to the destruction of the indigenous Khoisan pastoralist society. The British took control of the Cape Colony in 1806, leading, by the 1830s, to an exodus of Afrikaners north and east. The *Voortrekkers*, as they became known, arrived in the Transvaal in 1836, defeated the Ndebele people and in 1857 established the South African Republic. *Voortrekkers* also founded the Orange Free State in 1854, and over the next decades fought a series of wars against the indigenous African societies in the interior of the country. Similarly, in 1837 *Voortrekkers* inaugurated the Republic of Natalia, but in 1843 Britain annexed Port Natal and then colonized the region and fought a series of military battles with the Zulus.

The socio-economic basis of the pre-capitalist Khoisan and Bantu-speaking societies, based on pastoralism and shifting cultivation, was destroyed by two inter-related processes. The first was the gradual extension of merchant capital through trade in the eighteenth and nineteenth centuries. The second was the expansion of the frontier through the century-long series of wars between British and Boers moving north and east, and Africans.[15] These wars of conquest brought many African peoples, such as the Basutos and the Zulus, into the capitalist system. '*The land wars*', wrote Kenneth Jordaan, '*were also labour wars.*'[16]

Imperialist-fuelled industrialization followed a period of military struggle, dispossession and slavery, one characterized by marked regional variation, and with racial supremacy as its main ideological pillar. Diamonds were discovered in 1867; by 1870 there were an estimated 10,000 diamond diggers. Africans had traded in gold from the region for centuries; in 1871, however, a white man 'discovered' gold in the Eastern Transvaal. That supply was soon exhausted but in 1886 another deposit – this time, seemingly endless – was located at Langlaagte in the Transvaal. This precipitated the rapid development of the gold-mining industry and further military struggles, culminating in the Anglo-Boer War of 1899–1902, in which Britain defeated the South African Republic and the Orange Free State.[17]

British capital 'discovered' South Africa's mineral wealth before a significant proletariat existed; thus, it faced the critical problem of securing a labour force. The problem of labour scarcity had bedeviled the colonial authorities, the landed bourgeoisie and the Boer pastoralists throughout the nineteenth century. The social historian W. M. MacMillan, for instance, noted that an official report of 1876 asked the Government of the Cape Colony 'to survey mankind from China to Peru, in the hope of creating a class of cheap labourers who will thankfully accept the position of helots and not be troubled with the inconvenient ambition of bettering their condition'.[18] Following the mineral discoveries, both the colonial state and the capitalist class made various attempts to induce and coerce labour. As elsewhere in Africa, colonial law and taxation were used to great effect. Finally, they settled on what appeared to be a policy of halting proletarianization by combining the colonial reserve system, in which African ownership and occupation of land was restricted to specified areas, with the use of migrant labour.

Although the South African proletariat was largely a product of the rapid industrial development sparked by the mineral revolution, its antecedents could be traced back to the colonial era. In the Cape, for instance, the slave tradition of the seventeenth to nineteenth centuries contributed to the modern racial order, by fostering a coincidence between colour and class.[19] The racial hierarchy engendered by slavery protected poor whites from the competition of free black labour, albeit in a period where proletarians of any colour were a minority of the Cape labour force.[20] The reserve system was pioneered in the Cape Colony. There, as throughout the continent, the introduction of private property in the reserves accelerated the process of proletarianization. The limitations on the size of landholdings stunted the development of an African farming class in the reserves and at the same time led to loss of landholdings and to landlessness for many. As MacMillan explained, the Cape colonial government '*systematically planted its Africans in "reserves"* ', but spent little money to develop them, so that by the early twentieth century poverty was pushing Africans into the migrant labour system. After 1908 the Cape became the main area of mine labour recruitment in South Africa.[21] As African men were drawn into migrant labour, the historically prominent role which African women had played in subsistence production became accentuated. The responsibility for cultivation shifted disproportionately to women, who toiled under increasingly arduous conditions. The modern South African proletariat arose from the pores of the pre-existing social order.

Racial capitalist penetration in the countryside

British imperialism's quest for diamonds and gold set off a chain of reactions throughout South Africa and the entire Southern African region. The mineral revolution precipitated an agrarian revolution, as agricultural production, spurred by the needs of rapidly expanding urban and industrial areas on the Witwatersrand, came under the domination of the commercial market. This had dramatic social consequences. Black and white producers alike were pressured to produce for the market in order to retain their hold on the land, and small cultivators lost their access to land in the face of intense competition and land speculation. However, the rapid development of agrarian capitalism in the imperialist period followed a distinctly racial pattern in its interaction with the pre-existing colonial conquest society.

The 'poor white problem', as it was called, first appeared in the 1890s as the impact of the mineral revolution began to be felt in the countryside. Small-scale Afrikaner cultivators and pastoralists began to lose their land and livelihood due to land speculation and competition, which led to a concentration of landholdings. Larger landowners preferred the more productive African tenant farmers to Afrikaner share-croppers known as *bywoners*. In towns and on the mines, employers preferred cheaper black labour to unskilled white. Afrikaner proletarianization occurred largely through the workings of the market, although it was accelerated by the Anglo-Boer War. This process contrasted sharply with the coercive social engineering used to create a black proletariat and carried profound implications for the development of political consciousness and mobilization of these two sections of the South African proletariat.[22]

The Anglo-Boer War, in which the British brutally vanquished the Afrikaners, intensified Boer vulnerability to capitalist penetration, strengthening Afrikaner national identity against British imperialism. Huge numbers of Afrikaner women and children starved to death in concentration camps; the survivors were typically unable to start over again in their old rural occupations and drifted to unemployment in towns.[23] After the war, the rural sector came more firmly into the capitalist orbit, stimulating the growth of a market in land. Both agricultural production and property relations came under the domination of finance capital. The post-war boom was accompanied by overtrading, overspeculation, and overextension of mercantile credit, and the depression of 1904–1908, with its fall in agricultural prices, saw an increase in rural indebtedness and land alienation, especially to foreign owners. These years accelerated the impoverishment of rural Afrikaners, pushing many more into towns.[24]

Capitalism's penetration into the countryside, and the separation of producers from their means of production on the land, affected blacks very differently. The Western Cape wheat farms and vineyards had a tradition of slave labour dating from the seventeenth century, and Natal sugar plantations imported indentured Indian labour from the 1860s. In the Eastern Cape, servile and migrant labour worked the wool and ostrich farms; elsewhere in the Cape, small-scale cultivators were pushed into migrant mine labour.[25]

In the interior of the country, blacks laboured on capitalist farms as squatters and tenants. From the 1870s, a series of laws had curtailed African squatting on white farms, so that they had to sell increasing amounts of their labour-power to survive. Nonetheless, while *bywoners* rapidly lost their hold on the land, African cultivators gripped the soil tenaciously. In the late nineteenth century this posed no immediate threat to capitalist farmers and landowners on the Southern Highveld; indeed, their economic prosperity depended on black producers who were not completely proletarianized. Small black cultivators retained their means of production in the form of tools and cattle, they were experienced at commercial cultivation and, unlike *bywoners*, used the labour of women and children family members. Such productive capacity was important for the typically undercapitalized farms, and landowners relied heavily on sharecropping and tenant labour for commercial production. Black cultivators were not in every case as devastated by the Anglo-Boer War as Afrikaners. The post-war years sometimes found them in a position of relative economic strength *vis-à-vis bywoners* and landowners. The more productive black tenants outcompeted whites, and in some cases white landowners were economically dependent on the productive capacity of their black producers. Consequently, landowners often preferred black tenants and sharecroppers. Labour-intensive farming methods typically remained more profitable than capital-intensive ones well into the twentieth century.[26]

In the early years of the commercial market in agriculture, following the mineral revolution, the primary labour problem for capitalist landowners concerned extracting labour and produce from the largely self-sufficient black squatters. But whites protested bitterly against the independent African farming households that had settled on white farms after the loss of their land. These producers were brought under control through laws giving farm owners and employers extreme powers over black tenants and workers. Both the Master and Servants Ordinance of 1904 and the 1913 Land Act were formulated to increase the degree of exploitation of tenant labour. The 1913 Land Act, which represented the culmination of a wave of anti-black agitation, prohibited land sales to blacks outside reserved areas and, by outlawing sharecropping and squatting, increased the control and exploitation of black tenants. This made labour service the only legal means by which they could pay rent.[27]

The pockets of prosperous black cultivators that existed early in the century were too limited to contest the political and economic strength of white landowners. Any potential for the development of an African peasantry was stunted by the 1913 Act, leaving no intermediary black farming class to counter the weight of white landowners, backed by the state, against masses of small-scale and often impoverished sharecroppers and labour tenants. In these circumstances, class struggle in the countryside was played out largely along colour lines.

The development of a racially-divided industrial working class

While the reserves were still economically viable enough to provide bare subsistence, the cheap wages offered by mines were not sufficient to draw adequate supplies of labour from the reserves. The mines, therefore, had to rely heavily on foreign labour, and the industry's dependence on contract labour from southern Africa and China was particularly acute during the first decade of the twentieth century. The migrant labour system only became regularized in South Africa when the reserves were no longer able to provide for African subsistence. It became most effective only when economic pressures – depression and a series of agricultural disasters – compelled Africans in the reserves to seek wage labour on a regular basis.[28]

At the turn of the century black cultivators could still pay taxes through their agricultural production, despite widespread poverty. The difficulty of obtaining sufficient supplies of mining labour persisted throughout the decade following the Anglo-Boer War, due to the capacity of small-scale African producers to intensify their productive efforts. Hence, the Chamber of Mines, with government assistance, began using a variety of recruiting strategies together with direct coercion to obtain masses of unskilled labour.[29] Slowly and spasmodically, over the next decades, they developed a stable, though costly, system of labour recruitment.

While South Africa is rich in gold, the ore is low grade – a large supply of mined ore contains a relatively small amount of gold. The deposits are deep underground, and the industry uses deep-level mining with distinctive technological requirements. The mining industry's two-tier division of labour reflected its dual needs: on the one hand, a need for large numbers of workers who performed heavy work defined as unskilled, such as making small tunnels; on the other, a need for skilled craft workers – mostly from Britain and Australia – with experience sinking shafts, fitting pipes, installing lifts and operating machinery.[30] Initially, identities of colour and skill converged, reflected in a large wage differential: black labour was unskilled and cheap; white labour, skilled and expensive. The roots of this particular combination of colour and function in the labour hierarchy lay in the different socio-economic conditions that determined the value of black and white labour-power. These conditions included the proportion of the respective populations in productive labour, their retention of any independent means of production, their productivity and their social expectations, as well as the cost of living and the cost of training workers.[31]

The roots of cheap African labour date from the late nineteenth century when wages supplemented agricultural production rather than the reverse: African men initially turned to temporary migrant labour to pay fixed expenses, like taxes and marriage fees, while women farmed. The contingent nature of wage labour for Africans before the turn of the century operated to prevent the normal workings of supply and demand of labour through the wage system. Because of the continuous supply of temporary workers ready to accept low pay, the overall scarcity of permanent workers did not drive wages up. But starvation-level poverty, due to excessive fragmentation of landholdings, overgrazing and overpopulation – in short, land scarcity – undermined the productive capacity of the reserves, and began driving black men into low-paid migrant labour for longer periods of time. Now, wrote MacMillan, 'the stress under which people lived set the standard and kept it as near bare subsistence level as it was possible to be'. As Africans became more economically dependent on the wage and went to the mines in larger numbers, their real wages fell. In three decades the basic wage rate paid to African mineworkers barely rose.[32]

Skilled labour, by comparison, existed in very different conditions. In the early days of the mining industry, before the turn of the century, skilled mining labour from overseas had to be induced to perform dangerous and unhealthy work in a foreign country, and they commanded wages far higher than unskilled indigenous labour precisely because their skills were a scarce commodity in South Africa. Moreover, the wages of these white workers were established under conditions of complete proletarianization and urbanization and had to cover the costs of their social reproduction in cities.[33]

White workers brought their trade union traditions with them. The first trade unions on the Witwatersrand mines were craft organizations in which membership was restricted to workers who had obtained qualifications, generally through apprenticeship, in particular crafts, such as machine drilling. They aimed to control the classification system for determining rates of pay, to determine the tasks that workers performed and to control training through the apprenticeship system. They were most influential in South Africa in the two to three decades following the introduction of deep-level mining in the 1890s.[34] In Britain, the general unions that had emerged in the late 1880s had criticized the craft unions for their policies of exclusion. Transported to South Africa, craft-based exclusion became transformed into racial exclusion, initially in mining and then in manufacturing.

The coincidence of colour and skill gave the initial illusion that black and white wages were set in a single, national wage market. But even in the early industrial period, when the vast majority of both groups were defined as unskilled, two wage markets were operating along colour lines. Wages of white unskilled labour were set by reference to the relatively high wages of white skilled workers.[35] Urban black proletarians, by contrast, did not receive wages equivalent to those of comparably skilled white proletarians. Rather, their wage levels were set by the larger numbers of blacks migrating back and forth between the mines and reserves. Different social standards of what was acceptable for whites and blacks lay behind this dual wage market; black workers could be forced to live in conditions considered socially unacceptable for whites.

The fact that black labour was cheaper than comparable white labour at all levels – including unskilled Afrikaner labour – meant that the racial hierarchy was not merely a result of the law of supply and demand as it applied to skills. This colour-based, dual wage market reinforced the pre-existing racial division of labour and the racial antagonism on the mines since it meant that mine owners preferred cheaper black labour to unskilled and skilled whites. Social pressure to hire unskilled Afrikaners to solve the 'poor white problem' intensified after the Anglo-Boer war, yet the Chamber of Mines insisted that only cheaper black workers should perform unskilled labour. In 1903, not surprisingly, the Transvaal Labour Commission refused to use unskilled white labour due to its expense.[36] Moreover, although some black mineworkers had acquired skills, protectionist white unions excluded blacks in order to restrict the potential pool of skilled labour, thereby maintaining their high wage-rates. This suggests the salience of racial ideology, both for the direct interests of capital and white labour, and as a mechanism operating to preserve a particular class system.

In the craft era, white labour privileges corresponded to skills and colour. But the dependency on craft skills lessened as the mining labour process was restructured, and the skilled/unskilled division of labour, which had originally corresponded to colour, began to break down. Yet the racial division of labour, stemming from the pre-existing racialism of a colonial conquest society, and charged by the initial racial characteristics of the skilled/unskilled division of labour, continued, albeit transformed, into the industrial period.

The racial domination of the pre-industrial colonial period became racial competition in the industrial capitalist era, a competition suppressed by segregation and protectionism. This transformation was not only ideological, but reflected a change in the nature of social relations between the two historical periods. In the pre-industrial period, expropriation of surplus production was often through direct, coercive means, although in the Cape, with its longer integration into the world capitalist market, exploitation also took place through the market. Slavery, and indentured, apprentice and servile proletarian labour were typical forms for black labour. In the industrial period, by contrast, the intense competition and protectionism of white labour *vis-à-vis* blacks was due to their potential equivalence in the labour market. Craft unions opened their doors to unskilled whites, and skilled white workers combined with unskilled whites, increasingly basing their arguments for high wages on colour – and a presumption of innate competence – and not acquired skills. As the problem of labour supply eased in the 1910s, the labour question shifted to a struggle both between capitalists and workers and amongst workers over the terms of the labour relationship, leading to an intensification in the control and exploitation of producers.

Conclusion

The diverse socialist traditions from overseas had to confront this environment. Most significantly, they came to a land in which they lacked a social base. *Litvak* Jews lived in Yiddish-speaking ghettos in the fast-growing cities; but these remained tiny pockets isolated both from the majority of the black population in the countryside and from the majority of white workers in towns. Similarly, the 'religion of socialism' that a small number of British socialists carried with them, had developed amongst a cross-section of British society rather than being restricted to craft unions. Yet in South Africa, their apparent constituency was the craft unions, which were fighting for protectionist labour policies that excluded blacks. Syndicalism briefly found a resonance amongst certain strands of white labour in the early 1910s as they confronted state authority. But precisely because its central aim was 'one big union', it was the socialist tendency that was most receptive to the organization of black workers as they turned to collective protest at the end of that decade.

Because of their foreign origins, South Africa's earliest socialists were acutely attuned to developments within the international socialist movement. But the reverberations of the October 1917 revolution in Russia, which were felt in socialist movements around the world, had particularly strong repercussions in South Africa where the diverse and newly-imported socialist currents had not yet had sufficient time to root themselves.

Notes

*   The term 'black' refers to all people of colour in South Africa who were subjected to racial discrimination. The terms 'African', 'Coloured' and 'Indian' refer broadly to categories imposed by the South African state.

1. Hugh Seton-Watson, *The Russian Empire 1801–1917*, Oxford: Oxford University, 1967, 55, 273–4, 416, 493–4, 611.

2. Stephen Kotkin, *Magnetic Mountain: Stalinism as a Civilization*, Berkeley, Los Angeles and London: University of California, 1995, 385, n. 51.

3. Kotkin, *Magnetic Mountain*, 10; Seton-Watson, *The Russian Empire*, 495–6, 551–2.

4. Gideon Shimoni, *Jews and Zionism: the South African Experience (1910–1967)*, Cape Town: Oxford University, 1980, 4–5.

5. In Yiddish culture, *Litvak* refers to Jews who came from within the boundaries of the pre-1917 Tsarist Russian provinces of Kovno, Vilna, Grodno and Northern Suwalki – which were largely Lithuanian-Polish – and of Vitebsk, Minst and Mogilev – which were largely Belorussian-Russian. Shimoni, *Jews and Zionism*, 5–7, 18–19.

6. E. A. Mantzaris, 'Radical Community: The Yiddish-speaking Branch of the International Socialist League, 1918–1920' in Belinda Bozzoli, ed., *Class, Community and Conflict: South African Perspectives*, Johannesburg: Ravan, 1987, 160–76, 164; Taffy Adler, 'The Class Struggle in Doornfontein: A History of the Johannesburg Jewish Workers' Club, 1928–1950', paper presented at the African Studies Seminar, University of the Witwatersrand, 23 August 1976, 2–3.

7. British working-class males obtained the franchise incrementally in 1867, 1884 and 1918. For men, qualification for the franchise was based on whether they met the registration requirements, in which property rights played a significant role. For British women, the criterion was age. Most women over thirty obtained the franchise in 1918, and women over twenty-one in 1928. In the late 1960s, the age for the universal franchise was lowered to eighteen.

8. Chushichi Tsuzuki, *H. M. Hyndman and British Socialism*, Oxford: Oxford University, 1961, 57–87. The Democratic Federation was founded in 1881; in 1883 this was renamed the Social Democratic Federation, proclaiming adherence to Marxism.

9. Stephen Yeo, 'A New Life: the Religion of Socialism in Britain, 1883–1896', *History Workshop*, 4, Autumn 1997, 5–56, esp. 27.

10. Yeo, 'A New Life', 13.

11. Women, for instance, were actively involved at branch level, and a few became extremely popular speakers, drawing large numbers when they addressed meetings. Yeo, 'A New Life', 46.

12. For biographies of Olive Schreiner, see *inter alia*, S. C. Cronwright-Schreiner, *The Life of Olive Schreiner*, London: T. Fisher Unwin, 1924 and Ruth First and Ann Scott, *Olive*

Schreiner: A Biography, New Brunswick, NJ: Rutgers University, 1990.

13. Stephen Coleman, *Daniel De Leon*, Manchester and New York: Manchester University, 1990, quotes 20, 28.

14. Melvyn Dubofsky, *'Big Bill' Haywood*, Manchester: Manchester University, 1987, 8, 32–7, 63; Sheila Rowbotham, 'Rebel Networks in the First World War', *Friends of Alice Wheeldon*, London: Pluto, 1986, 5–107, esp. 12.

15. Monica Wilson, 'Co-operation and conflict: the Eastern Cape Frontier', in Monica Wilson and Leonard Thompson, eds, *A History of South Africa to 1870*, London and Canberra: Croom Helm, 1982, 233–71, esp. 234–56.

16. K. A. Jordaan, 'The Land Question in South Africa', *Points of View*, 1, 1, October 1959, 3–45, 12. Emphasis in the original. Extracted in Allison Drew, ed., *South Africa's Radical Tradition: A Documentary History, 1943–1964*, vol. 2, Cape Town: University of Cape Town, Buchu Books and Mayibuye Books, 1997, 325–39. See also W. M. MacMillan, *Africa Emergent: A Survey of Social, Political and Economic Trends in British Africa*, Harmondsworth, Middlesex: Penguin, 1949, 130.

17. Luli Callinicos, *Gold and Workers, 1886–1924*, Johannesburg: Ravan, 1981, 8–9.

18. W. M. MacMillan, *The South African Agrarian Problem and its Historical Development*, Johannesburg: Council of Education, Witwatersrand, 1919, 8.

19. Referring to the emancipation of the Khoikhoi and slave population between 1828 and 1838, T. R. H. Davenport notes that 'the habit of class and colour differentiation in the outlook of the socially dominant groups, and the tendency towards abjectness on the part of those accustomed to bondage, could not be legislated out of existence, and survived as social attitudes liable to be reasserted in times of stress'. See 'The Consolidation of a New Society: the Cape Colony', in Wilson and Thompson, eds, *A History of South Africa to 1870*, 272–333, quote 273.

20. Richard Elphick and Hermann Giliomee, 'The Origins and Entrenchment of European Dominance at the Cape, 1652–c.1840', in Richard Elphick and Hermann Giliomee, eds, *The Shaping of South African Society, 1652–1840*, 2nd edition, Cape Town: Maskew Miller Longman, 1989, 521–66, 542.

21. MacMillian, *Africa Emergent*, 120, emphasis in original, and 125–26.

22. MacMillan, *The South African Agrarian Problem*, 21, 63. Timothy Keegan, *Rural Transformations in Industrializing South Africa: the Southern Highveld to 1914*, Braamfontein: Ravan, 1986, 22; Charles van Onselen, *Studies in the Social and Economic History of the Witwatersrand 1886–1914*, vol. 2, Johannesburg: Ravan, 1982, 126ff describes the impact of this rapid proletarianization on Afrikaner consciousness.

23. MacMillan, *The South African Agrarian Problem*, 62.

24. Keegan, *Rural Transformations*, 46–47.

25. Timothy Keegan, 'The Dynamics of Rural Accumulation in South Africa: Comparative and Historical Perspectives', *Comparative Studies in Society and History*, 28, 4, 1986, 628–50, 631.

26. Keegan, *Rural Transformations*, 30 and 197. On the variegated impact of the Anglo-Boer War, regionally and for black South Africans, see Bill Nasson *Abraham Essau's War: A Black South African War in the Cape, 1899–1902*, Cambridge: Cambridge University 1991, esp. 1–11 and 169–92.

27. Jordaan, 'The Land Question', 18–19 and Keegan, *Rural Transformations*, 13, 182–4, 192–3.

28. Alan H. Jeeves, *Migrant Labour in South Africa's Mining Economy: the Struggle for the Gold Mines' Labour Supply, 1890–1920*, Kingston and Montreal: McGill-Queen's

University and Johannesburg: Witwatersrand University, 1985, 12, 15–16, and 55; Norman Levy, *The Foundations of the South African Cheap Labour System*, London and Boston: Routledge and Kegan Paul, 1982, 34–35. Saul Dubow, *Racial Segregation and the Origins of Apartheid in South Africa, 1919–36*, Basingstoke and London: MacMillan, 1989, 53–55, suggests that mine owners were far from unified regarding how to develop and stabilize the labour supply, and some hoped to establish stable African communities near the mines. The migrant labour system evolved through trial and error, and was a means by which mining capitalists adapted to conditions in which most people retained their access to land.

29. Jordaan, 'The Land Question', 16–17.
30. Callinicos, *Gold and Workers*, 15.
31. Karl Marx, *Capital: A Critique of Political Economy*, vol. 1, edited by Frederick Engels, New York: International, 1967, 559.
32. MacMillan, *Africa Emergent*, 172.
33. On white workers see, *inter alia*, Frederick A. Johnstone, *Class, Race and Gold: A Study of Class Relations and Racial Discrimination in South Africa*, London: Routledge and Kegan Paul, 1976; Robert H. Davies, *Capital, State and White Labour in South Africa 1900–1960: An Historical Materialist Analysis of Class Formation and Class Relations*, Brighton, Sussex: Harvester, 1979; MacMillan, *Africa Emergent*, 308–9; Levy, *Foundations*, 163.
34. Luli Callinicos, *Working Life: Factories, Townships, and Popular Culture on the Rand, 1886–1940*, Johannesburg: Ravan, 1987, 59–60.
35. This process was underlined by developments after the First World War. Although unskilled Afrikaners took over posts which had formerly been the domain of skilled British workers, white wages showed an upward stickiness, indicating the persistence of racial ideology in determining wages, and accentuated by the wartime shortage of white labour. See MacMillan, *Africa Emergent*, 309.
36. Levy, *Foundations*, 165, 177–90.

Chapter 2

'Rather a strange gospel': socialism in South Africa, 1900–1917

The first wave of South African socialism developed in a society marked by extreme regional parochialism in which national identity was in a state of flux. 'There is no cohesion or common bond among the people such as one finds, for example, in New Zealand', remarked the Scottish socialist James Keir Hardie when he visited the country in 1907. 'Each Colony is jealous of its neighbour, and fights for its own hand without regard to the interest of South Africa as a whole'. The pre-colonial African societies had only recently been militarily conquered, and there was as yet no broad sense of African identity. The overwhelmingly rural African population still thought of themselves as Zulus, Xhosas and Ndebeles, amongst others. Only in 1912 was the first African political organization that transcended tribal identity formed – the South African Native National Congress (SANNC), precursor to the African National Congress. By contrast, Afrikaners might have seen themselves as of Africa, yet they refused to consider the political incorporation of blacks. The British defeat of Afrikaners in the Anglo-Boer War hardened Afrikaners' resentment of foreigners and, particularly, of British imperialism. And immigrants from Britain saw themselves as part of the British Empire. Keir Hardie did not find South Africa appealing. The towns, he wrote, had been 'bled white by speculators' and the farms, ravaged by 'drought, pestilence, and locusts'. Only in India had he encountered such pessimism.[1]

Separated by vast distances, the three principal South African cities, Cape Town, Johannesburg and Durban, each developed a distinctive pattern of socialism. The Cape was the region both of longest European settlement and of earliest black political activity, with a non-racial qualified franchise. By the 1880s it was clear to many Africans that white expansion could no longer be opposed through military means. That decade saw an upsurge in African political activity, as well the first attempts to curtail the Cape African franchise. In the Eastern Cape John Tengo Jabavu, a mission-educated teacher and a future founder of the South African Native College, became editor of the influential *Imvo Zabantsundu* (*African Opinion*), which expressed the views of the emergent African middle class.[2]

Turn-of-the-century Cape Town had a very small African urban population and a high proportion of Coloured artisans and urban workers. Although some trade unions had a colour bar protecting white workers, others were open to Coloured workers. The African Political Organisation – later renamed the African People's Organisation (APO) – was formed in 1902. Its political identity was ambiguous. While calling for a qualified franchise for all men, regardless of colour, it nonetheless styled itself as 'an organization of the coloured people only' with responsibility for 'the rights and duties of the Coloured people ... as distinguished from the native races'. However, Dr Abdullah Abdurahman, its leader from 1905 to 1940, favoured joint Coloured–African political cooperation. A distinguished medical doctor who had trained at Glasgow University, in 1904 Abdurahman became the first black to win a seat on the Cape Town City Council. The Abdurahmans were part of Cape Town's social elite, their home open to visiting dignitaries and prominent South Africans of all colours.[3] Socialism in Cape Town and its environs reflected 'the elements of an integrated society'.[4] From its inception, Cape Town socialism had a non-racial element, a visionary quality and a propagandistic orientation.

The Witwatersrand, by contrast, was far more deeply polarized along racial and national lines. African societies had only been militarily defeated in the interior of the country in the past few decades; the region had been torn apart by the Anglo-Boer War at the turn of the century. Both the Transvaal and the Orange Free State had all-white electorates. White workers from Britain had brought their traditions of trade union organization; they dominated the labour movement and promoted a highly restrictive colour bar, despite a small number of skilled Coloured artisans and of Africans with industrial experience. According to Jack and Ray Simons, the key legal element entrenching the industrial colour bar was the Mines, Works and Machinery Ordinance of 1903: under its rubric colour bars were subsequently implemented in a range of skilled occupations.[5] Early socialists on the Rand were influenced by this racially-divided industrial environment: their views contained elements of syndicalism and of white labour protectionism. Reflecting its labour and trade union roots, socialism in Johannesburg placed a greater premium on trade union work and on gaining practical reforms than their more visionary Cape Town comrades.

Natal, too, was deeply polarized. Only in 1906 was the last Zulu uprising against British colonizers, led by Chief Bambatha, suppressed. Most Africans remained in the countryside. Indian indentured labour, primarily Hindu, had been imported to work on Natal sugar plantations between 1860 and 1911, with the last contract worked out by 1916. Most of these had only recently left the Indian countryside before coming to South Africa and, unlike imported white workers, had no tradition of trade union organization. They lived and worked under brutal conditions. They were forbidden from moving more than two miles beyond their place of work and, up to the early twentieth century, organizers were immediately transferred or repatriated.[6] 'Passenger Indians', by contrast, came voluntarily and became shopkeepers, traders and merchants. Most arrived in Natal between the 1870s and the 1890s; their entry was prohibited in 1913. Predominantly Muslim and Gujarati from western India, they initially styled themselves as Arab in the hope of distancing themselves both from Indian labourers and Africans.[7]

Natal had a qualified franchise with restrictions so stringent that the electorate was virtually all white. Its labour movement had a 'distinctly British flavour', dominated by white workers who pursued labour protectionist policies but who had little political influence.[8] Politically, Natal was dominated by a planter and landlord class. For the Labour Party to play a greater political role, advised Keir Hardie, 'it must clarify its views on the native and Asiatic questions'.[9] Of the three cities, Durban's socialist tradition was the weakest both in numbers and in continuity. A small number of socialists sought the attention of white workers and ran for elections on a socialist ticket.

The few accounts of the earliest years of socialism in South Africa belie the notion of a straightforward transition to a single centralized socialist organization and tell a story of a movement tinged with religious zeal and characterized by organizational and ideological eclecticism. The influence of British socialist traditions was predominant; most of the first socialist groups saw themselves as local branches of existing British organizations, and the early South African movement showed traces of the 'religion of socialism'. Religious motifs abound, for instance, in the memoirs of Wilfred H. Harrison, the 'Peter Pan of the Socialist movement' who came to South Africa from England in 1903 and lived in Cape Town. Syndicalism was also an important current, arriving chiefly by way of organizations of American origin. The period was marked by a distinct lack of an agreed socialist orthodoxy. On Sunday afternoons many of South Africa's first socialists – W. H. Andrews, William Freestone, David Dryburgh, and William Green – would congregate at Harrison's home, 'High Trees', in Lansdowne, just outside Cape Town, to discuss the relative virtues of industrial unionism, syndicalism, anarchism and parliamentary politics, debates that were simultaneously taking place around the world.[10]

Socialist circles in early twentieth-century South Africa

In Harrison's telling, socialism in South Africa 'had its beginning as a propaganda force from the plinth of Van Riebeeck Statue, Adderley Street, Cape Town, when it stood at the bottom of Dock Road in the latter months of 1903'. The early socialists were mainly middle-class white men 'with a sprinkling of the bohemian type from the university'.[11] One early agitator was J. L. Page, a Cockney orator of Hyde Park fame, and a french-polisher, sculptor and woodcarver. After hearing Page speak, Harrison approached him and they decided to establish a General Workers' Union, which collapsed after a brief, faltering existence. Soon thereafter, Harrison encountered another propagandist:

> The vicinity of the Van Riebeeck Statue at that time was the rostrum for all creeds and sects, who followed each other all through the day of Sunday, reminiscent of the Hyde Park gatherings. ... A stranger mounted the platform who, after giving expression to the purpose of the meeting, continued to describe himself as a Socialist. ... Loud cries of 'Stop that rubbish,' and other forms of dissent came from the promoters of that meeting.

The stranger was one Blagburn from London. Blagburn and Harrison decided to 'hold Socialist meetings every Sunday morning from the Van Riebeeck Statue plinth', postulating about the breakdown of capitalism from a soapbox. These became quite popular, and they soon added Wednesday business meetings to draw up a programme of action. Subsequently, Blagburn, Harrison and Jack Erasmus, a New Zealander who had left 'his native home, for the purpose of introducing Socialism to South Africa' and who penned a column called 'The Worker' in the *South African News*, decided to form a local branch of the SDF, reflecting the paradigmatic nature of the British experience for these early socialists.[12] In February 1905 the SDF held a packed meeting at Good Hope Hall for 'the Russian proletariat in revolt'. Olive Schreiner sent her support and kept in touch with occasional letters.[13]

Erasmus sent a report of the SDF's founding to *Justice*, the weekly newspaper of the SDF in Britain. 'We commenced with a membership of 10 only, but we had previously made open-air appeals for members', he recounted.

> For a month we held two meetings a week ... in a dining-room. When this became hardly large enough (there being only about 30 chairs), we hired a hall once a week for public meetings and retained the dining-room for our reading circle only. Thus we continued for about three months. All this time we were printing and distributing a thousand leaflets every week, and circulating books. At last we screwed up courage to engage a permanent room ... to be opened every evening.[14]

Cape Town socialists canvassed across the colour line. In 1904, a George Woollends had founded an ephemeral socialist party, arguing for the equality of all under socialism and citing the frequent examples that he had seen in Cape Town of cooperation across the colour line. Likewise, the SDF had Coloured members and sought to win the Coloured vote. Several SDF members belonged to craft unions and represented them on the Trades and Labour Council. Harrison was a delegate from the Amalgamated Society of Carpenters and Joiners; a Mr McKillop represented the Typographical Union and Tom Bolton, the Stone Masons' Union, even though the latter was racially restrictive. Harrison also represented the SDF on the Trades and Labour Council Parliamentary Committee; as he recalled, his critical stance on white labour's attitudes towards Coloured workers brought him into frequent conflict with the Trades and Labour Council bureaucracy.[15]

But the SDF displayed a tension between those seeing socialism as a vision to be obtained through propaganda and conversion, and those concerned with alleviating poverty. In the depressed years that followed the Anglo-Boer War, the SDF attracted the attention of the unemployed. Some of its members organized a soup kitchen in District Six, a predominantly Coloured area outside central Cape Town. This provoked some controversy within the ranks of the organization, as for the more radical, like Harrison, socialism was concerned with the hereafter, and not 'the petty grievances of the Capitalist system'. Nonetheless, the SDF 'multiplied in numbers and enthusiasm, and', as Harrison put it, 'became quite a religious institution, working for a grand ideal'. 'The early Socialist movement in South Africa', he wrote, 'did its propaganda work outside of all reformist institutions; we claimed to be the designers of a future order.'[16]

But practical labour issues could hardly be avoided in South Africa, where mining capital's overwhelming problem at this stage was one of securing an adequate labour supply. Almost immediately, the SDF was confronted with the controversy over the importation of Chinese labour. The atrocious working conditions made it difficult to recruit Africans, yet Lord Milner, High Commissioner for South Africa, did not believe that whites should perform unskilled labour and, moreover, the relatively high wages paid to white workers made that option economically unattractive to mineowners. The Chamber of Mines tried to redress the problem by importing indentured Chinese to labour on three-year contracts. In South Africa, the policy provoked much opposition from white labour representatives, notably Colonel Frederic Creswell, a staunch advocate of white labour who argued for the employment of unskilled whites.[17] The SDF protested against the Chinese Labour Ordinance on the grounds that the people of the country had no say in the operation of the mines, and demanded the collective ownership of the mines, the repeal of the Chinese Labour Ordinance, the voiding of Chinese labour contracts and the return of the Chinese workers to China. It also called for self-government in the Transvaal and Orange River Colonies and the extension of the franchise to all mineworkers.[18]

Overseas, British Liberals opposed the policy on a variety of grounds, ranging from racist cries of a 'yellow peril', to humanitarian concerns about the treatment of Chinese workers, to pragmatic calls for more British settlers to counterbalance the Boers. Both the Labour Representation Committee and trade unions opposed the Chinese labour policy on the grounds that it threatened achieved labour standards. The agitation was one of the issues leading to a comprehensive Liberal victory over the Tories in the general election of January 1906, with promises for an immediate end to the policy. Nonetheless, recruitment only stopped in November 1906. By 1910 the last contract had expired and virtually all Chinese workers had been repatriated.[19]

The SDF was in touch with other left groups in South Africa and with Russian radicals. Eastern European immigrants, like their British counterparts, formed South African branches of pre-existing organizations, and replicated Eastern European schisms. South African Jews rapidly polarized over the issue of Zionism. Branches of the *Yiddisher Arbeiter Bund* were formed in Cape Town and Johannesburg around 1900. They kept in close contact with developments in Russia, and after the anti-Jewish pogroms of 1905, members formed the Society of Friends of Russian Liberty, which clashed with local Zionists. In 1907, the *Yiddisher Arbeiter Bund* invited Sergius Riger of the Russian *Bund* to speak in South Africa, and the SDF helped organize engagements for him. However, there is no evidence of any further South African *Bund* activity after Riger's departure.[20]

Meanwhile, more South African branches of overseas socialist organizations were being formed. In Durban, two Scotsmen, Harry Norrie, a tailor who was later dubbed the 'pivot' of socialist organization in Durban,[21] and A. L. Clark, 'the father of railway trade unionism' and a leading figure in the Natal Labour Party,[22] were building up a small circle of socialists. Reflecting the pull of British experience, in 1903 Durban socialists formed a local branch of the Clarion Fellowship, an organization that provided recreational and cultural outlets within the tradition of ethical socialism. In its second year, it sold or distributed 429 books and 7479 pamphlets. By late 1907 local socialists had established a Durban branch of the SDF, of which Norrie was honourable secretary.[23] As well, noted Keir Hardie when he passed through Durban, the ILP was on the verge of forming a local branch. 'There is thus the nucleus of a good Socialist movement, the fruits of some very active propaganda work in the past', he enthused. 'One of the largest booksellers in the city devotes one window to the display of I.L.P. and Clarion and other Socialist publications, for all of which there is a ready sale.'[24]

As in Cape Town, Durban socialists held weekly propaganda meetings from a soapbox in the Durban Town Gardens and outside the railway gates. Nearby, at Pietermaritzburg, Lorrie Green established a small circle of socialists, and in 1905, J. Ross, Librarian at the Pietermaritzburg Public Library, agreed to display copies of *Justice* on the library's reading tables.[25] Yet the impact of this propaganda was limited. While in Britain socialist propaganda could be disseminated through the links between socialists and trade unions, the South African context made this strategy problematic. Not only was the Natal Labour Party politically weak, but Natal socialists, by all indications, were isolated from the local African and Indian population in these first years.

In Johannesburg, socialism's origins were more diverse. The experience of the American West was particularly important for the development of syndicalism, and it had a resonance in South Africa, in that both societies had experienced substantial waves of immigration, and both socialist movements faced the problem of adapting European socialist traditions to their local experiences. A South African branch of the De Leonite Socialist Labour Party (SLP) was set up in 1902. A South African branch of the IWW, another organization with American roots, was established in 1910 by radicals who had gained control of the tramway workers' union. This increased its membership after leading a successful one-day strike of Johannesburg tramwaymen in January 1911. Its local leader was Andrew Dunbar, a blacksmith by trade whom Sidney Bunting described as an 'industrial Cincinnatus at his forge'.[26]

In May 1906, a South African section of the British ILP was established on the Witwatersrand, with the trade unionist J. T. Bain of Pretoria as chairman. One of the ILP's notables was Archie Crawford, a Glasgow-born fitter who had come to South Africa in 1902 and had worked on the railways until dismissed for labour agitation in 1906. On 30 October 1907 Crawford was elected to represent Ward Five on the Johannesburg council – claiming to be the first socialist to be elected to any Transvaal public body. In October 1908 he founded the *Voice of Labour: A Weekly*

Journal of Socialism, Trade Unionism and Politics, which contained news on socialist activities around the country and which he co-edited with Mary Fitzgerald, whom he married. Fitzgerald's political roots were also in the white labour movement. Having worked for the Transvaal Miners' Association, the appalling rate of miners' phthisis had radicalized her. An advocate of 'direct action', in 1911 she was dubbed 'Pickhandle Mary' when, following police use of pickhandles to disrupt strike meetings, she, Andrew Dunbar and Thomas Glynn used pickhandles to disrupt the election meetings of aspirant anti-Labour town councillors.[27]

Crawford's position on the colour bar was ambiguous, like that of Fitzgerald, reflecting his own identification with white workers. The ambiguity of Rand socialists reflected a strategic dilemma: while hoping to gain the support of white workers, they nevertheless did not want to endorse their extreme racism. The first annual conference of the South African ILP was held in Germiston in late 1907, and 'an important discussion took place on the colour question'. While noting that '[t]he Transvaal public, as a whole, take a very narrow and prejudiced view of the colour question', the conference failed to reach a definite decision on the matter, 'although all were agreed that on principle no recognition could be made of race, colour, or creed'.[28]

Socialist ideas filtered into the smaller country towns as well. From East London in the Cape Colony, A. K. Soga, editor of *Izwi LaBantu* (*Voice of the People*), styled as 'A Kafir English Weekly' and 'The authority PAR EXCELLENCE on intelligent Native thought and feeling', sent his greetings to the *Labour Leader*. 'Our desire', wrote Soga in 1907,

is to educate the intelligent native mind on the principles of Labour and Socialism, which are beginning to penetrate the mind of the European workers. ... We are mostly enslaved here, both whites and blacks, and we in our humble way would like to study the literature of those who are, we believe, destined to play a large part in the government of the British Colonies and the coloured races under the British Crown in the fulness of time.[29]

Soga, a future founder of the SANNC, kept in touch with European developments. His mother was Scottish, and he had been educated there. The *Labour Leader* received copies of *Izwe LaBantu* and later that year reported on a 'Native Conference in South Africa' that had been held in East London 'to discuss subjects of vital import to the African race and to frame a common political platform to which members standing for native constituencies would be expected to adhere'.[30]

The following year Soga wrote to Keir Hardie with the aim of starting a correspondence on the 'cause of the workers, white, black, and coloured':

[W]e see no hope for the workers in South Africa outside of unity and cooperation between ourselves and yourselves, as the future hope of all the oppressed peoples of England and of the British Colonies. We are practically dominated by Pluto-aristocrats in the several Parliaments and are at present impotent.[31]

Trips to and from Britain strengthened the overseas ties. For British socialists on the move, South Africa became a stopping-off point en route from Australia. But the ideas of equality that visiting socialists preached were vehemently rejected by the white workers and labour organizations whom socialists saw as their natural constituency. Keir Hardie visited South Africa in 1907, en route from Australia and India, where he had been agitating for social and political equality. Both A. K. Soga and Archie Crawford had speculated on the reception Hardie would receive on account of the fierce propaganda campaign against his visit.[32] Their concerns were not unfounded. Hardie recalled his welcome to Johannesburg:

> The station, the approach leading thereto, and the bridge over the railway was one black mass of seething, howling demons. As the train drew up, young Crawford ... saw me, and signalled to a number of constables, who formed a cordon round the doorway, whilst a number of them surrounded me and led me by a by-path up from the station to where a cab was waiting. ... someone awoke to what was taking place, and with a shout the mob started in pursuit. Showers of stones smashed the windows, and both the driver and the police-man came in for some nasty cuts.[33]

Once in Johannesburg, Hardie came face to face with the implacable outlook of white labour. The meeting that the ILP organized for him quickly broke up. Speculating that Hardie had not realized the implications of asking white labour to eliminate the colour bar, Harrison pointed out that while 'some of the more responsible labour men there entertained him ... he dared not face the mob unprotect-ed'.[34] Hardie's own recollections of local attitudes were scathing:

> My suggestion was that the Unions should be thrown open to the coloured men, and that, as they would then claim the same pay as the whites ... their competition as cheap workers would end. It will scarcely be credited by those not on the spot, but this produced as much sensation as though I had pro-posed to cut the throat of every white man in South Africa. The capitalist Press simply howled with rage — there were, of course, exceptions — and at Ladysmith a mob, led by a local lawyer, wrecked the windows of the hotel in which I was staying.[35]

White labour's animosity towards black workers was felt in the more liberal Western Cape, as well. Although the Trades and Labour Council had invited Hardie to Cape Town, it refused to receive him after the agitation in Johannesburg. The SDF, however, gave him a warm reception at Socialist Hall in Buitenkant Street, where he declared: 'Socialism has no national or geographical boundaries. We are a world brotherhood.'[36]

The next few years saw sweeping political changes. The Union of South Africa was formed in 1910 – an amalgamation of two British colonies and two Boer republics – with the former Boer general, Louis Botha, its new prime minister. In anticipation, in 1909 a Native Convention was held in Bloemfontein to discuss the implications for Africans, while plans for a unified Labour Party were laid in 1908 and 1909. Archie Crawford was actively involved in this venture, reflecting the alliance orientation of the ILP.[37] The South African Labour Party was officially launched as the first national-level political party in January 1910, uniting the smaller regional Labour Parties. The Labour Party affiliated to the Second International. Its objective, as outlined in the Constitution and Platform adopted at its 1912–13 annual conference, was '[t]he socialisation of the means of production, distribution and exchange, to be controlled by a Democratic State in the interests of the whole community'. By community, however, it meant white people. Point 67 (a) of its platform called for '[t]he creation of conditions which will attract a free white population by prohibiting the importation of contract labour, white or coloured, and the abolition of the present indentured labour system'.

The Labour Party's Native Policy was premised on the '[s]eparation of native and white races as far as possible', and it called for separate political representation for Africans in reserved areas and for the provision of educational and agricultural training facilities for them.[38] Its 'Draft Report on Coloured Policy' stated:

Nothing should be done to attract coloured people to the Party at the expense of the white ideals. ... The white population must at present, and for a long time to come, bear the responsibility of guiding the destinies of the country, and this responsibility will not be lessened by the indiscriminate admission of large numbers of Coloured people in all stages of civilisation into our political institutions.

It then added, somewhat ambiguously, that 'any attempt to exclude civilised people merely on account of their colour is unjust and indefensible, and even suicidal. Separation from the white race – though most desirable in the case of the natives ... is an impossible policy in the case of the coloured population.'[39]

In 1911, Harrison went to England, visiting the London offices of the Social Democratic Party (SDP).[40] That was a key year for British socialism. The SDP, disenchanted members of the ILP and other localized socialist groups were discussing the possibility of unity as an alternative to the Labour Party, and Harrison undoubtedly took this in. A socialist unity conference was held in Salford in September 1911, launching the British Socialist Party. Archie Crawford attended and met Dora Montefiore, a wealthy British socialist and feminist, whom he invited to South Africa. When Harrison returned to South Africa later that year, he went to Pretoria and, along with two brothers, Robert and William Blake, and a Miss Hyatt, niece of the ethical socialist Edward Carpenter, launched a Pretoria Socialist Society. This held debates and linked up with the Pretoria Parliamentary Debating Society. Pretoria had already seen some socialist initiatives. A South African Socialist Federation had been launched in December 1909, led by the ILP's J. T. Bain. Although the Socialist Federation aimed to link up the various local groups around the country, Natal and Cape socialists never affiliated; like the British Socialist Party, it functioned on the

Rand and in Pretoria as an opposition group to the Labour Party.[41]

In Johannesburg, meanwhile, Philip Roux – father of the notable South African radical and historian Eddie Roux, active member of the Labour Party and an Afrikaans-speaking 'Britisher by adoption' – met Jock Campbell, a socialist who hailed from the west of Scotland and 'flourished in Johannesburg between 1905 and 1915' propagandizing for the SLP. In 1911 Philip Roux converted to socialism and gave his allegiance to the SLP. He owned a shop, and this became a meeting point for local socialists. Campbell, Eddie Roux tells us, ' is said to have preached unity between black and white workers. ... His meetings, however, were attended by white workers and not by Africans'.[42] In the slum of Ferreirastown, similarly, Jewish socialists agitated amongst local shopowners. The writer Bernard Sachs, a Lithuanian Jew who came to South Africa as a boy, told the story of one Jos. Gray who 'would declaim in ringing tones that echoed down the labyrinthine backyards of Ferreirastown, "*Sklaffen*, (slaves), why don't you fight for your freedom?"'[43]

On 23 February 1912, Dora Montefiore landed in Durban, having spent several weeks preaching socialism and meeting Labour Party officials in Australia. She spent several months on the Rand, working with Archie Crawford and Mary Fitzgerald on the *Voice of Labour*. Montefiore visited some gold mines and workers' compounds, 'though warned that white women went there at their own risk as to what they saw and heard'. The appalling conditions of the workers' lives imprinted themselves on her mind. '[A]s all sooner or later is paid for in this world,' she wrote many years later, 'when the day of reckoning comes between the black races and the white, the descendants of the present exploiters will have to answer for the greed and inhumanity of their forefathers.'[44]

She also became involved with the Pretoria Socialist Society, which organized a debate on socialism between Montefiore and Vere Stent, editor of the *Pretoria News*, held in the Pretoria Town Hall on 30 May. During the remainder of her time in Johannesburg, she spoke to the Jewish Workers' Union on the subject of Jewish industrial organization, and she held several meetings on female suffrage, given under the rather peculiar title 'Motherhood in the State'. Returning to Durban, she acted as election agent for Harry Norrie, who, running on a Socialist ticket, unsuccessfully tried to oust the Labour MP from his seat, and she addressed the local Women's Enfranchisement League. Later, in Cape Town, she gave a series of talks on female suffrage before sailing for England on 24 August.[45]

Montefiore arrived in South Africa at a particularly inauspicious moment for the feminist movement. Olive Schreiner had provided an inspiration for the South African women's suffrage movement, both through her writings and through her brief leadership of the Cape Women's Enfranchisement League, of which she was a vice-president at its founding in 1907.[46] But the movement was rent over the call for enfranchisement on the same basis as men. In Britain, such a qualification referred to class, educational status and age; in South Africa, it meant skin colour, at a time when black leaders were striving for a qualified franchise in the future Union of South Africa. In the Cape, Schreiner and a few other radicals resisted the idea of a racial franchise for white women. However, the Transvaal and Natal

Women's Enfranchisement Leagues insisted on calling for votes for white women only. As a step towards forming a national body, the majority in the Cape League finally agreed to that demand. Olive Schreiner resigned, scrawling her furious rejection on a leaflet: 'It was *not* a personal matter that made me leave that society. the women of the Cape Colony *all* women of the Cape Colony. these were the terms on which I joined.'[47] Her action was in marked contrast to that of Mary Fitzgerald, who co-edited *Modern Woman in South Africa* during 1909–10 under the auspices of the Women's Enfranchisement League, despite the exclusion of black women from its franchise demands.[48] Thus, by the time Montefiore visited South Africa, the women's suffrage movement was already racially divided.

The year 1912 saw another attempt to amalgamate the various South African groups – into a United Socialist Party. This effort followed British moves at socialist unity in 1911. But it also reflected the political unification of South Africa and the turn to national-level politics by all parties. A socialist unity conference was held in Johannesburg. Three delegates, including Harry Norrie and a Mr Knowler, represented Durban socialists; Archie Crawford and Mary Fitzgerald represented Johannesburg socialists; Dora Montefiore represented the Pretoria Socialist Society; and Harrison, the Cape Town SDF. Its draft constitution advocated 'the class war between the revolutionary working class and the reactionary exploiting class' and its membership was open to all socialists 'without discrimination as to race, sex, colour or creed'.[49] The United Socialist Party of South Africa, headquartered in Johannesburg, was formally launched on May Day 1912. Harrison valiantly publicized the organization and entreated socialists to overcome their differences. 'For denominational variety we almost excel the Christians', he complained, 'and with equal vindictiveness occupy almost as much time in vilifying each other's interest, as in philosophising on the ideal, and while these characteristics and doxology have obscured the real Christian teaching, the same reasons and opportunism have obscured scientific Socialism.' While noting that 'Freedom of method should certainly be recognized in local branches', he argued that a national body was necessary both for effective propaganda and 'to keep in touch with the International movement in other countries'.[50]

The United Socialist Party faltered for several months but the various local groups failed to agree on a constitution or on the relative merits of industrial unionism, anarchism and parliamentary politics. With the collapse of the *Voice of Labour* – the only socialist newspaper that was national in scope – late 1912 was not a particularly auspicious moment for South African socialism.[51] While socialism everywhere faced a rocky road, South Africa's racially-divided society made organization even more problematic.

Socialists and workers' struggles

The early 1910s saw further sweeping changes in the new 'for whites only' Union of South Africa as white supremacy was entrenched both in law and in practice.

These were measures that most whites, including white labour organizations, supported. In this climate, the SANNC was formally launched in January 1912 as a federated body of African organizations. Membership in the SANNC was open to African men over eighteen who could pay the annual membership fee; significantly, women could not be full voting members but were given auxiliary membership through the Bantu Women's National League. This was formed in 1913 as an outgrowth of the women's anti-pass protests that began that year in the Orange Free State. It was led by the indomitable Charlotte Maxeke, who had studied at Wilberforce University in the United States and was the first African woman from South Africa to receive a BA degree. Maxeke was not happy with the second-class status of women in the SANNC: 'They needed us to help by making the tea'.[52]

The SANNC's first major challenge was the 1913 Land Act, which became law in June. Protests against the proposed Land Bill had been taking place since 1910; black women had become involved in the campaign in 1912. The SANNC decided to petition the British King and Parliament, and it began raising funds to send a deputation to England; the 1914 deputation proved ineffectual. The Act precipitated mass evictions, frequently hitting the more prosperous, stock-owning tenants the hardest.[53] The evictions pushed more people into the reserves, causing overcrowding and making income from migrant labour increasingly necessary for survival in the reserves. As the supply of black mine labour increased and stabilized, this increased the anxiety of white mineworkers.

The working-class industrial struggle radicalized considerably in 1913. Despite socialist calls for 'one big union', their main focus was still organized labour – and this meant white labour. The tiny socialist movement was soon influenced by signs of growing militancy amongst some sections of white workers. While this appeared to be a positive development, especially as the more radicalized white workers demonstrated against symbols of state authority, it was, nonetheless, an ambiguous development, given white labour's attitudes towards black workers.

On the mines, white labour had been in a state of transition and turmoil for several years due to the reorganization of the labour process. Industrialization diminished the earlier skill differential between black and white, while management sought to cut the number of costly white workers employed. Acutely aware of their vulnerable position, in 1907 skilled craftworkers, still formally dominant in the labour hierarchy, went on strike against the mining companies' efforts to increase their supervisory workloads. Management broke the strike by replacing skilled white workers with cheaper, unskilled Afrikaners, brought onto the mines to supervise blacks.[54] This was possible because deskilling reduced the need for skilled craftworkers and because skilled and semi-skilled blacks, classified and paid as unskilled black labour, could take over many of the functions previously performed by skilled whites. Until 1907 unskilled Afrikaner labour had been used only on a short-term, experimental basis. This strike marked their permanent incorporation into the mining labour force.

At one level, the strike indicated the decline of craft-based privileges based on a monopoly of scarce skills and of craft unions. More importantly, it signalled a turning point in the nature of white labour and its relationship to black labour. Before 1907 white supervision of largely unskilled blacks rested in part on their position as skilled workers, as well as on the racial ideology whose roots lay in the colonial conquest period and that prevented any equality between black and white. Skilled English-speaking labour had performed supervisory tasks, and English and Afrikaner had stood in potential competition to each other as skilled and unskilled labour in a period of deskilling. The year 1907 marked the formal recognition of a process in which, hand in hand with industrialization, the privileged position of whites in the labour force was based less and less on skills and increasingly on their supervision of black labour. The potential for white unity, paradoxically, emerged out of their earlier competition. The strike's defeat signified the formation of a white working class, in which colour came to override distinctions of skills and nationality, where English and Afrikaner, skilled and unskilled, shared in common the potential to supervise black workers. The strike marked an important step in the structuring of white supremacy into the industrial capitalist system, in that white labour acquired a stake in the control of black labour at the workplace. The 1911 Mines and Works Act formalized this relationship by restricting skilled labour to whites.[55]

Despite the common interests of white workers *vis-à-vis* blacks, English-speaking whites saw themselves as British. Appeals 'to the brotherly feeling that should exist between the different sections of the Labour Party in the Empire' seemed but 'a hollow mockery' to white workers in the colonies, wrote G. J. Bruce of the Cape Labour Party in August 1908 to James Ramsay MacDonald, Labour MP in the British Parliament. Rather, he complained,

> it appears that the interests of the savage Zulus, the comfort of the Chinese criminals in the compound, & the convenience of the Indian coolies, seem to be nearer the heart of the English Labour Party than the continued oppression, physical ruin, & death by starvation of hundreds of their white brethren of the same flesh & blood in a British Colony.[56]

Despite the Cape Labour Party's entreaty for the 'protection & succour we are entitled to while the British flag flies over us', the British Labour Party prioritized the interests of the empire over those of white workers in any particular colony and refused to embroil itself in South Africa's internal affairs. Nor, Ramsay MacDonald tartly replied, would it pander to appeals for white solidarity.[57]

Industrialization on the mines had a contradictory effect on white labour. The 1907 strike had intensified the belief of many mine owners that the industry should begin to modify the strict racial hierarchy allowing cheaper black labour to perform semi-skilled and skilled work, thereby replacing more costly white workers. Although white social pressure had hitherto prevented any decisive move in this direction, the Chamber of Mines began moving to modify the colour bar in response to cost constraints. The next few years saw intense protest by white workers against the threat of black competition, and unskilled white labour relied heavily on the colour bar to protect its privileges as their potential for replacement by black labour increased.[58]

This tension culminated in the general strike of July 1913. In May 1913 white mineworkers at New Kleinfontein Mine in Benoni struck at the threat of losing their half-day holiday on Saturdays. Attempts to mediate and contain the strike failed. By 4 July 18,000 men were on strike at sixty-three mines; the Federation of Trades declared a general strike, and the government proclaimed martial law. By 5 July every mine and power station on the Witwatersrand was on strike.[59] Archie Crawford and Mary Fitzgerald of the ILP saw in the strike the possibility of a syndicalist revolution as the strikers defiantly attacked symbols of authority. The *Illustrated Star: Town and Country Journal* chronicled the escalating violence. It reported that led by Mary Fitzgerald, '[w]omen appeared to have assumed control: it was they who led the attack on the cars, and was they who led the crowd to the Power Station'. Later,

> with an overturned cab as a platform, the leaders held a meeting outside the Post Office in President Street. Mrs. Fitzgerald and Mr. Crawford both spoke. Mention was made of the railway men, and some said that the trains were still running. Rushing down Rissik Street yelling, 'We will burn Park Station!' the crowd swept aside the Police who guarded the station. ... after one or two futile attempts to set the place on fire, the flames took a good hold of the office, and spread with alarming rapidity.[60]

On 5 July representatives from the Federation of Trades met with Prime Minister Botha and Smuts and agreed to end the strike on condition that the government investigate the strikers' grievances. The strike effectively ended the following Monday, having remained concentrated on the Witwatersrand.[61] The strikers' grievances were subsequently incorporated in a document called the *Workers' Charter*. Although many of their demands for workers' rights and safe job conditions coincided with the parallel demands being voiced by workers around the world, they also included demands for the protection of white jobs from black competition.[62]

Hardly surprisingly, black organizations showed no real interest in the strike: at its July 1913 conference, for instance, the SANNC passed a resolution, drafted by Sol Plaatje, 'dissociating the natives from the strike movement'.[63]

Alongside the white labour protests of these years, the first wave of collective black working-class action swept the country in the early 1910s, moving from Natal to the Rand as far north as current-day Namibia, from the docks to the sugar plantations to the mines. For black mineworkers, the transition from individual protest over low wages and poor working conditions, generally through desertion, to collective protest coincided with the stabilization of the unskilled migrant labour supply in those years. This reflected the fact that by the second decade of the century, economic deterioration in the reserves meant that for most families the mining wage was an important source of income rather than a supplement to rural production.[64]

One significant repercussion of the 1913 white miners' strike was the immediate outbreak of a strike of black mineworkers. Two years before, in January 1911,

African mineworkers had struck at Dutoitspan, Voorspoed and Village Deep Mines. They were forced back to work by the police, who had the support of white workers, and were later imprisoned. Crawford's *Voice of Labour* angrily denounced those white workers who 'prostituted themselves into guardians of Capitalist plunder'.[65] Once again, in 1913, the struggle of black workers to improve their conditions met with antipathy from most whites. On 6 July meetings of African miners were disrupted by police; by 8 July 9000 miners on four mines refused to work, and the strike spread to other mines, involving about 13,000 men.[66] In Johannesburg, this caused 'all kinds of rumours ... as to a reported "rising" among the natives in various mining compounds'. These speculations were quickly dampened by the *Illustrated Star*, which went on to note that '[t]he would-be strikers contended that the white men had succeeded in their demands, and they considered it right that they should be treated in a similar fashion'.[67]

The government put a quick end to the strike. At City and Suburban Mine, mounted police and troops drove strikers into their huts. Later, the men were made to assemble according to tribe. Each group was told that their ringleaders would be arrested and that all those not going back to work the following day would be arrested. Alleged ringleaders were rounded up; sticks and other weapons were confiscated. Similar tactics were used at the other striking mines; the majority of workers agreed to return to work the next day.

Black organizations reacted angrily. The APO defended the right of black workers to strike and denounced the government's 'brutal savagery'. The SANNC called for government protection of African mineworkers in case of a general strike of white workers and argued that the 'strike leaders were being punished for "doing what their white overseers told them to do"'.[68]

This time, the actions of the black strikers made some impact on some white socialists. Two white trade unionists, George Mason and R. B. Waterston, had both exhorted black workers at Kleinfontein Mine to down tools, although they later indicated that they did not plan to help them organize and did not intend them to align with whites.[69] Seven years later David Ivon Jones, a founding member of the CPSA, would write that from the time of the 1913 black mineworkers' strike 'there has been a growing minority of white workers who realize that the emancipation of the white can be achieved only by solidarity with the native working masses'.[70]

Tensions among people of Indian origin were also mounting. Led by Mohandas Gandhi, who spent nearly twenty years in South Africa, the first major Indian *satyagraha* campaign had occurred in 1906, in protest against compulsory passes for Indians in Transvaal.[71] A host of other anti-Indian laws followed over the subsequent years. On 14 March 1913 the government's decision to invalidate non-Christian marriages, thus undermining the legal status of married Indian women, catalysed protests that led to the imprisonment of Indian women. Indian workers on the Newcastle coalmines went on strike over the women's imprisonment, and Indian indentured workers, led by Albert Christopher, began protesting against the renewal of their indenture contracts. Strikes erupted on sugar plantations, railways, factories and amongst Indian service workers in town, and continued throughout the year. Gandhi and other leaders were imprisoned but, following Gandhi's release from prison, the campaign was brought to a negotiated end with some concessions and reforms, and Gandhi left South Africa for good on 18 July 1914.[72]

The frustrations of white workers continued climbing through 1913 and into 1914. The *Illustrated Star* warned '[t]he Government is standing on the edge of a volcano',[73] while the Labour Party's organ, *Worker*, cautioned that a general strike 'now means something like a civil war'.[74] Tensions were especially acute in the railway industry, where white workers sought £1 day for skilled labour, a minimum wage for unskilled white labour and union recognition.

Catalysed by the government's decision to retrench railway workers on Christmas Eve, H. J. Poutsma, general secretary of the Amalgamated Society of Railway and Harbour Servants, declared a general strike of railway workers on 12 January 1914.[75] Martial law was imposed from 15 January through March 1914; the strikers gave up unconditionally. The government subsequently rounded up hundreds of trade unionists and strike supporters, including Colonel Creswell, MP and leaders of the Labour Party. On 30 January the government abducted nine alleged strike leaders – Archie Crawford, J. T. Bain, H. J. Poutsma, George Mason, R. B. Waterston, D. McKerrill, W. Livingstone, A. Watson and W. H. Morgan – and deported them without trial to Britain.[76]

The deported nine landed in England to a resounding welcome by trade unionists and Labour Party leaders: in contrast to the cold shoulder white South African labour leaders had received to their appeals for racial solidarity a few years earlier, the British labour movement was incensed over the issue of state repression. The renowned English trade unionist Tom Mann went to South Africa in March and spent several months there 'as the Ambassador of the Rank and File of Great Britain and Ireland', preaching syndicalism and revolution.[77] The strike leaders were repatriated back to South Africa later that year.

This ferment had a profound effect on socialists in South Africa, simultaneously inspiring hope for the ultimate victory of labour over capital – 'To me there seemed no doubt at all that socialism would soon be established' wrote Eddie Roux about the events of 1914 – while strengthening the bonds of kith and kin with socialists in Britain.[78] In fact, English-speaking socialists in South Africa still largely identified themselves as British. A manifesto entitled *Under Martial Law*, dated Johannesburg, 21 January 1914, and signed by six members of the South African Labour Executive – W. H. 'Bill' Andrews, H. W. Sampson, D. Dingwall, W. Wybergh, Sidney P. Bunting and F. A. W. Lucas – underlined the point, noting that '[w]e have tried on all hands – Federation of Trades, Labour party, and individuals – to send cables *home* since the proclamation of martial law, and even before, stating the true position of affairs from the strikers' standpoint'.[79]

Despite the collapse of the railway strike under martial law, the radicalization of white workers faced with state repression gave a push to the labour movement. Amongst whites, popular opinion swung towards Labour – not, however, to socialists – and a Labour victory was expected in the national elections of 14 October. '*But then*', wrote Bill Andrews, '*came the war*'.[80]

The impact of the First World War

The outbreak of war in August 1914 proved traumatic for socialist movements around the world. In Europe the willingness of labour movements to support their national war efforts gave final rest to the hope of international labour solidarity. The Russian revolutionary V. I. Lenin wrote his treatise on *Imperialism* in an attempt to explain the collapse of international working-class solidarity into nationalism.[81] The bulk of the British Labour Party supported the war, and several leading figures served in wartime coalitions. The ILP opposed the war and criticized the growing illiberality of the British state. In 1914, the majority of the leadership of the British Socialist Party, which incorporated both the SDP and dissident ILP members, was pro-war; in 1916 the British Socialist Party divided over the issue. The German Social Democratic Party split in 1917.

As part of the British Empire, South Africa was embroiled in the war. The South African government's formal declaration of war against Germany and its decision to invade the German colony of South West Africa kindled the alienation of Afrikaner nationalists and led to an aborted rebellion. But the war fuelled patriotic sentiments amongst organizations both of labour and of the nationally oppressed. The South African Industrial Federation, for instance, reversed its earlier anti-war position, and the SANNC agreed to suspend its protests against the 1913 Native Land Act once the war began.

South Africa's entry into the war created new schisms in its socialist movement, as socialists split between supporters and opponents of the war. For the diverse socialists who opposed the war, their common anti-war stance became a unifying bond, as some syndicalists and some proponents of political action submerged their strategic differences. A clearer distinction between some socialists and the white labour movement began to crystallize around opposing stances to the war. Olive Schreiner's vehement anti-war stance proved to be a barometer in signalling the centrality of the issue for South African socialists. In poor health, she spent the war years in Europe, feeling politically and personally betrayed by friends and socialists who now supported the war. Despite her sympathy for the SANNC and her previous support for Gandhi's *satyagraha* campaigns, she kept aloof from both Sol Plaatje, secretary-general of the SANNC, and from Gandhi while they were in England, due to their support for Britain's war efforts.[82]

On the war's eve, the Labour Party issued an anti-war statement that criticized 'the Capitalist governments of Europe in fermenting a war which can only benefit the international armament manufacturers' ring and other enemies of the working class' and called on 'workers of the world to organize and refrain from participating in this unjust war'.[83] Nonetheless, like Labour Parties elsewhere, the South African Labour Party changed its stance, led by Colonel Creswell and his 'See the war through' policy. In protest, in September 1914 a number of dissenters formed the War on War League within the Labour Party. A year later, in September 1915, about twenty dissenters, including Bill Andrews, Sidney Bunting and Yeshaya Israelstam, seceded from the Labour Party and formed the International Socialist League. The diverse backgrounds of these three white men typified the early socialist movement. Andrews, born in Suffolk, England, was a skilled worker who came to South Africa in 1893 and organized for the Amalgamated Society of Engineers (later, the Amalgamated Engineering Union) – a craft union. Bunting, from a prosperous English Nonconformist family, came to South Africa during the Anglo-Boer War and subsequently trained as a lawyer. Israelstam was an Eastern European Jew who had been involved with the Society of Friends of Russian Liberty. They were joined by members of the SLP and of the IWW.[84]

In Cape Town, the issue of whether or not to support the war caused such dissension within the SDF that initially it adopted a neutral position. Eventually, however, a pro-war faction formed the Constitutional Socialist League under H. Hiscox's leadership, while another pro-war member, H. A. Evans, turned to trade union work. The formation of the International Socialist League pushed the issue once more to the fore in the SDF, and on 6 September 1916 the anti-war members were able to push through a resolution opposing the war. The leading figures of this anti-war faction were Wilfred Harrison and Joe Pick, an Eastern European watchmaker who had a small shop on Waterkind Street. The SDF linked up with the International Socialist League and both began printing anti-war propaganda.[85]

The pattern of Durban socialism during the war years was different. There, socialism remained an extremely weak tendency and followed the lead of its British counterpart, the British Socialist Party. In 1914 the pro-war majority of the British Socialist Party's leadership controlled the party paper, *Justice*. Around 1914 the Durban SDF renamed itself the SDP, and when war was declared the SDP followed the majority position of the British Socialist Party leadership, and supported the war. In late 1915 a few International Socialist League members moved down from Johannesburg and opened an office. They began holding open-air meetings and organized some night classes that used works by Marx and Daniel De Leon. However, their opposing stances to war prevented any working relationship between the SDP and International Socialist League.[86]

Opposition to the war was hardly a popular position amongst whites generally. In Cape Town, Harrison remembered the temper of the crowds he addressed at the Adderly Street meetings during the war period: 'It took us all our time to keep the crowd from throwing us into the sea, which was then quite close to our rostrum, and many other damages they promised us.' Nevertheless, he went on, '[o]ur Adderly Street meetings grew in such numbers that we packed the Dock Road from the Flat Iron Building to the Carlton Hotel, which solicited a protest from the proprietor, and we were told to move our platform to the side of the building facing the pier'.[87]

Similar scenes took place in Johannesburg. Government harassment of anti-war socialists was stepped up. 'Detectives were always busy at the meetings with their note-books', Harrison recalled. He, for one, was fined and imprisoned for his authorship of a pamphlet entitled *War!*, which was published by the War on War League, and for selling the International Socialist League's new paper, the *International*.[88]

Syndicalist initiatives

Industrial unrest continued through the war and afterwards. Black mineworkers used strikes and boycotts to protest against the combined effects of rising prices and low wages. In December 1915 about 3000 black workers at the Van Ryn Gold Mine went on strike, and more strikes broke out at other mines in January and February 1916. In February 1917 a boycott of mines stores spread rapidly across the eastern Witwatersrand.[89]

Socialist responses to black working-class protests during these years were varied and equivocal, reflecting both the overwhelmingly white social composition of socialist organizations and the rigid racial division of the working class. Generally, the International Socialist League was more directly involved in trade union work than the propagandistic SDF, undoubtedly reflecting its organizational roots in the Labour Party. Two of the League's leading figures, Bill Andrews and C. B. Tyler, a shopfitter and an activist in the building workers' union who had come to socialism through the SLP, had long experience organizing white workers. They promoted the idea of industrial unionism to replace craft-based unions.[90] Despite the International Socialist League's commitment to industrial unionism, however, the few members who hoped to organize black workers had to confront the attitudes of their own comrades as well as the racially-divided labour force. For example, the International Socialist League supported the December 1915 strike of black mineworkers: the *International* called for an end to the pass and compound system and the use of indentured labour and appealed that 'as the first step to his safety the white worker must give the native a lift up to his own industrial status'. Nonetheless, the League's members held a range of views on 'the Native Question', and this was seen in its ambiguous compromise position to 'prevent the increase of the native wage workers and to assist the existing native wage workers to free themselves from the wage system' – a position that dovetailed with Labour Party policy.[91]

The influence of syndicalism on socialist organizers in the late 1910s, particularly those involved with black workers, is striking. Syndicalism was strongest in the Johannesburg area, although it had reverberations in Cape Town and Durban. In part this was due to the influence of the former SLP and IWW members. Syndicalist influence permeated the International Socialist League through SLP literature and documents from the United States and Britain. David Ivon Jones contacted the American SLP for copies of its constitution, platform and rules, and at its second conference in January 1917 the International Socialist League included the SLP's objective '[t]o propagate the principles of international socialism, industrial unionism, and anti-militarism'.[92] Bernard 'Benny' Sachs remembered Daniel De Leon's work on class struggle in Roman history as the most significant piece that he read during those years.[93]

As Jones recalled several years later, when he was firmly in the Bolshevik camp, the International Socialist League in its first days had 'been captured by the De Leonites' and was '[i]mbued with the ideas of De Leon, as popularized in the splendid series of Marxian pamphlets issued by the S.L.P. of America and Great Britain'.

The League, Jones continued, 'proclaimed the principal [sic] of Industrial Unionism' and sought 'to end parliaments, and to replace them by the class state of the workers functioning through their industrial unions'. Craft unions were 'odious' because they divided the workers, and 'the exclusion of the native workers from part or lot in the Labour Movement was denounced as a crime'. For members of the International Socialist League, declared Jones, 'the rather mechanical formula of De Leon's Industrial Unionism ... was made a living thing by its application to the native workers'.[94]

Early socialist approaches to black workers reflected this syndicalist orientation. A handful of International Socialist League members, most notably the veteran syndicalist Andrew Dunbar, Sidney Bunting and David Ivon Jones, played an important role in the early organization of black workers in Johannesburg through the formation of the Industrial Workers of Africa (IWA). This was modelled loosely on the IWW and had an ambitious slogan of '*Sifuna zonke!*' ('We want all!'). In 1917 the Johannesburg International Socialist League began making overtures to the Transvaal Native Congress, the regional branch of the SANNC, in an effort to pull in black workers, and in March 1917 it organized a meeting to protest against the Native Affairs Administration Bill. By July, the group that would later become the IWA held its first meeting in the shop of a Mr Neppe, attended by ten whites from the International Socialist League and twenty blacks, including two police spies. The group began holding weekly meetings, with attendance fluctuating between thirty and fifty. In September the group constituted itself as the Society of the Industrial Workers of the World, and on 11 October, after debates about the inclusion of whites, renamed itself the IWA. Its members included T. William Thibedi, a school teacher who became a socialist organizer; Kapan Reuben, who organized on the mines; and Reuben Cetyiwe and Hamilton Kraai, both of whom moved to Cape Town in 1919, setting up a Cape Town IWA and organizing dockworkers. Talbot Williams became an IWA organizer.[95]

By late November 1917 the IWA had produced and had printed about 1000 copies of a bilingual Zulu and Sesuto leaflet. The translation of the Zulu version began: 'Native workers! Why do you keep in Slavery? Why can't you get free as other men? Why are you kicked about and be [sic] spat on by your white employers?' And it exhorted them to unite and to '[f]orget all the distinction of nationalities. ... You must not say this is a Zulu, and this is a Msutu and this is a Shangaan. You are all workers. Bind yourself in a chain of being workers.'[96]

These were distributed in towns and on the mines across the Rand. IWA members were invited to address the APO, and by December, the IWA was holding joint meetings with the APO and the Transvaal Native Congress. Inspired by a successful strike in May 1918 of white power-workers, Johannesburg's black municipal workers, or 'bucket boys', went on strike. This had the support of the IWA and the International Socialist League. The strike was unsuccessful, and the 152 strikers were sentenced to two months' imprisonment. The alleged strike leaders were charged with incitement to violence but Bunting defended them and succeeded in getting the charges dropped. In the strike's aftermath, the IWA held a joint meeting with the Transvaal Native Congress and the International Socialist League, and in June a joint committee was formed to develop a plan of action in response to the continued unrest on the Rand. The joint committee organized a mass meeting attended by approximately 1000 blacks and forty whites. This launched a '1/- a day' campaign, which coincided with several weeks of labour protests and meetings on the Witwatersrand and represented the culmination of black protest on the Rand that year.[97]

The IWA functioned on the Rand for about another year. Roux suggests that constant police surveillance kept black workers away. And few Africans joined the International Socialist League directly at that time, most likely due to the predominance of whites.[98] Nonetheless, the IWA's influence was twofold: its propaganda permeated amongst black workers and probably pushed both the Transvaal Native Congress and the Transvaal APO to the left, and some of its original members played active roles in labour and socialist organizations for years to come.

Similar syndicalist initiatives took place in Durban. While Harry Norrie and comrades in the SDP evidently agitated amongst striking Indian workers, International Socialist League activists stressed trade union organization. In March 1917 a De Leonite socialist and International Socialist League member named Gordon Lee organized an Indian Workers' Industrial Union, along the lines of the IWW. This held open-air meetings and study classes. Bernard L. E. Sigomoney, a socialist, teacher and British-trained Anglican pastor, became its secretary and represented it at International Socialist League conferences. However, subjected to repeated harassment, the union foundered after a few years.[99]

Conclusion

Although the socialist movement remained tiny and marginal, the continued agitation of labour during the war, particularly black labour, inevitably pulled socialists along. As black labour unrest increased through the war, so did socialist interaction with black workers' struggles. Because South Africa's racial franchise largely precluded black electoral activity, syndicalism – as opposed to purely political action – provided a credible means of understanding and organizing black labour protests in this tumultuous period. Hence, the small number of socialists interested in organizing black workers were attracted to it.

Syndicalism's ready answer to racial divisions within the labour force was that such differences would be dissolved through class struggle. This was a naive supposition in South Africa, where the entrenched racial divisions in society and industry made the possibility of organizing all workers into one big union very remote. And the few socialists who were involved in organizing black workers still faced the scepticism of their comrades, who looked to white labour as the proletarian vanguard.

Notes

1. James Keir Hardie, 'In Cape Colony', *Labour Leader*, May 8, 1908, 292. See also Frederick Hale, 'Socialist Agitator, Traitor to the British Empire, or Angel of Peace? James Keir Hardie's visit to Natal in 1908', *Journal of Natal and Zulu History*, 14, 1992, 1–18.

2. Roux, *Time Longer than Rope*, 53–77; André Odendaal, *Vukani Bantu! The Beginnings of Black Protest Politics in South Africa to 1912*, Cape Town and Johannesburg: David Philip, 1984, 1–16.

3. Gavin Lewis, *Between the Wire and the Wall: A History of South African 'Coloured' Politics*, Cape Town and Johannesbug: David Philip, 1987, 57; Elizabeth Everett, 'Zainunnissa (Cissie) Gool, 1897–1963: A Biography', BA Honours, University of Cape Town, October 1978, 1.

4. Simons and Simons, *Class and Colour*, 73.

5. Simons and Simons, *Class and Colour*, 78.

6. Roux, *Time Longer than Rope*, 107; Fatima Meer, 'Indentured Labour and Group Formations in Apartheid Society', *Race and Class*, 26, 4, 45–60, esp. 46–9, 56; Maureen Swan, 'Ideology in Organised Indian Politics, 1891–1948', in Shula Marks and Stanley Trapido, eds, *The Politics of Race, Class and Nationalism in Twentieth-Century South Africa*, London and New York: Longman, 1987, 182–208, esp. 187–9.

7. M. K. Gandhi, *Satyagraha in South Africa*, Ahmedabad 14:Navajivan, 1972, 36; Frene Ginwala, *Indian South Africans*, London: Minority Rights Group Report No. 34, 1977, 5–7; Meer, 'Indentured Labour', 52.

8. Simons and Simons, *Class and Colour*, 102.

9. James Keir Hardie, 'South Africa: In Natal', *Labour Leader*, 17 April 1908, 244.

10. Harrison, *Memoirs of a Socialist*, xii, vii-x.

11. Harrison, *Memoirs of a Socialist*, xix.

12. Harrison, *Memoirs of a Socialist*, 4.

13. 'Social Democratic Federation: Annual Report', *South African News Weekly Edition*, 14 June 1905, 21; First and Scott, *Olive Schreiner*, 253; Harrison, *Memoirs of a Socialist*, 14.

14. 'Socialism in South Africa', *Justice*, 14 January 1905, 4.

15. Simons and Simons, *Class and Colour*, 73; Roux, *Time Longer than Rope*, 126; Harrison, *Memoirs of a Socialist*, 17.

16. Harrison, *Memoirs of a Socialist*, quotes 10 and xviii respectively.

17. Roux, *Time Longer than Rope*, 123; Bernard Wasserstein, *Herbert Samuel: A Political Life*, Oxford: Clarendon Press, 1992, 75–82; Allison Drew, ed., *South Africa's Radical Tradition: A Documentary History*, vol. 1, Cape Town: Buchu, Mayibuye and University of Cape Town, 1996, 71, nn. 6 and 8.

18. 'Social Democratic Federation'; 'Socialism in South Africa'.

19. Wasserstein, *Herbert Samuel*, 82.

20. Shimoni, *Jews and Zionism*, 53–54; Harrison, *Memoirs of a Socialist*, 65; 'The Worker', *South African News Weekly Edition*, 5 July 1905, 12.

21. Harrison, *Memoirs of a Socialist*, x.

22. Simons, *Class and Colour*, 103.

23. 'The Worker', *South African News Weekly Edition*, 22 March 1905, 18; Simons and Simons, *Class and Colour*, 102; Letter from Harry Norrie, Hon. Secy, Social Democratic Federation, Durban Branch, 14 May 1908 to Secy, Labour Party (London), James

Middleton Papers, SA/14, Labour Party Archives, National Museum of Labour History, Manchester.

24. Keir Hardie, 'South Africa: In Natal'.

25. 'South African Notes', *Justice*, 5 August 1905, 2.

26. Simons and Simons, *Class and Colour*, 103, 106, 141–8 and quote 216. See also John Philips, 'The South African Wobblies: the Origins of Industrial Unions in South Africa', *Ufahamu*, 8, 3, 1978, 122–38.

27. Katz, *Trade Union Aristocracy*, 54–55, 307–13; Simons and Simons, *Class and Colour*, 150.

28. A. Crawford, 'The Movement in the Transvaal', *Labour Leader*, 29 November 1907, 358.

29. 'Greetings from the South African Native Press', *Labour Leader*, 15 November 1907, 322.

30. 'Native Conference in South Africa', *Labour Leader*, 6 December 1907, 378.

31. Letter from A. K. Soga to Keir Hardie, 14 July 1908, Francis Johnson Papers, 08/281, (on microfilm, National Museum of Labour History, Manchester).

32. 'Greetings from the South African Native Press'; 'The Movement in the Transvaal'.

33. Keir Hardie, 'Stoned in South Africa', 1907 in Drew, ed., *South Africa's Radical Tradition*, vol. 1, 42–43. The reference to 'black mass' is of course to whites.

34. Harrison, *Memoirs of a Socialist*, 19–20.

35. Keir Hardie, 'Stoned in South Africa', 42.

36. Harrison, *Memoirs of a Socialist*, 20.

37. Roux, *Time Longer than Rope*, 108–9; Letter from C. H. Haggar to Ramsay MacDonald, 6 January 1909, Middleton Papers, SA/32.

38. South African Labour Party Constitution and Platform (as Amended by Annual Conference at Cape Town, 1912–13), quotes from II.2, XIV.64(a), and XIV.73 respectively, Middleton Papers SA/70.

39. 'Draft Report on Coloured Policy', Annexure to South African Labour Party Constitution and Platform, 16–18, quotes 18. See also Roux, *Time Longer than Rope*, 127–28.

40. In 1908 the British SDF became the SDP.

41. Harrison, *Memoirs of a Socialist*, 33–39; Simons and Simons, *Class and Colour*, 143–4, 151.

42. Roux, *Time Longer than Rope*, 129.

43. Bernard Sachs, *Multitude of Dreams: A Semi-Autobiographical Study*, Johannesburg: Kayor, 1949, 85; Mantzaris, 'Radical Community', 163–4.

44. Dora Montefiore, *From a Victorian to a Modern*, E. Archer, 1927, 146 and quote 148–9.

45. Montefiore, *From a Victorian to a Modern*, 150–51; Harrison, *Memoirs of a Socialist*, 35.

46. Cherryl Walker, 'The Women's Suffrage Movement: the Politics of Gender, Race and Class', in Cherryl Walker, ed., *Women and Gender in Southern Africa to 1945*, Cape Town: David Philip and London: James Currey, 1990, 313–45, 323; First and Scott, *Olive Schreiner*, 261.

47. First and Scott, *Olive Schreiner*, quotes 264 and 263 respectively.

48. Iris Berger, *Threads of Solidarity: Women in South African Industry, 1900–1980*, Bloomington and Indianapolis: Indiana University and London: James Currey, 1992, 37 and 308, n. 94.

49. Simons and Simons, *Class and Colour*, 152.

50. Wilfred H. Harrison, *What's up with the Movement?*, Johannesburg: Modern Press,

1912, Jack Simons Collection, Pamphlet Collection, P246, Manuscripts and Archives Department, University of Cape Town Libraries.

51. Harrison, *Memoirs of a Socialist*, 36–7; Simons and Simons, *Class and Colour*, 152.

52. Quoted in Miriam Basner, *Am I an African? The Political Memoirs of H. M. Basner*, Johannesburg: Witwatersrand, 1993, 23. Unlike the other provinces in the new Union, African and Coloured women in the Orange Free State were subjected to pass laws, which began to be tightened after 1910. Thomas Karis and Gwendolen M. Carter, eds, *From Protest to Challenge: A Documentary History of African Politics in South Africa 1882–1964*, vol. 1, Stanford, CA: Hoover Institution, 1972, 61. Cherryl Walker, *Women and Resistance in South Africa*, London: Onyx, 1982, 32–3; Peter Walshe, *The Rise of African Nationalism in South Africa: the African National Congress, 1912–1952*, London: Hurst & Co., 1970, 80, 206.

53. Brian Willan, *Sol Plaatje: South African Nationalist, 1876–1932*, London, Ibadan, Nairobi: Heinemann, 1984, 162–3; Solomon Plaatje, *Native Life in South Africa*, ed. by Brian Willan, Burnt Mill, Harlow: Longman, 1987, especially 49–66. Walker, *Women and Resistance*, 29–30; Keegan, *Rural Transformations*, 184.

54. Howard Simson, 'The Myth of the White Working Class in South Africa', *The African Review*, 4, 2, 1974, 189–203.

55. Although Simson, 'The Myth of the White Working Class', stresses the continuity in black and white labour relations on the mines during this period on the grounds that before and after the 1907 strike white labour had a supervisory relationship to blacks, the nature and basis of white supervision of blacks was transformed through the 1907 strike. Van Onselen, *Studies in the Social and Economic History*, 138–144, emphasizes the conflict between English workers and Afrikaner unemployed before and after the strike. Most other accounts see the 1922 Rand Revolt as the fundamental turning point for white labour.

56. Letter from the Cape Labour Party to James Ramsay MacDonald, 12 August 1908 in Drew, ed., *South Africa's Radical Tradition*, vol. 1, 43.

57. Letter from James Ramsay MacDonald to Mr. G. J. Bruce, Cape Labour Party, September 11, 1908, Middleton Papers, SA/24.i.

58. Callinicos, *Gold and Workers*, 74–7; Robert Davies, 'Mining Capital, the State and Unskilled White Workers in South Africa, 1901–1913', *Journal of Southern African Studies*, 3, 1, October 1976, 41–69.

59. W. H. Andrews, *Class Struggles in South Africa: Two Lectures Given on South African Trade Unionism*, Cape Town, 1941, 23–24; Harrison, *Memoirs of a Socialist*, 45; Simons and Simons, *Class and Colour*, 156; Elaine N. Katz, *A Trade Union Aristocracy: A History of White Workers in the Transvaal and the General Strike of 1913*, Johannesburg: African Studies Institute, University of the Witwatersrand, 1976, 411–14.

60. 'Story of the Strike', *Illustrated Star: Town and Country Journal*, 12 July 1913, 2.

61. 'Durban During Strike', *Illustrated Star*, 12 July 1913, 5.

62. Katz, *A Trade Union Aristocracy*, 324. The 1913 general strike revealed the continuing existence of ethnic tensions amongst whites, manifested through language question. A meeting on the first day of the strike discussed 'equality of language rights and the practical carrying into effect of clause 137 of the Constitution. ... One of the speakers held that it was a distinct breach of faith that the strike badges [which read "General Strike. Unity is strength."] should only be printed in one language. The badge should have been printed in Dutch on the other side, and should have read "Algemene Staking. Eendracht maakt macht." ... eventually it was decided that on future occasions Dutch

miners would refuse to come out, unless article 137 was carried out to the letter.' See 'Strike Snippets', *Illustrated Star*, 12 July 1913, 22.

63. Quoted in Willan, *Sol Plaatje*, 163.

64. P. L. Bonner, 'The 1920 Black Mineworkers' Strike: a Preliminary Account', in Belinda Bozzoli, comp., *Labour, Townships and Protest: Studies in the Social History of the Witwatersrand*, Johannesburg: Ravan, 1979, 273–97; Jeeves, *Migrant Labour*, 28–9; MacMillan, *Africa Emergent*, 308.

65. Quoted in Simons and Simons, *Class and Colour*, 154.

66. Bonner, 'The 1920 Black Mineworkers' Strike', 274–5; Johnstone, *Class, Race and Gold*, 169.

67. 'Natives on Strike', *Illustrated Star*, 12 July 1913, 6.

68. Simons and Simons, *Class and Colour*, 160; Baruch Hirson and Gwyn A. Williams, *The Delegate for Africa: David Ivon Jones, 1883–1924*, London: Core, 1995, 129.

69. Simons and Simons, *Class and Colour*, 159; Katz, *A Trade Union Aristocracy*, 425–6.

70. Quoted in Simons and Simons, *Class and Colour*, 159; cf. Hirson and Williams, *The Delegate from Africa*, 132.

71. Gandhi, *Satyagraha in South Africa*, 102–7 defined *satyagraha* as a soul force in which opponents were defeated through one's own suffering. Although tactically similar to passive resistance, *satyagraha* was premised on non-violence, while passive resistance, in Gandhi's view, was compatible with the use of force.

72. Gandhi, *Satyagraha in South Africa*, 251–2, 260–307; Andrews, *Class Struggles*, 27; Roux, *Time Longer than Rope*, 104–7.

73. 'Railway Unrest', *Illustrated Star*, 12 July 1913, 17.

74. Simons and Simons, *Class and Colour*, 160.

75. Harrison, *Memoirs of a Socialist*, 45–46; Andrews, *Class Struggles*, 25. Poutsma subsequently joined the South African Party and became its national secretary.

76. Andrews, *Class Struggles*, 25–26; Drew, ed., *South Africa's Radical Tradition*, vol. 1, 71, n. 3; Roux and Roux, *Rebel Pity*, 7–8.

77. Quoted in Chushichi Tsuzuki, *Tom Mann 1856–1941: The Challenges of Labour*, Oxford: Clarendon Press, 1991, 169; Montefiore, *From a Victorian to a Modern*, 179.

78. Roux and Roux, *Rebel Pity*, 8.

79. *Under Martial Law*, Johannesburg, 21 January 1914, Tom Mann Papers, Working Class Movement Library, Salford. My emphasis.

80. Andrews, *Class Struggles*, 27; emphasis in original.

81. V. I. Lenin, 'Imperialism, the Highest Stage of Capitalism' [1916], Henry M. Christman, ed., *Essential Works of Lenin*, New York, Toronto, London: Bantam, 1966, 177–270.

82. First and Scott, *Olive Schreiner*, 298–305; Hirson and Williams, *The Delegate from Africa*, 139, 153.

83. Quoted in Harrison, *Memoirs of a Socialist*, 51.

84. Bunting, ed., *South African Communists Speak*, 1–3, 16; Sheridan Johns, 'The Birth of the Communist Party of South Africa', *The International Journal of African Historical Studies*, 9, 3, 1976, 371–400, 373; Lungisile Ntsebeza, 'Divisions and Unity in Struggle: The ANC, ISL and the CP, 1910–1928', BA Honours, University of Cape Town, January 1988, 22–34; Shimoni, *Jews and Zionism*, 84, Mantzaris, 'Radical Community', 161.

85. Harrison, *Memoirs of a Socialist*, 50–52, 56.

86. Johns, 'The Birth of the Communist Party', 377; Evangelos A. Mantzaris, 'The Indian

Tobacco Workers Strike of 1920: A Socio-Historical Investigation', *Journal of Natal and Zulu History*, 6, 1983, 115–25, 117.

87. Harrison, *Memoirs of a Socialist*, 52–3 and 54.

88. Harrison, *Memoirs of a Socialist*, quote 60 and 60–62; Hirson and Williams, *The Delegate from Africa*, 151.

89. Bonner, 'The 1920 Black Mineworkers Strike', 275–6.

90. Johns, 'The Birth of the Communist Party', 373–4; *Report on Workers Organisation in S.A.*, n.d., Russian Centre for the Conservation and Study of Modern History Records (RTsKhIDNI), Moscow, 495.64.4.

91. Hirson and Williams, *The Delegate from Africa*, 152–53 and 153, respectively.

92. Hirson and Williams, *The Delegate from Africa*, 156–7, quote 157.

93. Sachs, *Multitude of Dreams*, 137–8; Daniel De Leon, *Two Pages from Roman History: Plebs Leaders and Labour Leaders; The Warning of the Gracchi*, Edinburgh: Socialist Labour Press, 1908; Coleman, *Daniel De Leon*, 159.

94. David Ivon Jones, 'Communism in South Africa' [part 2], *Communist Review*, 1, 4, August 1921, 63–71, 69.

95. Frederick Johnstone, 'The IWA on the Rand', in Bozzoli, comp., *Labour, Townships and Protest*, 248–72, 261; Ntsebeza, 'Divisions and Unity in Struggle', 35–42; Hirson and Williams, *The Delegate for Africa*, 161, 171–4; Roux, *Time Longer than Rope*, 154; Simons and Simons, *Class and Colour*, 203–4; P. L. Wickens, *The Industrial and Commercial Workers' Union of Africa*, Cape Town: Oxford University, 1978, 26; South Africa. Department of Justice Files, 1914–1928, School of Oriental and African Studies Library, University of London, (microfilm), 3/527/17 (1917 and 1919).

96. Johnstone, 'The IWA on the Rand', 265.

97. Johnstone, 'The IWA on the Rand', 257–63; Johnstone, *Class, Race and Gold*, 174–5; Hirson and Williams, *The Delegate for Africa*, 176–7.

98. Roux, *Time Longer than Rope*, 130–32.

99. Mantzaris, 'The Indian Tobacco Workers Strike', 116–18; Simons and Simons, *Class and Colour*, 203; Hirson and Williams, *The Delegate for Africa*, 171.

Chapter 3

'The Word was made flesh': the impact of the Russian Revolution on South Africa

As class conflict escalated in the late 1910s, the socialist movement began to experience profound changes stimulated by the Russian revolutions of February and October 1917. As elsewhere, the revolutionary developments in Russia had a decisive impact on the mentality of South African socialists and on the social composition and the development of the movement. The October 1917 revolution strengthened the appeal of socialism not just as a utopian vision but as a feasible alternative to capitalism. Eddie Roux, then just a boy, recalled: 'In 1917 came the great Bolshevik Revolution. To me this proved conclusively that Jock Campbell, my Dad and all the socialist writers I had read had been perfectly right'.[1] The International Socialist League was electrified. David Ivon Jones forecast in March that 'The Russian "elemental mass" was about to enter "the International class struggle for human emancipation"'. Seven months later, after the October revolution, the *International* intoned: 'The Word becomes Flesh in the Council of Workmen'.[2] In May 1918, Hamilton Kraai of the IWA exhorted its members: 'We should today do as these workers of Russia did ... The whole world should be owned by the workers'.[3] And Olive Schreiner wrote provocatively to Smuts in 1920, the year she died, '[w]e may crush down the mass of our fellows in South Africa today as Russia did for generations, but today the serf is in the Palace and where is the Czar?'[4]

Two profound reorientations began in the South African socialist movement after the Russian Revolution. These concerned firstly, the relationship between syndicalism and political action and, secondly, the demographic composition of the movement.

Syndicalism versus political action

The first reorientation began with the end of the war, as tensions between syndicalist-oriented socialists and those prioritizing political action began to resurface. This was linked to the emphasis that the Bolshevik Party and, after its formation in March 1919, the Comintern placed on explicitly political action. These bodies promoted the view that the Russian Revolution represented a victory of political organization over syndicalism and over the spontaneous or self-organized action of workers. Over the next few years, syndicalist tendencies fought their ground within socialist groups. Ultimately, however, affiliation to the Comintern both indicated and reinforced the marginalization of syndicalism within the revolutionary left in most societies.

Opposition to the war had provided the common ground that enabled syndicalist tendencies to coexist within the SDF and the International Socialist League. The end of the war saw a hiving-off of those who were sceptical of political action and had prioritized industrial unionism as the most direct means to achieve socialism. In May 1918 the SDF split again, with A. Z. Berman and Joe Pick forming the tiny Industrial Socialist League. Many of the Industrial Socialist League's leading figures and its most active members were Eastern European Jews, including A. Z. Berman, Joe Pick, Solomon Buirski, Barnett Sieff and Joe Fish, and many had been *Bund* supporters in Cape Town.

Opposing the SDF's primarily propagandistic orientation, the Industrial Socialist League tried hard to attract black workers. It moved out of central Cape Town and rented a hall in Ayre Street, District Six, hoping to organize Coloured workers. It aroused some local curiosity but later moved back to a more central locale at the corner of Plein and Longmarket Streets. Berman and M. Walt organized for the Harbour Branch of the newly-formed Industrial and Commercial Workers' Union (ICU); Buirski agitated amongst black workers in rural areas. The Industrial Socialist League made an unsuccessful attempt to establish links with the APO but in 1919 it established fraternal relations with the newly-formed Cape Town branch of the IWA, and it generated some interest amongst black trade unionists, a few of whom addressed its meetings. It linked up with the Jewish Socialist Society, which had emerged sometime after the founding of the SDF, and in 1919–20 published an ephemeral monthly called the *Bolshevik*. At some point, a few individuals split off from the Industrial Socialist League, calling themselves the Communist League.

In Johannesburg, this tension between syndicalism and political action paralleled developments in Cape Town. Syndicalists from the SLP and IWW who had joined the International Socialist League during the war now voiced their scepticism about the value of electoral participation. In 1919, a minority, led by Andrew Dunbar and R. MacLean, who had been in the pre-war SLP, set itself up as a faction within the International Socialist League and linked up with the Industrial Socialist League in Cape Town. Sometime in late 1919 or early 1920, a number of Yiddish-speaking members of the International Socialist League, disenchanted with its parliamentary orientation, broke away and linked up with the Communist League in Cape Town. In Durban, a tiny group splintered off from the SDP and formed the Marxian Club to study the relevance of Marxist thought for contemporary events.[5]

Demographic shifts

The second shift that the Russian Revolution precipitated within the South African movement was demographic, namely, an increase in the weight and influence of

Eastern European Jewish immigrants in the South African movement. This demographic shift was centred mainly in Johannesburg and Cape Town. Fewer Eastern European exiles went to Durban, where socialists were primarily English-speaking and of British origin. About 60 per cent of the Jewish population in Johannesburg were artisans or small shopkeepers. Most lived in the slum areas of Ferreirastown and Commissioner Street. Their standard of living having plummeted during the war, they struggled to make ends meet.[6]

By 1917, many of the International Socialist League's founding members, those who had been in the Labour Party, had left. After the February 1917 revolution, the International Socialist League experienced a substantial increase in Yiddish-speaking members from Eastern Europe, as well as attracting the attention of a few Afrikaners and Africans. An anti-Zionist Yiddish-Speaking Group of a few hundred members and sympathizers was formed in Johannesburg in February 1917 and began holding Sunday meetings. This decided to affiliate to the International Socialist League, taking the affiliation of the Jewish section of the Bolshevik Party, *Evsektsia*, as its model. The inaugural meeting of the Yiddish Speaking Branch of the International Socialist League took place on 24 August 1917. The affiliation significantly increased the International Socialist League's membership. This demographic shift led to a greater emphasis on the role of culture and national identities within the socialist movement – albeit with an Eastern European focus – than had been the case when English-speaking socialists had been predominant. The Yiddish Speaking Branch began to publish Yiddish propaganda and held meetings addressed by Yiddish speakers. It published several pamphlets on the revolution. Particularly successful was a Yiddish translation of *The Workers' Revolution in Russia* that sold about 7000 copies. It also sponsored a Russian-Literary Dramatic Circle, which held political discussions. However, it snubbed an invitation from the Yiddish Literary Association because it wished to have 'nothing to do with Yiddish bourgeois literature'. It also ran a small library, held Marxist study classes and collected funds for locked-out workers.[7]

Two sets of tensions were apparent in the Yiddish Speaking Branch by 1918. The first tension was that seen across the entire socialist movement – that between syndicalism and political action. The second concerned the question of Zionism. In November 1918 a number of Jewish immigrants, including the brothers Richard and Leibl Feldman, Jacob Judelowitz, E. M. Pincus and S. Kartun, formed a Johannesburg branch of the *Poalei Zion* (Workers of Zion). The *Poalei Zion* was founded in Russia at the start of the century as a Marxist wing of Labour Zionism, and in 1907 a World Union of *Poalei Zion* was formed. The South African *Poalei Zion* sought to combine socialism with Jewish nationalism. While it sympathized with aspects of Afrikaner nationalism, it also believed in a united struggle of black and white workers and participated in May Day Demonstrations. Initially, the Yiddish Speaking Branch had fraternal relations with the *Poalei Zion*'s left wing. However, Zionism had a strong pull on South African Jews, and the *Poalei Zion* began to rival the Yiddish Speaking Branch, attracting a few hundred members. Some members of the Yiddish Speaking Branch joined the *Poalei Zion*, while others were expelled for Zionist tendencies. This double set of tensions took its toll, and by about January 1920 the Yiddish Speaking Branch seems to have disintegrated, leaving the *Poalei Zion* as the main left-wing Jewish organization in Johannesburg.[8]

Black collective protest mounts

These organizational developments occurred against a backdrop of mounting class conflict. Jack and Ray Simons suggest that the transformation in the International Socialist League's social composition deprived it of labour activists, a loss that was not immediately compensated for by the zeal of the new recruits, leaving the organization more isolated than ever before. This was not the case. Alongside these organizational changes, a small circle of activists was beginning to support black workers and their struggles, and small numbers of blacks began to join the International Socialist League. In 1917, for instance, the group made a commitment to increase its activities amongst Indian workers in Durban; in 1919, it set up a branch in the diamond-mining town of Kimberley, enrolling twenty-seven Coloured members, including Johnny Gomas, who became a lifelong socialist and trade unionist.[9]

The post-war years saw an acceleration of organized collective black protest. In 1919 the Transvaal Native Congress launched a campaign against the migrant labour system and pass laws for African men, using the passive resistance method that African women had successfully used since 1913.[10] January 1919 saw the founding of the ICU, a trade union of black dockworkers, by Clements Kadalie of Nyasaland. Kadalie had graduated from secondary school and qualified as a teacher before deciding to travel around Southern Africa. In 1918 he went to Cape Town, where his brother worked, and subsequently became acquainted with a socialist named A. F. Batty who had recently formed a general workers' union called the Industrial Workers' Union and who inspired Kadalie to launch the ICU. Batty's union and Kadalie's ICU were two of several groups in the Cape Town area trying to organize unskilled black workers into general workers' unions. Hamilton Kraai and Reuben Cetyiwe formed a Cape Town branch of the IWA that year. Although the ICU and IWA vied for the same workers, they both cooperated during the impressive fourteen-day strike of black dockworkers in December 1919, which while unsuccessful, nonetheless catapulted the ICU to fame. At some point, the IWA merged into the ICU. The next year, 1920, saw a successful strike of Indian tobacco workers in Durban, which was supported by the International Socialist League.[11]

As inflation skyrocketed after the war, so did the protests of black mineworkers. This reflected the fact that despite significant wage gains for white miners during the post-war inflationary boom, black workers were denied upward mobility and their wages fell in real terms. These protests culminated in February 1920 with a massive strike of black mineworkers. Estimates of the number of strikers ranged from over 40,000 to 80,000. The strike brought many mines to a standstill and, as Phil Bonner has pointed out, lasted longer and involved more workers than the better-known 1946 African mineworkers strike.[12]

White labour remained antipathetic to the black strikers: the all-white South African Mine Workers' Union called upon its members to scab and defend the colour bar.[13] However, socialists were not blind to the strike's significance. David Ivon Jones described it as 'the most portentous event so far in the awakening of the native workers'. But the International Socialist League's response reflected the predicament caused by holding dual allegiances in a racially-divided society, as well as the limitations of political action in a society where only whites had the franchise. As Jones frankly admitted, the International Socialist League was then 'engaged in the general elections, printing literature on the Soviets and the Dictatorship of the Proletariat for its five candidates. The white workers were undecided as to their attitude towards the native strikers.'[14]

In going after the white vote, the International Socialist League had to be circumspect in its treatment of the native question, couching its arguments in a way that would not alienate white workers and that would appeal to their self-interest. Thus, instead of advocating direct support for the strike, it asked them not to scab. Its leaflet, *Don't Scab*, began with the appeal: 'Do you hear the new Army of Labour coming? The native workers are beginning to wake up. They are finding out that they are slaves to the Big Capitalists'. Pointing out that black workers were learning from the experiences of whites, it urged 'WHITE WORKERS! Do not repel them! The NATIVE WORKERS CANNOT RISE WITHOUT RAISING THE WHOLE STANDARD OF EXISTENCE FOR ALL.'[15]

The Industrial Socialist League's propaganda was couched in syndicalist terms. It railed against the Mine Workers' Union call for whites to scab as 'craft unionism in excelsis' and 'treachery to the working class'. Arguing that the black mineworkers' strike was a proletarian struggle that appeared to be racial precisely because white workers showed no solidarity, it warned: 'If we do not open our unions to them now... we shall find the natives fighting for the boss out here as they have already done in France, and Mesopotamia'.[16]

The strike was defeated by forcing the workers to work under threat of imprisonment and by arresting the leaders. In its aftermath, the Chamber of Mines opted for greater use of armed police to control black mineworkers, and mining companies began to discuss plans for modifying the job colour bar for semi-skilled blacks as a means to defuse the frustrations of this potential leadership stratum. The state initiated a two-pronged strategy to control the flood of black protest. It introduced laws such as the Native Urban Areas Act aimed at black labour, and programmes such as the Joint Council movement, geared to co-opt the black petty bourgeoisie. The Joint Council movement began following the visit of the Gold Coast educator J. A. E. Aggrey in 1921 on a Carnegie-sponsored project to study African education. Joint Councils of sympathetic whites and middle-class Africans were set up around the country to discuss issues relating to African welfare; these provided a rare forum for educated Africans to express their views. Separate Joint Councils were also formed for whites to meet with selected Coloureds and Indians.[17]

Where the state could not squash protests through beatings, intimidation and the arrest or co-optation of black leadership, it resorted to even more brutal methods. That same year, 1920, Samuel Masabalala began organizing Port Elizabeth municipal workers; in October a strike for higher wages seemed imminent. Attempts to defuse the situation with the help of the moderate Dr Walter Rubusana backfired. Masabalala was arrested; the police subsequently fired on a group of demonstrators protesting against his arrest, killing about twenty blacks and three white bystanders. The case provoked much sympathy amongst radicals. Olive Schreiner, then in her last year, raised money for Masabalala's defence at her boarding-house. Masabalala was acquited, and under pressure the government appointed a commission of enquiry.[18]

Similar violence was used at Bulhoek, near Queenstown in the Eastern Cape. There, government troops fired on members of the Israelite religious sect who, led by their prophet, Enoch Mgijima, had been squatting on common land for several months. In May 1921 the troops moved in, killing 163 people and wounding 129. Most whites were indifferent but radicals were aghast.[19] Jolted into action, Cape Town socialists held several mass protest meetings and drew up a leaflet that was reprinted in the *Cape Times* of 28 June 1921. As Wilfred Harrison revealingly commented, 'while we never attempted anything in the way of reforming the Capitalist system, we often made emphatic protests against many of their brutal deeds'. Four local socialists, including Harrison, were arrested for disseminating rebellious material but the charges were ultimately dropped.[20]

The impact of the Communist International

In the meantime, socialists were busy with other organizational issues. The formation of the Comintern propelled further changes, simultaneously pulling the South African groups towards unity while initially inspiring competition amongst them for recognition by the Comintern. Alongside the propulsion towards unity was a movement to marginalize those approaches not favoured by the Comintern.

At its Second Congress in July–August 1920, the Comintern adopted twenty-one points as conditions for admission. The points were premised on the idea that class struggle in Europe and America was approaching civil war, an assumption already outdated by political developments at the time of adoption. In these points, the Comintern put itself at the centre of the world socialist struggle. The Comintern's activities were directed by its Executive Committee (ECCI), whose composition reflected the disproportionate influence of the Russian Communist Party. All national parties were expected to adhere to the Comintern's policies, and within national parties, factions were to be subordinated to the Central Committee. Democratic centralism meant that the party centre was to have 'complete power, authority and ample rights'. Social democratic and social pacifist principles were to be replaced with Communist ones. Reformists and centrists were to be removed from leadership posts in all labour organizations and replaced with Communists, even at the costs of replacing experienced with inexperienced personnel. Parties were to propagandize against the International Federation of Trade Unions (IFTU)

– also known as the Amsterdam International – in support of a proposed Red International of Labour Unions (RILU). These points were the subject of intense debate by South African socialists.[21]

Both the International Socialist League and the Industrial Socialist League decided to apply for affiliation to the Comintern, only to learn that it would give official recognition to only one organization. The two organizations had frequently worked together, and the idea of unity was not anathema. They certainly saw themselves as holding compatible positions on the colour bar. Aside from the International Socialist League, Bill Andrews wrote to the English socialist and feminist Sylvia Pankhurst, the Industrial Socialist League was the only group 'which clearly and fearlessly stands by the principle that no revolution can be successful without a recognition of the rights of the Native workers to full participation'.[22]

The first tangible merger initiatives came from the Industrial Socialist League, principally through the efforts of Manuel Lopes. The Lopes brothers, Manuel and Francis, were the sons of Portuguese Catholic immigrants. Of the two brothers, Manny, a tramwayman, had the reputation as the more adept at Marxist analysis. Following the Russian Revolution, Manny Lopes began to rethink the anti-political approach. In October 1920 the Industrial Socialist League merged with the Communist League and a few members of the SDF to form the CPSA, with branches in Cape Town and Johannesburg, and of which Manny Lopes became secretary. Notably, it still maintained a strong syndicalist orientation. While endorsing the organization of all workers regardless of colour, it nonetheless opposed electoral politics. In January 1921 the Jewish Socialist Society joined the CPSA.[23]

As part of this movement towards unification, in late 1920 the International Socialist League invited other socialist groups and individuals to attend its January 1921 annual conference in order to discuss the prospects of unity. A number of organizations sent delegates or statements of support. Andrew Dunbar represented the CPSA. In 1920 the World Union of *Poalei Zion* split into left and right factions, with the left seeking affiliation to the Comintern and the right continuing in the Labour Zionist tradition. The South African *Poalei Zion* followed the left faction in the international split and in January 1921 participated in the unity talks. The conference exhibited a broad range of views, but by the time it had ended, the delegates had adopted the International Socialist League's statement on socialist unity, which reflected the influence of the twenty-one points. A Unity Committee was established, with three of the five members from the International Socialist League.

Similar moves went on in Cape Town, with meetings between the SDF, the CPSA and the Constitutional Socialist League. To bring in the CPSA, its constitution was used as the benchmark. But divisions soon emerged. A section of the CPSA withdrew from the unity talks opposing the endorsement of political action; the Constitutional Socialist League pulled out, objecting to the idea of a proletarian dictatorship. Nonetheless, in March 1921 the SDF, together with a section of the CPSA and various individuals, formed a United CPSA that endorsed the twenty-one points. The next month the remainder of the CPSA joined but five individuals – Cecil Frank Glass, Joe Pick, S. H. Davidoff, E. Reynolds and A. Brown –

launched the minute Communist Propaganda Group, which opposed political action. This, too, sought affiliation to the Comintern. The Communist Propaganda Group briefly maintained its organizational independence but held joint meetings with the United CPSA following the arrest of some of the latter's members for protesting the Bulhoek massacre.[24]

Back in Johannesburg the Unity Committee that had been formed at the International Socialist League's annual conference held its first meeting on 19 January and its second on 27 March, Easter Sunday. Each socialist group was allowed to send two delegates to the Easter meeting. The twenty-one points were thoroughly discussed and adopted, with qualifications on point 3, concerning the creation of an illegal organization, and point 7, stipulating a break with reformism. Interestingly, the Johannesburg CPSA, led by Andrew Dunbar, did not attend the Easter conference, and objected to the twenty-one points, particularly to the support of political action. Nonetheless, Bill Andrews had the impression that 'the major part of his Party are anxious to fall into line on the twenty-one Points, but Dunbar is as impossible as ever and it is doubtful whether if he is willing to join we would have him in the Party as he is a pure and simple anarchist saboteur'.[25]

However, the CPSA's anti-political stance created discord within its own ranks and led to the expulsion of a few dissenters. In Durban, too, the twenty-one points met with a mixed reaction – approval from the Marxian Club and the Durban International Socialist League and rejection by the SDP.[26] But William Thibedi, probably the only African member of the International Socialist League at the time, was enthused about the prospects of unity. Andrews reported that

> the Natives have formed what they call a 'Little Group' at Natal Spruit and wish to become a Branch of the new Communist Party, Thibidi [sic] is at the head of it.*

> *I have just received a note from him to the effect that he is threatened with the sack if he does not leave the I.S.L. he is a good school teacher as you know.[27]

The SDP took a characteristically social democratic position, arguing that the twenty-one points were anti-democratic. It believed that the requirement to break with all labour organizations that did not accept the twenty-one points would be purely divisive for the working-class movement. It felt that the Comintern's pressure for a speedy decision regarding affiliation and its insistence on subordinating factions to central authority were antithetical to free thinking and discussion and would mean 'constant suspicion, distrust, strife, and the stifling of all personal generosity within any movement imbued with the spirit of the Third International'. The Comintern's aim, continued the SDP, 'is bureaucratic-authority centralised in the hands of officials', which 'will make possible a dictatorship of the proletariat – not a dictatorship "by" the proletariat as many believe'.[28]

The pull of the Russian Revolution and the beliefs that it was a result of political action and, in consequence, could be replicated in other countries, ultimately prevailed amongst South African socialists. On 30 July 1921 the CPSA (Section of the Communist International) was formed – after almost a year of discussion and planning involving more than ten groups. The Durban SDP remained outside, but constitutional amendments submitted at the conference indicated that it was not alone in its scepticism of centralization. Amendments proposed by the Durban Marxian Club, and by Joe Pick and Frank Glass of the former Communist Propaganda Group in Cape Town, suggest a wider concern about the Comintern's centralising tendencies. However, none of these amendments carried, with the exception of an amendment to exclude Central Executive members from automatic delegate status at the annual congress. Given the previously eclectic nature of the South African movement, acceptance of the twenty-one points was a large leap. The delegates at the new Party's launch represented no more than 175 members out of a country of 7 million, and there is no doubt that they felt themselves immeasurably strengthened through their relationship with the Comintern.[29]

Conclusion

From the point of view of those members of the new CPSA who traced their lineage back to the International Socialist League, unity came to be seen as the logical outcome of the development of the most advanced socialist tendency. David Ivon Jones, for instance, had spoken of 'true Communist policy' in his statement on *Communism in South Africa* presented to the Executive of the Third International on behalf of the International Socialist League.[30] From other perspectives, this unity was contested, just as other South African socialists would have undoubtedly disputed any International Socialist League claim of a monopoly on true Communism. The organizational unity of the new CPSA provided it with a coherent profile during an era of national politics, and its affiliation to the Comintern gave it an international legitimacy in an era when international revolution still seemed feasible. However, the contested nature of the CPSA's unity left the new organization with an element of instability, the spectre of which would be seen in the spate of dissensions and expulsions that took place in the 1920s and 1930s.

Unity of the new party, however, was seen as a necessary prelude to a greater unity – solidarity of the working class across colour lines. In June 1920 Manny Lopes had written that 'to the task of fighting against the prejudices + ignorance of the masses (a task common to the Communists of all lands) we have this terrible task of combatting the widespread growth of race prejudice, nay even of race hatred'.[31]

It was a view amplified by the report of Sam Barlin and David Ivon Jones, the two South African delegates to the Comintern's Third Congress, on the eve of the CPSA's founding. They were keenly aware of the limitations imposed by the new party's social composition. 'Normally, all the activity of the South African Communists is among the whites', they acknowledged, although the subject matter of propaganda largely includes the native labour question. Our members and supporters find themselves in white Trades Unions, and are preoccupied with the fight against class collaboration there. There are hardly any native linguists among the white Communists. ... On the occasions when we have issued leaflets in the native languages we have had to depend on native translators. All Communist activity among the native Africans has to be mainly illegal. For this, the Communist Party organisation, besides being inadequate, is wholly unsuited.

South African socialists were enthusiastic about their acceptance into the new international community of revolutionary socialists, and Barlin and Jones appealed to the Comintern to send a representative to South Africa to study the 'Negro question and its relation to the Communist Party' and to provide financial assistance. 'What is required', they argued,

is to assure economic sustenance to a few native workers as agitators and organisers, such as Cetiywe, Mashabala [sic] and others who have already made attempts, some successful, to organise their brothers. This primitive mass is waiting to be stirred. Given the necessary funds and a comrade like Bunting who is a capable administrator and journalist, we are convinced that great results could be achieved.[32]

As part of the new Communist International, South African socialists felt sure that they could reap the benefits of the Bolsheviks' wisdom.

Notes

1. Roux and Roux, *Rebel Pity*, 14.
2. Simons and Simons, *Class and Colour*, 201.
3. Quoted in Johnstone, 'The IWA on the Rand', 262.
4. Quoted in First and Scott, *Olive Schreiner*, 323.
5. E. A. Mantzaris, 'The Promise of the Impossible Revolution: The Cape Town Industrial Socialist League, 1918–1921', *Studies in the History of Cape Town*, 4, 1981, 145–73, 148–53; Harrison, *Memoirs of a Socialist*, 68; Shimoni, *Jews and Zionism*, 53–4; Johns, 'The Birth of the Communist Party', 376.
6. Mantzaris, 'Radical Community', 162–3.
7. Quoted in Shimoni, *Jews and Zionism*, 54; Johns, 'The Birth of the Communist Party', 375–9; Mantzaris, 'Radical Community', 166.
8. Shimoni, *Jews and Zionism*, 84–5, 173–5; Mantzaris, 'Radical Community', 167.
9. Simons and Simons, *Class and Colour*, 210; Mantzaris, 'The Indian Tobacco Workers Strike', 117; Doreen Musson, *Johnny Gomas, Voice of the Working Class: A Political Biography*, Cape Town: Buchu, 1989, 21.
10. Andrews, *Class Struggles*, 27–32; Roux, *Time Longer than Rope*, 117, 130–31; Simons and Simons, *Class and Colour*, 220–43.

11. Wickens, *The Industrial and Commercial Workers' Union*, 23–34; Clements Kadalie, *My Life and the ICU: the Autobiography of a Black Trade Unionist in South Africa*, ed. by Stanley Trapido, London: Frank Cass, 1970, 39–49; Helen Bradford, *A Taste of Freedom: The ICU in Rural South Africa, 1924–1930*, New Haven and London: Yale, 1987, 1–20; Roux, *Time Longer than Rope*, 155; Musson, *Johnny Gomas*, 27; Mantzaris, 'The Indian Tobacco Workers Strike', 120.

12. Bonner, 'The 1920 Black Mineworkers' Strike', 274, 280–85; Roux, *Time Longer than Rope*, 132; Jones, 'Communism in South Africa' [part 2], 67; South Africa. Department of Justice Files, 6/757/20, 6/757/20/1, 1A, 1B and 1D (1920).

13. Roux, *Time Longer than Rope*, 132–4; Simons and Simons, *Class and Colour*, 229–31.

14. Jones, 'Communism in South Africa' [part 2], 67.

15. 'Don't Scab.', reprinted in *International*, 27 February 1920. See also 'The Great Native Strike', *International*, 27 February 1920 in Drew, ed., *South Africa's Radical Tradition*, vol. 1, 45–6.

16. 'Trade Union Notes' in Drew, ed., *South Africa's Radical Tradition*, vol. 1, 46.

17. Jones, 'Communism in South Africa' [part 2], 67; Roux, *Time Longer than Rope*, 132; Johnstone, *Class, Race and Gold*, 182; Bonner, 'The 1920 Black Mineworkers' Strike,' 274, 286–8; Karis and Carter, eds, *From Protest to Challenge*, vol. 1, 150–51.

18. Jones, 'Communism in South Africa' [part 2], 67; First and Scott, *Olive Schreiner*, 322–3; 'The Exclusion of the Bantu', Address by the Rev. Z. R. Mahabane, President, Cape Province National Congress, 1921, in Karis and Carter, eds, *From Protest to Challenge*, vol. 1, 291: Simons and Simons, *Class and Colour*, 241–2.

19. Roux, *Time Longer than Rope*, 136–9; Simons and Simons, *Class and Colour*, 253; Address by Selby Msimang, President Industrial and Commercial Workers' Union of South Africa, July 23, 1921, in Karis and Carter, eds, *From Protest to Challenge*, vol. 1, 317–20, 320.

20. Harrison, *Memoirs of a Socialist*, 73, 76–80; Simons and Simons, *Class and Colour*, 255.

21. 'The Twenty-one Points – Conditions of Admission to the Communist International' as adopted at the second Comintern congress in 1920 and appended to the constitution of the Communist Party of South Africa by its founding conference in 1921, in Bunting, ed., *South African Communists Speak*, 58–62, quote 60; see also McDermott and Agnew, *The Comintern*, 225–6.

22. Letter from W. H. Andrews to Sylvia Pankhurst, 19 March 1920, RTsKhIDNI, 495.64.1; Harrison, *Memoirs of a Socialist*, 71.

23. 'Communist Party of South Africa', *Bolshevik*, October 1920, 1; Johns, 'The Birth of the Communist Party', 382–3, 388; Interview with Charles van Gelderen, Cottenham, Cambridge, 23–24 July 1997.

24. Johns, 'The Birth of the Communist Party', 386–9, Shimoni, *Jews and Zionism*, 175; Mantzaris, 'The Promise of the Impossible Revolution', 164.

25. Letter from W. H. Andrews to Sam Barlin, 27 April 1921, RTsKhIDNI, 495.64.5.

26. Johns, 'The Birth of the Communist Party', 391–3.

27. Letter from W. H. Andrews to Sam Barlin, 27 April 1921.

28. Durban Social Democratic Party, 'Socialist Unity in South Africa', *Communist Review*, 1, 4, August 1921, 73–6.

29. Johns, 'The Birth of the Communist Party', 397–9. Evidently, the *Poalei Zion* never actually joined the CPSA, despite its initial interest. Agenda and Minutes of the Second National Congress, CPSA, April 28 & 29, 1923, RTsKhIDNI, 495.64.16.

30. Jones, 'Communism in South Africa' [part 2], 66.

31. Letter from M. Lopes, Industrial Socialist League of South Africa to Dear Comrade, 24 June 1920, RTsKhIDNI, 495.64.1.
32. Memorandum to the Small Bureau of the Comintern on the Situation in Africa from D. Ivon Jones and Sam Barlin, South African delegation to the Third Congress of the Communist International, 16 July 1921, quotes 2 and 3 respectively, RTsKhIDNI, 495.64.25.

Chapter 4

Searching for the socialist road: the Rand Revolt and the turn to black labour

Headquartered in Johannesburg, the new CPSA proselytized on the rostrum of the City Hall steps. For decades, the blacksmith Andrew Dunbar held forth there, first for the IWW, then for the Labour Party, then the International Socialist League and now for the CPSA, the words flying from his mouth 'red hot, like sparks from a forge'. His style was constant but his successive organizational affiliations charted the metamorphoses of the South African left. The likes of Bill Andrews, Harry Haynes, Issy Diamond, Sidney Bunting, Eddie Roux, Willie Kalk and Bernard and E.S. 'Solly' Sachs – all men and all white – also held their own on the steps. Issy Diamond, the red barber, would fling his arms wildly, taunting passers-by seeking to kill a little time. When challenged with the usual racist: 'Would you let your sister marry a Kaffir?', his standard retort, 'Yes, if I had the needle to the Kaffir', was generally enough to prompt a few chuckles and sidetrack the racist. Bunting alone used notes, clenching them behind his back and pausing every so often to study them. In his cultured English accent he would pursue dense themes, using words well beyond the scope of his audience. An especially sombre pronouncement that 'This situation is egregious and grotesque', made one Chaim Zvick turn to Bernard Sachs and ask: 'Vot's he saying?', while others slipped away. In those turbulent times in that rowdy city Communists preached truth and enlightenment to any who would listen for a moment.[1]

The 1920s marked a critical turning point in the relationship between the state, capital and workers in South Africa. As the decade opened, white labour continued its militant protests against both state and capital, its confrontation with authority finally culminating in the Rand Revolt of 1922. This was crushed by the state, leaving the white trade union movement in a state of despair and disarray. The election in June 1924 of the Pact Government formed by the Labour and National Parties and the ensuing implementation of white – or 'civilized' – labour policies represented the state's co-optation of white labour representatives following their industrial defeat. With white labour firmly co-opted into the racial capitalist polity, the state was able to turn its energies to black labour. The most striking sign of the latter's development was the trajectory of the ICU, which shot across the South African landscape, from Cape Town north and east, becoming, by 1927, a mass movement that embraced both town and country folk. The state sought to break the back of this movement, along with that of the Western Cape ANC, which organized rural farm workers. By 1931, it had effectively halted these movements.

Despite the accord that developed between the state, capital and white workers in the 1920s, white labour's racial consciousness displayed striking continuity. The protectionism that white English-speaking craftworkers had demonstrated in 1907 was extended subsequently into the protectionism of white, increasingly Afrikaner, industrial workers threatened by competition from cheaper black labour of equivalent skills. This same white labour protectionism became a hallmark of the Pact Government. Racial ideology was a thread connecting the craft and industrial periods.[2]

In the 1920s, with its belief in the feasibility of socialism intact, the CPSA's main concern was how to promote socialist revolution in South Africa. While the CPSA looked to the Comintern as the ultimate authority on socialist doctrine, the Comintern itself had little interest in South Africa until the late 1920s and aside from periodic circulars, the CPSA received scant communication from it during these years.[3] From 1920 on the Comintern became increasingly centralized and bureaucratized under Russian dominance and developed methods facilitating the intervention of its Executive Committee in local parties.[4] Nonetheless, South Africa was geographically remote and of marginal political significance to the Comintern in this period. Until the late 1920s the South African Communists were generally left alone to implement Comintern policies as they thought best. Beset with regional tensions between the more liberal Cape Town branch and the Johannesburg headquarters, the CPSA underwent a tortuous reorientation in its first half-decade, as events forced Communists, firstly, to recognize the limitations of their initial belief in the vanguard potential of white labour, and secondly, to turn towards black labour.

The 1922 Rand Revolt

Within six months of its formation, the CPSA was catapulted into a labour struggle whose aftermath would force the Party's members to clarify their stance towards black workers. The 1922 Rand Revolt by white workers was the culmination of a period of challenge to capital that had begun in 1907. During the war, white labour had been in a strong bargaining position due to the exodus of many of the English. Despite the defeat of the 1913 miners' strike and the government's implementation of the Riotous Assemblies Act, in 1914 the Chamber of Mines granted recognition to the South African Industrial Federation (SAIF), marking the entry of industrial as opposed to craft-based trade unionism on the mines. The social composition of white mine labour changed dramatically between 1907 and 1918: deskilling, which allowed the replacement of craft labour with cheaper, unskilled Afrikaners, coincided with the departure of English workers for the war, and by the war's end, 80 per cent of the underground white labour force were South African-born Afrikaners. In 1918, still feeling the scarcity of skilled workers, the Chamber of Mines conceded a Status Quo Agreement, retaining the prevailing ratio of white to black mine labour and ceasing the replacement of whites by blacks in specified jobs.[5]

Over the next few years, however, the South African state was faced with a series of protests that it took as challenges to its hegemony: the 1920 black mineworkers' strike, the Bulhoek land occupation of May 1921, the Bondelswart tax revolt of May 1922, and the 1922 white miners' strike that began in January and culminated in March in the Rand Revolt. The violent response of the Smuts Government to these protests must be viewed against the backdrop of international working-class struggles: the ripples of the Russian Revolution were felt as far away as South Africa by both imperialist interests and organized labour. Both capitalists and Communists of the time employed the discourse of international socialist revolution, however inaccurately, likening the Rand Revolt to a Bolshevik-inspired revolt.[6] Nonetheless, the judicial enquiry that followed the revolt belied the allegation of a 'communist plot'; only a few Communists were actively involved, and non-Communist Afrikaners bore the brunt of the government's wrath after the strike.[7]

These challenges occurred in a period of economic uncertainty. The farming and gold mining industries were hard hit by the global recession that followed the post-war inflationary boom. The world market price for South African agricultural commodities fell, and between 1920 and 1922 the premium gold price dropped significantly. As the recession deepened, the Chamber of Mines sought to cut its labour costs by abrogating the Status Quo Agreement.[8] It announced its decision to restructure underground work and to cut the wages and the numbers of white workers, estimating a retrenchment of 2000 white workers. The wage cuts were justified by reference to events in Britain, where in July 1921 coalminers had suffered a heavy defeat. Prime Minister Smuts argued that 'wage cuts "have been accepted by the English miners that go far beyond anything proposed in this country"'.[9]

White labour's response to the Chamber of Mines ultimatum was swift. Fearing that the actual retrenchment of white workers could reach 10,000, trade union leaders saw this as a prelude to either driving down white wages to the level of black workers or eliminating the higher-paid white workers from the mines altogether. As one sympathetic account argued, the key issue was 'whether free European labour should be displaced by the extension of Negro slave labour on contract at the unfettered discretion of the Chamber of Mines'.[10] Both the South African Mine Workers' Union (SAMWU), which adamantly refused to accept black members, and the SAIF made it clear that their struggle was '"to protect the White race", "to maintain a White standard of living", and "to preserve White South Africa"'.[11] Indeed, the only banner seen at demonstrations on the Rand bore the notorious slogan, 'Workers of the World Fight and Unite for a White S.A.'[12]

Yet the SAIF was in no position to provide leadership to a strike. To the amazement of other trade unionists, Archie Crawford, the SAIF's leader, came out in support of the proposal to cut wages, arguing wrongly that mineworkers in Britain had accepted a similar fate without complaint. Many of the unions involved were not members of the SAIF, and on 31 December 1921 union executives set up an Augmented Executive comprised of both SAIF and non-SAIF members. From that point on, R. K. Cope claims, the SAIF had little if any control over events. Crawford tried to get the SAIF General Council to disown the strike, arguing that the Augmented Executive was unconstitutional.[13]

Several new organizational structures emerged during the dispute. First was the Central Strike Committee, which coordinated all the local strike committees. This Central Strike Committee was, ostensibly, answerable to the Augmented Executive. Second was the Council of Action, a 'loose, unofficial organisation' that functioned from 10 January. This was led by a number of miners who had been expelled from the SAMWU for engaging in unauthorized strike activities, including Harry Spendiff, Percy Fisher and Ernest Shaw; later, Bill Andrews joined. Third were the commandos, structures used by rural Afrikaners during the Anglo-Boer War that were adapted, allegedly by George Mason and J. T. Bain, for use in an industrial setting where Afrikaner workers predominated. Roux and Cope claim that the commandos were Afrikaner nationalists and openly hostile to blacks, while the Council of Action, by contrast, especially through the efforts of Spendiff and Fisher, tried to restrain anti-black sentiments.[14]

The City Hall steps bore silent witness to the many assorted strands bundled together in this revolt and to the extent to which resistance was powered by structures beyond those of formal trade unionism. 'The City Hall steps became the focus of life', wrote Bernard Sachs, 'and there poured forth from it nightly a spate of wrath compounded of hatreds, spites, disappointments, empty dreams, ambitions'. 'Fight till you drop', exhorted Harry Haynes, recalling the Bolsheviks, while Ernie Shaw uttered only 'Comrade chairman' before collapsing, coughing blood from his phthisis-ridden lungs. Spendiff and Fisher vowed, on the steps, that they would never be captured alive.[15]

By March, as the state turned to bombs, tanks and machine-guns, the strike transformed into an armed struggle for which the strikers were militarily unprepared. On 5 March Bill Andrews called for a general strike in response to the government's use of extreme force. The strike, however, failed to generalize either across industrial sectors or regions. Railway workers, typographic printers and other workers refused to come out. In Durban, a few hundred workers struck; in Cape Town there was no response at all. Instead, on 7–8 March pogroms against blacks took place in Johannesburg and elsewhere. On 10 March, the government proclaimed martial law, imprisoning about 1500 strikers. Half an hour after the proclamation, wrote 'F', a member of the CPSA who worked as a typist for Andrews,

> a large posse of mounted police surrounded the Trades Hall. The detectives poured into our [CPSA] office arresting all that were there but myself, – Comrades Andrews, G. Mason + Ernest Shaw; when they took them away, I had to look on while they ransacked the office. This time seemed the signal for all the shooting that went on continually for five days throughout the town. – aeroplanes, bombs, machine + Louis guns.[16]

The heaviest fighting took place at Fordsburg, where Bernard Sachs lived, and where he watched as government planes rained leaflets stipulating immediate evacuation prior to an artillery bombardment scheduled the next day. Spendiff and Fisher were based there; true to their word, they committed suicide just before troops stormed the area.[17]

On 16 March, after several days of bombs, machine-guns, artillery and tanks, the Augmented Executive called off the strike. Overall, about 230 to 250 people died as a result of violence during the strike, about thirty of whom were black. Close to 5000 people were arrested, forty-six were charged with murder, and of these, eighteen were sentenced to death and four executed.[18]

Contemporaries put forward various interpretations of the revolt. The 1922 strike, wrote W. M. MacMillan, was the first major white mining strike after the entry of unskilled Afrikaners into the mines, and accordingly, the first mining strike led by the SAIF, rather than the craft unions, which had until then remained aloof from the industrial unions. Just as craft workers had felt the threat of semi-skilled blacks and unskilled whites in 1907, so these newly proletarianized workers, 'fresh from the farms', felt their vulnerability to replacement by cheap black labour if the colour bar were modified; hence, their militancy.[19] Yet far from being forward-looking, MacMillan thought, the Rand Revolt looked back to an idealized past of Afrikaner self-sufficiency before British domination. '[T]here was certainly much talk of a Republic – ostensibly a Workers' Republic', he wrote. 'There is no doubt, however, that the Republic dreamt of by the men who actually took up arms was the Boer Republic of former times.'[20]

Such 'republican' ideology would, indeed, appeal to newly-urbanized men under the threat of replacement by lower-paid workers. The earlier republics were societies where, before the commercial economy undermined their position on the land, Afrikaner *bywoners* possessed independent means of subsistence. The imagery evoked by MacMillan coincides with the anti-black, anti-*uitlander* ideology of Afrikaner proletarians who had only recently been forced to leave their rural origins. This interpretation is borne out by the reports of rural support for the strikers:

> [T]he call to preserve a White South Africa swept through the rural areas where the strikers, not vainly as it proved, had hoped for moral and material support. Food and promises of further aid began flowing in from the Platteland. *Ons Vaderland* reported that the strikers were receiving cattle from the farmers as outright gifts or as purchases on deferred terms. Shopkeepers were allowing them generous credit.[21]

In fact, wrote Andrews, once the state resolved to smash the strikers with force, support from the countryside appears to have dried up.[22] Despite their criticism of the government, the relationship between the Labour Party and National Party, and between English-speaking and Afrikaner workers, remained ambiguous. The Augmented Executive appealed for aid from the National Party and called for an overthrow of the government. In early February, a meeting of the National Party and Labour Party was held in Pretoria, dubbed 'Roos's Parliament'. On 5 February, R. B. Waterston, Labour MP and leader of the Brakpan Commando, asked the National Party to proclaim a republic and to form a provisional government, a proposal that met with acclaim at a Johannesburg rally but that the National Party coldly rejected.[23]

The CPSA walked a tightrope. It aligned itself most closely with the Council of Action, which was headquartered in the Party's office, and it supported the white workers' struggle against wage cuts and retrenchments while trying to convince them not to attack blacks. 'The white miners are perfectly justified in fighting to keep up the numbers and pay of holders of blasting certificates', claimed Andrews. 'They would get native support ... if they also insisted on higher pay and better treatment of the blacks. ... FOR A SECTION WHICH POSES AT THE SAME TIME AS BOTH MASTERS AND WORKERS MUST SOONER OR LATER COLLAPSE', he warned.[24]

Bunting, too, tried to resolve the moral dilemma posed by the strike's clearly racialist content, using the *International* to make his points. Although Cape Town Communists were generally more critical of the Rand strikers than their Johannesburg comrades, no doubt due to the pressure of local black radicals, Bunting's belief in the need to organize blacks put him well in advance of most Johannesburg Communists. Yet, while acknowledging that the colour bar was unfair to blacks, he argued that if repeal of the colour bar regulations led to a fall in white wages, black wages could never rise.[25] To Bunting, the 'Rand revolt was not the proletarian revolution: at the most it was only a prelude, or rather a preliminary study'. For him, the episode raised two tactical questions, both of which concerned the problem of how to fight an armed state without arms: firstly, whether strikes could ever succeed in conditions where the state habitually resorted to armed force; secondly, whether strikes could ever surmount capital's use of force and ideological resources to divide workers. Bunting saw little solidarity between English and Afrikaner workers, despite their common interests against black competition. But the greatest obstacle, in his view, was discord across the colour line.[26]

From Moscow, David Ivon Jones saw the revolt not so much in terms of the problem of ever achieving proletarian unity across the colour line but as a possible transition in the political development of the working-class movement. 'It remains to ascertain', he speculated 'whether the conflict is the last revolt of a non-revolutionary white working class driven to arms by the very insecurity of their economic position over against the native masses'. If so, he added, 'the conditions for a Communist Party based on white militants have disappeared, and the Comintern will henceforth have to take over the direct responsibility for the native masses'.[27]

In fact, the strike deepened the polarization of black and white workers. Thousands of black miners lost their jobs during the strike, sent back to the reserves by the Chamber of Mines. Racial attacks on those who remained in the compounds and upon black city-dwellers on the Rand fuelled the animosity of blacks towards whites. In Cape Town, while white trade unionists canvassed in support of the strike, the ICU and other black organizations condemned the 'White South Africa' agenda and called for the abolition of the colour bar and for government protection of blacks. At an ICU meeting, a CPSA resolution to support the strike was defeated.[28]

The Rand Revolt had a contradictory consequence for the CPSA. As Jack and Ray Simons note, white labour's betrayal of the black mineworkers' strike a few years earlier meant that when the CPSA supported this struggle, they were seen by black radicals as supporting white labour and thus, indirectly, the repression of black labour.[29] Yet, a number of white youths became politically activated as a direct consequence of the strike. Radicalized by the state's ruthless repression of the strikers, some of them would become principal actors in the Party's turn to black labour. 'The Govt is talking about its friendship + protection for the Black Workers against the Strikers banner for a "White S. Africa"', wrote 'F'. 'You will know how our tiny ship "Communism" has been tossed about from rocks to heavy seas', he continued.

> Is it to sink? As I approach some of our well dressed Members ... they say 'Oh the Party is finished now, quite finished in *this* country'. But again Communism approaches as a dusty dishevelled Worker you have hardly seen before comes + grips your hand with 'By god, Comrade, we've got some organising work in front of us now'.[30]

The aftermath of the Rand Revolt

The white labour movement emerged from the Rand Revolt in a sorry state. Trade union membership plunged from a high of 135,000 in 1920 to 82,000 in 1923. The SAIF fell apart after the Rand Revolt, replaced in 1925 by the South African Association of Employees' Organisation (SAAEO), later renamed the South African Trades Union Congress (TUC), which functioned until 1931. White trade unions were severely restricted. In the key mining industry, mine owners assumed far greater control over production, no longer recognizing shaft and shop stewards. Strikes and direct shop-floor involvement in negotiations were prohibited. The 1918 job reservation agreement was annulled, and in 1923 the colour bar regulations of the Mines and Works Act were declared invalid. Through the introduction of new technology, whites were restricted to supervisory duties. The Chamber of Mines reduced white wages, increased the ratio of black to white workers, and replaced whites with skilled and semi-skilled blacks at the lower black wage rates. White wages were reduced by 25–50 per cent, and by 1925 black wages were driven down to close to pre-1920 rates. While these laws curtailed white labour militancy, government reconstruction efforts pacified white workers through housing and employment schemes.[31]

Although white labour's movement to control the subordination of black labour on its own terms was violently crushed, the movement for white labour protectionism was not destroyed. In this pessimistic climate, white labour turned to electoral politics and to negotiation and accommodation with the bourgeois state. That laid the basis for the class alliance of white workers and landowners that formed the social basis of the Labour Party-National Party electoral Pact.[32] White labour politics had always taken the existence of the capitalist state for granted. But the election of the Pact government in 1924 marked the formal incorporation of white labour representatives into state structures, tying their interests more formally to the state's preservation. Practically, there could be no harking back to the Boer republics. The development policies pursued by the state after 1924 had tremendous significance in structuring white supremacy into state-sponsored industrialization.

Some socialists were swept along with the racialist tide. The Labour Party moved to the right, although Colonel Creswell failed, at its January 1923 conference, to get the socialist objective deleted from the Party's programme. In December 1923, Harry Haynes, Durban's left-wing stalwart, wrote to the CPSA's Central Executive objecting to what he saw as the Party's native policy being imposed on white workers and proposing that the Party dissolve and that its members join the Labour Party. In 1924 he resigned from the CPSA and became editor of *Forward*, an independent Labour paper, and used it to promote pro-white labour positions. At the Labour Party's annual conference in January 1925, Gabriel Weinstock, a founding member of the War on War League and now *Forward*'s manager, proposed that blacks be banned from employment in white eating establishments and licensed premises, a view echoed by A. Z. Berman, former leader of the Industrial Socialist League.[33]

However, not all socialists went along with this. The CPSA had been profoundly demoralized by the strike's defeat, and the *International* did not appear between March and late May 1922. Hoping to revive the flagging trade union movement, the CPSA invited veteran trade unionist and Communist Tom Mann to visit South Africa and, together with a number of trade unions, set up a Tom Mann Tour Committee in its Johannesburg office. This was Mann's third trip to South Africa, and his objectives were to promote the Comintern's united front policy and to drum up support for the RILU, the Comintern's trade union arm.[34]

At its Third Congress in June–July 1921 the Comintern had endorsed the united front thesis put forward by the Russian delegation. The united front policy reflected the Bolshevik perception that working-class revolution in Europe was no longer imminent and, accordingly, that it was necessary to ease relations between the Soviet Union and capitalist states in order to allow Soviet economic reconstruction. One symptom of European stabilization was the continuing support which the great majority of the European working class gave to non-revolutionary parties. The united front called for joint struggles between Communists and all sections of workers – not organizational unity with their leadership. It was hoped that joint activity would expose the limitations of social democratic politicians and of reformist trade union leaders and promote the acceptance of Communist methods. RILU was launched in July 1921 to promote the united front policy within the international trade union movement and to counteract the influence of the IFTU, denounced scathingly by Tom Mann as ' the reformist yellow Amsterdam beloved of Crawford and Co.'.[35]

Landing in Cape Town on 2 October, Mann was greeted at the docks by a large demonstration of trade unionists and Communists. One of Mann's first acts was to appeal for clemency for those sentenced to death in the aftermath of the Rand Revolt. A South African Strikers' Defence Committee had been formed after the revolt to campaign against the death penalty for strikers. The appeal was taken up by the Class War Prisoners Release Committee in London, where the racial over-tones of the strike were not readily apparent.[36] But so deeply did the colour line cut into South African society that even an appeal for mercy carried racial implications. Carel Stassen's case was notorious: a Rand striker sentenced to hang for shooting two Africans in Sophiatown on 8 March, calls for clemency came not only from Nationalists and Labourites, but also from Tom Mann.[37] Yet to the APO, which had looked forward to Mann's visit, this smacked of hypocrisy: whites were rou-tinely allowed to escape responsibility for hurting or killing blacks, and the APO saw this as one more case.[38]

Stassen was hung. So were Herbert Hull, David Lewis and Taffy Long. Long had been condemned for the killing of Johannes Marais, himself convicted by a strikers' court for being a police spy. In his own defence Long is said to have stated:

> Only a few years back I lay drenched in water and soaked in blood in the trenches of Flanders. ... But what did we find when we got back from the hell of war? ... What do the mine-owners care about our homes and the dignity of our lives? If they thought they could grind an ounce of gold from the Union Jack they would put it through the mills of their mines.[39]

On the morning of the hangings, 17 November, a crowd of people stood outside the prison keeping vigil. They and the other prisoners heard Long, Hull and Lewis walk to their death, the words of 'The Red Flag' on their lips: 'The people's flag is deepest red, It shrouded oft our martyred dead ... '. 'This prison episode', wrote Bernard Sachs, 'set the country aflame'. The funeral the next day, reportedly attend-ed by 50,000 people, was the largest up to that time in South Africa. A massive demonstration against Smuts took place outside Johannesburg City Hall with thou-sands singing 'The Red Flag'.[40] The young Fanny Klenerman, who joined the CPSA in the mid-1920s, criticized the strikers' racism. But for her the greatest lesson was 'the unforgettable punishment meted out to members of trade unions [which] will always be remembered in the history of time, as long as there is a working class'.[41]

When Tom Mann first arrived in South Africa, he saw white workers as his nat-ural constituency, appealing to them that Africans 'ought to be treated as fellow humans and not as slaves'.[42] But his presence at the ICU's third annual conference in January 1923 catalysed a change in his views on the colour question. Hitherto Mann had seen blacks as 'natives'. Now, through contact with the ICU, he saw them as workers. 'White and black are going to shake hands ... We have begun to climb the mountain and we had to start from the bottom', he told the ICU.[43] Thereafter, he was more sharply critical of white workers, 'many of whom would indignantly denounce any such conditions in any part of the world for whites, yet here, they have no compunction in imposing unbelievable tasks upon the blacks'.[44]

There is no doubt that the local Communists thought Mann's trip a success. 'We had touched rock bottom before you came and now a more buoyant spirit is in the air', Andrews wrote to him.[45] Nonetheless, Communists were far from united in their approaches to labour in this period. The years 1922–24 saw a significant shift within the CPSA in regard to white labour. On the one side were trade union stalwarts like Bill Andrews and Frank Glass, who continued to believe in the vanguard potential of white workers. Manny Lopes believed that white workers' numerical predominance in the industrial workforce, combined with their trade union tradition, necessarily made them the working-class vanguard. On the other side were many of the Cape Town Communists, and in Johannesburg, Sidney Bunting, joined by Willie Kalk and Eddie Roux of the Young Communist League who were increasingly concerned with the organization of black workers.

Andrews and Bunting exemplified two polar types in the socialist movement, both in their backgrounds and in their political styles. Bunting's forefathers were Wesleyan ministers, carriers of a tradition that combined puritanism with struggles against injustice. His father, Percy William Bunting, musician, campaigner for women's rights and founding editor of *Contemporary Review*, was knighted in 1908, three years before his death, for his work for the Liberal Party. Bunting's mother, Mary Hyett Lidgett Bunting, worked amongst the poor in London, founding a society for women servants. Their home became a venue for an array of political refugees and promoters of unpopular causes. Bunting imbibed this political and cultural background from his early years. A brilliant scholar as well as a musician, in 1897 he won the Chancellor's Prize for classical languages at Oxford University, before training as a solicitor. In 1900 he went to South Africa as a British officer in the Anglo-Boer War. He decided to remain, and set up a legal practice in Johannesburg. Over the course of his lifetime, Bunting's views went through a significant development; yet, at the same time, he changed slowly – he had a certain rigidity. Only gradually did he become involved with politics, joining the Labour Party in 1910. But from that point, politics became his life. He became radicalized during the 1913–14 strikes and subsequently made the decision to oppose participation in the war, becoming a founding member of the War on War League and the International Socialist League. In 1916, against her family's wishes, he married Rebecca Notlowitz, a Russian Jewish émigré whom he had met in the International Socialist League. In what Bunting fondly called their 'International Socialist marriage', they travelled and campaigned together for the promotion of socialism.[46]

By contrast, the working-class Andrews, described by Mann as 'absolutely straight, a bit abrupt in manner, + perhaps soured a bit, but true as steel',[47] was a fitter and turner by trade who rose up through the trade union movement. In 1902 he helped form the first Trades and Labour Council. In 1909 he became the first chair of the Labour Party and was elected an MP in 1912. He was a founding member of the War on War League and the International Socialist League. Later, in

1925, he became the first secretary of the Trades Union Congress (later renamed the Trades and Labour Council).[48]

Their political differences were accentuated by their contrasting physical appearances: Bunting, noted for his gawkiness, Andrews, for his 'marmorial dignity and solidity'. But perhaps the most important difference in understanding the political psychology of these two outstanding men was that Bunting, the intellectual, had only one political home, the Party, while Andrews, who had risen through the trade union movement, had two homes, the trade union movement and the Party. Thus, Andrews could, and did, distance himself from the Party when it decided to follow a path that he found difficult, and he was able to weather the stormy period when the Party expelled him in 1931. In contrast, expulsion broke Bunting, who had single-mindedly dedicated himself to building the CPSA. 'If Bunting was the middle-class, humanitarian Jaures of the South African Socialist movement,' wrote Bernard Sachs, 'Andrews was the working class Bebel.'[49]

The CPSA and the united front policy, 1922–24

In June 1922 Sidney and Rebecca Bunting left South Africa, landing first in England and later making their way to Russia, where they attended the Fourth Congress of the Comintern in Moscow. They left Moscow on 20 November, spent several months in England, and arrived back in Cape Town in March 1923. Between the Comintern's formation in 1919 and its Second Congress in July 1920, it had begun to re-examine its position on 'the national and colonial question'. As the prospect of a socialist breakthrough receded in industrialized countries, the colonial issue became more acute, as did the national question within the Soviet Union, and at the Second Congress the main issue concerned the political content and significance of national liberation movements for the achievement of socialism. Lenin and M. N. Roy of India were the main protagonists in the debate. Lenin argued that the Comintern should seek temporary alliances with bourgeois democratic movements in the colonies, while Roy stressed the difference between such movements and movements of peasants and workers. Lenin conceded the politically ambivalent nature of bourgeois democratic movements and changed his position to one of support for national revolutionary movements. Two years later, in 1922, with international socialism clearly in retreat, the main issues at the Congress were 'immediate demands' and 'united fronts', clearly matters of import for South African socialists in the wake of the Rand Revolt. Along with the continued concern with the national and colonial question, the Comintern began to focus more attention on the struggle for black liberation, and at the Fourth Congress it produced its 'theses on the Negro question', which argued that the exploitation of black people was a result of imperialism.[50]

Bunting tried to develop a South African strategy that would dovetail with the Comintern's line on the national question and its united front policy. At this stage, he was still trying to straddle and unite both black and white sections of the labour movement. This aim flowed from his assessment of the Rand Revolt – that discord across the colour line was the main obstacle to the overthrow of capitalism. But while Lenin, by comparison, insisted on the right of national self-determination for oppressed people as a fundamental democratic principle, Bunting saw the struggle for equal rights as a pragmatic step needed to achieve working-class cooperation across the colour line: 'The point is not equality but solidarity', he argued. Accordingly, 'in-as-much as inequality is a bar to cooperation, an attempt must be made before, not after, the revolution to mitigate it so far as necessary to facilitate cooperation'.[51]

Racial polarization was still acute a year after the Rand Revolt. Bunting's initial optimism that the '1922 experience will induce white organised labour to repent of its previous rejection of communist advice and to respond to such native advances [as wage increases]', was quite off the mark.[52] Instead of working-class unity, racialism increased in the next few years. White workers, reported Bunting to the Comintern, still had a 'damned nigger' attitude. Bunting, himself, had been branded a '*kafir boetie*' for his legal defence of Africans, and his return to South Africa stirred some controversy in the local press.[53] '[A] leader urged that he should not be allowed to land owing to his policy of educating + organising the native workers', wrote Andrews to Mann in December. '[T]hey are on the war path all right. + so are we so that's all right', he added.[54]

Within the CPSA, proponents of work amongst blacks – chiefly Bunting, a few Young Communist League members from Johannesburg and some of the Cape Town branch – had been marginalized by the Rand Revolt and the state's brutal reaction. The trauma of the Rand Revolt was still vividly felt by Johannesburg Communists, and articles about the revolt and tributes to those who had died – 'Class War Heroes' – figured prominently in March 1923, the first anniversary of the strike's defeat.[55] In stark contrast, at the APO's conference in Cape Town in April 1923, its president, Dr Abdurahman, echoed the same sense of betrayal by the state expressed by Taffy Long the year before: that having fought for the empire in the world war, the state had repudiated them. But while Long had targeted capital, Abdurahman claimed that 'the greatest exploiters of coloured labour on the Rand are the white workers, and their "solidarity" has resulted in our being kept down at unskilled work'.[56]

Leading figures in the Party began pushing the united front policy actively in 1923. From Russia, David Ivon Jones helped launch the united front bandwagon with an article in the *International*. Manny Lopes wrote on the need for a united front during the period of socialist retreat, and Bunting argued that the age of splits was almost gone, claiming, naively, to have found no splits in the Communist Party of the Soviet Union. The approach did not go uncontested. From Cape Town, Wilfred Harrison argued that a united front with the reformist Labour Party would dilute the CPSA's revolutionary goals. To that Bunting responded: 'It should be our privilege not to stand on a Capetown dunghill and crow that we know better' but to march with the united front.[57] Grudgingly, the *International* printed Harrison's reply, with the admonition: 'No further controversy on this subject will be printed in the "International." Action, not debate, is the need of the moment.'[58]

The united front became CPSA policy at its Second Congress, held in Johannesburg on 28–29 April 1923. The debate on the CPSA's relationship to the Labour Party proved more controversial. Sam Barlin reported that Moscow supported the motion for affiliation. However, Wilfred Harrison argued that the Labour Party's parliamentary atmosphere would have a harmful effect on the revolutionary members in the CPSA, while T. Chapman claimed that the Labour Party was declining while the CPSA was growing. Bunting opposed the motion on the grounds that, unlike its British counterpart, the Labour Party had no provision for affiliation, that it was not a mass party but excluded Africans and that it only existed for fighting elections. Nonetheless, the congress agreed, by thirteen votes to six, to apply for affiliation.[59]

It was hardly a propitious time for a united front policy premised on an alliance between the CPSA and the Labour Party. In July, the CPSA learned from the *Guardian* that its application had been rejected, with only one dissenter, on the grounds that the CPSA's alleged adherence to the violent seizure of power conflicted with the Labour Party's organic approach to change.[60] Undaunted, the CPSA gave critical support to the Pact candidates and devoted much of its attention over the course of the year to the election campaign. 'Vote Pact', urged a CPSA manifesto that appeared in May 1924, about a month before the election, 'not for the sake of the "Pact" but ... as a step towards WORKERS' CONTROL OF THE WHOLE MEANS OF PRODUCTION and SELF-DETERMINATION IN A WORKERS' REPUBLIC!'[61] However, it also argued that the Pact must end after the election. In May 1923 Bill Andrews had given up his positions as general secretary and editor of the *International* to take up a seat on the Comintern Executive in Moscow. Upon his return in February 1924, he vainly tried to convince the Labour Party not to enter the Cabinet.[62]

The Party's stance towards black organizations during this period was ambiguous: while believing the African National Congress (ANC) to be dominated by 'instruments of the ruling class', it was unsure whether the ICU was a 'fit and proper body' to deal with the tasks it set on its own agenda.[63] Moreover, the huge educational and skills differential between blacks and whites meant that the Party found it very difficult to find and recruit African organizers. The few educated Africans were quickly co-opted by the state – or, as Bunting put it, 'snapped up by the enemy'. When the Comintern asked the CPSA to suggest a few African delegates for a planned Negro Conference and for the Fifth Comintern Congress, Bunting reported that they could not find anyone. 'Here, while I would not say they are all crooks,' he baldly began,

> yet they are so well cultivated by the other side, or so much under bourgeois influence, that I should not care to enter into any confidential arrangement with any of them, it would ... be reported to the police or to the agents of the Chamber of Mines, posing as parsons or friends of the natives or what not. ... The rank and file, ignorant and half civilised aa [sic] they are, unable to speak any but their native languages, are the most class conscious elements,

but what can you do when it comes to getting a representative of them to travel through the world?

The difficulty in finding educated Africans willing to work for the CPSA impeded the Party's organizing efforts. It seemed to be trapped in a vicious circle. 'Work *among* the natives has been attepted [sic] from time to time, with a little success, but it has never lasted', wrote Bunting; 'they fall away quickly as soon as the police get wind of it'. Bemoaning the fact that 'we have not yet got hold of any able and trustworthy native "missionaries" to do it among their compatriots', Bunting was nonetheless convinced that 'someday we shall succeed'. 'But the best propaganda', he went on, 'will be not by Communists as such, but a case in which in a strike of natives the white workers openly stand by them.'[64]

However, it became clear that the new Pact Government was just as racist as its predecessor, and hopes that white labour organizations would reach out to blacks were doused – an outcome already foreshadowed in October 1923 when the SAMWU executive had dissociated itself from a plan to organize black miners.[65] The entrenched racism of white trade unions strengthened the hand of those wishing to give more attention to the organization of black workers. The contest came to a head at the Party's Third Congress, held in Johannesburg in December 1924.

The generational challenge

The CPSA's turn to black labour in the mid-1920s was facilitated by the entry of a number of young people into the socialist movement who were concerned with organizing those outside the traditional orbit of trade unions: black and women workers. The Young Communist League was pivotal in the Party's turn towards black labour. It was launched 'in the purity of enthusiasm' one Sunday morning in Johannesburg, shortly after the CPSA's formation.[66] About fifteen young people were there, all white, and mostly male. The group drifted until its members got swept up in the waves of meetings and demonstrations for the 1922 Rand Revolt.

In the aftermath of the revolt, the Young Communist League revived through the campaign to free the strikers, chalking its slogan, 'Release the Strike Prisoners', all over town. It affiliated to the Young Communist International and followed its directive to campaign against military training. Eddie Roux remembers that as he became more and more caught up in practical work, convinced of the need for a Communist Party, his father Philip, who had introduced him to socialism, was now disillusioned with politics and argued that capitalism would collapse of its own accord, without the need for a vanguard party. Like many fathers and sons, the idealistic youth and his cynical father had frequent arguments: for one thing, Philip Roux spurned Bunting's turn to black workers with the remark that '[h]aving failed to get the support of the white workers, they now go and preach to the Natives'. But Eddie was impressed with Bunting, and scrupulously followed his writings in the

International. Eventually, sometime in 1923, when Eddie refused to leave the Young Communist League, his father locked him out of the house.[67]

Aside from Roux, the Young Communist League's notables included Willie Kalk, the South African-born son of a German social democratic immigrant, and a furniture-maker by trade; Victor Danchin, a university student; and the brothers Bernard Sachs, a writer, and Solly Sachs, who became a leader of the Garment Workers Union. In 1923 the Young Communist League began duplicating a monthly paper called the *Young Communist.* This ceased in August 1923 and was followed by the *Young Worker,* the name taken from the British counterpart, which had just renamed its own organ. The Young Communist League tried running study classes on Marxism; these proved unpopular and led to an exodus of members. The group included workers, clerks and shop assistants, and a few students. They were mostly men, and the few women generally kept a low profile.[68] It was also still solidly white at this stage, which Willie Kalk and Eddie Roux bemoaned amongst themselves and sought to remedy. It is Kalk whom Roux credits with putting him in touch with black workers. After that, Roux began dropping by the office of the ANC's paper, *Abantu-Batho* (*The People*). There he met Stanley Silwana, a teacher, and Thomas Mbeki, a worker, both of whom he invited to a Young Communist League meeting. Through Silwana and Mbeki, Roux came into contact with the ICU, and began to address its meetings.[69]

By early 1924, Kalk and Roux were trying to convince other Young Communist League members of the need to admit blacks. Initially stymied by Solly Sachs, their most articulate and forceful opponent, who argued that blacks should be recruited into a separate organization, they eventually won the day, both through perseverance and because Solly Sachs left on a trip to Europe. The Young Communist League's turn to blacks dovetailed with the Comintern's growing interest in the Negro question; Roux reported on the situation to the Young Communist International, which sealed the matter by endorsing the proposal to recruit blacks.

The debate in the Young Communist League paralleled the contest within the CPSA, which culminated at the Party's Third Congress. '[I]f our Conference accomplishes no more than to remove mutual aloofness on the subject of native affairs, it will have justified itself', argued Bunting. The entire labour movement, he went on, 'is paralysed and stultified by its failure to tackle its "native question"'. The CPSA 'should strenuously resist any tendency to a similar paralysis'. The Party resolved not to apply for affiliation to the Labour Party but '[t]hat the relations of the C.P. to the S.A.L.P. be on the United Front basis' and 'that the overthrow of capitalism can only be achieved through the joint endeavours of all the workers and therefore urges all branches to help to the utmost all the attempts of the native workers to organise industrially'.[70] Its programme demanded the abolition of the indentured labour and pass systems and the repeal of restrictions on the right to strike; 'equal pay for equal work', regardless of colour, sex or age; the nationalization of mines and banks; the expropriation of big estates in favour of landless workers and the provision of land for Africans; and votes for women.[71]

Many of those who favoured an emphasis on white workers either left or drifted away. In February 1925 Andrews resigned his position as general secretary and editor of the *International*. Archie Crawford, Andrews' chief political adversary in the white labour movement, had died in December 1924, and in March 1925 Andrews became secretary of the SAAEO. In June he resigned from the CPSA's Central Executive, although he remained a Party member. Roux took his place as general secretary.[72] In February 1925, Frank Glass gave up his posts as treasurer and Central Executive member, arguing that the new policy 'involves the complete isolation of the Party from the rest of the Labour Movement' and that he could not 'conscientiously take part in the carrying out of a policy with which [he] totally disagreed'. The following month, he became treasurer of the SAAEO. In May Glass resigned from the Party altogether, claiming that his membership was 'a stumbling-block' to work in the white labour movement and that the CPSA was a 'sect – nothing more, and is regarded by the average European worker as an anti-white party with some justification'.[73]

Ambiguities of gender

The CPSA's position on women's rights was even less developed than its position on blacks. There were few women in either the Young Communist League or the CPSA in the early 1920s, and those few generally played secondary rather than leadership roles. 'The woman question', a subject of burning interest for socialists two decades earlier, was of secondary concern for the Comintern, which sent occasional circulars to its affiliates urging them to organize women as a means of building working-class solidarity.[74] The diminished status of this issue for the Comintern reinforced the numerical predominance of men in the South African movement. The *International* printed occasional reports of or by women members, like Alice Harrison or Jessie Chapman, who in October 1923 ran as Communist candidate for Ward Three in the Benoni municipal elections. The *Torch*, an abortive CPSA organ dedicated to the unemployed of South Africa, featured an appeal 'To the Women' in its first issue.[75]

South African women did not yet have the right to vote, and most white feminists had already accepted the exclusion of black women from their demands for the franchise. The 1920s saw the beginnings of a convergence between the movement to disenfranchise the minority of Africans who had a qualified franchise and the women's suffrage movement. Many whites supported suffrage for white women on the basis that it would further diminish the significance of the black vote. In February 1924 the *International* responded to the debate on the Woman's Suffrage Bill with an article called 'Votes for (Native) Women', which indicated the CPSA's convoluted response to the issue. '"Votes for women" has become a capitalist cry in most countries', it claimed inaccurately, 'because by control of women's "education" and psychology capitalism has succeeded, or thinks it has, in turning most women into tame and ignorant servants of its own regime.' As it appealed to white workers on the basis of their own prejudices and self-interest to support the struggle of black labour, so it couched its argument on female suffrage to appeal to working-class derision of 'middle-class' women:

> After all, how many white women (to say nothing of men) are capable of political judgment? Hear these 'ladies' childish chatter, watch their empty-headed snobberies, see their complete mental enslavement to current bourgeois slosh, and then compare them with the native women at Bloemfontein, for instance, who resisted the proposal to make them carry passes. Which have the soundest political judgment?

Nevertheless, the CPSA supported women's suffrage on the instrumentalist line that only through the fullest possible democracy could capital be overthrown. Thus, instead of waiting until after the establishment of socialism to enfranchise women and blacks, political education through popular enfranchisement would help the struggle for socialism. And it entreated Labourites to '[f]ace the facts, grasp the nettle, and insist that the bourgeoisie, if it wants to enfranchise its women, pays the price to the last penny by enfranchising ... the maximum number of proletarian and peasant women too!'[76]

The fragmentation of women by colour and class in the wider society and the Comintern's ambiguity about women's rights provided little basis for female solidarity amongst the few women Communists. A small number of young women turned to socialism in the mid-1920s, as part of the generational shift, although even fewer were primarily interested in organizing women. Fanny Klenerman was one of those few women. Like her male counterparts, she had felt acutely the demoralization affecting the labour movement after the Rand Revolt. A Russian Jewish immigrant, Fanny Klenerman came to South Africa with her family as a small girl. Her grandmother had been left behind in Russia. As a consequence, Fanny's mother spent most of her time taking care of the household, only picking up English slowly. Her father, a socialist shopkeeper, had a number of friends with whom he used to discuss politics, and, unusually for a young girl, Fanny was included in these discussions. She studied jurisprudence at the University of Cape Town, where she became a prominent speaker and student leader. After university, her father put her in contact with Gabriel Weinstock in Johannesburg, where she began working for the Labour Party. But revulsion over the colour bar – she recounted, for instance, her distress at the conditions of the Coloured school where her friend Eva Green taught – led Klenerman to leave the Labour Party and join the CPSA. She continued to study jurisprudence through evening classes at the University of the Witwatersrand. But she eventually dropped out. 'The work I had now determined to do', she recalled, 'was the work of organising working class women – who were then without any means of safeguarding their positions as workers.'[77]

This was not the first attempt to organize women workers. In 1920 the ICU and the APO had made a stab at organizing black women and had convened a meeting in Cape Town attended by about fifty women. The ICU reiterated its commitment to organizing women workers at its annual conference in January 1923.[78] But

Klenerman's main constituency was white women. In the aftermath of the Rand Revolt, many rural Afrikaner communities became destitute, and young Afrikaner women began flocking to towns to earn a living. With few skills and limited English, many became seamstresses or waitresses. Assisted by Eva Green, Klenerman organized the South African Women Workers' Union and became its secretary. A similar union had existed before the strike but had collapsed around the time of the Revolt amidst allegations of financial irregularities. Klenerman organized in numerous factories, particularly in the sweets industry, where white women performed the unskilled work while white men worked on speciality sweets and received far higher wages. Just as white male workers had opposed the organization of black men for fear that their wages would be driven down, so they opposed the organization of white women. But Klenerman convinced them that 'there was no reason why all men's wages should come down when women's go up. And I also said no union would exist for five minutes if forming a union for women brought down the wages of the men.'[79]

In 1925 Klenerman attended the annual conference of the SAAEO, requesting assistance and affiliation for the Women Workers' Union. Bill Andrews was the SAAEO's secretary, and Klenerman sensed his ambivalence, as a man who had come through the craft union tradition, towards women workers. He was, in her words, 'an excellent official, a clever man & a man who understood politics – not only Trade Unionism'. Nonetheless, she had her reservations: 'I felt he was not a kindly-disposed man; I do not think he liked women. But we did get a certain amount of assistance from him.'

Andrews helped her polish a manifesto with the union's demands for improved wages, working conditions and holidays, and in the upshot, sweet-workers' wages were scaled up. Although initially denied affiliation because of its structure, the Women Workers' Union later split into two organizations, a Waitresses' Union and a Sweet Workers' Union, each of which gained recognition. In addition to her work for the Women Workers' Union and its offshoots, Klenerman also lobbied for women's issues in the SAAEO.[80]

Molly Zelikowitz Wolton's career in the CPSA took a very different path. Whereas Klenerman's decision to organize women workers allowed her to develop a political identity outside the CPSA, Molly Wolton was a polemicist and agitator who followed the Comintern's shifting policies and never developed an independent political identity. A Lithuanian Jew and a cousin of A. Z. Berman, she came to South Africa in 1919 and joined the CPSA in 1925. There she met and married Douglas Wolton, who arrived in South Africa in 1921 from Yorkshire. Douglas Wolton had originally come to South Africa to participate in a Cape to Cairo walk. Instead, he began working as a journalist and drifted into politics. Molly Wolton was described by Roux as 'petite, vivid, excitable, and a magnificent public speaker', and until the early 1930s when she left South Africa following a complete collapse, she was one of the few women to play an active role in the Party's leadership.[81] But she showed little interest in the direct organization of women. In a rare statement on the woman question, she articulated a position that paralleled the view held by the Party's majority on the national question until 1928 – that the franchise for women was a means to an end. It focused attention on problems facing women but it did not provide any real solution to their oppression. The only real way to emancipate women was through industrial organization.[82]

Bolshevization and the turn to black workers, 1925–27

The CPSA was relatively more successful in addressing the needs of black workers than those of women. The Party's decision in December 1924 to actively recruit black workers led to significant changes. Notably, the change dovetailed with the Comintern's policy of Bolshevization, announced at its Fifth Congress in June–July 1924 and revised by the ECCI in March–April 1925. The Bolshevization policy was a reaction to the defeat of the attempted German revolution in 1923. It also reflect-ed power struggles in the Russian Communist Party between the Zinoviev–Kamenev–Stalin triumvirate on the one side, and Leon Trotsky on the other. The ECCI, led by Zinoviev, ultimately decided that the fiasco in Germany was due to a 'right deviationist' leadership that had been soft on social democracy – and to which the triumvirate sought to link Trotsky. Bolshevization represented an attempted left turn to correct the alleged right deviation. In essence, the ECCI argued that successful revolution was predicated on the national affiliates applying the successful Bolshevik model to their own situation.

The Fifth Comintern Congress stipulated that a Bolshevized party 'must be a real mass party' and 'must be a centralised party, permitting no fractions, tendencies or groups'. The old style of ostensibly social-democratic organization, in which a few branch members did the work while the majority were inactive, was out. A Bolshevik party must be governed by a central committee, which, in principle, would be divided into a political bureau and an organizing bureau. The line of command was to run from the central committee to district committees and then to local groups. The model also proposed organizational precepts for Communists operating outside Party institutions. Within trade unions and similar bodies Communists should form a fraction seeking to advance Party policy and to win elections to posts. The formulation and application of this strategy required thor-ough conformity with both Party policy and discipline. Party members within a specific workplace were also required to operate in an organized fashion. Such a group was characterized as a nucleus and, once again, acted under Party discipline.[83]

1925 was a difficult year for the CPSA as it attempted to implement Bolshevization alongside its turn to black workers. Discussions about the Party's reorganization began in force in the second half of the year. Two British Communists, Jimmy and Violet Shields, arrived from Britain and spent the next couple of years in South Africa; Jimmy Shields helped the Party to introduce the new policy. The proposed changes were limited at this stage and included the regu-larization of agendas for the monthly aggregate meetings, the setting up of study classes for members, and the establishment of a clear dividing line between members and sympathizers, with the former having specified duties. The following year, 1926, Solly Sachs returned from Moscow, where he had represented the Young Communist League. He brought back recommendations for further changes involving the specialization of functions within the Party; accordingly, the CPSA set up Agitprop and Agrarian departments.[84]

Problems were already apparent by the CPSA's Fourth National Conference in Cape Town in December 1925. Many of the Party's white followers had been alienated by the emphasis on the Native question, and many of its most active members had lost interest, reported Sidney Bunting. The two main branches had suffered dissension, although the Cape Town branch was more plagued with resignations and expulsions than Johannesburg. There was a high turnover both in the general membership and on the Central Executive. Of the delegates to the fourth conference, only Sidney Bunting and Joe Pick had been delegates at the first conference.[85] But these difficulties should not deter a true Bolshevik Party, Bunting insisted. 'Bolshevisation', he exhorted,

> consists in espousing the cause of the native workers. The S.A.L.P. has no future although the 'white S. Africa' slogan is still popular with whites on the Rand. ... It still remains that many of our members are reluctant in this matter – 'our most Bolshevik work'. If carrying on this work offends the white trade unionists we should still go ahead with it.[86]

The shift towards black workers inevitably antagonized white workers, and this took its toll on CPSA activists, particularly those trying to organize white workers. The debate at the Fourth National Conference reflected the diversity of views on the matter. Willie Kalk began by arguing that 'Com. Roux should not say at public meetings in Jobg that natives should walk on the pavements, etc. That is what causes trouble at the meetings.' To this Bunting swiftly retorted: 'Com. Roux does not say foolish things at the meetings. Com. Kalk has no business to blame Com. Roux for attacks at the meetings. The capitalist class is responsible for attacks on us, not "lack of tact" on our part'. But Pick agreed with Kalk: 'Continual hammering at the native question is not a good policy: a variety of subjects should be discussed at meetings'. Thibedi in turn countered: 'You cannot draw back from mentioning the natives at open air meetings'. This led Molly Wolton to exclaim: 'Surely you must adapt yourself to the psychology of your audience!' R. de Norman concluded: 'Someone should write a dictionary of tact. We should and must stand firm on the native question whatever the consequences.'[87]

Indeed, the Party was not about to renege on its earlier decision, and it began a series of activities geared to attract black workers: night school, trade union work, meetings and public gatherings. Until 1925, the only African member had been William Thibedi, a veteran of the IWA and International Socialist League. By 1928, the Party claimed about 1600 African members out of approximately 1750, and in the middle to late 1920s it recruited a number of significant black leaders. Many of those who rose up the hierarchy came from a background that valued education; a number, including Thibedi, John B. Marks and Albert Nzula, had been teachers. Gana Makabeni, Johannes Nkosi and Moses Kotane, however, were workers who acquired their education in the Party night school. The majority of blacks who joined the Party, particularly in the Transvaal, were workers from small semi-rural locations.[88]

Thibedi, the son of a Wesleyan minister, taught in a Wesleyan school in Johannesburg. He was an invaluable organizer. He 'scurried all over the place all the time like a mouse', recalled Moses Kotane.[89] Roux described him as 'a genius at getting people together, whether workers in a particular industry, women, location residents, or whatever was needed at the moment'.[90] Thibedi certainly used novel approaches: in November 1923, for instance, he requested approval from the Central Executive to form a Christian Communist school 'to bore within religious circles' – to which request the executive chose to remain neutral.[91]

In 1925 the CPSA started a night school under Thibedi's direction. This became extremely successful at attracting and training African cadres; it attracted forty students in its first year. Initially, classes were held by candlelight at an African church in Ferreirastown. The programme was heavy going, covering Bukharin's and Preobachansky's *A.B.C. of Communism* and Bukharin's *Programme of the World Revolution*. Johannes Nkosi, who joined the Party in 1926 and became its first martyr three years later at the age of twenty-five, attended the night school. So did Moses Kotane – who had learned of the night school through Thibedi – and Edwin Mofutsanyana, both of whom later lectured there. Later the night school moved to slightly better premises on Fox Street, where the Party office was based.[92]

The CPSA also began using its paper more strategically, despite the fact that its printing press was suffering severe financial difficulties.[93] On 2 July 1926 its paper was renamed the *South African Worker*, its masthead now bearing the figures of a shirtless black miner and a skilled white worker. It increased its coverage of issues affecting black workers and began running educational articles. The 27 August issue announced that 'A Communist Primer for South Africa', was to be serialized in the paper to replace the Eurocentric *A.B.C. of Communism*.[94] In February 1926 the Central Executive Committee had discussed the possibility of publishing Bantu-language articles and decided that Thibedi 'should submit an article as an experiment'; by 1928 about two to three pages per issue were written in Bantu languages.[95]

Party activists also turned their attention to the ICU. In 1923 this began to spread 'like a veld fire over the Union of South Africa', with branches set up first in the coastal towns of Port Elizabeth and East London, then in the rural areas of the Cape Province and in the Orange Free State and the Transvaal. Thomas Mbeki and Stanley Silwana joined the Young Communist League, and in 1924 they and other members set up the Johannesburg branch of the ICU. Despite opposition from the Cape Town branch, in 1925 Kadalie moved the ICU headquarters to Johannesburg, purchasing and revamping the Workers' Hall.[96] Because of its success – Kadalie was always being interviewed by journalists and asked to speak at other trade union meetings, recalled Fanny Klenerman – the ICU began attracting the attention of a number of black leaders and activists who had heretofore remained aloof. Alex M. 'Max' Jabavu, the second son of John Tengo Jabavu who took over the editorship of *Imvo Zabantsundu* from his father, became a senior vice-president; Allison W. G. Champion, who had been involved with the Mine Clerks' Union, became leader of the ICU's Natal branch. The CPSA's Durban branch was practically defunct in 1926, leaving the field open for the ICU. So rapidly did the Natal branch of the ICU grow that by 1926 it was the leading section, both financially and in terms of membership. The ICU showed the possibility of a radical mass mobilization – an achievement that necessitated a response from the CPSA.[97]

By 1926, five black Communists had gained prominent posts in the ICU: Jimmy La Guma, Eddie Khaile, Johnny Gomas, R. de Norman and Thomas Mbeki were on the ICU's National Council, and Thibedi was an ICU shop steward and an organizer at Viljoens Drift. Paradoxically, that same year the CPSA's Central Executive Committee felt that the time was not opportune to appoint an African organizer for the Party's own work.[98]

The ICU drew support from a few white activists as well. Bill Andrews of the TUC, former Communist Frank Glass of the Witwatersrand Tailors' Association and Fanny Klenerman of the Waitresses' Union addressed an ICU meeting at Workers' Hall in August 1926. In March 1927 Andrews and Glass lambasted the government's repressive racial policies at an ICU conference, their speeches causing an outcry in the press and in Parliament.[99] Glass became a temporary financial officer for the organization, and Klenerman taught English and basic knowledge to workers at the ICU's school, so that 'they should know that they were part of something already practiced in Europe for many years' and that elsewhere 'workers such as themselves had won status and recognition of rights by the state'.[100]

The ICU and left politics

But the Communists had competition in their quest to influence the ICU, for it attracted the interest of other white liberals and socialists, and Kadalie cultivated their support. Chief amongst these was the author Ethelreda Lewis, who would shoot to international fame with the publication of *Trader Horn* in 1927. Lewis lived in Johannesburg and made the ICU her *cause célèbre*, organizing lectures at the Workers' Hall, raising funds and trying to drum up support from other leading whites.[101] She had a horror of Communism and hoped to mould the ICU into a force for moderate trade unionism. It was 'surely better to have Kadalie, with his undoubted power over fifty thousand natives, on the side of the reasonable trade union ambitious [sic] for the black man', she believed, 'than to leave him as a useful catspaw to men of the Moscow type who within the last twelve years have done untold harm to South Africa by means of the native'. She was dismayed at Glass's association with the ICU, claiming that 'he has stolen some hundreds of pounds' and simply appalled when she met his wife, Fanny Klenerman, 'a Russian Jewess with a scarlet dress and a B.A. degree. ... teaching natives to "read and write" etc *every night* down there' and 'glibly expounding "red" principles'.[102] At the same time Lewis felt keenly the limitations of the Joint Council movement, which those on the left saw as liberal paternalist talk shops that were woefully inadequate to deal with the pressing social needs of the black majority. As Lewis saw it, Kadalie was 'likely to be of far more use in South Africa tha[n] if he were a docile nonentity amongst a small group of natives who are content to be influenced by the Joint Council'.[103] Yet Lewis's own political outlook was imbued with all the paternalism of the English literati. The myth of the rural idyll was central to much British socialism and to many intellectuals of the period, and Lewis romanticized the South African countryside. Believing that rural Africans needed to be protected from the disruptive effects of imperialism and of city life, she hoped to convince Kadalie that the ICU should restrict itself to urban areas: 'perhaps the greatest future for the I.C.U., lies in the perfect organising *of town labour* throughout South Africa. To concentrate on that first: and having established (eventually) schools and colleges for manual even more than mental training – *then* to organise the country labour.'[104]

Ethelreda Lewis introduced Kadalie to the English author and journalist Winifred Holtby, who came to South Africa in January 1926 at the age of twenty-eight and spent six months as a League of Nations lecturer. Holtby was both mesmerized and appalled by South Africa's stark contrasts, ranging from the world 'of witty, agreeable, intelligent and generous people whose like might be met in Chelsea, Vienna, New York, Paris or Rome' to the half-hidden world that she found 'in every town that she visited. ... At dawn its citizens poured from the locations into the mines and workshops; they polished the parquet flooring in the Parktown bungalows; they emptied the ash-bins and cleaned the streets, they drove the carts drawn by limpid-eyed, softly treading donkeys.'[105] From that time on until she died in 1935, she campaigned for the ICU and for the organization of blacks in South Africa and against racism in Britain.

Ethelreda Lewis's counterpart in Durban was Mabel Palmer, a Fabian socialist and a university lecturer. Palmer contacted Sidney Webb on behalf of the ICU and put Kadalie in touch with Arthur Creech Jones, assistant secretary of the British Transport and General Workers' Union and member of the Independent Labour Party who would in the late 1940s become Colonial Secretary in the Labour Government.[106] The Independent Labour Party, an affiliate of the British Labour Party, still represented in the mid-1920s a broad spectrum of socialist opinion. Its members generally emphasized socialist morality more than Communists, who stressed the primacy of economics. By 1927, following the experience of the first Labour Government and the general strike and miners' lockout, it was becoming unambiguously left wing. Until 1928 some of its members cooperated with Communists. But subsequently, due to the Comintern's shifting policies, relations between the two organizations deteriorated dramatically.

Upon Holtby's return to England, she contacted Creech Jones and other prominent socialists on behalf of the ICU, including Dr Norman Leys, an authority on Kenya; James Maxton and Fenner Brockway of the Independent Labour Party; and

Lord Olivier, a Fabian and Secretary of State for India in the 1924 Labour Cabinet. Holtby and Palmer also launched a book drive to set up an ICU library.[107] This venture was initially quite successful. Fanny Klenerman remembered the library as a 'treasure-house', with 'all the literature that one could desire on the labour movement'. But the ICU lacked the administrative procedures and the skilled personnel to care for such a collection, and Klenerman gradually 'saw the shelves becoming more and more empty'.[108]

The ICU's very success contained the seeds of its demise. On the one hand, its growth was so rapid, as followers flocked to it, that it was unable to establish adequate structures to sustain its sprawling organization. With ambitions of enrolling 100,000 members by 1927, the ICU hired inexperienced and unskilled organizers. This led to financial irregularities and to corruption. There were also serious problems of personal rivalry and factionalism amongst its leadership. On the other hand, it faced severe repression from the state. In March 1926, Kadalie was banned from entering Natal, and other ICU officials were subjected to continued harassment and intimidation, both by the government and by hostile whites.[109]

By late 1926 the cordial relationship between the ICU and CPSA was beginning to sour. Not surprisingly, the ICU was no longer achieving concrete gains for its members, despite the dues that were flowing in. There had been no strikes or mass campaigns since the dock strikes in Cape Town and Port Elizabeth. Thus, there was significant internal pressure for a clear policy and programme of action. Communists on the ICU's National Council called for checks on the power of the leaders and for financial controls. The situation came to a head at the end of the year. At a meeting of the ICU's National Council on 16 December 1926 a resolution was passed by six to five that 'No member of the I.C.U. shall be a member of the Communist Party'. CPSA members on the National Council were forced to choose which organization they would remain with. Of the Communists on the Executive, Jimmy La Guma, Eddie J. Khaile, and Johnny Gomas refused to resign from the Party and were expelled from the ICU. Mbeki and de Norman choose to remain with the ICU and resigned their Party membership.[110] Although Kadalie subsequently tried to justify his action on African nationalist grounds, the problem was not one of colour: the expelled Communists included both Africans and Coloureds. As Thibedi described the scene to Roux, who was then studying at Cambridge, 'Kadalie, Champion, Thomas Mbeki, James Dippa, Theo B. Linjiza, De Nor, B.C.R. Mazingi, H.D. Tzamsashe + Co have left the revolutionary camp and moved to the Law + Order camp. There is no freedom of speech in the I.C.U. at all more especially who are known to be in the revolutionary camp.'

The National Council's expulsion of the Communists did not go without protest from the CPSA and from the ICU's branches, although the decision was not rescinded. Nonetheless, Thibedi, for one, was able to maintain some contact with ICU branches: 'I am asked ... to speak in Pretoria on the 30/1/27 by the I.C.U. branch there', he wrote to Roux. 'Kadalie Champion and Co does not know that I have been invited by that branch.'[111] In Vereeniging, members of the ICU branch were denied recognition by ICU headquarters for condemning the expulsions;

Thibedi organized some of these disgruntled members into a CPSA branch, recruiting Jacob Tjelele. And in Johannesburg, he reported, a group of African Communists had formed a 'Centre Forward' group to work within the ICU.[112]

Ethelreda Lewis was clearly relieved, if surprised, at the expulsion of the Communists.[113] Indeed, she appealed to General Hertzog 'to suggest that the recent action of the secretary of the I.C.U. in trying to suppress Communism in the ranks of his trade union would make him worthy of some approving message' – advice that, not surprisingly, Hertzog failed to heed.[114]

The ICU was effectively an outcast organization in South Africa, vilified and repressed by the state and rejected by white labour. The Communist presence in the ICU gave both the state and white labour organizations an excuse for their actions, with the latter claiming that the ICU was a political or racial movement rather than a bona fide trade union organization. Taking advice from its Independent Labour Party contacts in Britain, at its December 1926 conference the ICU committed itself to seek allies outside South Africa, and it applied for and received affiliation to the IFTU in Amsterdam. Kadalie hoped that international recognition might give the ICU more credibility at home and improve its bargaining position with white labour organizations. After corresponding with Creech Jones and Winifred Holtby, in May 1927 he sailed for Europe to develop contacts with European trade unions and to attend the International Labour Organisation conference in Geneva.[115]

Kadalie was overwhelmed by his reception in Europe. He attended the IFTU Congress in Paris and labour conferences in Amsterdam, Berlin and Vienna. In Britain Kadalie met with members of the ILP and its Imperialism Advisory Committee. In July 1927, despite protests by the TUC, the Labour Party, the ICU and the IFTU, the South African government passed the Native Administration Act, a law that severely impeded black labour and political organization. The ILP launched a campaign around the issue. In July the ILP Imperialism Advisory Committee sponsored a weekend lecture school and conference on 'Socialism, Imperialism and "Subject" Races', at which Kadalie lectured, and in October Kadalie addressed an ILP forum entitled 'Is South Africa to be a Slave State?'[116]

The Imperialism Advisory Committee advised Kadalie to establish the ICU on a firm trade union basis and to build up support in Europe. The vision offered by Creech Jones coincided with Holtby's, as well as with that of Ethelreda Lewis. 'The Union', he advised Kadalie, 'must not be side-tracked by Communism, and should not attempt to put itself in the position of being an industrial movement one minute and a political party the next.' However, he added, 'the natives must attempt to secure political redress. The oppressive laws must be revoked.' The ICU, he emphasized, must proceed step by step in its attempt to establish itself as a legitimate trade union. Hence, it must appeal firstly to the Labour Party for affiliation; if the appeal were rejected, then there would be a case for applying to the Labour and Socialist International and to the League against Imperialism.[117] In September 1927 Kadalie attended the British TUC in Edinburgh. This TUC marked a significant attack on the left, especially the Communist Party of Great Britain (CPGB), in the aftermath of the general strike of 1926 and deteriorating left–right relations;

it could only have reinforced Kadalie's own views about Communist participation in the ICU.

Behind the antagonism that many British socialists and trade unionists displayed towards Communism in the late 1920s was the preference for evolutionary socialism, a belief in its feasibility in the British context and, consequently, a belief that the Soviet model was inappropriate for Britain. Lord Olivier, for one, believed that the Fabian approach was the only effective means of superseding capitalism. 'Those of us in England who have understood the native cause', he wrote to Roux,

> have been trying to strengthen the I.C.U. as a force in South Africa and take the same line with regard to the Communist party there as we do in Europe. I desire to see the I.C.U. relieved of its Communist propagandists, and I hope it will be strong enough to run genuine Labour Socialist candidates of its own.[118]

By 1927 the ICU was mainly a rural movement that gave little attention to urban black workers. That year it applied for affiliation on the basis of a claimed 100,000 members to the South African Trades Union Coordinating Council, a joint body representing the all-white Johannesburg-based Trades Union Congress and the Cape Federation of Labour Unions, whose affiliates included some Coloured members. In reality the ICU had nowhere near 100,000 members and could not have paid the affiliation fee for such a number. The Coordinating Council rejected the ICU's request, fearing that its white affiliates would feel 'swamped'. Instead, it suggested joint discussions and the possibility of future affiliation on the basis of 5000 members, a suggestion endorsed by the executive of the TUC. Kadalie rejected the offer, although the ICU subsequently did hold joint discussions with the TUC.[119]

During Kadalie's 1927 trip to Europe, Creech Jones had suggested that the ICU employ an experienced British trade unionist to overhaul its organization and administration.[120] Kadalie pursued the suggestion, and in 1928 the thirty-four-year-old Scotsman William Ballinger was appointed as advisor to the ICU. From a poor, working-class background, Ballinger had been Secretary of the Motherwell Trades and Labour Council, the second largest trades council in Scotland, since 1921. He was a member of the Amalgamated Engineering Union, a propagandist for the Independent Labour Party and an activist in the Workers' Educational Association and in public affairs. Through the Motherwell Trades and Labour Council he had worked with Communists. Creech Jones had certain reservations about Ballinger, due to his lack of senior experience in a big trade union, but, he told Kadalie, 'common sense in a cautious Scotsman might make good this lack of experience'.[121] And Creech Jones confided to Winifred Holtby that '[h]e seems of the right type – W.E.A., I.L.P., Socialist propagandist, energetic, enthusiastic, trades council work, labour party secretary, trade union delegate, etc.'. In other words, Ballinger belonged to the respectable side of the British labour and socialist movements.[122]

Ballinger, himself, was eager for the challenge. 'It is a man's job', he told Winifred Holtby, 'I'm willing to try it.' While the complexities of Motherwell politics necessitated skill at pragmatic bargaining – and Ballinger had excelled at that – he envisioned his role in Africa very much in idealistic terms. When he was twelve, he told Holtby, his father had taken him to Blantyre, the birthplace of explorer David Livingstone. The story of Livingstone's work in Africa had made a profound impression on him.[123] Now, Ballinger's desire to assist black workers in South Africa could be seen both as a testament to the memory of his father and their journey to Blantyre and as an example of the idea of 'service to others', which had a resonance in Scottish radicalism. 'I think the post will offer a splendid opportunity for an understanding between the White and Black workers', he subsequently wrote to Winifred Holtby,

> as the right person could set out to become a liason [sic] officer between the two unions in Africa. ... If our Black comrades are refused the assistance of their White brothers, then it means a fearful internicine [sic] struggle with a certain still further lowering of the 'Whites' standard of living ... [124]

The news of the appointment of a British trade unionist as ICU advisor caused quite a stir in South Africa. 'I.C.U.'s New Plans: Trade Unionism Only', reported the Johannesburg *Star*.[125] Despite Ballinger's hope to 'slip into Africa as quietly as possible',[126] when he landed at Cape Town in June 1928, he was informed that he would be detained as an 'undesirable alien' and only after much negotiation was he given a temporary landing permit.[127]

The ICU's situation, Ballinger discovered, was far worse then he had been told. He found the organization in financial and administrative disarray, facing debts and legal actions. He implemented some financial and administrative reforms and dismissed some of the corrupt officials. Its officials had not been paid for several months; indeed, the ICU's promises to reimburse Ballinger's travelling expenses and to pay his salary came to nought, and for years he relied on local and international support for his livelihood. Despite Ballinger's attempts to re-establish the ICU on sound administrative lines, the organization became factionalized and splintered. In 1928 the Cape Town branch seceded and Champion established the ICU *yase* Natal. Relations between Kadalie and the other ICU officials deteriorated, and in January 1929 he was forced to take a one-year leave of absence. Shortly thereafter he launched an Independent ICU but this soon foundered, and he faded from active politics, consumed by ill health and drink.[128]

Ballinger, himself, contemptuous of the South African Labour Party as 'the most conservative psuedo [sic] Labour group I have ever run up against', was squeezed between the Communists on one side and the Joint Council movement, whose members saw him as 'a Communist in disguise', on the other.[129] In 1929 individuals in the Joint Council movement founded the South African Institute of Race Relations, a research body concerned with the effects of segregation and discrimination and led by J. D. Rheinallt Jones. Ballinger was highly critical of the paternalism behind these two groups; he regarded the Institute of Race Relations as 'a dangerous philanthropic movement'. Although Ballinger still maintained in 1930 that '[t]he ICU is today the greatest Native force in South Africa despite its deplet-ed numerical strength', over the next few years he distanced himself from the trou-bled organization. In part this was due to a serious illness that incapacitated him for eighteen months in 1930–31. But he became increasingly involved in other pro-jects, notably research on the British protectorates of Basutoland, Bechuanaland and Swaziland, and the development of consumer and producer cooperatives.[130] Similarly, Ethelreda Lewis withdrew from active support for the ICU in 1931, fol-lowing the death of her husband. Her novel, *Wild Deer*, published in 1933, repre-sented her attempt to come to terms with the ICU's demise.

Like the CPSA, the ICU was caught in a dilemma between class and colour in South Africa: insufficiently militant for the CPSA; too black for the white labour movement. After their expulsion from the ICU, Communists generally portrayed it as an organization manipulated by a corrupt and reformist petty-bourgeois leader-ship. By 1928 Roux was arguing that the CPSA should support the ICU in so far as it supported the working class but that the collapse of the ICU would not be against the Party's interests. Yet, after Kadalie's resignation, the CPSA evidently con-sidered the possibility of re-entering it: when Roux asked Ballinger whether he would agree to the readmission of Communists to the ICU, Ballinger unequivocal-ly replied in the affirmative.[131]

Instead, after its activists were expelled from the ICU, the CPSA concentrated on the direct organization of black trade unions and on building up its own branch-es. In early 1927 William Thibedi and Ben Weinbren established a number of industrial trade unions that were the nucleus of the South African Federation of Non-European Trade Unions formed in March 1928. In March 1927 Thibedi became the Party's first African organizer. His duties included, amongst other things, writing, translating and reporting 'on observations at the law courts, com-pounds, native townships, prisons, etc.' for the *South African Worker*, subscriptions and sales; 'hunting up backsliders'; 'learning to type, especially articles in native lan-guages for the printers'; and 'tabulating the list of scholars at the Study Class and collecting their dues'.[132] He and Jimmy Shields also helped to build up the branch-es in Vereeniging and South East Transvaal. When Thibedi and Shields visited the South East Transvaal Branch, whose members were farmworkers who 'met periodi-cally, in a religious atmosphere',

they had prolonged discussions with a stream of visitors, followed next day by a meeting of over 400 on the veld, with many visitors from towns and dis-tricts 30 miles or more away. They secured the adhesion of three headmen, on which the crowd insisted, and 115 gave in their names for membership.

Moreover, reported Thibedi and Shields, the people were using the CPSA's Pass Law leaflet 'as a text book' and desired literature in Xhosa and Zulu. Thibedi and Shields advised them to hold monthly meetings and to form a united front with the ANC and ICU, despite evident criticism of these organizations for their lack of policy and 'only demanding money or cattle'.[133] In the vacuum left by the perceived weaknesses of the ANC and the ICU, there was certainly scope for Communist organizers. Despite great obstacles, the Party seemed to be on the upswing. Thus, in September 1927 when the CPSA's Central Executive Committee received a lengthy thesis from the ECCI outlining the Party's purported problems, it agreed that it was 'not a correct bird's eye view of local problems'.[134]

Conclusion

After the demoralization that followed the Rand Revolt, the 1920s were generally years of cautious optimism for South African Communists. The CPSA's brief united front period represented a transition between its earlier white labour focus and its turn to black labour from 1924. However faltering its first steps, the Party's reorientation towards black labour was a consequence of internal dynamics in South Africa – notably the accord between white labour and the state coupled with the remarkable growth of black protest organizations. However, the turn also dovetailed with Comintern policy that placed growing emphasis on the national and colonial question and on the Negro question. Although the Comintern was gradually increasing its involvement with the CPSA, it had not yet begun to intervene in the South African affiliate to the extent that it had in its European and Asian affiliates. Thus, during these years the CPSA operated with relative autonomy from the Comintern. Nonetheless, the CPSA used the Comintern's changing policies as a guide for its own activities and beliefs, and individuals in the Party referred to the Comintern to shore up their own positions against their critics. Communist scepticism about the role of the British Independent Labour Party in the ICU, for instance, reflected the broader political tensions within the international socialist movement. Despite the CPSA's ousting from the ICU, Communists believed that the Party's fortunes were on the rise, as indicated both by the growth of its membership and of its trade unions. The CPSA's solution to South Africa's national question paralleled the responses of Communist Parties around the world to the problems of national and sexual oppression: the emancipation of blacks, like that of women, lay through the emancipation of organized labour. That, they were convinced, was the road to socialism.

Notes

1. Bernard Sachs, 'The City Hall Steps', *South African Personalities and Places*, Johannesburg: Kayor, 1959, 118–21, quotes 117, 118 and 117 respectively.
2. The years 1922–24 are often seen as a turning point in the political consciousness of white workers. Simons and Simons, *Class and Colour*, 617–18, see 1922 as a transition point between the early class consciousness of white workers and their subsequent degeneration into colour consciousness. Davies, *Capital, State and White Labour*, 4–5, argues that once white workers moved into state structures, they became white wage-

earners, rather than workers, that is, part of a new petty bourgeoisie that included workers, supervisors and other intermediary strata. See also Simson, 'The Myth of the White Working Class'; Robert Davies, 'The "White Working-Class" in South Africa', *New Left Review*, 82, November–December 1973, 40–59; and Harold Wolpe,'The "white working class" in South Africa', *Economy and Society*, 5, 2, 1976, 197–240.

3. S. P. Bunting, 'Statement presented at the Sixth Comintern Congress, 23 July 1928', in Drew, ed., *South Africa's Radical Tradition*, vol. 1, 77–80, criticized the Comintern's lack of contact with the South African affiliate.

4. McDermott and Agnew, *The Comintern*, 23–4.

5. For other discussions of the Rand Revolt see, *inter alia*, W. M. MacMillan, 'The Truth about the Strike on the Rand', *New Statesman*, 19, 474, 13 May 1922, 145–6; Edward Roux, '1922 and all that', *Trek*, 11 February 1944, 12; Robert Davies, 'The 1922 Strike on the Rand: White Labor and the Political Economy of South Africa', in Peter Gutkind, R. Cohen and J. Copans, eds, *African Labour History*, Beverly Hills and London: Sage, 1978, 80–108; Rob Davies, 'The 1922 Strike and the Political Economy of South Africa', in Bozzoli, comp., *Labour, Townships and Protests*, 298–324; Baruch Hirson, 'The General Strike of 1922', *Searchlight South Africa*, 3, 3, October 1993, 63–94; Jeremy Krikler, 'Women, Violence and the Rand Revolt of 1922', *Journal of Southern African Studies*, 22, 3, September 1996, 349–72; Jeremy Krikler 'The Commandos: The Army of White Labour in South Africa.' *Past and Present*, 163, 1999, 202–44.

6. Simons and Simons, *Class and Colour*, 252–5, 271–99, and 303; Norman Herd, *1922: The Revolt on the Rand*, Johannesburg: Blue Crane, 1966, 19–20.

7. S. P. Bunting, *'Red Revolt': The Rand Strike, January–March, 1922*, CPSA: Johannesburg, 1922, 32–3; Johns, *Raising the Red Flag*, 139–43.

8. S. P. Bunting, 'The Rand Revolt: Causes and Effects', R. K. Cope Papers, A953/6a, 3–6, Historical Papers Library, University of the Witwatersrand. Despite white labour's prosperity relative to blacks, Bunting noted, p. 4, that 'artisans from England often say they live no better in Africa than at "Home"; and many white miners are in some respects worse off than, until recently, their fellows in Wales, who at least escape the deadly South African "miner's phthisis", and are not so directly liable to be displaced by the advance of cheap non-european labor'. See Simons and Simons, *Class and Colour*, 271, for a less sympathetic Communist view.

9. Cope, *Comrade Bill*, 230–31.

10. *The story of a crime, being the vindication of the Transvaal Strike Legal Defense Committee in connection with the Great Strike on the Witwatersrand in 1922*, 28 May 1924, 18, African Collection (South Africa), Box 37, folder 683, Manuscripts and Archives, Yale University Library.

11. Simons and Simons, *Class and Colour*, 278.

12. The slogan, 'Workers of the World Fight and Unite for a White S.A.', which appeared on a banner evidently held up by white workers and their wives, was most emphatically not a CPSA slogan nor is there any evidence that Communists supported it. See *Through the Red Revolt on the Rand: A Pictorial Review of Events, January, February, March, 1922*, compiled from photographs taken by representatives of *The Star*, Johannesburg: Central News Agency, 1922, 1st and 2nd editions.

13. Cope, *Comrade Bill*, 232–6; 'The Enemy Within', *International*, 27 January 1922, 1.

14. Roux, *Time Longer than Rope*, 148; Cope, *Comrade Bill*, 244.

15. Sachs, 'City Hall Steps', quotes 119 and 120 respectively.
16. Letter from F. to Ivon Jones, 16 March [1922], RTsKhIDNI, 495.64.159.
17. Roux and Roux, *Rebel Pity*, 23. A scrawled comment inserted on the letter from 'F' to Ivon Jones, 495.64.159, claims Spendiff and Fisher were killed by shrapnel.
18. Bunting, *'Red Revolt'*, 22–3; Herd, *1922*, 47–48; Simons and Simons, *Class and Colour*, 294–6.
19. MacMillan, 'The Truth about the Strike', 145. See also Jeremy Krikler, 'William MacMillan and the Working Class', in Hugh MacMillan and Shula Marks, eds, *Africa and Empire: W. M. MacMillan, Historian and Social Critic*, London: University of London, Institute of Commonwealth Studies, 1989, 35–71, esp. 61–8.
20. MacMillan, *Africa Emergent*, 310.
21. Herd, *1922*, 31.
22. W. H. Andrews, 'Foreward' to Bunting, *'Red Revolt'*, 3.
23. Cope, *Comrade Bill*, 239–40.
24. Quoted in D.I. Jones, *Re General Strike in South Africa*, n.d., RTsKhIDNI, 495.64.9. See also South Africa. Department of Justice Files, 3/1064/18 (1921–23).
25. Bunting, *'Red Revolt'*, 7, 39–41; '"White South Africa". Two Voices', *International*, 27 January 1922, in Drew, ed., *South Africa's Radical Tradition*, vol. 1, 48–50; Roux, *S. P. Bunting*, 92–3, 100.
26. Bunting, *'Red Revolt'*, 36–7, quote 37.
27. D. I. Jones, *Further Statement on the South African Situation*, 25 March 1922, 2, RTsKhIDNI, 495.64.6.
28. Roux, *Time Longer than Rope*, 150–51.
29. Simons and Simons, *Class and Colour*, 299.
30. Letter from F. to Ivon Jones, March 16th, [1922], RTsKhIDNI, 495.64.159.
31. Simons and Simons, *Class and Colour*, 321; Davies, 'The 1922 Strike', 95–8; Andrews, *Class Struggles*, 37–41; Bonner, 'The 1920 Black Mineworkers' Strike', 289; Bunting, 'The Rand Revolt', 16–17. Bunting speculates that the drop in black wages was due to greater recruitment from surrounding regions outside South Africa, where labour was cheaper.
32. Simons and Simons, *Class and Colour*, 303–4.
33. Cope, *Comrade Bill*, 286; Simons and Simons, *Class and Colour*, 323–4; *The Communist Party of South Africa and the question of relations with the Labour Party*, [1924?], RTsKhIDNI, 495.64.28; Minutes of the CPSA Central Executive Committee held on 14 December 1923, RTsKhIDNI, 495.64.17.
34. Tsuzuki, *Tom Mann*, 209–12; Roderick Martin, *Communism and the British Trade Unions 1924–1933*, Oxford: Clarendon Press, 1969, 1–12.
35. 'Tom Mann in South Africa', *All Power*, December, 1922, 8. Tom Mann Papers, Box 4, 1922–23, MSS 334, University of Warwick Modern Records Centre; McDermott and Agnew, *The Comintern*, 27–38, esp. 31–2.
36. Class War Prisoners Release Committee, Committee, *SHALL SOUTH AFRICAN MINERS BE MURDERED?*, 1922, Mann Papers, Working Class Movement Library.
37. 'South Africa To-Day', by a Comrade on the Rand, *The Workers' Dreadnought*, September 16, 1922.
38. 'The World Struggle', *A.P.O.*, 7 October, 1922, 4. See also letter from David L. Dryburgh to Tom Mann, Mann Papers, Working Class Movement Library.
39. Quoted in Bernard Sachs, 'The 1922 Rand Revolt', *South African Personalities*, 15–32, 28–9.

40. Sachs, *Multitude of Dreams*, 122–3; Andrews, *Class Struggles*, 36.

41. Fanny Klenerman, 'Jan Smuts', unpublished memoirs, Fanny Klenerman Papers, Historical Papers Library, University of the Witwatersrand.

42. *Tom Mann's Message. To the Workers of South Africa*, Johannesburg: I.S.L. Press, 1922, 3 and 8.

43. 'White and Black Shake Hands', *Argus*, 17 January 1923; 'Mr. Tom Mann and the Coloured Workers' and 'Mr. Tom Mann on the Parade', both in *Cape Times*, 18 January 1923.

44. Tom Mann, 'S. African Natives and Coloured Men', *All Power*, March 1923, 8.

45. Letter from W. H. Andrews to Tom Mann, 26 December 1922, in Drew, ed., *South Africa's Radical Tradition*, vol. 1, 54–5.

46. Sachs, *Multitude of Dreams*, 134–6; Roux, *S. P. Bunting*, 40, 57–61 and quote, 187, n. 15. See also Brian Bunting, ed., *Letters to Rebecca: South African Communist Leader S. P. Bunting to his Wife, 1917–1934*, Bellville: Mayibuye, 1996.

47. Letter from Andrews to Mann, 2-1-23, Mann Papers, uncatalogued MSS 334, University of Warwick Modern Records Centre.

48. Ivan L. Walker and Ben Weinbren, *2000 Casualties: A History of the Trade Unions and the Labour Movement in the Union of South Africa*, Johannesburg: SATUC, 1961, 285–6; Drew, ed., *South Africa's Radical Tradition*, vol. 1, 71, n. 9.

49. Sachs, *Multitude of Dreams*, 137.

50. Roux, *S. P. Bunting*, 96–9; Sheridan Johns, 'The Comintern, South Africa and the Black Diaspora', *Review of Politics*, 37, 2, 1975, 200–34, 211–13.

51. S. P. Bunting, 'The "Colonial" Labour Front', 23 October 1922, in Drew, ed., *South Africa's Radical Tradition*, vol. 1, 51–4, quote 53.

52. Bunting, 'The Rand Revolt', 23.

53. Letter from S. P. Bunting to I. Amter, Communist International, 24 November 1923, RTsKhIDNI, 495.64.14; Roux and Roux, *Rebel Pity*, 26.

54. Letter from W. H. Andrews to Tom Mann in Drew, ed., *South Africa's Radical Tradition*, vol. 1, 54–5.

55. *International*, 9 March 1923, 1–2.

56. Quoted in S. P. Bunting, 'The Bitter Cry of Outcast Africa', *International*, 13 April 1923, 3.

57. D. I. Jones, 'Some Remarks on the United Front', *International*, 5 January 1923, 2; M. Lopes, 'The United Front', *International*, 16 March 1923, 2; S. P. Bunting, 'An Open Letter', *International*, 13 March 1923, 4. See also Roux, *S. P. Bunting*, 99–100.

58. 'An Open Letter', *International*, 13 April 1923, 4; Harrison, *Memoirs of a Socialist*, 98–101.

59. CPSA Second National Congress, April 28 & 29, 1923. Agenda, Delegates to Congress, and Minutes, RTsKhIDNI, 495.64.16. The Party officers elected at the congress included Julius First as chair and Sam Barlin as vice-chair; Sidney Ward as treasurer and C. F. Glass as organizer. The Central Executive included A. Goldman, R. Gelblum, H. Lee, S. Rubin, E. Roux, R. Rabb and W. Ward.

60. 'Affiliation with the L.P.', *International*, 25 May 1923, 2; 'Keep out the Communists: S.A. Labour Party Baulks Again', and 'Communist Affiliation: Letter from the Labour Party', both in *International*, 27 July 1923, 2 and 4 respectively. See also Cope, *Comrade Bill*, 286–7.

61. 'Communist Party, S.A.: Election Manifesto', *International*, 16 May 1923, 6–7.

62. CPSA, *A Vital Issue. Shall Labour enter the Cabinet?*, 25 June 1924, British Library, Colindale; Cope, *Comrade Bill*, 287–91.
63. 'An "African Labour Federation"', *International*, 11 January 1924, 3. In 1923 the SANNC was renamed the African National Congress.
64. S. P. Bunting to I. Amter, Communist International, 24 November 1923, RTsKhIDNI, 495.64.14. See also letter from Provisional Secretary for Calling the Negro Conference to Executive Committee of the CPSA, 23 July 1923 and letter from the Secretary for Calling a Negro Conference to the Executive Committee, CPSA, 15 November 1923, RTsKhIDNI, 495.64.19.
65. 'In Quest of Reason', *International*, 26 October 1923, 3.
66. Roux and Roux, *Rebel Pity*, 147.
67. Roux and Roux, *Rebel Pity*, 24–28, quote 27.
68. 'Young Communist Notes', *International*, 18 July 1924, 8.
69. Roux and Roux, *Rebel Pity*, 30–37; 'Young Communist Notes', *International*, May 9, 1924, 8; 'Our Social Composition', *Young Worker*, 2, 1, January 1924, 4.
70. *CPSA Third Congress, Johannesburg, 27–30 December 1924*, quotes 14 and 20, RTsKhIDNI, 495.64.33. The first (amended) motion was proposed by T. Chapman and seconded by Roux; the second motion proposed by S. Buirski and seconded by S. A. Rochlin. See also Roux, *S. P. Bunting*, 104–6.
71. Draft Communist Party Programme adopted by the Party conference on December 30, 1924, for submission to the branches, in Bunting, ed., *South African Communists Speak*, 80–84.
72. Letter from E. R. Roux to the ECCI, 27 June 1925, RTsKhIDNI 495.64.40; Simons and Simons, *Class and Colour*, 325–6; Roux, *S. P. Bunting*, 105–6; Roux and Roux, *Rebel Pity*, 38–9.
73. Letter from C. F. Glass to the General Secretary, Communist Party of South Africa, 9 May 1925, Fanny Klenerman Papers.
74. For a discussion of early socialist debates on the woman question see Hal Draper and Anne G. Lipow, 'Marxist Women versus Bourgeois Feminism', in Ralph Miliband and John Saville, eds, *The Socialist Register 1976*, London: Merlin, 1976, 179–226.
75. 'To the Women', *Torch*, 1, 1, July 1923, 1; N. Lenin, 'Freeing the Women', *International*, 4 April 1924, 2; Walker, *Women and Resistance*, 46–7.
76. 'Votes for (Native) Women', *International*, 22 February 1924, 2.
77. Klenerman, 'How the S.A. Woman [sic] Workers' Union Began', unpublished memoirs.
78. Walker, *Women and Resistance*, 59; Bradford, *A Taste of Freedom*, 3–4; Industrial and Commercial Workers' Union of Africa, *Annual Conference Agenda*, 18 January 1923 in Drew, ed., *South Africa's Radical Tradition*, vol. 1, 56.
79. Klenerman, 'How the S.A. Woman [sic] Workers' Union Began', unpublished memoirs.
80. Klenerman, 'How the S.A. Woman [sic] Workers' Union Began', unpublished memoirs. Her memoirs refer to her attendance at the Trades Union Congress in 1927. Jon Lewis, *Industrialisation and Trade Union Organisation in South Africa, 1924–55*, Cambridge: Cambridge University, 1984, 61–2; Berger, *Threads of Solidarity*, 92–4.
81. Roux, *S. P. Bunting*, 113; Elizabeth Ceiriog Jones, 'Inkululeko: Organ of the Communist Party of South Africa, 1939–1950', in Les Switzer, ed., *South Africa's Alternative Press*, Cambridge: Cambridge Univ., 1997, 331–72, 366, n. 14.
82. Molly Wolton, 'Votes for Women in South Africa', *South African Worker*, 11 March 1927, 2.

83. McDermott and Agnew, *The Comintern*, 44–6, quotes 46. Henry Pelling, *The British Communist Party: A Historical Profile*, London: Adam and Charles Black, 1958, 21–2. See also South Africa Department of Justice Files, 3/1064/18 (1923–26 and 1926–27).
84. CPSA Central Executive Committee Minutes, 6 August and 20 August 1925, RTsKhIDNI, 495.64.42; Letter from E. S. Sachs to General Secretary, CPSA, 21 November 1925, RTsKhIDNI, 495.64.40; CPSA Central Executive Meeting Minutes, 22 April 1926, RTsKhIDNI, 495.64.53.
85. *Fourth National Conference of the Communist Party of South Africa held at 145 Long Street, Cape Town, on December 26–28, 1925*, RTsKhIDNI, 495.64.43; see also Cape Town branch report to Central Executive Committee for 1925, RTsKhIDNI, 495.64.45.
86. *Fourth National Conference of the Communist Party of South Africa*, 17.
87. *Fourth National Conference of the Communist Party of South Africa*, 27.
88. Roux, *Time Longer than Rope*, 214–16, argues that African intellectuals were more overtly nationalist than workers and were, accordingly, more sceptical of the visible presence of white leaders, especially in towns. As well, he adds, African intellectuals were often politically ambitious and the CPSA did not offer much scope for that. See also Roux, *S. P. Bunting*, 52, 126; Johns, *Raising the Red Flag*, 126; Robin D. G. Kelley, 'The Religious Odyssey of African Radicals: Notes on the Communist Party of South Africa 1921–34', *Radical History Review*, 51, 1991, 5–24. Sonia Bunting, interview with Moses Kotane, October 1972, Brian Bunting Collection 8.2.2.1, Mayibuye Centre Historical Papers Archive, University of the Western Cape.
89. Quoted in Bunting, *Kotane*, 44.
90. Roux, *S. P. Bunting*, 116; Robert Edgar, interview with Edwin Mofutsanyana, Roma, Lesotho, July 1981, 20–21.
91. Minutes of CPSA Central Executive held on 15 November 1923, RTsKhIDNI, 495.64.17.
92. Roux, *S. P. Bunting*, 107–8, 113–14; Roux and Roux, *Rebel Pity*, 68, 92, 128, 144; Roux, *Time Longer than Rope*, 132, 225; *Fourth National Conference of the Communist Party of South Africa*, 37.
93. Central Executive Committee Minutes, 22 October 1924, RTsKhIDNI, 495.64.42; Letter from S. P. Bunting to Secretary, ECCI, 3 November 1926, RTsKhIDNI, 495.64.48.
94. 'A Communist Primer for South Africa', *South African Worker*, 27 August 1926, 3.
95. CPSA Central Executive Committee Minutes, 4 February 1926, RTsKhIDNI, 495.64.53.
96. Kadalie, *My Life and the ICU*, 19, 81; Wickens, *Industrial and Commercial Workers' Union*, 93.
97. Kadalie, *My Life and the ICU*, 72–3; CPSA Central Executive Minutes, 9 September 1926, RTsKhIDNI, 495.64.53.
98. 'Obey Orders', *The Workers' Herald*, 14 September 1926, 2; CPSA Central Executive Committee Minutes, 21 June 1926, RTsKhIDNI, 495.64.53.
99. 'White Trade Unionist and Kadalie's Ban', *The Workers' Herald*, 14 September 1926, 5; Wickens, *Industrial and Commercial Workers Union*, 131; Baruch Hirson, 'Death of a Revolutionary: Frank Glass/Li Fu-Jen/John Liang 1901–1988', *Searchlight South Africa*, 1, September 1988, 28–41, 34.
100. Klenerman, 'The I.C.U. and night schools', unpublished memoirs. Glass and Klenerman were married in 1927.

101. For background on Ethelreda Lewis see T. J. Couzens's introduction to Lewis's novel, *Wild Deer* [1933], Cape Town: David Philip, 1984.

102. Lewis to Holtby, 4 April 1928, Winifred Holtby Collection, file 4.9, item 9, Kingston upon Hull Local Studies Library.

103. Lewis to the Honourable Prime Minister, 3 January 1927, Holtby Collection, file 4.9, item 69.

104. Lewis to Kadalie, 10 January 1927, Holtby Collection, file 4.9, item 66. Lewis, *Wild Deer*, xvii.

105. Vera Brittain, *Testament of Friendship: The Story of Winifred Holtby* [1940], London: Virago, 1980, quotes 211, 213.

106. Kadalie to Holtby, 10 September 1926, Holtby Collection, file 2.40. Roux, *Time Longer than Rope*, 156–8, 202; Johns, *Raising the Red Flag*, 172–3.

107. Lewis to Holtby, 27 July 1926, Holtby Collection, file 4.9, item 1; 'International Support for the I.C.U.: A Modern Library for Headquarters from England', *The Workers' Herald*, 14 September 1926, 3.

108. Klenerman, 'The I.C.U. and night schools', unpublished memoirs.

109. Wickens, *Industrial and Commercial Workers' Union*, 97.

110. Roux, *Time Longer than Rope*, 159–67; 'The Communist [sic] and the I.C.U.: Expulsion of Communist Members', *South African Worker*, 24 December 1926, 1 and 'More Expulsion Moves', *South African Worker*, 14 January 1927, 4.

111. Letter from T. W. Thibedi to E. R. Roux, 27 January 1927, in Drew, ed., *South Africa's Radical Tradition*, vol. 1, 57; see also CPSA Central Executive Committee Minutes, 9 September 1926, RTsKhIDNI, 495.64.53; RESOLUTION ADOPTED AT MEETING OF PRESIDIUM ON MARCH 26, 1927, RTsKhIDNI, 495.64.58.

112. CPSA Central Executive Committee Minutes, 17 February and 3 March 1927, RTsKhIDNI, 495.64.63.

113. Lewis to Holtby, 12 January 1927, Holtby Collection, file 4.9, item 4. Lewis speculated that Kadalie might have been jealous of the selection of La Guma to attend a labour conference in Europe and that this may have been behind his attacks on the Communists.

114. Lewis to the Right Honourable Prime Minister, 27 January 1927 and Letter from the Prime Minister's Office to Mrs Lewis, 3 February 1927, Holtby Collection, file 4.9, items 64 and 65; Wickens, *Industrial and Commercial Workers' Union*, 129.

115. Kadalie to Walter Citrine, undated [c. June 1927] and Kadalie to Holtby, 10 September 1926, Holtby Collection, file 2.40.

116. Wickens, *Industrial and Commercial Workers' Union*, 136–40; Independent Labour Party Imperialism Committee, Week-end Lecture School and Conference on 'Socialism, Imperialism and "Subject" Races', 9–10 July, London, flyer, Edward R. Roux Papers, item 6, Institute of Commonwealth Studies, London; Independent Labour Party, *Is South Africa to be a Slave State?*, flyer, Holtby Collection, file 4.5, item 47. See also 'Miss Holtby and the Native Bills', *Star*, 23 February 1928; 'Union Native Policy: Miss Winifred Holtby on Government's Bills', *Cape Times*, 24 February 1928; 'Our Native Policy: A Denunciation by Miss Winifred Holtby', *Friend*, 24 February 1928; all Holtby Collection, file 4.6, items 1, 2 and 3. Foreign pressure provoked anger in the local press, particularly after the IFTU got involved. See '"International" Impertinence: South Africa taken to task – Amsterdam conducts our politics', *Natal Mercury*, 26 April 1927, Holtby Collection, file 2.40, item 87.

117. Creech Jones to Kadalie, 15 September 1927 and Creech Jones to Kadalie, 18 November 1927, Holtby Collection, file 2.40.

118. Lord Olivier to E. R. Roux, 6 January 1929 and 10 May 1929, Roux Papers, items 9 and 13.

119. Roux, *Black and White Trade Unionism in South Africa*, in Drew, ed., *South Africa's Radical Tradition*, 63; South African Trades Union Congress, Minutes of Special Meeting of National Executive Council held in No. 15 Trades Hall, Kerk Street, Johannesburg on the 8th December, 1927, Holtby Collection, file 2.40, item 45.

120. Creech Jones to Kadalie, 15 September 1927, Holtby Collection, file 2.40.

121. Creech Jones to Kadalie, 5 April 1928, Holtby Collection, file 2.40.

122. Creech Jones to Holtby, 15 February 1928, Holtby Collection, file 2.40, item 55.

123. Brittain, *Testament of Friendship*, 243.

124. Ballinger to Holtby, 11 February 1928, Holtby Collection, file 2.40, item 53.

125. 'I.C.U.'s New Plans: Trade Unionism Only', *Star*, 16 November 1927, 11.

126. Ballinger to Creech Jones, 3 May 1928, Holtby Collection, file 2.40, item 71.

127. Brittain, *Testament of Friendship*, 245; Wickens, *Industrial and Commercial Workers' Union*, 169.

128. Winifred Holtby and Ethelreda Lewis raised funds for Ballinger's salary, which was administered through the accountant Howard Pim. Wickens, *The Industrial and Commercial Workers' Union*, 161–2, 169, 180–84.

129. Quotes from Ballinger to Holtby, 6 August 1930 and Ballinger to Holtby, 25 March 1931, Holtby Collection, folder 4.12, items 16 and 29.

130. Ballinger to Holtby, 23 July 1930, Holtby Collection, folder 4.12, item 15; W. G. and M. L. Ballinger, *The British Protectorates in South Africa. Should they be transferred to the Union?*, [British] Labour Party, International Department, Advisory Committee on Imperial Questions, no. 155, April 1935.

131. Roux, *Black and White Trade Unionism*, and Letter from E. R. Roux to W. G. Ballinger, 19 March 1929 both in Drew, ed., *South Africa's Radical Tradition*, vol. 1, 62–3 and 65–6, respectively; W. G. Ballinger to E. R. Roux, 12 June 1929, Roux Papers, item 15.

132. CPSA Central Executive Committee Minutes, 31 March 1927, RTsKhIDNI, 495.64.63.

133. CPSA Central Executive Committee Minutes, 21 July 1927, RTsKhIDNI, 495.64.63.

134. CPSA Central Executive Committee Minutes, 29 September 1927, RTsKhIDNI, 495.64.63.

Chapter 5

The one best way: the Comintern's hand and the Native Republic thesis

By the late 1920s the CPSA was overwhelmingly black in membership, although a small number of whites still played a disproportionate role in the Party's leadership. As a CPSA report to the ECCI explained, 'so far the effectiveness, the "specific gravity" as it were, *per head*, remains greater among the white members'. Thus, it continued, the Party's Central Executive Committee 'contains only 3 or 4 native members out of a total of 13, simply for want of more efficient native comrades available *as yet*'. The Party had been trying to develop a black cadre for several years, it assured the ECCI, and there was no doubt that the efforts would eventually bear fruit.[1]

Most South African Communists, even the whites, were disillusioned by the passivity and bureaucracy of white trade unions under the Pact Government, and they favoured more practical work amongst black workers. Yet, many still believed that the participation of white workers was fundamental for a successful working-class revolution. The dominant view saw national liberation and democratic rights as reformist goals that were inherently subordinate to the class struggle. Thus, participation in national liberation organizations was seen as a tactic rather than the expression of a democratic principle, a view reinforced by the ICU's expulsion of Communists and the ANC's equivocal stance towards the Party.

But the CPSA's ambivalent attitude on national liberation was challenged by the Comintern, which in 1927 and 1928 agitated for the adoption of the Native Republic thesis in South Africa. This external pressure pushed the CPSA very painfully towards a reinterpretation of the relationship between the socialist and national liberation struggles and between the urban working class and the rural majority. The Comintern's imposition of the Native Republic thesis in 1928 marked a shift in the balance between national and international influence in the formulation of South African Communist policies – a portent of the future.

The origins of the Native Republic thesis

Behind the Comintern's decision to intervene decisively in the affairs of South African Communists were a series of profound changes that followed the defeat of the attempted German revolution in 1923 and the Bolsheviks' recognition that Russia's revolution would very likely remain isolated. The German defeat simultaneously reinforced the prestige of the Russian Bolsheviks – as having produced the one successful socialist revolution – and enhanced their dominance within the Comintern. The lesson that Soviet leaders – especially the political triumvirate of Zinoviev, Kamenev and Stalin – sought to instill was that other Communist Parties must follow the Russian model if they were to implement successful revolutions. This lesson was codified at the Fifth Comintern Congress in June–July 1924 when it adopted the concept of 'Bolshevization' and when Stalin replaced Trotsky in the ECCI.

Between 1924 and 1928 the Comintern implemented its policy of Bolshevization, a process that simultaneously entailed the concentration of power in the hands of the Russian party delegates to the ECCI and the vilification of Trotsky and 'Trotskyism'. Within the Comintern, the key criterion for the selection of leaders became loyalty towards authority rather than particular policy stances; 1924 saw a spate of expulsions throughout the Comintern. Increasingly, foreign Communist delegates ratified decisions that had already been taken by the Russian delegates. Soviet political disputes overshadowed the Comintern's deliberations, particularly from 1926. The Comintern became a terrain in which political struggles within the Soviet regime were played out. Interpretations of Comintern policies 'zig-zagged' back and forth following these power struggles.

As the prospects of revolution in Europe waned, the Comintern gave more attention to anti-colonial and national liberation struggles, which were seen as a means of weakening imperialism. In 1926 and 1927 the central figure on the Comintern was Nikolai Bukharin. He pointed to three stages of capitalist development in postwar Europe and introduced the concept of a Third Period. The first stage had been one of revolutionary upheaval; the second was a period of relative capitalist stabilization characterized by united fronts; the Third Period, which was in its incipient stage, would be one in which the contradictions of capitalist stabilization were becoming more acute and in which the European working class was becoming more radical. In 1927 the Soviet Union's foreign policy was beset by disasters. Deteriorating relations with Britain culminated in the Conservative Government breaking off diplomatic relations. Stalin's policy of accommodation with Chinese nationalists led to a catastrophe for Chinese Communists. Debate over responsibility for the Chinese débâcle fed into the broader antagonism between Stalin and Trotsky over revolutionary strategy. Bukharin's emphasis on national liberation struggles developed in this context. The Native Republic thesis, which the Comintern pushed both in South Africa and in the United States, was one such example. By the time of the Sixth Comintern Congress in July–August 1928, Bukharin's fortunes had waned. Nonetheless, his Third Period argument still held sway within the Comintern. As Comintern officials anticipated a working-class radicalization, they began implementing the New Line.[2]

While the theoretical roots of the Native Republic thesis were in Moscow, South Africa provided fertile soil for the slogan to take root.[3] Jimmy La Guma became a critical link in transplanting the slogan to South Africa. Born in Bloemfontein in 1894 and orphaned as a child, La Guma was subsequently taken to Cape Town and apprenticed as a leatherworker. In 1910 he went to South West Africa (Namibia) and ended up working in the diamond fields. By the end of the decade he had founded an ICU branch in Luderitz. Returning to Cape Town, he rapidly became a leading figure in the ICU. He joined the CPSA in 1925 and was elected to its Central Executive Committee the next year.[4] In February 1927 La Guma attended the League Against Imperialism conference in Brussels as a CPSA delegate, along with two other South Africans, Daniel Colraine of the TUC and J. T. Gumede of the ANC. There La Guma discussed the national question with other leaders of anti-colonial struggles. The conference adopted two resolutions. The first, submitted by the South African delegation, called for '[t]he right of self-determination through the complete overthrow of capitalism and imperial domination'. The second, a general resolution on the Negro question, demanded 'full freedom, equality with all other races, and the right to govern Africa'.[5]

After the Brussels conference, La Guma, Colraine and Gumede visited Moscow and met with representatives of the ECCI. The Comintern's concern with the Negro question had been translated into a call for black self-determination through independent statehood. This call, Comintern officials believed, was applicable to blacks both in the United States and in Africa.[6] La Guma agreed with Bukharin and other Comintern officials that South Africa was a colony or semi-colony of Britain and that the South African struggle was primarily anti-imperialist in nature. The Brussels resolutions were reformulated into a draft resolution on South Africa that called for 'an independent Native republic, as a stage towards a workers' and peasants' government'.

The Native Republic thesis proposed national self-determination through a struggle against British imperialism, but this was an imperialism defined not so much by its capitalist nature as by its colonial character, which included both foreign and racial domination. From its emphasis on the proclaimed colonial character of South African society, flowed the assumption that the land-hungry peasantry was the moving force of the South African revolution. By prioritizing the satisfaction of black land-hunger, argued the Comintern, South African Communists would persuade rural blacks to align themselves under proletarian leadership, as in the Russian Revolution. The land question, then, was the core of the South African struggle and laid the basis for strategy on the national question.[7] Although Marxist debates had often seen national struggles in instrumentalist terms, preceding Comintern policy on national self-determination emphasized the right to self-determination as a democratic principle: nations that had suffered national oppression should be free to decide their own destiny rather than have a particular policy imposed upon them. By contrast, the Native Republic thesis offered a particular solution to South Africa's national question: majority rule as a stage towards socialism.

The debate within the CPSA

When the ECCI's draft resolution was first sent to the South African comrades in September 1927, the majority on the Party's Central Executive rejected the idea of an 'independent native republic'. Most found the slogan strikingly close to Marcus Garvey's 'Black Republic' and 'Africa for the Africans' slogans, which the CPSA had campaigned against for several years. The Garvey movement, a worldwide movement to imbue blacks with a shared sense of national and racial identity, was vigorously opposed by Communists for its racial exclusivity and nationalist orientation, and most of the Central Executive Committee members saw the Native Republic thesis in the same light. This response did not follow colour lines: prominent black activists such as William Thibedi and, initially, Johnny Gomas both opposed the thesis.[8]

La Guma returned to Moscow for the October celebrations – evidently against the wishes of the Central Executive Committee[9] – and in December 1927 submitted a *Report on the South African Situation in the Party*, informing the Comintern that the CPSA's Central Executive disagreed with the Native Republic thesis. Noting 'the opposition on the part of rank and file of European labour to cooperation with Blacks', he argued that the Party leadership had given black members the impression that it 'considers the mass movement of the natives should be held up until such time as the white worker is ready to extend his favour'.[10]

A thorough discussion within the CPSA was postponed until La Guma's return to South Africa and his report to the Central Executive Committee in Johannesburg in February and March 1928. At a special meeting of the Central Executive Committee on 15 March, significant opposition to the slogan remained. Thibedi called the slogan 'Garveyism and Racialistic'. Gana Makabeni argued that it 'may be alright later on but was not suitable now. It does not take into consideration the wishes of the people.' Phooko maintained that it would be a means of 'placing power in the hands of the chiefs who will use it for their own ends'. And while Rebecca Bunting conceded that '[a] black republic is inevitable. ... The launching of the slogan now', she added, 'will mean the hostility and antagonism of the entire white working class.'[11]

But La Guma had two key supporters in Johannesburg: Douglas and Molly Wolton. Douglas Wolton had been invited to replace Jimmy Shields on the Central Executive Committee when the Shieldses departed for Britain in November 1927.[12] Although a relative newcomer to the Party, Douglas Wolton soon became its general secretary and editor. He and his wife, Molly Wolton, were in a minority on the executive in their support for the thesis; Douglas Wolton had already warned La Guma to come to Johannesburg 'adequately prepared for a battle of logic and a good deal of nonsense'.[13] Wolton argued that because the slogan 'Workers of the World Unite' could not be readily understood by blacks 'in face of daily oppression at hands of white workers' there was a need for a slogan 'reaching out to native masses especially'. And Molly Wolton felt that the slogan had been misinterpreted and rejected the idea that whites would be 'driven into the sea'. After all, she pointed out: '[e]ven a Native Bourgeois Govt would mean improvements for the native worker and the limited freedom secured would be an advance on present conditions'.[14]

In April Jimmy Shields wrote from England stating that he now supported the thesis. Bunting, for his part, conceded certain points made by the supporters but argued that '[w]e cannot tell on what lines the liberation of African Workers will take place. A slogan of a Workers South Africa, – Liberation – Freedom, etc, is and would be more popular and to the White Workers also.'[15] The Central Executive Committee asked the Johannesburg and Cape Town branches to submit majority and minority reports. In May, Bunting and Wolton submitted respectively the majority and minority positions for the Johannesburg branch. And Bunting made it undiplomatically clear to the Comintern that he was frankly tired of the matter: 'Our discussion on the slogan has largely been due to our great respect for E.C.C.I. decisions, (without however attributing pontifical infallibility to them). But it has monopolised too much of our time.'[16] No report was received from Cape Town, despite La Guma's earlier claim that since his return to Cape Town, ' we have had very hot arguments on the thesis supported by the entire black membership'.[17]

Bunting, on one side, and La Guma, supported by the Woltons, on the other, were the initial protagonists in the ensuing debate. Bunting argued that the road to democracy lay through socialism won by joint black and white proletarian class struggle. He believed that the CPSA's work in African nationalist organizations had come to a dead end and that the white working class was potentially more revolutionary than the virtually non-existent black bourgeoisie. The Native Republic thesis, he believed, by equating all whites with imperialism, would neutralize the prospects of working-class unity across the colour bar and forestall the prospect of a socialist struggle. Thus, Bunting proposed as an alternative slogan: 'All power to the soviets of workers and peasants – black and white'.[18]

La Guma, by contrast, believed that the road to socialism lay through majority rule established through a national liberation struggle. He argued that black South Africans were developing a national consciousness and that anti-imperialist national liberation movements were inherently revolutionary, no matter what their class leadership. The Native Republic thesis, he thought, would help educate white workers that their future lay in unity with blacks.[19] White workers had consistently opposed black equality and their chauvinism should not be appeased. Should the Party now tell blacks: 'Yes, you will be allowed to march into the promised land at such time as it can be considered without wounding the susceptibilities of the "Baas"'?[20]

Both the ICU and the ANC were then distancing themselves from the CPSA because of its apparent radicalism. At the ANC's second annual convention of chiefs, held in Bloemfontein in April 1928, mention of the CPSA caused such an uproar that the meeting had to be recessed. When it was reconvened, the ICU leaders insisted the ANC renounce its relationship with the CPSA, to which the chiefs unanimously agreed. Gumede's sympathetic stance towards Communists was clearly atypical within Congress: at his resumé of his trip to Moscow, in which he mentioned the overthrow of the tsar, a voice taunted: 'Do you intend to kill our chiefs?' At the subsequent joint meeting of the ICU's National Council and the ANC's Executive Committee, the two organizations confirmed their desire for mutual cooperation. The meeting unanimously resolved that the ANC 'hereby repudiates its association with the South African Communist Party, which of late has openly identified itself with the Congress'.[21] Gumede, it was reported at the CPSA's Central Executive Committee, was considering withdrawing from the ANC and setting up a branch of the League Against Imperialism. The Party's leadership, however, thought it advisable for him to remain in the ANC.[22]

The furious debate over the Native Republic thesis overshadowed other developments. The CPSA was putting more efforts into reaching black workers, and these were paying off. In December Charles Baker, an English schoolmaster, described by Roux as 'a fiery little man, an ex-Roman Catholic and now a violent atheist', had been appointed to run the Party's night school.[23] Thibedi was involved in organizing and tutoring in the country branches and, along with Ben Weinbren, in building the newly-formed South African Federation of Non-European Trade Unions (FNETU). The Party had finally sold its printing press for a sum that enabled it to pay its creditors in full. At Thibedi's suggestion its paper, *South African Worker*, was to be published in several languages, with the first two pages in English and the third and fourth in Sesuto and Xhosa.[24]

Moreover, La Guma had also brought back from Moscow the news that ten spaces had been reserved for black South African students to study at the Eastern Workers Communist University. It was decided to send five students immediately and the other five when they could be spared. Initially, Gomas and Thibedi were at the top of the list. In May, the Central Executive Committee decided that Gomas, Thibedi and Ndobe would leave with the Buntings when they went overseas to attend the Sixth Comintern Congress. This did not work out. Passports proved a difficulty: in June Thibedi reported that his application for a passport had been rejected. In the meantime, Victor Danchin and Willie Kalk were selected to attend the Lenin School[25] – a decision that irked La Guma, who wrote to A. Bennett, secretary of the Comintern's Anglo-American Secretariat, stating that 'I tell you frankly I have no confidence in them to return from Moscow and do any Party work. Both of them ... are useless to the Party at present.'[26]

The Sixth Comintern Congress

Sidney and Rebecca Bunting and Eddie Roux represented the CPSA at the Comintern's Sixth Congress in July–August 1928. They encountered an atmosphere markedly different to the comradeship that Rebecca Bunting had felt at the Comintern's Fourth Congress in 1922. Now, observed Roux, 'there were numerous factions and cliques, each trying to curry favour with the powers at the top. ... Comrades were afraid to discuss things openly for fear of being accused of political deviations'. Moreover, the South African delegates sensed that they 'were deliberately cold-shouldered by some of the delegates. ... The story had gone round that the South African delegates were "white chauvinists".'[27] Indeed, La Guma, embittered by the CPSA's resistance to the Native Republic thesis, had been corresponding with various Comintern officials, predicting that the thesis would likely lead to 'a split on colour lines again or prove a very strong purgative'.[28] He was particularly critical of Bunting's administration of the Party's affairs and his influence over others. 'The crowd led by Bunting are unable to divorce their feelings from the parasitical white worker who are using the black worker now as a catspaw', he wrote in August to Bennett, who was chair of the South Africa session at the Sixth Congress. 'I am going to make every effort at the next Congress of the CP of S.A. to change the leadership', he added.[29]

The three South Africans simply had no idea how to manoeuvre in this situation. Sidney Bunting and Roux put forward the Party's majority view. The main thrust of their argument was that there was no objective basis for prioritizing a black national struggle when there was so much potential for the development of black working-class consciousness.

Bunting emphasized the proletarian character of colonial peoples, which, he argued, the Comintern's colonial theses and the Native Republic thesis overlooked. South Africa was neither a pre-capitalist nor a peasant society, but a white settler society with an imperialist-financed gold industry, as well as iron and steel industries. Its peasantry was actually a migrant labour force, he maintained. While a black nationalist movement should not be opposed, Bunting argued, the struggle was not only anti-imperialist, it was also anti-capitalist. The African workers of South Africa, and the colonial labour force more generally, were not merely a component of a nationalist, anti-imperialist force, but were an important force in the struggle against capitalism. Yet the Comintern's draft programme, Bunting complained, did not allow the colonial proletariat to play its full role. Its reference to colonial 'masses', counterposed to the European 'proletariat', reeked of the same racial chauvinism as white South African labour. The essence of the white worker's prejudice, he argued, 'is not that he wants to kill the black worker, but that he looks upon him not as a fellow-worker but as native "masses"'. Communists must come to terms with the proletarian nature of the colonial working class so that it could take its place in the international proletarian movement.[30]

Roux stressed South Africa's distinctive class structure, which, he argued, the Native Republic thesis failed to recognize. The colour bar allowed little chance for a black bourgeoisie and intelligentsia to develop, and the proposed thesis, he declared, did not admit '[t]he possibility of the *complete telescoping* of the bourgeois nationalist revolution and the development of the proletarian revolution in the *absence* of a native bourgeoisie'. Given the lack of a black bourgeoisie, maintained Roux, leadership of the political struggle inevitably devolved to the CPSA. He optimistically predicted that the Party, 'if it succeeds in training the necessary number of capable native organisers will grow into a mass party in a very short time'. Believing that the Native Republic thesis would negate the Party's previous efforts to build working-class unity, Roux proposed instead an '*Independent Workers and*

Peasants Republic with equal rights for all toilers.[31] Not surprisingly, this proved to be a non-starter with the Comintern.

In his final address to the Congress Bunting reiterated that the proposed Native Republic slogan mechanically applied the Comintern's general model for colonial struggles – that of a peasant-based, anti-imperialist struggle – to South Africa's specific conditions. But the agrarian struggle was not the nexus of the South African struggle, Bunting contended. South Africa's white population included an exploited working class and peasantry, with the former displaying the most militant behavior. Similarly, he asserted, the rapidly increasing black proletariat has shown greater militancy than the black rural population.

The presence of a white proletariat complicated the political struggle, Bunting continued. If white labour could be won to a position of neutrality rather than antagonism *vis-à-vis* blacks, it could act as a shield in circumstances where the black working-class movement bordered on illegality. He feared that the Native Republic thesis would alienate white workers, exacerbating the contradiction between the class and national movements, even pushing some whites towards fascism. Thus, concluded Bunting, the majority of South African comrades, ' while standing for proletarian equality and for majority rights ... [were] against the CREATION of any special nationalitic [sic] slogan ... except of course the liberation of the native people from all race oppression and discrimination and separation from the British Empire'.[32]

Rebecca Bunting spoke on the need to organize women. Her forthright declaration that '[t]his Congress is evidence in itself that not enough work is done among women. Why are there so few women delegates here?' and her contention that the organization of women should be taken up by men comrades as well as women, would scarcely have endeared her to the Comintern officials and delegates, despite the periodic circulars on the matter that the Comintern sent to their affiliates.[33]

In an attempt to get some official understanding of their view, Rebecca Bunting convinced her husband to write articles for *Pravda*, which she translated into Russian. Nonetheless, the Comintern officials were not swayed by their arguments and the Native Republic slogan became 'law'. This was hardly surprising: Roux and Bunting assumed that the road to any form of democracy lay through a socialism built by a united black and white proletariat; the Native Republic thesis assumed that the road to socialism lay through the achievement of a formal political democracy. A loyal Communist, Bunting resolved to accept the thesis, and on the boat home he wrote a pamphlet called *Imperialism and South Africa*. This contained, he thought, his best efforts to come to terms with the slogan's anti-imperialist thrust and to explain the slogan's basis in South African political economy.[34] Roux, likewise, returned to his studies at Cambridge and began trying to convince himself of the correctness of the thesis, putting the blame on the alleged theoretical backwardness of the South African comrades.[35]

The debate within the CPSA resumed

Back at home, the Party's leadership had become embroiled in a controversy that reached destructive proportions. Between June and December 1928 Central Executive meetings were the scene of vituperous fighting. The Central Executive was small, with attendance generally between eight and ten. This meant that political differences became intertwined with personal antagonisms and flourished in a hothouse environment. But what distinguished Communist Parties from other political parties was that ultimate authority lay in a foreign country. Warring factions could appeal to the Comintern to vindicate their positions, and South African supporters of the Native Republic thesis had Moscow to back them up.

The tension crystallized around the personalities of Jimmy La Guma and Douglas Wolton, staunch proponents of the Native Republic thesis, on the one side, and William Thibedi, an ardent opponent, on the other. In June the Central Executive asked La Guma to come to Johannesburg to organize for the FNETU. From the beginning, there were tensions between La Guma, who as secretary of FNETU received a salary of £6 per month, and Thibedi, who as organizer earned £4 per month. By September La Guma was claiming that there was sabotage within the federation, although it was unclear whether he attributed this to Thibedi.[36] The relationship between Wolton and Thibedi rapidly deteriorated. Wolton, backed by Edwin Mofutsanyana – who had recently joined the Party while working as a checker on the mines – alleged that Thibedi was trying to turn Mofutsanyana against another activist, named Shadrach Kotu. Thibedi denied the allegation and, in turn, accused Wolton of plotting against Bunting and of calling one of Bunting's speeches 'that of a Cresswellite'.[37] The matter reached a head on 20 September, when Thibedi claimed to have found a document written by Wolton and sent to the Comintern that stated:

> Financially the Party depends on donations from S. P. Bunting or some of those who aim to visit Russia eventually and claim allegiance to the movement. A definite non-European section of the Party is persistently clamouring for recognition and accordingly the white members of the Party see their privileged monopoly being threatened. Definitely hostile acts are being resorted to in order to stem the development of non-europeans within the Party.

Thibedi also claimed that Wolton had told him that '[f]or the last ten years some members had been trying to get the Buntings out of the Party – this is now their chance'. And he alleged that Wolton and La Guma were carrying on intrigue within the Party. Wolton and La Guma denied the allegations; Wolton claimed that he was preparing a report to the Comintern but had not yet sent it, while La Guma admitted that he had been in frequent contact with the Comintern Executive.

A motion was passed '[t]hat the C.E. hereby warns all those concerned that this squabbling and antagonism be stopped otherwise the suspension of such members will be enforced.' The Central Executive Committee agreed to accept Wolton's and Mofutsanyana's accounts over Thibedi's. A motion proposed by Danchin and seconded by Molobi that the evidence regarding the Kotu matter was inadequate to reach a decision was lost; Thibedi was reprimanded.[38]

Despite the pressure on Thibedi, he and Weinbren remained hostile to the Native Republic thesis. In vain, Weinbren attempted to convince officials in the International Trade Union Committee of Negro Workers, a section of the RILU, that 'the Comintern theses will certainly not help us. ... Even the native workers are against it and state that they desire a republic of all workers irrespective of colour or creed'.[39] And although the FNETU was close to the Party, he reported that 'a resolution was unanimously passed at the last meeting of the Federation disassociating themselves from the slogan of a "Black Republic" as same is pernicious to the relationship between the black and white workers of S.A.'[40]

Not surprisingly, when Bunting returned to South Africa, he soon wrote to Roux complaining that

> we found the party split sideways and endways with quarrels, intrigues, backbiting etc to incredible lengths. ... Woltons and La Guma versus all the rest, but some of the rest also versus Thibedi; the branches also bewildered at this excess of partisanship at head office, and the Trade Unions quite paralysed especially by disagreements between La Guma & Thibedi.

He also learned of Thibedi's allegations that the Woltons had been undermining him behind his back. 'We left them last June', he confided to Roux,

> despite differences of opinions, on the best of intimate terms, but in our absence they have worked up a case against us to make you shudder ... it has destroyed all the real confidence between us. ... we see now that our very unpleasant experiences... [in Moscow] were the result of a violent secret preparation in the shape of reports which as you know Bennett & Co never showed us.[41]

However, despite Bunting's criticisms of events at the Sixth Congress, he nonetheless defended the doctrinal authority of the Comintern. With some arm-twisting on Bunting's part, the Native Republic thesis was adopted by the CPSA at its seventh annual conference on 29 December 1928 – 2 January 1929. '[T]hough some wanted to move amendments', Bunting explained, 'I felt bound, while allowing full discussion ... to disallow these as contrary to the Comintern statutes, enjoining unreserved acceptance'.[42] On 1 January 1929, the CPSA formally endorsed a version of the thesis that read: 'An Independent South African Native Republic as a stage towards the Workers' and Peasants' Republic, guaranteeing protection and complete equality to all national minorities'.[43]

The final South African consensus was an effort to combine democracy and socialism in one stage. As Bunting explained to Roux, 'We agreed on interpreting the slogan as meaning much the same as a (predominantly & characteristically native) Workers & Peasants republic, and not meaning a black dictatorship'.[44] As the Party's programme explained:

> If we are to achieve real labour unity we must first remove the greatest obstacle to it, viz, the unequal, subjected, enslaved status of the native workers and people. Hence race emancipation and class emancipation tend to coincide. Hence too the conception and realisation of native rule merges into that of the Workers' and Peasants' Republic, non-imperialist, non-capitalist, non-racialist, classless and in effect Socialist.[45]

And in response to the oft-posed query: 'Won't your black republic fall under Imperialist influence?' Bunting's reply was

> that this language about 'stages' represents sociological rather than chronological sequences (though I think it was dictated by the analogy of a bourgeois democratic native revolution in China, but of course I couldn't say that) as really no black republic in SA could be achieved without overthrowing capitalist rule. And in fact I think the 'stage' part of the forumula *is* verbiage.[46]

There was still grumbling about the thesis, particularly by trade union activists. La Guma had dropped out of the FNETU and returned to Cape Town in late 1928, temporarily retiring from politics. This left the Federation in the hands of Weinbren and Thibedi who, wrote Bunting to Roux, were 'still irreconcilable to the slogan, especially W, who is leading the native T.U.'s against it'. Immediately after the Party's conference, Thibedi had picked up the pen to appeal to the Comintern to

> quickly reconsider their decision on the matter. ... Tell Comrades Losovsky, Bukharin, Stalin and the CI Secretariat for dealing with the Negro problems ... the Federation of Non-European Trade Unions... consider the Black Republic slogan a mistake, and that a 'Workers and Peasants Republic' would really rally the black and white workers in this country.[47]

Bunting, himself, was a pragmatist: 'I also think the slogan defective', he added, 'but we can get along with it, and *may* make a hit'.[48]

But in 1929 the political climate took a turn for the worse. The Pact Government was re-elected on a 'Black Peril' campaign, and the state intensified its attacks on black organizations. In turn, the ANC moved defensively to the right. The hostile climate gave the Native Republic thesis greater credibility and some of those who had originally opposed the thesis, such as Johnny Gomas, changed their views.[49] The ultimate goal of most Communists, particularly the minority of whites who remained in the Party, was still unity of the proletariat across the colour line, believing always that such unity was the only road to socialism. But they came to accept the argument that racial inequality obstructed such unity. Hence, in challenging racial inequality, the Native Republic thesis was seen as a means to promote working-class unity.

Organizing under the Native Republic banner

The most palpable and immediate impact of the adoption of the Native Republic thesis was that the CPSA began to give more attention to rural organizing. Bunting was quite correct in criticizing the Comintern's neglect of the proletarian movement in South Africa. But his contention that '[t]he native agrarian masses as such have not shown serious signs of revolt. ... [and] a live agrarian movement has still to be organised in South Africa' was seriously off the mark in the late 1920s. By then South Africa had seen numerous serious rural uprisings, starting with a wave of rural anti-tax protests that were sparked off by the 1921 Bulhoek uprising, described about a decade later by Albert Nzula 'as the first attempt by the peasantry to seize and occupy land'. In 1922 women in Herschel and in the Transkei organized a successful boycott against the exorbitant prices charged by traders in the reserves.[50]

Indeed, in 1928 when Bunting dismissed rural movements, the ICU had just passed its peak. Although no longer focusing on urban workers, and despite its expulsion of Communists in 1926, the ICU gave a voice to black sharecroppers and labour-tenants seeking to retain possession of their meagre means of production. That both the Western Cape ANC and its radical successor, the Independent ANC, were decimated by the early 1930s reflects the harsh reaction of white farmers and the state towards any attempts to organize black farmworkers.[51]

Likewise, Bunting's belief that blacks could not be readily mobilized on a nationalist, anti-British imperialist slogan was wrong. The late 1910s and early 1920s were years of urban black working-class militancy that in turn radicalized sections of the black petty bourgeoisie. In this climate the Garveyist movement, with its calls for a 'Black Republic' and 'Africa for the Africans', struck a resonant chord amongst some black South Africans. The quest for self-determination encapsulated by Garvey's 'Black Republic' slogan anticipated the Native Republic thesis in its twin goals of African self-determination and independence from British imperialism.[52]

Yet, in the repressive climate of the late 1920s, it is not surprising that, as Bunting reported, the ICU was 'inclined to repudiate' the Native Republic thesis and the ANC remained 'silent'.[53] Far from rejecting British imperialism, the ANC looked to Britain for support against Afrikaner nationalism, with the Cape ANC reaffirming its 'faith in the Union Jack'.[54] In 1930 the South African Garveyite James Thaele, who had a few years before captured the rural proletarian upsurge in the Western Cape, expelled two activists, Bransby R. Ndobe and Elliot Tonjeni, for 'Bolshevistic tendencies'. Ndobe and Tonjeni went on to form the Independent ANC, which spanned the Cape Province, organizing farmworkers for better wages and work conditions under the banner of a 'Native Republic' and 'Africa for the Africans'.[55]

Bunting's polemical exaggerations were corrected in practice as the CPSA began campaigning under the banner of the Native Republic. Cape Africans still had a qualified franchise, and the Party put forward two candidates in the 1929 parliamentary electoral campaigns. Douglas Wolton ran as a candidate in the Cape Flats, which most Communists presumed would be the easier contest, and Bunting, now suspect because of his initial criticism of the Native Republic thesis, was temporarily exiled to the Transkei, to campaign amongst the Tembuland electorate. It was, given the harsh material conditions and the political repression in the Transkei, a test of both physical and political fortitude. Bunting took up the challenge, eager to atone and demonstrate his loyalty.[56]

Hitherto the Party had been urban-based, with the exception of some activity in Basutoland, where Communists had contact with the *Lekhotla la Bafo* (League of the Poor). Bunting's campaign was the Party's first foray into the reserves. He arrived in the Transkei on 8 March 1929, accompanied by Rebecca Bunting and by Gana Makabeni, taking advantage of a legal loophole that outlawed 'Native agitators' from entering Tembuland but made no provision against white agitators. They addressed large crowds, and faced continuous police harassment and arrests, and many local Africans were intimidated.[57] Indeed, Bunting was apparently protected by local people who, hearing rumours that he was going to be murdered, 'kept a constant guard at his residence'.[58]

During the Tembuland campaign, the Buntings and Makabeni founded a League of Native Rights – later known as the League of African Rights. Given the thumbs-up by Paul Merker, a German Communist who visited South Africa in June 1929 on behalf of the Comintern, the League of African Rights was an affiliation of local groups around the country that aimed to unite Africans against the government's proposals to curtail their economic and political rights. Drawing on the tradition of Britain's nineteenth-century Chartist movement, the League of African Rights drew up and circulated around the country a petition of democratic rights under the slogan, '*Mayibuye!*' (Let Africa Return!). It demanded the franchise for blacks on the same basis as for whites; universal free education for black children on the same basis as whites; abolition of all pass laws; and the rights of free speech and public meeting irrespective of race. The League, Roux reported, was 'a big success from the start. Political fever among Africans was still running high.'[59] That it was able to draw in representatives from the ANC and ICU indicated its catholic appeal, given that both organizations had rejected the Native Republic thesis as too radical.

Both Communist candidates lost decisively, although Bunting obtained enough votes to save his deposit, whereas Wolton forfeited his. Wolton explained the failure of his campaign as due to the weakness of local African Communists, the treachery of several leading Party members and the failure of the Party to do preparatory work in a constituency where other parties had long experience of campaigning. 'In future campaigns', he advised the Party's Central Executive Committee, 'the choice of constituency must be carefully considered and preferably a straight fight between SAP or Nationalist, and C.P. selected. The success of such campaigns will largely be a reflection of the strength and organised experience of native Party members in shouldering the bulk of the work amongst native voters.'[60] To Bunting's supporters his electoral defeat was a personal triumph, not only over the hardships of the campaign but also because of his achievement in the founding of the League of African Rights. Yet Rebecca Bunting worried that Bunting's relative success over Wolton exacerbated the deterioration of their relationship. As the Woltons left South Africa in July 1929 for Britain, giving no indication that they would be returning, her concern seemed unnecessary. Nonetheless, as events over the next few years would tell, it was a fear that did, indeed, have some foundation.[61]

Conclusion

The Native Republic thesis was premised on a peasant-based colonial model that differed in important respects from South Africa of the late 1920s. The absence of a black bourgeoisie raised the possibility that the weight of the working class and impoverished rural masses would push the national liberation movement towards socialism. In the late 1920s the overwhelming majority of Africans lived and worked in the countryside. Most rural Africans lived in the reserves where they had access to small plots of land. They could not be neatly categorized as self-sufficient peasants, however. Men based in the reserves were contract or migrant workers on farms or mines. Typically, by the 1930s, a third of the total male population was absent from the reserves. In some areas, like the Ciskei, this reached close to 70 per cent, and it meant that the burden of cultivation fell increasingly on women. Outside the reserves, the rest of the rural population worked on mostly white-owned farms as wage-workers, squatters and tenant farmers. The *de facto* proletarianization of reserve-dwellers who depended on wage-labour strengthened Bunting's argument against the Comintern's notion of a peasant-based revolution. As he reported back to his comrades, 'these territories ... are to-day mere appurtenances of the Chamber of Mines. The people ... can only subsist by sending their men to the mines.'[62]

There was an urban African proletariat as well. Of the total number of workers employed in private manufacturing in the late 1920s, for example, 81,233 or 44 per cent were Africans, who performed unskilled, manual labour, while 69,757 or 38 per cent were white, typically performing skilled or supervisory work. Coloureds and Indians were intermediary strata, performing unskilled, semi-skilled, and especially in the Western Cape and Natal, skilled artisanal work. But there was no African bourgeoisie able to accumulate capital by exploiting the labour-power of others, and less than 1 per cent of Africans could be described as formally-educated and trained professionals.[63]

The Native Republic thesis reoriented the CPSA away from a class-based approach that had arguably been too abstract and had not dealt adequately with the problem of the racially-divided working class. It forced Communists to put South Africa's pressing social problems, the national and the land questions, at the top of their political programme and to reconcile the slogan with their scenarios for social revolution. Nonetheless, although South African Communists interpreted the Native Republic thesis in a manner that allowed them to speak of compressing the national and class struggles, by introducing the language of 'stages', the thesis had limitations as a mobilizing device for socialism.

The thesis underestimated the potential impact of class divisions amongst the black population on the evolving social struggle, assuming that rural Africans constituted a homogenous, undifferentiated peasantry. Similarly, the analysis overlooked the consequences of the changing sexual division of labour in the reserves, as growing numbers of African men were drawn into migrant labour, leaving rural cultivation increasingly in the hands of women. Its proposal to eliminate laws restricting the development of a black farming class would mean the formal dismantling of the reserve system. But the thesis did not address the needs of the large numbers of virtually proletarianized reserve-dwellers who depended on migrant labour income and who could not afford to buy land, even if it were a legal option. Nor did it address the needs of farmworkers, whose demands were generally those of proletarians seeking control of their working conditions rather than those of aspirant peasants.[64] Presupposing national self-determination for a predominantly agrarian black colony conquered by white foreigners, its implicit concept of the South African nation was a racial one. It neglected the question of whether capitalist development in South Africa was creating conditions for a national identity that was no longer rooted in the period of white colonial conquest of blacks.

Aside from its political content, the Native Republic thesis represented the first experience of aggressive Comintern intervention in the CPSA's affairs. It indicated the pitfalls of applying policies derived overseas to South Africa. More importantly, it raised in an acute form a question that dominated the CPSA for the next decade: in a movement that looked for doctrinal authority to the Comintern, how was it possible to remain loyal to one's local comrades?

Notes

1.   *ECCI Resolution on S. Africa*, n.d., 9–10, RTsKhIDNI, 495.64.76.
2.   McDermott and Agnew, *The Comintern*, 42–54, 68–71.
3.   For other discussions of the Native Republic thesis in South Africa see, *inter alia*, Martin Legassick, 'Class and Nationalism in South African Protest: the South African Communist Party and the "Native Republic," 1928–1934', *Eastern African Studies*, 15, July 1973; Baruch Hirson, 'Bunting vs. Bukharin: the "Native Republic" Slogan', *Searchlight South Africa*, 3, July 1989, 51–65; Baruch Hirson, 'The Black Republic Slogan – Part II: the Response of the Trotskyists', *Searchlight South Africa*, 4, February 1990, 44–56; Nyawuza, 'The Road to the "Black Republic" in South Africa', *African Communist*, 122, 3rd quarter 1990, 42–50, 92; Nyawuza, 'Left, Right on the Road to the Black Republic', *African Communist*, 123, 4th quarter 1990, 52–61. See also Roger E. Kanet, 'The Comintern and the "Negro Question": Communist Policy in the United States and Africa, 1921–41', *Survey*, 1973, 19, 4, 86–122; and Johns, 'The Comintern'.

4. Karis and Carter, eds, *From Protest to Challenge*, vol. 4, 53. La Guma, *Jimmy La Guma*, 17–23.
5. Simons and Simons, *Class and Colour*, 389. See also David J. Mason, 'Race, Class and National Liberation: Some implications of the policy dilemmas of the International Socialist League and the Communist Party of South Africa, 1915–1931', MSc, University of Bristol, 1971, esp. 25–36.
6. Johns, 'The Comintern', 217–19.
7. Resolution on 'The South African Question' adopted by the Executive Committee of the Communist International following the Sixth Comintern congress, in Bunting, ed., *South African Communists Speak*, 91–7, esp. 94–6.
8. Roux, *S. P. Bunting*, 89, 101 and 105; Simons and Simons, *Class and Colour*, 396; La Guma, *Jimmy La Guma*, 35–42; Musson, *Johnny Gomas*, 48. Robert A. Hill and Gregory A. Pirio, '"Africa for the Africans": the Garvey Movement in South Africa, 1920–1940', in Marks and Trapido, eds, *The Politics of Race, Class and Nationalism*, 209–53.
9. CPSA Central Executive Committee Minutes, 29 September 1927, RTsKhIDNI, 495.64.63. La Guma, *Jimmy La Guma*, 42–4.
10. J. La Guma, REPORT ON THE SOUTH AFRICAN SITUATION IN THE PARTY, 2/12/27, RTsKhIDNI, 495.64.61.
11. Minutes of special meeting of the Central Executive Committee held on Thursday 15 March in Ahsers [sic] Buildings at 8 pm, RTsKhIDNI, 495.64.75.
12. CPSA Central Executive Committee Minutes, 10 November and 10 December 1927, RTsKhIDNI, 495.64.56.
13. Quoted in Simons and Simons, *Class and Colour*, 399. See also Letter from Douglas Wolton to Jack Simons, 23 August 1967 and Statement of Douglas Wolton, 23 August 1967, Simons Collection, South African Communist Party, 6.7.
14. Minutes of special meeting of the Central Executive Committee held on Thursday 15 March in Ahsers [sic] Buildings at 8 pm, RTsKhIDNI, 495.64.75.
15. CPSA Central Executive Committee Minutes, 12 April 1928, RTsKhIDNI, 495.64.75.
16. *ECCI Resolution on S. Africa*, n.d., 30, RTsKhIDNI, 495.64.76.
17. Letter from J. A. La Guma to Victor, 10/1/28, RTsKhIDNI, 495.64.77; Simons and Simons, *Class and Colour*, 395; CPSA, Central Executive Committee Minutes, 10 May 1928, RTsKhIDNI, 495.64.75.
18. S. P. Bunting, *An Independent Native Republic for South Africa* [1928], quoted in Simons and Simons, *Class and Colour*, 395–7.
19. J. A. La Guma, *A Native Revolutionary Movement of Black South Africa* [1928], summarized in Simons and Simons, *Class and Colour*, 398.
20. J. A. La Guma, *Who's for the Third International Thesis on S.A.* [1928], quoted in Simons and Simons, *Class and Colour*, 409. La Guma, *Jimmy La Guma*, 45–8.
21. 'African National Congress: Convention of Chiefs at Bloemfontein', *Umteteli wa Bantu*, 14 April 1928, 3.
22. CPSA Central Executive Committee Minutes, 19 April 1928, RTsKhIDNI, 495.64.75.
23. Roux and Roux, *Rebel Pity*, 67.
24. CPSA Minutes of Central Executive Committee held in Ashers Buildings on 5 January, 19 January, 26 January, 2 February and 9 February 1928, RTsKhIDNI, 495.64.75.
25. CPSA Special Executive Meeting Minutes, 17 March, 3 May, 10 May, and 14 June, 1928, RTsKhIDNI, 495.64.75.
26. Letter from J. A. La Guma to Comrade Petrovsky, 22 August 1928, RTsKhIDNI, 495.64.77.

27. Roux, *S. P. Bunting*, 123.
28. Letter from J. A. La Guma to Victor, 10 January 1928, RTsKhIDNI, 495.64.77.
29. Letter from J. A. La Guma to Comrade Petrovsky, August 22, 1928, RTsKhIDNI, 495.64.77. See also Letter from Douglas Wolton to the Secretary, Colonial Commission, c/o the Anglo-American Secretariat, Comintern, 23 May 1928 and Letter from Douglas Wolton to the Secretary, British Section, Comintern, 1 August 1928, RTsKhIDNI, 495.64.77.
30. S. P. Bunting, 'Statement presented at the Sixth Comintern Congress, 23 July 1928', 79.
31. E. R. Roux, 'Thesis on South Africa', presented at the Sixth Comintern Congress, 28 July 1928, in Drew, ed., *South Africa's Radical Tradition*, vol. 1, 81–4, quotes 81, 83, 84. Emphasis in the original.
32. S. P. Bunting, 'Statement on the Kuusinen Thesis', in Drew, ed., *South Africa's Radical Tradition*, vol. 1, 86–93, quote 93.
33. 'Discussion on the Report of Comrade Bukharin. Comrade Rebekka Bunting (S. Africa)', Sixth World Congress of the Communist International, Ninth Session, 25 July 1928 (afternoon), *International Press Correspondence*, 8, 48, 11 August 1928, 839.
34. Letter from S. P. Bunting to E. R. Roux, 5 December 1928, in Drew, ed., *South Africa's Radical Tradition*, vol. 1, 98–101; Simons and Simons, *Class and Colour*, 386, 410–11.
35. Roux, *S. P. Bunting*, 125–9.
36. CPSA Central Executive Committee Minutes, September 6, 1928, RTsKhIDNI, 495.64.75. La Guma, *Jimmy La Guma*, 48–9.
37. CPSA Central Executive Committee Minutes, 13 September 1928, RTsKhIDNI, 495.64.75.
38. CPSA Central Executive Committee Minutes, 20 September 1928, RTsKhIDNI, 495.64.75.
39. Letter from Ben Weinbren, Amalgamated Laundry Cleaners' and Dyerrs' [sic] Union, 14 December 1928 to James W. Ford, International Trade Union Committee of Negro Workers, RILU, RTsKhIDNI, 495.64.78.
40. Letter from Ben Weinbren to Comrade Losovsky, RILU, Moscow, 23 December 1928, RTsKhIDNI, 495.64.78.
41. Letter from S. P. Bunting to E. R. Roux, 5 December 1928 in Drew, ed., *South Africa's Radical Tradition*, vol. 1, 98–100, quotes 98 and 99 respectively.
42. Letter from S. P. Bunting to E. R. Roux, 9 January 1929, in Drew, ed., *South Africa's Radical Tradition*, vol. 1, 101.
43. 'Programme of the Communist Party of South Africa adopted at the seventh annual conference of the Party on January 1, 1929', in Bunting, ed., *South African Communists Speak*, 100–6, 104; La Guma, *Jimmy La Guma*, 49–50.
44. Letter from S. P. Bunting to E. R. Roux, 9 January 1929, 101.
45. 'Programme of the Communist Party of South Africa adopted at the seventh annual conference of the Party on January 1, 1929', 102.
46. Letter from S. P. Bunting to E. R. Roux, 5 December 1928, 100.
47. Copy of letter from T. W. THIBODI [sic], General Secretary, South African Federation of Native Trade Unions; Johannesburg, 7 January 1929; see also Extract from letter received from E. S. Sachs, Secretary, Witwatersrand Tailors' Association, Johannesburg. Dated Jan. 30th, 1929, both in RTsKhIDNI, 495.64.80.
48. Letter from S. P. Bunting to E. R. Roux, 9 January 1929, 101.
49. Musson, *Johnny Gomas*, 54.

50. A. T. Nzula, I. I. Potekhin and A. Z. Zusmanovich, *Forced Labour in Colonial Africa*, ed. and intro. by Robin Cohen, London: Zed, 1979, 208–9.

51. On the Western Cape ANC and Independent ANC see Willie Hofmeyr, 'Rural Popular Organisation Problems: Struggles in the Western Cape, 1929–1930', *Africa Perspective*, 1983, 26–49 and Willie Hofmeyr, 'Agricultural Crisis and Rural Organisation in the Cape: 1929–1933', M.A., University of Cape Town, 1985; Nzula et al., *Forced Labour*, 210–11.

52. Hill and Pirio, '"Africa for the Africans"'; Philip Bonner, 'The Transvaal Native Congress, 1917–1920: the Radicalisation of the Black Petty Bourgeoisie on the Rand', in Shula Marks and Richard Rathbone, eds, *Industrialisation and Social Change in South Africa*, London: Longman, 1982, 270–313.

53. Letter from S. P. Bunting to E. R. Roux, 5 December 1928, 100.

54. Roux, *Time Longer than Rope*, 237–8; Simons and Simons, *Class and Colour*, 393.

55. Roux, *Time Longer than Rope*, 236–43; Hofmeyr, 'Agricultural Crisis', 155ff and 320ff; Hill and Pirio, '"Africa for the Africans"', 230–34.

56. Sachs, *Multitude of Dreams*, 161; Roux, *S. P. Bunting*, 135.

57. Roux, *S. P. Bunting*, 135–40; Simons and Simons, *Class and Colour*, 411–13. Laurens van der Post, *In a Province*, London, Hogarth Press, 1934, 309–34, describes a fictional campaign in Bambuland (Tembuland) by a socialist trade union organizer which government provocateurs turned into a riot.

58. [Anderson Khumani Ganyile], *Notes on the Pondo Struggle Against Bantu Authorities: the Background to Resistance.* [c. 1962?], 34, Ruth First Collection, 9.1.2, Institute of Commonwealth Studies, University of London.

59. Roux, *S. P. Bunting*, 142; Roux, *Time Longer than Rope*, 226–7; League of African Rights, in Drew, ed., *South Africa's Radical Tradition*, vol. 1, 103.

60. COPY OF REPORT SUBMITTED BY CAPE FLATS CANDIDATE TO EXECUTIVE BUREAU C.P.S.A. *Report on Cape Flats Communist Election Campaign*, RTsKhIDNI, 495.64.81.

61. Roux, *S. P. Bunting*, 135–40.

62. Roux, *S. P. Bunting*, 137.

63. Sheila T. van der Horst, 'Labour', and Department of Economics, Natal University College, 'The National Income and the Non-European', both in Ellen Hellmann, ed., *Handbook on Race Relations in South Africa*, Cape Town, London and New York: Oxford University, 1949, 109–57 and 306–47 respectively.

64. Hofmeyr, 'Agricultural Crisis', 321–8.

Chapter 6

The New Line:
fighting the scourge of
Buntingism

If the Native Republic thesis subordinated the struggle for socialism to the prior achievement of national liberation and bourgeois democracy, the implementation of the Comintern's New Line in South Africa began to swing the pendulum back. With fascism seemingly secure in Italy and the left in retreat elsewhere in Europe, the Comintern now argued that the crisis of capitalism had reached its Third Period, one in which the contradictions of the capitalist system were rapidly leading to its collapse. The immiseration of the working class, it was assumed, would lay the conditions for revolutionary proletarian class consciousness. With world-wide Communist revolution imminent, social-democratic and reformist policies were seen as particularly dangerous counter-revolutionary attempts to divert the working class from the struggle against capitalism. Hence, the Comintern's repudiation of united fronts from above and its introduction of the New Line of independent leadership and of 'class against class'. This slogan highlighted the working-class struggle against social democracy and its capitalist allies. But if the Great Depression from 1929 could be seen as confirmation of the Third Period thesis, subsequent events in Europe and South Africa failed to confirm the Comintern's corollary assumption that deepening economic crisis would radicalize the working class and strengthen Communist support.

The emergence and victory of the New Line can certainly be traced to the domestic and foreign policies of the Communist Party of the Soviet Union, and to the ongoing power struggles of its leaders. Trotsky and Zinoviev were expelled from the Russian Communist Party in December 1927, and Stalin finally won his battle against Bukharin in the autumn of 1928. As the New Line became law, the old and allegedly 'social-democratic' and 'right-deviationist' leaders were ousted. Political conformity and loyalty to Stalin became paramount; ideological diversity was no longer tolerated. Both the Comintern's central bureaucracy and its national affiliates were rent by denunciations and expulsions, beginning with Bukharin's removal in July 1929.

But the New Line's acceptance by the Comintern's affiliates can also be understood in part as a reaction to the strengthening of right-wing and anti-Communist practices within European trade unions and social-democratic parties. Excluded from united fronts with labour and social-democratic organizations, Communist

Parties hoped to pull workers away from those organizations and to form united fronts from below. These conditions gave the New Line a certain credibility amongst Communist activists.[1]

In South Africa, similarly, the CPSA was excluded both from the Labour Party and from black organizations. In June 1929 General Hertzog's National Party came to power, inaugurating a reign of white terror. By 1930 the South African state had smashed the latest wave of collective black working-class protest. The ICU, not having systematically organized its branches around the country and unable to prevent the proletarianization of its largely rural constituency, was disintegrating. With the significant exception of the Western Cape, the ANC, under pressure from anti-African legislation, and with no counterweight from the African working class, distanced itself even further from the CPSA. At the ANC's annual conference held at Bloemfontein in April 1930, it deposed the then-radical Gumede and elected a conservative slate of officials led by Pixley ka Izaka Seme.[2] The CPSA's political marginalization gave the call for independent leadership some credibility.

But the New Line meant that nationalism and democracy were once again subordinated to the class struggle of black and white workers and that alliances with national liberation organizations were shunned. And the call for proletarian unity to fight reformism, while seemingly radical, was ill-suited for South Africa's racially-divided class structure where democratic reforms were desperately needed. Given the enormity of racial oppression, which stifled the development of even a tiny black bourgeoisie, black political leaders were scarcely in a position to align with the white bourgeoisie. Their social class position was not analogous to that of the trade union and political party bureaucracies of the West, even assuming that the New Line's dismissive depiction of the latter was adequate. Furthermore, white labour in South Africa derived economic, political and social benefits from the super-exploitation of black people, meaning that, with rare exceptions, working-class unity across the colour line was virtually impossible. The only feasible organizational possibilities that did not concede to white chauvinism were the direct organization of black workers and the alliance of all blacks on a common democratic platform.

The imposition of the New Line in South Africa occurred at a time when the CPSA's internal relations were in a state of turmoil, particularly in the Johannesburg headquarters. Political relationships in the CPSA were fraught and complex, characterized by shifting alignments over political issues and complicated by personal rivalries. In part this reflected the fallout from the Native Republic disputes. Now, long-time friends and comrades became enemies, ratting on each other, using the discourse of the New Line to settle old scores. The New Line also gave new Party recruits – generally Africans – the opportunity to rise rapidly in the Party hierarchy through a policy of Africanization and to displace the veteran socialists who had founded the Party. The denunciation of Sidney Bunting and of 'Buntingism' became the prime test of loyalty.

Latent promises

At first glance, the CPSA seemed to be in a relatively promising position in 1929. The twenty black and ten white delegates attending the Party's seventh conference at the start of the new year claimed to represent nearly 3000 members.[3] But its seeming success masked serious organizational difficulties. Finances were a major problem. 'I have never come across a Party as poor as that of South Africa', reported a Comintern representative – probably Paul Merker, a German Communist and trade unionist who had worked in the RILU – who visited South Africa in June 1929. In its first years the Party had counted on contributions from radical white members and sympathizers. This source had dried up as the Party turned towards black workers, and it had never been able to organize regular payments of dues by its black members or effective fund-raising drives. 'The comrades have hitherto been extremely lax in the collection of funds among the masses', the Comintern representative explained. 'The argument is that we must not show that we appeal to them for money.' Bunting, however, while keenly aware of the problem, had a somewhat different interpretation: 'Our party cannot get either its African members (non European) to pay party subscriptions for the most part (there is a certain atmosphere of let the white men pay)', he wrote in response to a query about whether the CPSA had formed a local branch of International Red Aid, 'or its white ones, they are not too regular either and they are a rapidly dwindling number, for revolutionary white workers and emigrants from different parts of the former Russian Empire rapidly become counter revolutionary in this slave state'.[4] Whatever the cause, the Party's financial woes were a source of simmering tensions on its Central Executive Committee.[5]

The Party's modest expansion was also a source of stress. In 1929 the CPSA was growing in a number of key branches. Durban's militant environment provided fertile conditions for the Party's growth there. The ICU *yase* Natal was still a force to be reckoned with. 1929 saw a popular boycott movement against 'Native' beer halls that spread to a number of towns in Natal and lasted several months. The mobilization was instigated by African women who brewed beer as their main source of income and saw these beer halls as a threat to their business. The CPSA was able to capitalize on this militant mood, due chiefly to the efforts of Johannes Nkosi, a young cook and an ICU organizer who joined the Party in 1926 and became extremely popular with his comrades, both for his wit and his storytelling talent.[6]

The Party also gained a foothold in the rural town of Potchefstroom, where Edwin Mofutsanyana organized from 1928 to 1931. The Party grew rapidly there because it was able to link up with a local struggle against lodgers' permits that lasted several years, and in which women were particularly active. Josie Mpama, a domestic worker, came to the fore as a leader with a particular interest in organizing women. Originally active in the local Wesleyan Church, she left the church for the Party, and became its local branch secretary.[7] Similarly, in Bloemfontein Sam Malkinson, who recruited a large number of Africans, was invaluable in building the local branch.

In the Western Cape, the Party had links with the militant Western Cape ANC, led by Bransby Ndobe and Elliot Tonjeni. The Cape Town branch also gained an important new member around this time. On 6 November 1929 fifteen-year-old Ray Alexander walked off the boat at Cape Town, still homesick for Riga. But on one of her first forays around town, she went to a factory and, finding that its workers were not unionized, made up her mind that this was 'virgin soil'. On her first weekend, she met the local Communists, and on the following Monday she was invited to join the Cape Town District Party.[8]

But the rapid influx of new members was undercut by the lack of experienced cadre. Douglas Wolton's retrospective report of September 1929 had pointed to this problem in the Transkei, where significant numbers of previously unorganized peasants had sought to join the Party following Bunting's electoral campaign. 'This created a very serious problem ... in that local Party groups had to be left in control of elements completely inexperienced in elementary understanding of Party work', he noted. In some cases the Party was able to send in experienced comrades – notably Gana Makabeni – in order to hold the new groups together, 'but in the other cases the Party influence was lost after the propagandists had left the areas concerned'.[9] The report of the visiting Comintern representative underscored the predicament. New members had streamed into the Potchefstroom and Vereeniging branches – in Potchefstroom well over 1000 had joined in one day – but this was not a real membership, he argued: people were joining out of enthusiasm but were politically inexperienced and had no intention of regularly paying dues.[10]

The League of African Rights that Bunting had founded offered a vehicle for such untrained but enthusiastic people. But with the New Line, the Comintern directed the Party to cease work in so-called reformist organizations; in October 1929, just as the League of African Rights was gaining ground, the Comintern ordered its disbanding on the grounds of possible fusion with reformist organizations or leadership.[11] The CPGB firmly endorsed the Comintern's stance. The Scottish Communist Aitken Fergusson had already complained to the Comintern that '[t]he Anti Bolshevik nature of our C.P.S.A. leadership is shown by their founding of the "League for African Rights", (a title which by the way reveals the essentially liberal nature of their outlook) and by the programme of this league'. He emphasized that, contrary to the claims of the CPSA, the CPGB 'vehemently attacks the whole conception'.[12]

In vain Eddie Roux, the CPSA's general secretary, tried to convince the Comintern of the League's value. Canvassing for the petition entailed mass meetings and discussions, activities that threatened the white establishment and from which moderate black leaders generally remained aloof. 'In fact', Roux wrote to the Comintern, 'the reformists have already taken fright at the petition and are boycotting it accordingly'. The League of African Rights was a practical way of spreading Communist influence in country towns, particularly important in the likely event that the Party was banned. It could, moreover, help bring together various potentially anti-imperialist organizations into a federal organization.[13] But the Comintern was adamant. 'At a time when the natives are proving their revolutionary determination to struggle by openly violating the slave laws', it remonstrated, 'the Party, through the agency of the League, puts forward an extremely mild reformist programme'.

The Comintern took Bunting's and Roux's attempts to justify the League as an example of their desire 'to lay a theoretical basis for reformist views' and 'to revive the theory of South African exceptionalism'.[14] Despite its obvious value and initial success on the ground, the CPSA finally disbanded the League at the Comintern's insistence. But it was clearly a traumatic episode for the South African affiliate. For the next year the Comintern disparaged the local Party for having formed such an organization and, following this cue, the local Communists berated themselves for having done so.[15] However, although the Comintern was definitely letting the South African affiliate feel its boot, the CPSA did not always passively accept this. '[W]e would ask you not to be always seeking occasion for vilification of us on the one hand or public laudation of yourselves at our expense on the other', complained Albert Nzula to the ECCI. 'It is not impressive nor is it comradely. ... we do not only our best but better than, if we may say so, you can teach us to do when it comes to local details.'[16]

The first portent: the case of Comrade Thibedi

The CPSA was squeezed between the pressure of increasing legal repression, on the one hand, and organizational weakness coupled with increased intervention by the Comintern, on the other. Under those circumstances, it was virtually inevitable that the CPSA's leadership and main activists would begin to turn on each other as their perceptions of the Party's situation began to diverge. In 1929 the Johannesburg headquarters was beset by tensions that were manifested in the apparent rivalry of Thibedi, now FNETU's general secretary, and Albert Nzula, a protégé of Wolton. Thibedi still opposed the Native Republic thesis; in March 1929 Roux chided that 'Thibedi is an ass about changing the slogan. It would be rather amusing though if he could meet Stalin!'[17] Nzula, who had been a teacher at the African Methodist Episcopal Mission School at Wilberforce in the Transvaal, and a court interpreter, found himself drawn to radical ideas and joined the CPSA in August 1928. Intellectually gifted, and a talented speaker and writer, he was groomed by Wolton and in 1929, following the latter's departure, briefly became the CPSA's first African general secretary. During his short stint as general secretary, Nzula recruited Moses Kotane, who had been attending the Party's night school at Thibedi's encouragement, and who would become a pivotal ally of Nzula. However, Nzula was an alcoholic and often came to Party meetings drunk, alienating other Party members. Ultimately, this would be his downfall.

Moreover, Thibedi and fellow trade unionist Ben Weinbren fell out. In April 1929 Weinbren asked Roux to take over FNETU's organizational and secretarial tasks, claiming that Thibedi 'is useless for this job'. The African secretaries, he noted, were 'weak', and the unions 'are at present not in the best conditions'.[18]

Nonetheless, he was confident about the potential of the trade union movement. 'Things are brightening up', he wrote to Roux in June. 'We are expecting "Lehotla le Bafo" a Basutoland organisation to apply for affiliation to the Federation, + I am in touch with many Unions in the Cape re affiliation.'[19]

The personality problems immersed the Party's eighth conference at the end of December 1929. Thibedi was suspended from the Party and then hurriedly expelled for allegedly mismanaging trade union funds. The precise circumstances were never clearly explained, and a number of people, including Bunting, had doubts about the fairness of the treatment meted out to him.[20]

Nzula took over Thibedi's position at FNETU, and in January 1930 Weinbren resigned as FNETU's chairman and moved to Cape Town. But Nzula lacked trade union experience, and Bunting moaned that 'Nzula, as the virtual successor of [Thibedi] and Weinbren in the Federation, has so far accomplished nothing; indeed the unions are at a very low ebb. We are very short of good "functionaries"'.[21]

Yet Thibedi's case was far from over. He applied for reinstatement to the Party. Bunting appealed on his behalf to the Executive, which finally wrote to him in June that

> your potential abilities in the movement are still recognised no less than your shortcomings and ... once it becomes clear that they would once again as heretofore be wholeheartedly and honestly devoted to the single purpose of loyally working for, in and under the Party, the Executive for its part would gladly take up the question of your reinstatement. ... [22]

Thibedi had his pride, however, and he never replied. But he still had a constituency amongst African workers, and in August 1930 Nzula and Kotane called a meeting of FNETU 'because the Trade Unionists demanded Thibedi's return' and '[t]he workers could not see that Thibedi was a thief'. Thibedi had evidently been expelled by Weinbren and the Laundry Workers' Union but not from the Federation as a whole, which wanted him back. Nzula and Kotane, in turn, were criticized by other members of the Central Executive Committee for calling the meeting without its permission. However, in September Thibedi was accepted back into the Federation, reportedly, unanimously.[23] By then Bunting had become quite irritated at Thibedi's 'defiance of the Party since, amounting to very serious mischiefmaking'. He noted with irony that 'probably however the affair will be "liquidated" by an undertaking from him to be a good boy henceforward – the value of which must remain a matter of opinion meanwhile'.[24] Nzula, by contrast, reportedly put the treatment not only of Thibedi but also of himself and Kotane down to white chauvinism.[25]

The close relationship between the CPSA and the FNETU that the RILU required became a straightjacket. The CPSA faced the predicament of dealing with an organization run by a former member who refused to kowtow to the Party. Thus, when the FNETU requested financial and material assistance from the CPSA, the Party Executive was divided – along racial lines – and finally reached a compromise position that included a statement of censure.[26] Despite Bunting's earlier sympathy for Thibedi, he endorsed the Party line. He chided FNETU for appointing an expelled member of the CPSA as its general secretary and cautioned 'that until the intolerable situation thus created has been liquidated it is very difficult for the Party, ardently as it desires to assist the Trade Unions, to deal normally with them or the Federation'.[27] In practical terms, the CPSA could hardly cut off all support for the FNETU just because it did not approve of its general secretary. As Bunting noted, 'the Party is somewhat in the position of a person being blackmailed, as, if on account of Thibedi it runs counter to the Federation, it is denounced as an enemy of the workers'.[28]

The Party lost the support of a number of black activists around this time, including La Guma, Ndobe and Tonjeni. Likewise, it lost Manny Lopes, who had been a thorn in the CPSA's side for a number of years. Voracious readers, Manny and Fracis Lopes were the best customers of Modern Books, a radical bookshop in Cape Town run by Paul Kosten. They subscribed to a number of international papers, and when Manny Lopes read about Stalin's thesis of socialism in one country, he opposed it. He also remained vehemently opposed to the Native Republic thesis, believing that white labour's numerical predominance in the industrial workforce and its trade union tradition made it the more advanced section of the working class. In September 1930 the CPSA expelled him for 'unreliability'.[29]

Increasingly, the perceptions of the leading activists diverged. Tension revolving around Bunting's leadership and accusations of white chauvinism mounted in 1930; the meetings of the Central Executive Committee and of the Johannesburg branch frequently collapsed into vicious recriminations. Ironically, Bunting had been a key advocate of the turn to black labour. Yet in personality and style he appeared ponderous and slow to change – particularly in the eyes of the Party's more recent African recruits. He also had very high standards – which he applied to himself as well as others – and which he expressed in a moralistic tone. By 1930 more Africans were assuming leadership positions in the Party, and Bunting's missionary style irked them. Moreover, Comintern communiqués were critical of Bunting because of his past positions. To the relatively new members Bunting became characterized as an obstacle to change. Kotane, for instance, wrote that if Bunting resigned 'that will desist the Buntingites of their influence in the party as a whole. We are accused of a serious charge a charge of racialism. It was the acuteness of chauvinism in the past that has driven us to adopt racial lines and attitude.' He berated Bunting's discussion of financial matters at Central Executive Committee meetings, adding, '[m]y little intellect always brings me to the conclusion that Bunting was in the Party for creating a title for himself. ... in a word the fellow is a rogue. ... It might perhaps be due to the fact that he is a solicitor of capitalist system or otherwise.'[30] A spate of letters found their way to Moscow in late 1930 criticizing Bunting's leadership. Some were meant for Comintern officials. Others were sent to the Woltons, who were then in Moscow. These latter letters made their way into the Comintern files.[31] The cumulative effect of the correspondence to and from Moscow was to undermine Bunting's credibility in the Party.

The Ninth Party Conference

The principal figures responsible for the implementation of the New Line were Douglas and Molly Wolton and Lazar Bach. In July 1929 the Woltons had sailed for England, where Douglas Wolton helped to organize black workers in Liverpool and assisted the CPGB's Colonial Department. The next year the Woltons made their way to Moscow in the hopes of attending the fifth conference of the RILU in August. Initially, their application was rejected, and they were requested to leave Moscow. However, with the help of the CPGB, Douglas Wolton was eventually given a consultative vote enabling him to participate in discussions on the South African question at the RILU conference.[32] The Woltons helped the Comintern Executive draft two directives on the 'right-wing danger' in South Africa. In September 1930 Douglas Wolton was instructed to return to South Africa 'and had the general political line to be pursued in South Africa laid down'. Molly Wolton stayed in Moscow to study at the Lenin School.

When Wolton arrived back in November, the CPSA was preparing for the upcoming Dingaan's Day demonstrations. Dingaan's Day was the anniversary of the Battle of Blood River on 16 December 1838, when Zulu chief Dingane and 100,000 Zulu warriors were defeated by *Voortrekkers* on the banks of the Ncome River in Natal, triggering a civil war in the Zulu kingdom. Wolton remained aloof from the preparations. As he reported the situation,

> the Party [was] in a very bad state. The Party centre was on the point of being moved from Johannesburg to Capetown, the Party membership had declined to a mere handful of 40 or 50, and the white chauvinist Bunting leadership was firmly entrenched in the leading positions. Except for occasional loosely organised mass meetings, no activities whatever were being conducted.[33]

Accordingly, he concentrated on preparing for the CPSA's upcoming ninth conference, scheduled for December 1930, circulating the Comintern resolutions on the right-wing danger. This right wing, it was alleged, had opposed the Native Republic thesis and was now preventing Africans from playing a leadership role.

The discussion at the Party's ninth conference centred on two problems. First was the intense repression faced by Party activists, especially Africans, who were subject to various forms of intimidation, including imprisonment, eviction and the loss of their jobs. Secondly, the acute stress that African Communists faced inevitably led them to criticize the leadership, personified by Bunting, for failing to deal adequately with this problem.

The leadership was criticized on two grounds: first, in Nzula's words, for its 'disbelief in the natives masses having the spirit to fight for their rights', causing the Party to lag behind the masses instead of providing guidance; and second, for failing to train African cadre. As John Marks exhorted: 'We must have some of our African leaders educated.' Nzula underlined the point: 'The old leaders have not taught the new members like myself and the native members. ... We need a new leadership, without it we are going to commit the same errors, we are going to commit the same mistakes as in the past.' But Fanny Klenerman would not accept this. '[W]e are told the trouble in the T.U.s is not Thibedi but white chauvinism', she observed. 'What constitutes white chauvinism?', she wanted to know. 'If the comrades accept and practice the slogan, where is white chauvinism.'[34]

The dispute did not simply follow racial lines, however. Makabeni defended Bunting, claiming that Nzula was only concerned with squabbles, and adding, '[t]here is no discipline at all in the Party, there are natives who are given work to do by the meeting and they do not do it'. Rebecca Bunting insisted that the CPSA had loyally followed the Comintern line. 'When mistakes were pointed out', she noted, 'those mistakes were corrected. ... The leadership is only a reflection of the state in which the whole country is in, politically and economically.'[35]

Two appeals by expelled members for reinstatement were considered: that of Josiah Grey, who had been expelled for slandering the Party and that of Thibedi. The newly-formed control commission granted Grey's appeal, which, it determined, was 'of a trivial nature'. But despite the lingering ambiguity over Thibedi's guilt, his former supporters had dropped him and his request was denied. The decision seemed to have broad support. Although some felt that the original charge against Thibedi had reflected a racial double standard, the general mood was aptly expressed by Kotane's assertion that 'I am now satisfied that Thibedi is not prepared to work in the interests of the Party and the masses and I therefore agree with the Control Commission'.[36]

The organizational changes required by the Comintern settled the political issues. Wolton nominated a Presidium; this was agreed by the delegates. In turn, the Presidium's suggestions for the credentials commission, control commission, the panel commission and the trade union commission were accepted. The panel commission's recommendations for the twenty-four members of the Central Committee were, similarly, approved. As Eddie Roux recalled, Wolton's request that the list of names he submitted 'be voted for *en bloc*' came 'with a broad hint that anyone who voted against the list was disloyal to the Party and the Comintern'.[37] The method certainly posed no problems for the new, predominantly African, leadership. Nzula, for one, insisted that if a Communist Party's policy meant anything, 'it means that everybody has to agree to it, if everybody does not agree to it then it means there is no discipline'.[38] Wolton became the new general secretary, assisted by three whites, Solly Sachs – who despised Bunting, Charles Baker and Eddie Roux, and by nineteen Africans. The 'rightwing elements' – Bunting and Malkinson – were carefully excluded.[39] Finally, Wolton outlined the necessary conditions for a Bolshevik organization: democratic centralism; iron discipline (meaning payment of dues); the direct participation of all members, the formation of factory, mine and farm cells; the training of professional revolutionaries; the elimination of fractions; and self-criticism.

Purifying the Party

Propagating the New Line entailed the centralized control of information and knowledge. One of Wolton's first acts upon his return had been to take control of the Party paper. Until 1930 the paper had been published in Johannesburg. However, the branch's political turmoil hampered production and it became irregular. In early 1930 Roux persuaded the Party's Executive to let him move the paper to Cape Town. Away from the Johannesburg squabbles, the paper thrived. Roux renamed it *Umsebenzi* (*Worker*), added a new feature of linocut cartoons, and printed half the paper in English and the rest in a variety of Bantu languages. He began with a circulation of 3000 and at the end of the year this had grown to 5000.[40] But Wolton convinced Roux that the paper should be transferred back to Johannesburg under the direct control of the Executive. For all Roux's political honesty, he had a weakness for strong leaders. 'I found I did not share Bunting's dislike of Wolton', Roux admitted.

> He seemed to have just those qualities in which Bunting was lacking. Here was a man with a definite theory of revolution, with a clear-cut doctrine and a programme of action – all beautifully co-ordinated and tabulated. Next to him Bunting appeared a mere empiricist. I was impressed. I was prepared to work with him.

In December 1930 *Umsebenzi* ran a two-part statement from the Comintern detailing the CPSA's 'right opportunist' mistakes. Increasingly dense theoretical statements – 'Imprecor language' – replaced popular articles on issues of interest to black workers.[41] Within a year after the transfer to Johannesburg, production became irregular and circulation fell. Black workers had to husband their meagre resources carefully and could ill afford needless expenditures. Fanny Klenerman recalled that for a while she and Eva Green sold *Umsebenzi* in the Johannesburg slum of Rooiyard on Friday afternoons, and that 'numerous men and some women bought it. But a larger number declined to pay the modest price.'[42] As one Leipke Sender archly noted to Benny Sachs about his efforts to sell *Umsebenzi* in Sophiatown, 'I stopped a Blackman and asked him to buy the Umsebenzi. I told him that it was the light, and that he could buy it for a penny. But he replied that for one penny he could buy a candle.'[43]

With the new leadership in place and in control of the paper, the CPSA was able to cleanse itself of the right-wing elements who were seen as impeding the Party's progress. Heretofore, the CPSA had escaped the complete Bolshevization that had taken place in the Comintern's other affiliates. Now, the new leadership busied itself with Bolshevizing the Party and implementing the New Line. Behind the scenes was the triumvirate of Douglas and Molly Wolton and Lazar Bach. Although Roux naively believed that theoretical mastery was the key to success, obedience, not theory, was the order of the day. Molly Wolton returned in 1931 – a brilliant agitator with an authoritarian personality. Ray Alexander was impressed with her speaking skills but did not think much of her organizational ability nor her articles – she constantly exaggerated the numbers of black workers attending meetings and demonstrations.[44] To Roux, she was 'easily our most gifted orator, brilliant in repartée so that hecklers thus made to look foolish soon came to have a wholesome respect for her'. However, Roux added, she combined an impatience of routine and of office work with an inflexibility about getting her own way: 'She could not endure contradiction, not even in the smallest detail. She had to be right, always right.'[45] To Charlie van Gelderen, she was a demagogue – the real boss – of whom they were all terrified.[46] The Woltons were assisted by a Latvian émigré named Lazar Bach, a leatherworker in his early twenties, who arrived sometime in late 1930 and joined the CPSA in 1931. Bach, a small, quiet man with an eye for the ladies, was a master of Comintern doctrine. Together, the triumvirate acted as the Comintern's interpreters, pointing the finger at all those who had at any time challenged authority. Thibedi and Lopes were but the first in a long list.

The year 1931 saw a spate of expulsions of those who, over the previous decade, had built the Party. Many years later Douglas Wolton told Jack Simons that the decision to expel these people came entirely from the CPSA, and not from Moscow. No doubt, he believed this. Nonetheless, the Woltons were precisely the type of local leaders chosen by the Comintern during the New Line years for their loyalty to authority above all else, and they had been empowered by the Comintern. The case against Bunting had been built up by both the Comintern and South Africans Communists over several years.[47]

But Sam Malkinson's case came first. Following the Party's Ninth Conference, Malkinson sought an explanation for his having been dropped from the restructured and reconstituted Central Committee. After several months he received a reply from Wolton that claimed, Malkinson wrote, 'that I did not accept the new line. When I retorted that he knows very well I did ... he said there was some vagueness about it in my mind'. Consequently, Malkinson *charge[d] the Secretariat with acting in a non-Bolshevik manner in victimising me on purely personal grounds*.[48] Roux had been sent by the Secretariat to explain the situation to the Bloemfontein branch but as far as the branch members were concerned, 'Com. Roux failed to give satisfactory explanations and replies as regards the charges against Com. Malkinson'. They further complained that Nzula had been writing letters about Party matters to an ex-member whom they believed to be associating with the local Criminal Investigation Department. 'Such action is not commendable, the PB should show an example to the contrary', the branch chided. 'We trust the PB will in future discontinue it, and communicate direct with the BFN DPC.'[49]

The Politburo did not take kindly to such uppity behaviour. Its reply was straightforward. Expelling Malkinson for factional activities, it appealed to the Bloemfontein branch to 'detach itself from the actions of Com. Malkinson' and 'to recant and isolate disruptive elements within the Party and to align itself with the Leninist leadership of the Party'.[50] The local branch refused to comply, claiming that Malkinson had been unfairly treated, that the branch had 'nothing to recant on' and that it was 'disgusted at the threat ... of the liquidation of the local DPC'.

It was also alarmed at 'the Mussolini-like attitude adopted by the PB and [upheld] the Leninist principle of self-criticism'. The Politburo never replied.[51]

Malkinson explained the troubles that lay behind his expulsion as a power struggle between the 'Nzula-ites' and the 'Buntingites'. 'Although ... there were culprits on both sides ... nevertheless the orginiating [sic] and mostly contributing factor to the disorderly meetings was the drunkenness of Nzula', Malkinson claimed. Nzula 'used to interrupt, shout and generally make the meetings look ridiculous'. Moreover, Malkinson alleged, Nzula had instigated anti-Semitic attitudes in the Party. 'Epithets were flung by the Nzula-ites against the Jewish members of the Party. ... I am glad to say there were [sic] no corresponding retaliation, although, as mentioned, fights were threatened, with hammers, etc.'

Trying to mediate the situation, Malkinson had prepared a report to Party headquarters that argued that whatever the causes, Nzula's behaviour had led to 'a complete chaos'. He urged the Party to 'purge itself of such elements, as they are dangerous to the Party, particularly as leaders'. However, he added, what lay behind this disgraceful state of affairs was the Party's 'criminal neglecting of the livelihood of leaders (Nzula and Baker) who were starving, the concentration of the little money that there is in one's hands (Bunting's)'. Malkinson did not deny that the whites had chauvinist attitudes, which were 'probably not sufficiently realised ... but the struggle for power, as to who was going to be the leader, predominated the issue'.

Somewhat naively, Malkinson had hoped that this explanation would solve the problem. Instead, not surprisingly, it led to a complete breakdown in his relationship with Nzula. Malkinson claimed that Wolton had removed him from the Central Executive Committee 'because Nzula was against me, and Wolton had to support him'.[52] But Malkinson's explanation did not improve the situation: the Bloemfontein branch members became demoralized and the branch declined.[53]

Douglas Wolton assumed the role of high priest at the Central Committee meetings. In July 1931 Wolton warned against the right danger revealed in Com. Bunting's legal work, cautioning that 'We must view these questions very seriously as they now border on counter-revolutionary activities'. Yet, although the local Communists accepted the authority of the Comintern's directives, they nonetheless questioned some of Douglas Wolton's political interpretations. Moses Kotane, for instance, queried whether the Independent ANC was really a reactionary organization. 'I do not intend to defend these people', he hastened to add, 'but I want to know whether we are accusing them wrongly.'[54]

African Communists familiar with regions such as the Transkei also questioned the abstract and idealized notion of rural class divisions and consciousness put forward by Wolton. When Gana Makabeni observed that people in the Transkei did 'not wish to be organised into subsidiary organisations like peasant organisations but direct into Party', Wolton replied that the Party needed an agrarian programme which distinguished 'between rich, middle and poor native farmers'. But Kotane countered that '[t]here are no rich farmers. ... What he [the peasant] wants is a better price for his meal. He does not receive cash from the storekeeper only payment in kind.' And Makabeni explained that '[b]y agricultural workers I mean those who work in the towns but live on their plots because they cannot subsist on their plots. There are no rich farmers who hire labourers. ... There is no question of over-stocking.'[55] The classical Marxist conception of rural class structure did not exist in the Transkei, and the Communists who organized in the region were clearly aware of this.

But the concern with local issues and the recognition of local specificities could not overpower the trajectory of the New Line. Personal interactions became vicious. Benny Sachs remembered 'a certain Party meeting – a veritable Witches' Sabbath – with everybody shouting Bunting down and calling him 'Lord' Bunting. ... An elderly woman, whom Bunting had befriended over years, turned her posterior towards him with her dress lifted high'. Why, Sachs pondered, did this woman behave like this? It was not a question of her own self-advancement in the Party, as 'she was only one of our strays'. Yet the venemous atmosphere infected her. Benny Sachs knew his own departure from the Party was fated. He recalled attending a Party social where one Sarah Lewis made an embarassing scene singing 'Down Among the Dead Men'. Sachs burst out laughing, whereupon Sarah Lewis went up to him and, pointing her finger, spat the words 'Down Among the Dead Men' in his face. A week later, she attended a Party meeting, waving a banner with the words *Daloi Predachi* (Down with the Traitor) above Sachs's head.[56]

The Wolton–Bach leadership counted for support on the Jewish Workers' Club, a cultural club whose members were recent immigrants from Eastern Europe, earnest Communists or fellow-travellers with little knowledge of South African pol-itics or of the CPSA's inner dynamics. As Roux remarked: 'They were told by Bach that Bunting was a traitor and that was enough for them.'[57]

In September 1931, Bill Andrews, C. B. Tyler, Solly Sachs, Fanny Klenerman, Ben Weinbren and Sidney Bunting were ousted from the Party. Aside from Bunting, all were leading trade unionists, expelled on charges of using reformist and social-democratic methods and of neglecting the red trade unions. Bunting, it was alleged, had continued to engage in right-wing activities: he had appealed for leniency while defending unemployed demonstrators arrested at a May Day rally; he had persuaded Issy Diamond, charged with contempt, to apologize to the court; he had appeared on the same platform as the ICU and ANC; he had sought Thibedi's reinstatement to the Party.[58] As Bunting later tried to explain to the Comintern, his expulsion was due to Wolton's 'increasing obsession with him since he gained the ear of powerful allies oversea [sic]'. Bunting, himself, never lost his faith in the Comintern – only in its local interpreters.[59]

The purges strengthened a climate of intimidation: the Johannesburg expulsions were emulated in other branches, as long-standing friends and comrades turned on each other, hoping to prove their own ideological purity. The year before, in October 1930 – prior to Douglas Wolton's return – Johnny Gomas and Eddie Roux had heard rumours of an attempt to oust Bunting from the Central Executive Committee; the Cape Town branch immediately asked for a full explanation from the concerned parties and expressed its sympathies for Bunting. Now, a year later, the Cape Town District Party Committee, led by Gomas and Roux, took up the gauntlet thrown down by Johannesburg and expelled its own 'right wing': Joe Pick – for 'fractional activities against the leadership', Mr and Mrs Plax, Wilfred Harrison, J. Raynard and S. Fridman went in the first batch; La Guma was next, having only recently been reinstated after apologizing for opposing Wolton's parliamentary campaign. La Guma's expulsion order was signed by Johnny Gomas, his long-time friend. And in 1932 Roux reported to the Politburo a putative link between Bunting and Thibedi – who had written to Trotsky and had started a new socialist group outside the CPSA – leading to a new round of allegations against 'Buntingism' and Trotskyism in *Umsebenzi*. Only Gana Makabeni stood by Bunting and defended him, briefly protected from Wolton's wrath because he was African and because of his success as a trade unionist – until his own expulsion on charges of 'Buntingism'.[60]

The Durban branch was in disarray in 1931. The success of the 1929 beer-hall boycott had led to a clampdown by state authorities that continued into the next year. The Dingaan's Day demonstration in December 1930 had taken place in an atmosphere of tension and intimidation, culminating in violence. As the police charged the demonstration, Johannes Nkosi, leading activist of the Durban CPSA, was shot and stabbed. After Nkosi's murder, a succession of Party activists were sent down to Durban by the head office, including Gana Makabeni and Edwin Mofutsanyana, only to be arrested and deported. When Roux went to reorganize the branch in March 1931, he found the city in a state of terror and the local Party, 'a practical non-entity. … There were no contacts worth speaking of in the factories, docks, etc. … There was no office or rendezvous whatsoever where members could get in touch with the Party or obtain Umsebenzi.' In October the Durban District Party Committee endorsed the Johannesburg purges: its very weakness precluded it from standing up to authority.[61]

The CPSA also resolved the dilemma posed by Thibedi, even though it entailed FNETU's destruction. In January 1931, under Wolton's guidance, Thibedi had been expelled from the FNETU, which the Party reconstituted as the African Federation of Trade Unions (AFTU). 'The Communists have crashed', commented William Ballinger. 'Their industrial wing the S.A. non-European Fed. of Trade Unions is defunct. They are attempting revival under a new name "The African Fed. of Trade Unions".'[62] AFTU, along with two other newly-formed organizations, *Ikaka labaSebenzi* (Workers' Shield or Labour Defence) and Friends of the Soviet Union, were essentially fronts for the CPSA, designed to attract potential members. *Ikaka labaSebenzi* was the South African section of International Red Aid that provided legal assistance for Africans. The Friends of the Soviet Union was formed to counter anti-Soviet propaganda. AFTU's aim was to provide 'an alternative revolutionary leadership' for the trade unions and to expose the bankruptcy of the offical trade union leaders.[63]

AFTU never got off the ground. Nzula ran it as a political movement, its members taking part in rallies and demonstrations for the unemployed. Ballinger was sympathetic to Nzula, despite the fact that he 'represents no one. He is trying to rebuild on the ruins of the old [FNETU]. But he is a good man and is at the moment probably the only non-self-seeking Native agitator.' But Nzula was not adept at building bridges across the racial divide. In 1931 he addressed the Trades and Labour Council's conference in Durban on behalf of the AFTU. The Trades and Labour Council, he claimed, 'has betrayed the masses in general strikes' and was 'sabotaging and betraying joint black and white workers strike struggles in the factories of Johannesburg'. Hence, the need for AFTU's 'alternative leadership, built and based upon militant class struggle'. Not surprisingly, his speech was not a big hit with his audience: 'The White T. Unionists will not invite him again', noted Ballinger dryly.[64]

By 1932, AFTU was decimated, with only two remaining affiliates, the African Clothing Workers' Union and the African Laundry Workers' Union. It had abandoned the Mine Workers' Union at City Deep, presumably because it had been started by Bunting and his African comrades. The CPSA continued to intervene in the affairs of AFTU's affiliates. In March 1932 AFTU became embroiled in a dispute with the African Clothing Workers' Union, run by Gana Makabeni. Its parallel white union was the Garment Workers' Union (GWU), led by Solly Sachs. The GWU was on strike, and the CPSA claimed that Sachs had refused to provide strike pay for members of the African Clothing Workers' Union although they had been locked out for their support of white strikers. AFTU therefore insisted that the African Clothing Workers' Union break links with the GWU. Makabeni refused to do this and was expelled from the CPSA and AFTU. Similarly, according to Makabeni, relations between the African Laundry Workers' Union and AFTU deteriorated. By late 1932 AFTU's numbers had evidently dwindled to about 200.[65]

Dissenting voices

The autocratic methods and the expulsions did not go unchallenged. The critics were divided between those who continued to believe in the legitimacy of the Comintern and the possibility of reforming the Party by changing the leadership, on the one side, and others who no longer believed that internal reform was a viable option. Gana Makabeni was one of those hoping to reform the Party from within. In November 1931 he and other members of the Johannesburg branch convened a meeting at the Party Hall to which they invited the Politburo. The critics lashed out at the leadership for 'having taken a holiday in organising the oppressed, exploited and voiceless masses in South Africa … while considering who should be expelled in the next issue of Umsebenzi'. In fact, some of those expelled, they continued, were 'not reported in Umsebenzi because of their unimportance and inferiority or because they are mostly Blacks'. A fight broke out. The branch members succeeded in evicting the Politburo members and called a conference at Inchcape Hall for 27 December.

This, too, was far from peaceful. A report prepared by the dissident members and signed by Gana Makabeni criticized the autocratic methods of the leadership, particularly Wolton. 'The Party members who have the machine of the Party in their own hands would do anything detrimental to either movement or workers in order to keep their positions regardless of consequences', the report charged. Moreover, racism was rife, it claimed. 'Native masses are not only neglected and no agitation is carried in their localities, but [they] are abused by the officials of the Party of being barbarians "from the long grass". ... black comrades [are] expelled for daring to hold any views of their own.' As a result, '[t]he Party has become mainly a white man's affair, almost completely in the hands of the Jewish Workers Club (mostly petty bourgeois)'. Many of the original white members of the CPSA had left the Party 'when it adopted the true policy of the Communist Party to embrace all nationalities of workers' claiming 'that it was not time yet, to combine with natives'. Now, the report continued, we see '[t]hese whites resuming their old seats in the Party because probably "kaffirs" have been swept away'. The conference delegates still accepted the Comintern's authority, however. They designated a committee to draw up a report to send to 'Headquarters' in Moscow 'in full confidence in the International' and decided that, in the meantime, 'no opposition of any nature must be carried or allowed to prevail in the Party'.[66]

The protests against the Party's leadership provoked a harsh response at the Central Committee meeting at the end of December. Makabeni, whom Sam Malkinson had described as, 'the most self-sacrificing member of the Party and liked by all', was the chief target.[67] Joseph Sepeng charged that Makabeni, 'has shown himself in his true colour'. And Charles Baker argued that the Politburo had been weak in its handling of the right danger. Some of those involved in 'the raid on the Party hall' had subsequently been expelled but '[t]he main engineer, Makabeni, was left untouched', he complained. 'To say that because he is a native, he sould [sic] be dealt with leniently is wrong. We are not whites, blacks or coloured, we are communists. Ignorance cannot be pleaded by Makabeni. He is a traitor.' Josie Mpama echoed the sentiment, demanding: 'Anyone who does wrong should be expelled, no matter what his colour is'.[68]

The poison in the Party seeped into the Friends of the Soviet Union and *Ikaka labaSebenzi*. Sidney Bunting and other purged Communists were marginalized and expelled from the Friends of the Soviet Union. Makabeni, who had been elected chair of *Ikaka labaSebenzi*, was stripped of his office without notification and allegedly beaten up by John Marks when he demanded an explanation. In March 1932 Makabeni was expelled from the Party. By April William Thibedi had organized a new group outside the Party that called itself the Communist League of Africa and that made contact with Trotsky and his overseas supporters.[69]

In November Makabeni and eight other African delegates met to discuss the current state of affairs in the Party. Also present were the Buntings and I. Stein. Two of the Africans, Frans Mopu and Lucas Malupi, had been involved with Thibedi's Communist League of Africa. Despite this, Thibedi's request to attend the meeting was denied on the grounds that 'it was a meeting of those who had always been against forming any opposition organisation, whereas Thibedi had formed one'.

Although disappointed at the Comintern's failure to reply to their earlier missive, 'especially as such non-reply has been construed as a slight on the African People', they resolved to send a report of their previous meeting to the Comintern. But the group failed to reach agreement on their future strategy.[70]

Bunting, on the one side, believed that the desire to oust him had been the cause of the Party's troubles and therefore asked the group to cut him out and 'to carry on as if he did not exist'. But he also stressed his opposition to forming a separate organization outside the Party. 'The C.I. and its sections rightly claim a monopolistic position – there can be only one machine, and isolated groups only confuse the masses.'[71] On the other side, Solundwana argued that 'We must have a centre at which branches can meet and give or obtain advice. We can't work with head office. It fights against us.' This view was endorsed by Stein, who stated, 'Bunting's advice will not result in any good but only in justifying the leaders' mistakes. Let us organise separately and see who is right.' Makabeni came down in the middle, 'oppos[ing] the return to the party pending reply from Moscow. We Africans are flouted by the white members of the party. We must organise ourselves as a race. ... I am against going back to the party until it is put in order. Rather let us thrash those who have spoilt it. The natives at head office are not champions of the black man, they are there only for their pay and have to say and do what they are bid.' Hence, the decision as to whether or not to try to work within the Party was postponed 'pending reply from the C.I.'[72] But evidently no reply was forthcoming, and the idea of trying to form a ginger group to reform the Party from within was dropped.

Following the New Line

In 1931 and 1932 the Party became thoroughly Bolshevized, its few remaining members seemingly secure in their ideological purity. Those now preaching on Sunday evenings on the City Hall steps included Molly Wolton; Issy Diamond; Eddie Roux; Gideon Botha, an Afrikaaner and an ISL veteran who floated uneasily between Afrikaner nationalism and Communism; Nzula, so poised a speaker that no one ever jeered him; and occasionally John Marks. The state clamped down heavily on protest activity and Communists paid the price. Many of the Party's leading members suffered imprisonment and banishment in the early 1930s. In consequence, the Wolton–Bach leadership stressed secrecy. At one point most of the Party's open work was done by Roux and by Louis Joffe, an ardent disciple of the Comintern line who was desperate to belong and to feel valued – and rather ridiculous in his own sense of self-importance.[73] Those who survived the purges still believed it necessary to trust the leadership.

For those who toed the line, there was even less intellectual autonomy in the Party after the purges than before, indicated by the reception given by the leadership to the Comintern's new interpretation of the Native Republic thesis. At a meeting of the Central Committee in December 1931 Joseph Sepeng introduced the new version, which called for 'a Government of the Bechuana, of the Basutos, Swazis etc. and all of these will federate in one Union, free from the domination of any one nation, as is the case in the U.S.S.R., where every nation has the right of nationalism, to speak its own tongue, the right to maintain its own customs and traditions'. Molly Wolton explained that the new version would ensure that the various South African tribes did not have to worry about the possibility of domination by any single tribe. Moreover, she added, it would not dilute the Party's socialist objective, as the struggle would not simply stop with the achievement of national liberation for the various groups.[74]

Washington Nchee's was the sole dissenting voice, arguing that 'there are too many tribes and we would have too many republics. ... if German, French, English and other people can live together why cannot we be a contented nation.' He also referred to Basutoland, where 'there was never peace ... because they are divided under so many chiefs'. Finally, he pointed to the example of the ICU, where 'All the different tribes were combined under the I.C.U. and then Champion tried to form a Zulu republic by forming the I.C.U. Yase Natal'.[75] But Johnny Gomas, convinced 'that the Federation of Republics is the only solution', rejected Nchee's contention that the whites were united, adding that '[t]he Dutch would not have had an official language if the Nationalists had not come into power. ... There can be no unity under capitalism. One nation is forced to acknowledge the rule of the dominating nation.'

Ultimately, Nchee's cynical concession only underlined the lack of tolerance in the Party: 'We had this discussion in Durban and I was beaten and given to understand there', he stated. 'I only brought this up for discussion and thought I might get support, but I now give up.'[76] This new variant of the Native Republic thesis was even more out of touch with South African conditions than its predecessor – the ANC, for example, was striving to unite Africans across tribal lines, not to fragment them – but that did not prevent the Central Committee from endorsing the new version.

Protected by the myth of their own political superiority, the Party's leadership even tried to encroach on the personal lives of its members. When Eddie Roux and Winifred Lunt wanted to marry, Roux was instructed that as a revolutionary, he should not do so – this despite the presence of a number of married couples in the Party hierarchy – while Winifred was informed that as a 'petty bourgeois intellectual' she was not suited to be a revolutionary's wife. On this occasion, they defied Party discipline. Winifred Lunt had been a student at Liverpool University and a member of the local Fabian Society. She later travelled to South Africa, began working as a schoolteacher and, shocked at the segregation and treatment of blacks, joined the CPSA in late 1931. She and Eddie discussed the purges and the lack of internal democracy between themselves. But they were both inclined towards practical work, and the Party gave them a political home.[77]

The Comintern now kept a tighter rein on the CPSA. Moscow's hand was felt via the Lenin School and the Eastern Workers Communist University (KUTVU). In 1931 renewed efforts were made to enable African Communists to study in Moscow. They were generally unable to obtain passports in their own names and had to travel under assumed identities. After some difficulties, Nzula finally arrived in Moscow on 25 August 1931, and Moses Kotane arrived about a month later. Edwin Mofutsanyana, John Marks and B. Nikin, who later became a trade unionist, arrived thereafter. Gana Makabeni had initially been selected to study in Moscow as well but he never made the trip.[78] Several Lenin School or KUTVU graduates subsequently rose in the Party hierarchy, notably Kotane, who returned to South Africa at the start of 1933, Mofutsanyana and Marks. In contrast, Albert Nzula never returned to South Africa. He spent the last two and a half years of his life in Moscow, studying at the KUTVU and co-authoring a volume entitled *The Working Class Movement and Forced Labour in Negro Africa* with A. Z. Zusmanovich and I. I. Potekhin, two Soviet Africanists who worked in the Africa Bureau of the KUTVU. He also worked for the International Trade Union Committee of Negro Workers and edited the *Negro Worker*. However, he became increasingly disenchanted with the Soviet regime and was reputedly overtly critical when he was drunk. He died, evidently of pneumonia, on 14 January 1934 and was buried in Moscow.[79]

Two foreign emissaries came to propagate Comintern policy in 1932. An American Communist named Eugene Dennis, who used the pseudonym Russell, oversaw the implementation of the New Line in 1932–33.[80] Polish-born Gina Medem came to discuss Jewish land settlement in Bira Bidjan in the Eastern Soviet Union, while promoting the Comintern line more broadly.[81] But there were indications that the Party's leadership was seen as having been overly zealous in its implementation of the New Line. One report to the Comintern chided the CPSA's leadership for trying to justify the drop in membership as a political cleansing when in fact it represented a divorce from the masses.[82] Harry Pollitt of the CPGB criticized the CPSA's 'expulsions from above' and its setting of the red unions against white workers – an indication from a Communist leader that the Wolton–Bach triumvurate had gone too far.[83]

The CPSA's depleted membership precluded any large-scale activities. Anticipating that the poverty of the depression years would radicalize white workers, the CPSA, under Wolton's direction, now tried to organize unemployed workers across colour lines. The Party ran a soup kitchen in Ferreirastown and organized unemployed people to raise funds for it. Yet, aside from a notable demonstration on May Day 1931, the attempts at joint black–white activity were largely unsuccessful; one effort, at least, almost led to a riot. Gideon Botha concentrated on the white unemployed but the growing poverty of Afrikaner peasants and workers was not reflected in a non-racial consciousness. 'The problem', Roux noted, 'was always to get white and Native unemployed to march together in a demonstration.' Despite the best efforts of the Communist organizers to unite black and white in one procession, 'by the time they arrived anywhere … most of the whites had vanished'.[84]

But as Ballinger saw it, '[t]he "C.Pers" have overexploited the situation and in consequence the poor unemployed Blacks are the sufferers'.[85] Makabeni was scathing. He claimed that the CPSA's attempt to organize unemployed blacks had foundered after one week. He also pointed to the absence of May Day celebrations in 1932 and noted that the only time recently that an African comrade appeared on the City Hall steps, on 30 April, those responsible for protecting the white Communist speakers failed to protect the African from a trouncing by the police. 'This gave some suspicion even to the "hangers on" of the Party that the Party had nothing in common with natives', Makabeni noted. The Party's announcements of demonstrations, he concluded cynically, 'only means a white people's meeting to be held at City Steps where a "nigger" cannot have his share at the meeting'.[86]

In 1932 Lazar Bach went to Durban to try to organize black trade unions. Late in the year he was recalled to Johannesburg, and the Woltons went to Cape Town. Eddie and Winifred Roux seized the opportunity to revive *Umsebenzi*. They now tried a new strategy: to aim the paper at the black intelligentsia: teachers, ministers, clerks, officials and traders whom Communists had earlier labelled as reformist. This worked: *Umsebenzi* soon outsold its two rivals, *Umteteli wa Bantu* (*People's Mouthpiece*) and *Bantu World*. The Rouxs also started a monthly magazine called *Indlela Yenkululeko* (*Road to Freedom*), which they posted to various institutions around the country, including Fort Hare.[87]

A by-election was held in Germiston that same year. The previous incumbent had been a member of the National Party, which favoured keeping South Africa on the gold standard, while the South African Party, under Smuts, wished to take the country off gold to suit the Chamber of Mines. The CPSA decided to use the election to protest against the fact that Africans did not have the vote in the Transvaal and could not run for Parliament. The Party put forward John Marks, a black man, as a 'demonstrative candidate'. Despite the rigid controls on the African location at Germiston, the CPSA was able to attract huge crowds. In the event, Marks's candidature was not accepted by the election authorities, and the CPSA's top local white activists – Issy Diamond, Douglas Wolton, Willie Kalk and Eddie Roux – along with former Communist Solly Sachs, were banished from the Witwatersrand for a year. Eddie Roux remained and operated clandestinely. The South African Party won an overwhelming victory, and Communist attempts to hold protest meetings in the African location were squashed with violence.

The CPSA's tiny numbers meant that its activists were disproportionately subjected to the threat of police harassment and arrest. This increased the chances of political burn-out. In 1933 Molly Wolton had 'a complete physical and mental breakdown'. In order to recuperate, avowed her husband, 'she needed complete removal from the sense of responsibility which was ever-present wherever she was in South Africa'. Thus, when Wolton's brother wrote to him in August 1933 about a job on the *Yorkshire Times*, the Woltons left speedily for England. In a subsequent explanation to both the CPGB and the Comintern about their unauthorized departure, Douglas Wolton remained utterly convinced that he and his wife had done their utmost for the CPSA.[88]

Conclusion

The Native Republic thesis and the New Line were the first two experiences of direct Comintern intervention in the CPSA's affairs. Both indicated the pitfalls of applying policies derived overseas to South Africa. The Native Republic thesis reoriented the CPSA away from a primarily class-based approach towards a mechanical view of the relationship between national liberation and socialism. The New Line depleted the Party's membership and set the black trade union movement back several years. From a claimed peak of almost 3000 members in early 1929, by April 1931 the Party's membership had plummeted to 100, Eugene Dennis reported, and by January 1932 it had dropped to about sixty.[89]

The sometimes acrimonious discord that had characterized the South African socialist movement from its earliest days should not be underestimated. Nonetheless, perhaps the greatest legacy of the Comintern's intervention was that it corroded the sense of trust and comradeship that South African socialists had previously felt. It promoted the value of exclusion rather than inclusion – the sense of us versus them – even within the tiny left. Internally, the Party was wracked by faction fights, as the Comintern's dominant role in the CPSA led to the stifling of discussion and debate, which was replaced by the correct interpretation of dogma, by the use of personal abuse against dissenting voices and by the expulsion of dissidents. Democratic practice was subordinated to loyalty to authority. Responsibility for formulating socialist theory and policy was given to the Comintern. Those who survived in the Party either toed the line or became skilful tacticians and dissimulators, carefully navigating until the next change in the political tide. Most of those who were expelled ultimately accepted the decision; Bunting was the only key figure to continue fighting for reinstatement. Some of those ousted from the Party never found another political home and withdrew from politics. Others, like Andrews and Makabeni, took refuge in trade union work. Still others formed Trotskyist groups in opposition to the dominant Party.

Notes

1. Martin, *Communism and the British Trade Unions*, 102–3, 108; McDermott and Agnew, *The Comintern*, 71–2, 83–4.
2. Bradford, *A Taste of Freedom*, 272–8; Hofmeyr, 'Agricultural Crisis', 289–304; Simons and Simons, *Class and Colour*, 427–9.
3. Roux, *Time Longer than Rope*, 217.
4. Letter from Chairman of the CPSA to the Secretaries (H. Desmond and Rubin), I.R.A., 26 February 1930, RTsKhIDNI, 495.64.99.
5. *REPORT OF COMRADE X (ECCI REPRESENTATIVE IN SOUTH AFRICA).*, 25/9/29, 6, RTsKhIDNI, 495.64.81.
6. Sachs, *Multitude of Dreams*, 153–4.
7. Luli Callinicos, *Working Life, 1886–1940: Factories, Townships and Popular Culture on the Rand*, Johannesburg: Ravan, 1987, 190–91; Edgar, interview with Mofutsanyana,

12–20; Julie Wells, interviews with Josie Palmer [Mpama]. Orlando West, 19 and 26 October 1977. My thanks to Julie Evans, Institute of Commonwealth Studies, for sending me copies of these interviews.

8. Interview with Jack and Ray Simons, Cape Town, October 1994.

9. D. G. Wolton, REPORT ON SOUTH AFRICA, 20 September 1929, RTsKhIDNI, 495.64.81.

10. *REPORT OF COMRADE X*, 2.

11. Roux, *S. P. Bunting*, 141–2.

12. Letter from A. Fergusson, to [address cut off], n.d., [date stamped 4 Jan 1930], RTsKhIDNI, 495.64.85.

13. Letter from the Executive Bureau, CPSA to the Executive Committee, Comintern, in Drew, ed., *South Africa's Radical Tradition*, vol. 1, 108–10.

14. Letter to the Communist Party of South Africa from the Presidium of the ECCI, 7.5.1930, RTsKhIDNI, 495.64.89.

15. See, for instance, Nzula's *Resolution on South Africa* in the Report on Ninth Annual Conference of the Communist Party (South Africa), held at 41a Fox Street, Johannesburg, on the 26th, 27th and 28th December, 1930, 10, RTsKhIDNI, 495.64.96.

16. Letter from A. Nzula on behalf of Executive Bureau, CPSA to the ECCI, 11 December 1929, RTsKhIDNI, 495.64.85.

17. Letter from E. R. Roux to Victor Danchin, 6 March 1929, in Drew, ed., *South Africa's Radical Tradition*, vol. 1, 102.

18. Ben Weinbren to E. R. Roux, 27 April 1929, Roux Papers, item 12.

19. Letter from Ben W[einbren] to Ed [Roux], 7 June 1929, S. P. Bunting Papers, A949, Historical Papers Library, University of the Witwatersrand.

20. According to one account – presumably by Wilhelmina Taylor, a staunch critic of Bunting – Weinbren had accused Thibedi of mismanaging the Federation's funds after the latter revised his position on the Native Republic thesis, and a committee to investigate the matter was bypassed in favour of a critical report by Julius First. Letter to 'My dear Molly', 26 August 1930, RTsKhIDNI, 495.64.99. Bunting himself was unhappy about Thibedi's treatment; see Roux, *S. P. Bunting*, 145.

21. Roux, *S. P. Bunting*, 145.

22. Letter from S. P. Bunting to the South African Federation of Native Trade Unions, 20 September 1930 in Drew, ed., *South Africa's Radical Tradition*, vol. 1, 66–7, quote 67.

23. Letter to 'My dear Molly', 1.

24. Letter from S. P. Bunting to the Secretary, Communist Party of South Africa, 22 September 1930 in Drew, ed., *South Africa's Radical Tradition*, vol. 1, 69–70, quote 69.

25. Letter to 'My dear Molly'.

26. Communist Party of South Africa, Memo on S.A.F.N.E.T.U., 1930 in Drew, ed., *South Africa's Radical Tradition*, vol. 1, 68.

27. Letter from S. P. Bunting to the South African Federation of Native Trade Unions, 67.

28. Letter from S. P. Bunting to the Secretary, Communist Party of South Africa, 22 September 1930, 69.

29. Simons and Simons, *Class and Colour*, 424, 442; interview with Charlie van Gelderen.

30. Letter from Moses M. Kotane to Dear Comrade Willy, 22/11/1930, RTsKhIDNI, 495.64.99.

31. See, for instance, REPORT from A. Green, 8 October 1930 and letter from [Solly Sachs?] to Comrades, July 24, 1930, RTsKhIDNI, 495.64.100.

32. Letters from [Campbell] to Political Commission, ECCI, 15 and 16 August 1930, RTsKhIDNI, 495.64.92.
33. REPORT OF COMRADE D. G. WOLTON (Late S.A.) TO E.C.C.I., 13 March 1934, 1, RTsKhIDNI, 495.64.132.
34. Report on Ninth Annual Conference of the Communist Party (South Africa), held at 41a Fox Street, Johannesburg, on the 26th, 27th and 28th December, 1930, quotes 11, 4, 11–12 and 12, respectively, RTsKhIDNI, 495.64.96. Fanny Klenerman is referred to as F. Glass in the report.
35. Report on Ninth Annual Conference of the Communist Party, 13a and 15–16.
36. Report on Ninth Annual Conference of the Communist Party, 18 and 19.
37. Roux, *S. P. Bunting*, 149; Johns, *Raising the Red Flag*, 267.
38. Report on Ninth Annual Conference of the Communist Party, 11.
39. Simons and Simons, *Class and Colour*, 443.
40. Roux, *Rebel Pity*, 74, 81–82; Simons and Simons, *Class and Colour*, 442.
41. Roux, *S. P. Bunting*, 149 and 153.
42. Klenerman, 'Distributing newspapers with Eva Green', unpublished memoirs.
43. Quoted in Sachs, *Multitude of Dreams*, 195.
44. Simons and Simons, *Class and Colour*, 451; interview with Jack and Ray Simons.
45. Roux and Roux, *Rebel Pity*, 96.
46. Interview with Charlie van Gelderen.
47. Statement of Douglas Wolton; Bunting, *Kotane*, 56.
48. Letter from S. Malkinson, 10 March 1931, emphasis in original, RTsKhIDNI, 495.64.109.
49. Letter by the Bloemfontein DPC to the Politburo, sent 12 March 1931, signed Dambula, Acting Secretary, RTsKhIDNI, 495.64.109.
50. Letter from Moses Kotane for the CPSA Politburo to the Bloemfontein DPC, 20 March 1931; letter from the CPSA Political Bureau to S. Malkinson, 20 March 1931, both in RTsKhIDNI, 495.64.109.
51. Letter from the DPC Bloemfontein to Secretariat, Johannesburg, passed 24 March 1931 and dispatched 26 March 1931, RTsKhIDNI, 495.64.109.
52. S. Malkinson, *EXPLANATION*, 2 June 1931, RTsKhIDNI, 495.64.109.
53. Roux, *Rebel Pity*, 98; cf. Simons and Simons, *Class and Colour*, 447.
54. MINUTES OF CENTRAL COMMITTEE held at 41a Fox Street, Johannesburg, on 4th July 1931 at 3 p.m., 1–2, RTsKhIDNI, 495.64.113.
55. MINUTES OF CENTRAL COMMITTEE held at 41a Fox Street, Johannesburg, on 4th July 1931 at 3 p.m., quotes 11, 12 and 12 respectively, RTsKhIDNI, 495.64.113.
56. Sachs, *Multitude of Dreams*, 164–5.
57. Roux and Roux, *Rebel Pity*, 103, 109.
58. Roux, *S. P. Bunting*, 157–8; Simons and Simons, *Class and Colour*, 448.
59. S. P. Bunting, Letter to Dear Comrades of the Communist Party, draft, September 1931, RTsKhIDNI, 495.64.118.
60. Roux, *S. P. Bunting*, 158, 163–4; Simons and Simons, *Class and Colour*, 449; La Guma, *Jimmy La Guma*, 56–7.
61. MINUTES OF CENTRAL COMMITTEE held at 41a Fox Street, Johannesburg, on 4th July 1931 at 3 p.m., 495.64.113; Roux and Roux, *Rebel Pity*, 99; Simons and Simons, *Class and Colour*, 449. See also Shula Marks, *The Ambiguities of Dependence in South Africa: Class, nationalism and the state in twentieth-century Natal*, Johannesburg: Ravan, 1986, 85–6; the estimate, 150, n. 49, reported by a Criminal Investigation Department detective of 6000 CPSA members is wildly exaggerated.

62. Ballinger to Holtby, 25 March 1931, Holtby Collection, file 4.12, item 29.

63. Johns, *Raising the Red Flag*, 274–6.

64. All quotes Ballinger to Holtby, 14 April 1931, and attached Report on Meeting of South African Trades & Labour Council, Durban, Easter 1931, Holtby Collection, file 4.12, item 31.

65. Simons and Simons, *Class and Colour*, 444, 457; *INTRODUCTORY OF THE REPORT* (re the Conference of the 27th December 1931) and *REPORT TO THE SECOND CONFERENCE OF PARTY*, MEMBERS DISSATISFIED WITH THE PARTY POSITION, signed by Garner Makabeni, 7–8, RTsKhIDNI, 495.64.108; Johns, *Raising the Red Flag*, 282; Nzula et al., *Forced Labour*, 9–10, 130–37.

66. *INTRODUCTORY OF THE REPORT*, 4, 4, 12 and 2.

67. S. Malkinson, *EXPLANATION*, 2.

68. REPORT OF MEETING OF THE CENTRAL COMMITTEE OF THE C.P.S.A., held at Johannesburg, on the 28th, 29th and 30th, December, 1931, 3 and 21, RTsKhIDNI, 495.64.113.

69. *INTRODUCTORY OF THE REPORT*, 6–7, 12; Roux, *S. P. Bunting*, 163–4.

70. *MINUTES OF A MEETING OF COMMUNIST DELEGATES* At the Albert Street Hall, on the 13th November, 1932, quotes 1 and 3 respectively, RTsKhIDNI, 495.64.122. Eugene Dennis claimed that Bunting's African support was based in Vereeniging, Brakpan and Prospect Township but that by mid-May 1932 the CPSA had won most of them back. See letters from Dennis, 16 July 1932, 5 and 16 November 1932, 7, RTsKhIDNI, 495.64.120.

71. *MINUTES OF A MEETING OF COMMUNIST DELEGATES*, 3 and 5; see also Roux, *S. P. Bunting*, 168.

72. *MINUTES OF A MEETING OF COMMUNIST DELEGATES*, quotes 3, 4, 6 and 5, respectively.

73. Roux and Roux, *Rebel Pity*, 111–13.

74. REPORT OF MEETING OF THE CENTRAL COMMITTEE OF THE C.P.S.A., held at Johannesburg, on the 28th, 29th and 30th, December, 1931, 3 and 13; see also Bunting, *Moses Kotane*, 41 and Simons and Simons, *Class and Colour*, 473.

75. REPORT OF MEETING OF THE CENTRAL COMMITTEE OF THE C.P.S.A., held at Johannesburg, on the 28th, 29th and 30th, December, 1931, 14, 15 and 16.

76. REPORT OF MEETING OF THE CENTRAL COMMITTEE OF THE C.P.S.A., held at Johannesburg, on the 28th, 29th and 30th, December, 1931, both quotes 16.

77. Roux and Roux, *Rebel Pity*, 131–2, 127–8. A similar double standard was seen in the CPSA's alleged rejection of Tilly First's request for membership on the grounds that she was the wife of a factory owner. In fact, her husband, Julius First, had been a founder member and chair of the Party. Slovo, *Every Secret Thing*, 274, and letter to author, 5 September 1997. In another example of the culture of intrusion into personal affairs, Ray Adler Harmel described how she was criticized by the Jewish Workers' Club for wanting to participate in the religious wedding ceremony of a friend, *Ray's Story*, Unpublished Memoirs, London, January 1993, 33–4.

78. Bunting, *Kotane*, 44, 46, 58–59, 117. Kotane spent about a year and Mofutsanyana, two and a half years. Edgar, interview with Mofutsanyana, 26–8.

79. Nzula et al., *Forced Labour*, 12–15. Despite controversy about the cause of Nzula's death and rumours that he was murdered by agents of Stalin, there is no evidence of this. However, Mofutsanyana believed that the Soviet authorities were well aware of Nzula's criticisms of Stalin and that there was talk of sending him to the United States

because they feared he would promote an anti-Soviet view if he returned to South Africa. Edgar, interview with Mofutsanyana, 30–31. Charlie van Gelderen recounted a story that shortly before George Padmore was due to go to the Soviet Union, Nzula sent him a telegram, via Latvia, telling him not to come. This was allegedly one week before Nzula's death. Van Gelderen added that Johannes Moses Beyers, who joined the CPSA in 1933 and was sent to the KUTVU, claimed to be at a meeting at which Nzula was called out, never again to be seen alive, and that Beyers said that Nzula had warned him not to express critical views while in the Soviet Union. Jomo Kenyatta told a similar story to C. L. R. James, according to Cohen in Nzula et al., *Forced Labour*, 15.

80. Dennis became general secretary of the American Communist Party in 1948, and chair in 1959. Simons and Simons, *Class and Colour*, 453; Roux and Roux, *Rebel Pity*, 143.
81. Interviews with Charlie van Gelderen and with Lilian Dubb, Cape Town, July 1999.
82. [Eugene Dennis?], *URGENT QUESTIONS ON THE WORK OF THE CP OF SOUTH AFRICA*, (Letter from South Africa), 21/6/32, RTsKhIDNI, 495.64.119.
83. Bunting, *Kotane*, 62; letter from Dennis, 16 July 1932; Minutes of the Fourth Plenum of the Communist Party (South Africa), 47.
84. Roux and Roux, *Rebel Pity*, 131; Simons and Simons, *Class and Colour*, 456; Minutes of the Fourth Plenum of the Communist Party (South Africa), 6–8 February 1933, 41, RTsKhIDNI, 495.64.129.
85. Ballinger to Holtby, 20 April 1932, Holtby Collection, file 4.12, item 35.
86. *INTRODUCTORY OF THE REPORT*, 5 and 9.
87. Roux and Roux, *Rebel Pity*, 130.
88. SUPPLEMENTARY REPORT OF COMRADE D.G. WOLTON TO E.C.C.I., March 13, 1934, RTsKhIDNI, 495.64.132. See also Letters from CPSA to M. Wolton, 7 July 1933, and from J. W. Macauley to Secretariat, CPGB, 12 September 1933, RTsKhIDNI 495.64.126; Roux, *S. P. Bunting*, 169–70. Although Douglas Wolton reported back to the CPGB there is no evidence that the Woltons joined the British affiliate following their final departure from South Africa.
89. Letter from Dennis, 16 July 1932, RTsKhIDNI, 495.64.120, 2–3.

Chapter 7

A new prophet, a new prophecy: the origins of South African Trotskyism

Communists everywhere had pinned their hopes on the feasibility of an international socialist revolution; by the late 1920s that vision had faded. In the Soviet Union, Joseph Stalin sought to justify the regime's long-term viability with the notion of socialism in one country, which the Comintern adopted as its programme at its Sixth Congress in 1928. This conception, that socialism could thrive in international isolation, was vehemently rejected by Stalin's antagonist, Leon Trotsky. Instead, Trotsky continued to argue on the basis of his theory of permanent revolution. This theory posited that all social struggles were interconnected due to their common reproduction in the capitalist system, so that the resolution of one struggle shaped the outcome of others. Social change developed continuously and unevenly, rather than proceeding through discrete stages, enabling a proletarian revolution to occur in a relatively undeveloped country like Russia before it took place in more advanced capitalist countries. Since capitalism was an international system, social revolution in one nation was immanently part of an international struggle. Therefore, the contradictions within a relatively undeveloped socialist state could be resolved through world revolution. Building on these propositions, Trotsky argued that just as capitalist development of the productive forces necessarily transcended state boundaries and that socialism necessarily carried on the development of the productive forces started by capitalism, so the interdependence of the international economy made the idea of socialism in one country utopian. Accordingly, he emphasized, the protection of the Soviet Union as an isolated state would inevitably lead to the destruction of the international Communist movement.[1]

Trotsky was successively marginalized and vilified in Soviet politics in the late 1920s, culminating in his expulsion from the Soviet Union in 1929. A Left Opposition, in which Trotsky became the principal figure, had been formed within the Russian Communist Party in 1923. With Trotsky's exile, the political struggles between Stalin and the Left Oppositionists spilled into the international arena. In the South African affiliate, as in Communist Parties around the world, they led to a series of defections and expulsions. Between 1929 and 1934 the CPSA expelled members of varying political hues based on a variety of allegations. Some of these expulsions formed the nucleus of the early Trotskyist movement. Former Communists, joined by small numbers of other socialists, loosely grouped themselves under the banner of Trotskyism.[2]

The principal differences between the Party and those it expelled concerned the Comintern's expanded role in internal policy, the lack of internal democracy and disputes over the Native Republic thesis. Trotskyists, like certain Communists a few years earlier, argued that the thesis subordinated working-class interests to those of the peasantry and aspirant peasantry and presupposed the existence of a black bourgeoisie, while simultaneously reinforcing racial divisions in the labour force. Instead, they argued, socialists should strive to unite the working class across colour lines.

Despite these differences, many similarities remained between early Trotskyists and Communists. Both socialist tendencies in the early 1930s were victims of the repressive social conditions that also crushed black organizations. The CPSA entered this period already weakened by its own internal dynamics of extreme policy swings and purges. In its difficulty in gaining a foothold in the working-class movement, the Trotskyist movement reflected the period of retrenchment in which it was born.

The CPSA was held together by centripetal force, its inner turmoil masked by the Comintern's strong hand and intolerance of differences. Abrupt policy shifts, intense faction-fighting and expulsions, rooted in or justified by Comintern politics, hampered practical work. At several points the Party's membership and influence were virtually decimated by this turmoil, and it had to rebuild itself almost from scratch. Despite the Comintern's destructive impact it retained its prestige, and members sought its advice in mediating internal differences, often using its statements to support their own arguments. The Comintern's existence as an external authority helped to ensure the CPSA's organizational unity and continuity.

In contrast to the CPSA's internal suppression of factions, Trotskyism in South Africa was characterized by a centrifugal tendency. The overriding aim of South African Trotskyists in the 1930s was to develop the programmatic and organizational unity necessary to lay the foundations for a working-class party. For a variety of reasons, they failed to do this. At the end of the decade the Trotskyist movement was organizationally fragmented, and had still not developed a unified programme of action and a common set of tactical slogans based on South African conditions. This disunity continued in the 1940s, and at the war's end Cape Town and Johannesburg Trotskyists stood on opposing sides in trade union disputes. By contrast, while the CPSA was periodically depleted by political vacillations and internal disputes, in the 1940s it recouped organizationally and helped to resuscitate the ANC.

The timing of Trotskyism's origins in South Africa exacerbated the impact of regionalism, which in turn reinforced its organizational fragility. Each Trotskyist group had a perspective coloured by specific regional peculiarities, focusing on aspects of South African society. In Cape Town, rival Trotskyist factions competed for the support of the black intelligentsia, which they saw as a means of disseminating political ideas to the urban and rural masses. Urban Trotskyists tended to argue for the significance of the proletariat, while those who organized in the countryside stressed the weight of the peasantry. On the Witwatersrand, Trotskyists were more active in trade unions than those in the Western Cape, where trade union work in the 1930s was the province of Communists.

Born in a period when the black protest movement had recently been crushed for its first efforts at collective class action in the late 1910s and 1920s, and when the socialist movement in South Africa was extremely weak, Trotskyists had great difficulty building a sustained relationship with the black working class, as did the CPSA through most of the 1930s. Organizational instability accentuated this problem. Trotskyists were caught in a vicious circle: on the one hand, their intense theoretical discussions of the 1930s reflected their search for a political programme of action. But their tiny numbers and their relative isolation from working-class struggles limited their ability to develop a concrete analysis based on experience and eventually led them to elevate theoretical abstractions to a programmatic level. Each Trotskyist group came to believe that they had found the correct theoretical blueprint for building socialism, and in this respect they replicated the dogmatic approach of the Comintern. Yet, while both Communists and Trotskyist laid their rival claims to the Russian Revolution, only the Communists could lay claim to the enduring Soviet state. For decades, this gave Communist Parties around the world a legitimacy that Trotskyists lacked.

The emergence of South African Trotskyism

Some of the socialists who rejected or were expelled from the CPSA quickly turned to the international Trotskyist movement. Frank Glass and Manny Lopes were in contact with Trotskyists overseas by 1930. They wrote to the *Militant*, organ of the Communist League of America (Opposition), criticizing the CPSA's lack of internal democracy and its position on the national question. Glass believed that the colour bar was relaxing and still saw white workers as the most advanced section of the working class; he blamed the Native Republic thesis for alienating them.[3]

For a couple of years in the early 1930s the Cape Town left retained some fluidity. There was still a degree of diversity and eclecticism amongst Cape Town socialists. In 1931 an array of socialists came together to form the International Socialist Club. Regulars included expelled Communists, such as Manny and Francis Lopes; Wilfred Harrison, who now styled himself a philosophical anarchist; Joe Pick; and David Dryburgh; together with assorted anarchists and social democrats and a few individuals from the Douglas Credit movement. The Lopes brothers ran a restaurant on Longmarket Street, which socialists frequented. By law the restaurant was divided into black and white sections but Francis Lopes would more often be found in the black section. Despite his expulsion from the CPSA, Manny Lopes continued to hold great sway amongst Cape Town socialists: he was able to grasp complex ideas of Marxist theory and explain them to others in an accessible manner. Two young brothers, Charlie and Herman van Gelderen, began attending the International Socialist Club. The van Gelderens were twin brothers of Dutch Jewish background, an unusual combination in South Africa, which meant that they did not fit in either with the overwhelmingly Calvinist Afrikaner community or with the predominantly Yiddish-speaking, Eastern European Jewish community. Raised in Paarl, around 1929 the van Gelderen family moved to Cape Town, where the brothers had their first contact with blacks as fellow workers. Like most South Africans, their point of entry into politics was through nationalism, specifically Zionism. In 1930 a Fabian Society was formed in the Western Cape, and Julius Lewin introduced the brothers to Fabian ideas; from that point they became interested in socialism.[4]

The International Socialist Club was a propagandistic group with a strong international orientation; in September 1931, for instance, it protested against Japan's invasion of Manchuria. The *Militant* circulated around the International Socialist Club's members, and a number of individuals decided to form a self-consciously Trotskyist study group, called the Marxist Educational League. This included Manny Lopes, Joe Pick, Moshe Noah Averbach, the Lunn brothers, the van Gelderens, a Coloured worker named Johannes Moses Beyers who joined the CPSA, studied in Moscow but moved to Trotskyism upon his return,[5] and a quiet man named Max Gordon.

Local anti-Trotskyism on the left was rife. In October 1932 Gina Medem arrived in South Africa at the invitation of the *Gezelshaft far Erd* (*Gezerd*), a predominantly Jewish, Yiddish-speaking CPSA-aligned organization meaning 'Go Back to the Land'. A brilliant Yiddish orator, Medem's mission was to promote the settlement of Russian Jews in Bira Bidjan. She also sought to eradicate the Trotskyist pestilence inside the CPSA and its linked organizations. Her impact on the South African Jewish community and on the Jewish left was extremely divisive. At a public meeting of the *Gezerd* Medem reputedly announced: 'Comrades of Trotsky cannot be our comrades. They are all expelled.' M. N. Averbach, who owned a small grocery shop in District Six, was treasurer of the Cape Town branch and refused to hand over the books; these were taken from him by force. The expelled members of the *Gezerd* set up a group called the Lenin Club – officially launched on 29 July 1933 – which was mainly Yiddish-speaking. Its main intellectual figures were Averbach and Yudel Burlak, a bookkeeper for a tobacco company who had allegedly been a member of the Lithuanian Soviet. Although neither was an effective public speaker, they were both impressive as lecturers and teachers in small groups, and each quickly attracted a number of acolytes.

Communist intolerance was seen in other circles as well. On 7 November 1932 the Marxist Educational League held a public meeting to commemmorate the anniversary of the Russian Revolution. The occasion was, Charlie van Gelderen recalls, his first introduction to 'Stalinism in the raw'. When members of the Marxist Educational League arrived at their pre-arranged venue, they found that local Communists had arrived there first and that Douglas Wolton was in the process of addressing a meeting. As the van Gelderens began distributing leaflets, Molly Wolton 'descended down on [Charlie van Gelderen] like bomb', and tore the leaflets out of his hand with the cry: 'Why are we allowing these agents of Lopes and Pick here?' A brawl ensued.[6] Van Gelderen's account was corroborated by none other than Eugene Dennis, the Comintern representative, who wrote to his superiors in Moscow that 'on the basis of our instructions, the DPC mobilized a large number of Party + non-Party workers and decisively smashed the gathering ... sending all leaders to the hospital. And that is that.' He hastened to add, however, that 'our struggle against the renegades is not confined to "smashups" but is basically an ideological campaign'.[7]

The Yiddish-speaking core of the Lenin Club was soon joined by individuals from the International Socialist Club and the Marxist Educational League, which both faded away. The Lenin Club included a number of Jewish intellectuals and workers, a few Coloured professionals and workers and several radicals from the University of Cape Town. Some of the regulars at its monthly meetings included the van Gelderens; David Schrire; J. G. Taylor, a psychologist, and his wife Dora Taylor, a writer. Two of those who attended its meetings, George Sacks and Benjamin Farrington, later became Communists. Farrington attended briefly, and lectured on dialectics, before departing for England and joining the CPGB.[8]

Isaac Bangani Tabata, who later led the Non-European Unity Movement, started attending meetings around 1933 with Goolam Gool and his sister Janub 'Jane' Gool. Tabata was the first African member, although he was soon joined by S. A. Jayiya.[9] Tabata, born near Queenstown, was educated at Lovedale and Fort Hare, where he had studied with Professor D. D. T. Jabavu. In 1931 he left university and moved to Cape Town, where he worked as a lorry driver, joining the Lorry Drivers' Union and becoming a member of its executive. He also joined the Cape African Voters' Association.

The Gools, like the Abdurahmans, to whom they were linked through marriage, were part of Cape Town's Coloured elite, 'singular exceptions in the general scheme of Coloured poverty', their home open to visiting dignatories such as Mohandas Gandhi and white artists and intellectuals.[10] Yet even for this stratum higher education was becoming more and more racially restrictive. When Dr Abdullah Abdurahman had been young, he had attended the South African College, the country's first secondary school, which later became the University of Cape Town. Subsequently, however, the South African College implemented a colour bar, and Abdurahman and his brothers finished their education in Britain. The extension of the colour bar in education motivated Abdurahman to help found Trafalgar High School in 1913. Seven of its first class of eleven students were Gools. Goolam Gool and his brother Abdul H. Gool later trained as medical doctors in Britain; their sister, Jane Gool graduated from Fort Hare, an environment that had kindled her interest in African politics, and taught primary school in District Six.[11]

In early 1934, a few individuals joined from the Independent Labour Party, an ephemeral offshoot of the local Cape Town Labour Party, which had broken from its national parent over its racial restrictions and which Manny Lopes had helped to found. These included Paul Kosten, an American sailor who landed in Cape Town in 1931 and who ran Modern Books, and Clare Goodlatte, a retired nun. Goodlatte was born in Ireland in 1866. She went to South Africa to teach in 1886, and was principal of the Grahamstown Training College from 1904–21. After her retirement she moved to Woodstock, Cape Town and became involved in local community affairs. She joined the local branch of the Joint Council of Europeans and Natives in 1930 and became its secretary in 1931. Around 1933 she met Manny Lopes and, increasingly attracted to socialism as an answer to the social injustice she saw all around her, joined the Independent Labour Party and became its general secretary. 'I cannot imagine any country *further* from Socialism than our South Africa', she noted at the time, 'but it is good to be at constructive work again and my heart is in it.' The next year, she moved to the Lenin Club. 'I feel wonderfully at home in the "Lenin Club"', she enthused to one of her former students. 'A learned Professor (of Classics!) at the University popped in one evening when we had a special lecture, and he said to me he had never met such a friendly mixture of all ranks and races.'[12]

In its first two years, the Lenin Club engaged in varied activities. Jane Gool and Millie Matthews ran a socialist Sunday school for children. The Club held a study class in District Six, at the offices of Abdul Gool. In 1934, the centenary of the abolition of slavery in South Africa, it organized a May Day rally on the Greenpoint common, producing its only known publication, *Workers of South Africa, Awake!*[13] On Wednesday evenings it held open-air meetings in Castle Street, outside the old Post Office.

Relations with the CPSA deteriorated. Cape Town Communists started a rival discussion circle called the October Club and that, like the Lenin Club, sought to attract and provide Marxist training for black workers.[14] The Lenin Club criticized the CPSA's intellectual intolerance, its lack of internal democracy and its subservience to Moscow but it nonetheless operated within the same political frame of reference. Its theoretical differences with the CPSA were often rhetorical. Thus, while it rejected the Native Republic thesis on class rather than colour grounds, arguing that peasants could not play a vanguard role in any South African revolution, it fell back in line with the CPSA's abstract conception of unity among black and white workers. Its argument was virtually identical to that made by Bunting at the 1928 Sixth Comintern Congress. The Lenin Club recognized the strong racial, economic and political divide between black and white workers, but believed that 'unless the white worker takes his courage in both hands and assists the Native to a position by his side', he – or she – would eventually face the same economic immiseration as the black worker.[15]

Like the CPSA's expulsions of Trotskyists and other dissidents, the early splits among Western Cape Trotskyists reflected political struggles and debates then taking place in Europe, sometimes centred around theoretical disputes, rather than programmatic differences regarding South Africa. William Ballinger attended a meeting in early 1935 but was not impressed. 'Wooly theoretical communists or rather Leninists', he described them. 'Critical of Communism and my "reformism". I challenged them to openly and publicly repudiate me. They are now left guessing. They are just academic theorists.'[16]

Despite the eclectic traditions that had merged into the Lenin Club, the promise of tolerance was not realized and the group was soon rent by internal tensions. Although couched in strategic and tactical terms, the growing rift coincided with personality differences and personal rivalries, revolving around Averbach and Burlak. According to Charlie van Gelderen, the precise reason for the initial division in the Lenin Club was inspired by the 1934 'French turn', which caused splits in Trotskyist organizations worldwide.[17] In 1934 the group divided into two factions. In early 1935 the Lenin Club formed the Communist League of South Africa (CLSA) but this split almost immediately when a faction led by Burlak, and joined by a number of Johannesburg Trotskyists, constituted itself as the Workers' Party of South Africa. This new group took over publication of the *Spark*, which had been in the planning stages since 1934; the first issue appeared in March 1935. In June 1935 the Workers' Party withdrew from the Lenin Club altogether and began running its own Spartacus Club and Spartacus Bantu Study Class to rival the Lenin Club.[18] The remaining members of what became the minority faction, grouped around Averbach, continued as the CLSA, with Goolam Gool in the chair. This ran the Lenin Club as a forum for public lectures and discussion, and from August 1935 to 1936 it produced a monthly called *Workers' Voice*. A few members made occasional excursions to the locations on Cape Town's outskirts that were reserved for Africans working in town. Whites were not allowed into the locations but as a medical doctor Goolam Gool had access to these areas, and Joe Pick and Charlie van Gelderen made semi-clandestine forays into Langa Location, hidden in the back of Gool's car.[19]

In Johannesburg, Trotskyism followed a slightly different path and was more oriented towards trade union work. Frank Glass had owned a bookshop there, which was the sole supplier of left-wing literature from overseas. In 1931 Glass left South Africa and turned over the bookshop to his wife, Fanny Klenerman. She reopened the bookshop on 17 April 1931 under the name Vanguard Books and continued to supply Trotskyist and radical literature.[20]

William Thibedi, who had been expelled from the CPSA in 1930, came into contact with Trotskyist ideas through the *Militant*. In early 1932 Thibedi formed a group that became known as the Communist League of Africa. The group was atypical of most subsequent Trotskyist groups in that all of its members were Africans; indeed, it was reputedly intended to be 'purely in African hands'. Thibedi evidently claimed to have about fifty members in Krugersdorp, Vereeniging, Brakpan and the Northern Transvaal.[21] The group began making contacts with Trotskyists overseas, and in April 1932 it wrote to the Communist League of America in New York, asking for additional copies of the *Militant* and for other political material and expressing particular interest in the Chinese situation.

Thibedi claimed that the racially-divided working class was the greatest obstacle to socialist mobilization in South Africa. They were an all-black group not by choice, he explained, but because of the paternalistic attitudes of white South African socialists. 'Comrades', wrote Thibedi, 'do not be worried in seeing all these applicants being negro and think that we are purposely refusing to unite with European comrades, no we are not. ... Negro workers are generally considered inferior even on such matters as revolutionary organizations, and as usual European workers are considered superior.'[22]

The American group forwarded copies of Thibedi's letter to Trotsky and to the International Secretariat of the Left Opposition in Berlin.[23] Both the American Left Oppositionists and Trotsky agreed that within revolutionary parties no distinction should be made between black and white. Trotsky was explicit on this point, cautioning that 'if the proletarian group works in a district where there are workers of various races, and in spite of this, it consists only of workers of a privileged nationality ... are we not dealing with the workers' aristocracy? Isn't the group poisoned by slave holding prejudices active or passive?' But Trotsky continued, '[i]t is quite a different matter when we are approached by a group of Negro workers. ... because of their whole position they do not and cannot strive to degrade anybody, oppress anybody, or deprive anybody of his rights. They do not seek privileges and cannot rise to the top except on the road of the international revolution.'[24]

The Communist League of Africa published a single issue of *Maraphanga*, then flickered out of existence. According to the Bolshevist Leninist League of Johannesburg, which appeared on the scene two years later, the Communist League of Africa 'finally collapsed through lack of experience, of political leadership and of perspectives'. Attempts to revive the group failed, although a training class for African workers was formed. The Bolshevist Leninist League was formally launched in April 1934 and included a few individuals recently expelled from the CPSA. Some of the members organized African bakery and laundry workers. In mid-1934 the group contacted the Lenin Club and in 1935 it merged with the majority of the Cape Town-based Lenin Club to form the Workers' Party. Thibedi continued to organize trade unions and spent a number of years organizing mineworkers, temporarily rejoining the CPSA in 1935.[25]

The issues that divided the Workers' Party and the CLSA were largely theoretical, rather than problems of immediate practical concern necessitating programmatic divergences or an organizational break. In fact, the theoretical similarities of the two organizations, and of all South African Trotskyist groups in the 1930s and 1940s, far outweighed their theoretical differences. Both saw the Soviet Union as a degenerated workers' state and believed that Stalin's regime was the political manifestation of this degeneration. Both endorsed the theory of permanent revolution. They believed that while the rural population would play a critical supporting role, only the urban working class could provide revolutionary leadership. Like Frank Glass a few years earlier, they believed that South African capitalism was heading towards a crisis that would force the bourgeoisie to break its historic pact with the white working class; that white workers and Afrikaner *bywoners* would be forced down to the economic level of blacks, and that it was the task of socialists to mobilize those groups for a common working-class struggle, rather than letting poor whites succumb to fascist ideology. Consequently, like Bunting and Roux in 1928, they rejected the Native Republic thesis on the grounds that it would alienate white workers and thus impede the development of a working-class movement united across the colour line.

The real difference between the two groups boiled down to one of emphasis on the nature and degree of peasant consciousness amongst the rural population and the degree of black proletarian development. The Workers' Party believed that social mobilization should be based on people's perceptions of their problems. The CLSA argued that socio-economic trends like proletarianization and urbanization should be the guideline for developing strategy. These two perspectives were not necessarily incompatible. The difference in emphasis and perspective stemmed from the fact that the two groups were focusing on distinctive aspects of the same broader phenomenon during a period of rapid socio-economic change in which social classes were in a state of flux. However, in elevating these different analytical perspectives to a level of importance that required an organizational split, they displayed the same intolerance of difference that the Comintern had promoted in the CPSA.[26]

The 1935 unification of Trotskyists in Cape Town and Johannesburg into the Workers' Party masked the real meaning of the Lenin Club's split. Whereas the CPSA demonstrated its intolerance of democratic debate and differences through expulsions, Trotskyist groups demonstrated theirs through splits. Almost from its inception the movement was displaying the traits that were to characterize it throughout subsequent decades. Trotskyist factions and groups used theoretical differences that generally had no programmatic implications and that would have been tolerated, and even welcomed, in a democratic and dynamic socialist organization, as a pretext for continuous splits. These splits weakened the movement's capacity to perform effective practical work. Such ineffectiveness in turn increased the propensity to split. Thus, despite sporadic intersections of the Trotskyist movement with popular upsurges, the movement was frequently isolated from significant struggles.

The Workers' Party and the land question

In 1934 the two factions of the Lenin Club drew up position papers on a number of issues – the Native question, the trade union question, the war question and the organizational question. Burlak wrote the theses for the majority faction; Averbach wrote the minority theses. The principal differences between the two factions were over the native question and the organizational question.

For the majority faction, the agrarian problem was at the root of the Native question. Influenced by Rosa Luxemburg's discussion of South Africa in *The Accumulation of Capital*, the majority faction took as its point of departure the distorted social relations on the land.[27] These were, it argued, the material basis for the oppression of blacks, for the racial division of the working class and for South Africa's economic stagnation. The skewed racial distribution of landholdings meant landlessness for the majority of blacks, forcing them to labour on mines and on white-owned farms. This huge pool of ultra-cheap black labour in turn was used to threaten white job security and push white wages down. Finally, the extremely low level of economic development of the majority restricted the domestic market and stunted industrial development. Burlak characterized the rural black population, even the agricultural proletariat, as a landless peasantry, and contended that black land-hunger would be the mobilizing force and the pivot of a permanent revolution, which must be led by a united black and white working class. 'Only the Revolution can solve this agrarian question, which is the axis, the alpha and omega of the revolution', he argued. 'It must be made clear to the workers and intelligentsia of South Africa, that the Native Problem, the Agrarian Problem, is *their* problem, that the liberation of the Native is *their* liberation.'

Despite the similarity between this argument and the Native Republic thesis, the majority faction argued that the Native Republic thesis subordinated the class struggle to the national struggle and insisted that '[a] man needs first of all bread, and then liberty. The Native needs first of all land, and then national emancipation. The national question is not the fundamental problem of our revolution; the agrarian question is and will remain the basic task.' Accordingly, the majority faction proposed two slogans around which they hoped to mobilize the black majority: 'Land to the Natives' and 'Every man has the right to as much land as he can work'.[28]

The African population was indeed overwhelmingly rural in the 1930s. Close to 83 per cent of all Africans lived in rural areas, either in reserves or other areas scheduled for Africans, or on white farms, and over 62 per cent of the men and 86 per cent of the women worked in agriculture and forestry.[29] Nonetheless, this in itself did not mean that their consciousness or aspirations were fixed in the countryside, given that the population was in a state of flux because of the migrant labour system. The thesis suffered from an overly quantitative analysis, overemphasizing the agrarian struggle because the black population was still predominantly rural, and overemphasizing the role of white labour because of its quantitatively greater role in urban industry. It assumed that political consciousness and aspirations flowed directly from material conditions.

The Communist League: fighting the colour bar

While the majority faction anticipated that continued rural stagnation would retard industrial development and proletarianization, the minority believed that economic development was actually hastening proletarianization. But like Burlak's group, the minority optimistically maintained that these objective processes would eventually equalize the conditions of black and white workers and translate into a class consciousness that would transcend colour divisions. The colour bar was seen as the foremost threat to the working class because it prevented a united anti-capitalist movement. Consequently, this became a focal point for the CLSA, as it urged socialists to organize black workers and fight the colour bar in exising trade unions. If white labour would not admit blacks, then black labour should organize independently.[30]

The solution to South Africa's pressing social problems lay not in agrarian revolution, the minority thesis argued, but in the direct overthrow of British imperialism, which underpinned the mining companies and their repressive labour policies. In the style of Bunting, the minority faction downplayed the progressive potential of rural blacks, claiming that the peasantry was politically backwards and 'has not once succeeded in offering resistance to the cruel oppression of the white slaveowners'.[31] The proletariat, it stated, was by far the most militant and organizable section of the black population. Nonetheless, urban workers needed the support of the countryside, and it envisioned that the Afrikaner peasantry would play an important anti-imperialist role due to its historic, anti-British sentiments. Since the national (Afrikaner) bourgeoisie had an interest in fighting the domination of British imperialism, 'the anti-imperialist sentiment of the countryside' must be used to overthrow British rule.

In its hope for a progressive role for Afrikaner nationalism, the CLSA underestimated the potential for this nationalism to be diverted to a purely reactionary path due to its racism. Thus, despite the CLSA's apparent rejection of the Workers' Party's stress on the land struggle as the pivotal point of the revolution, it in effect came to a similar position when it concluded that the the rural anti-imperialist struggle against British imperialism

> is the *first* stage of the struggle. Once, having got rid of the biggest bandit, we can turn our attention to the lesser bandit – the local capitalist class. We can then rally the workers of South Africa for the *final* struggle, the overthrow of capitalism and the setting up of workers' rule.[32]

Aside from the particular reference to the Afrikaner peasantry and bourgeoisie, this passage is remarkably close to the Native Republic thesis in its conception of an initial national, rather than class-based alliance against imperialism. In effect, both Trotskyist factions endorsed a two-stage revolution.

These theoretical arguments, which provoked acute political divisions, stemmed from the different vantage points and conceptions about the speed of economic development adopted by these groups in their analyses of South African political economy. The arguments of both groups rested on conceptions of proletarians and peasants mechanically transposed from what they believed to be Russian conditions, rather than derived from an observation of social classes in South Africa. These were then translated into strategic maxims. While the faction that formed the CLSA overestimated the ease with which black workers could be organized, those in the Workers' Party hardly discussed the issue. The CLSA's assertion that the black peasantry had never offered significant resistance was controverted by the fact that the major social upheavals across South Africa in the late 1920s had been rural protests: squatters and labour-tenants resisting proletarianization as well as agricultural workers fighting for better working conditions. By the same token, the Workers' Party's assumption that the Africans were predominantly a landless peasantry to be mobilized on the basis of land-hunger was probably too simplistic even in the 1930s, given the existence of an African proletariat, the rapid pace of industrialization and urbanization and the impoverishment on the reserves that was forcing people to accept wage-labour as their chief means of livelihood.

Both worked from a similar conception that economic development would eventually break through the fetters of racism. Their stress on the need for a united working-class movement of black and white workers, a viewpoint with which the CPSA concurred, underestimated both the enduring racism of the white working class and the material basis for that racism. Poor and working-class Afrikaners were indeed willing to break their formal links with British imperialism, but they steadfastly refused to give up the possibility of continued white privileges to align with black workers: in the mid-1930s white labour refused to associate with organizations that even called for black democratic rights, a harsh riposte to the expectations of both groups.

Linking the land and national struggles

By 1935 both factions, in the quest for programmatic unity, were asking the international Trotskyist movement to help mediate their differences.[33] The response of the International Secretariat to the majority thesis on the Native question, was written under the pseudonym of Dubois by Ruth Fischer, a founding member of the Austrian Communist Party and a leader of the left wing of the German Communist Party in the 1920s. The flaw of the thesis, Fischer argued, was that it failed to target British imperialism as the key problem. Although there was nothing inherently wrong with the slogan 'Land to the Natives', it was nonetheless inadequate because it was not linked to any other political slogan except the rhetorical call for a 'South African October'. In effect, she maintained, the majority faction's conception of the agrarian revolution lacked political content because it neglected the national question. The agrarian revolution, wrote Fischer, is inextricably linked to the national question. 'The thesis, instead of indicating the connection, neglects it, separating the two sides of the *same* question quasi-independently of one another.' For this reason, she concluded, the thesis was abstract and did not offer tactical guidelines.

The thesis spoke of the need to develop the class consciousness of black workers, without stressing the same need for white workers. Yet, the development of class consciousness amongst white workers would be signalled by their rejection of white privileges and their support for the struggle against British imperialism. Accordingly, Fischer maintained, the seemingly nationalist Native Republic thesis might not be antithetical to the socialist movement, given the absence, in the 1930s, of a black bourgeoisie.[34]

Fischer's argument represented one pole within the International Secretariat, which in 1935 acknowledged the 'two clashing viewpoints' its members held on the South African question. The first position endorsed the slogans 'Africa for the Negroes' and 'Independent Negro Republics'. Since, in this argument, all whites directly or indirectly exploited black labour, the social struggle would inevitably unfold along colour lines. While conceding that the black movement might be dominated by nationalist ideology, in all probability the class structure of the black population would push the movement in a socialist direction. But even a black nationalist solution was considered far less dangerous than white nationalism, which rested on racial privileges and the power of British imperialism.

The other viewpoint argued for 'the undiluted Marxist idea of the class struggle (the exploited and the oppressed against the exploiters and the oppressors)'. South Africa's white proletariat, it maintained, distinguished it from colonial countries like India or China. Although it was a labour aristocracy, white labour was nonetheless vulnerable to capital. Accordingly, black and white workers must unite against black and white nationalism on the basis of an agrarian revolution.[35]

Trotsky responded to the Workers' Party thesis in April 1935. He began his letter noting the dual nature of the South African polity: a dominion for whites and a slave colony for blacks. It was this social contradiction, he suggested, which gives the mass movement for democratic rights its revolutionary potential. Rejecting the claim that the national struggle was not the domain of socialists, Trotsky insisted that the proletarian party, one with a working-class base representing the distinct class interests of the proletariat, 'should in word and in deeds openly and boldly take the solution of the national (racial) problem in its hands'. The national liberation movement and the proletarian party were, he underlined, mutually interdependent: on the one hand, the democratic demands of the majority could be solved only through socialist revolution; on the other, the proletarian party could seize power only with the help of the oppressed majority. What distinguished the proletarian party from reformist organizations like the ANC, Trotsky maintained, was that its solutions were based upon working-class independence and the method of class struggle. While the proletarian party could cooperate tactically with populist organizations and must support them against state repression and racism, including the racism of white trade union bureaucrats, it must retain its own programmatic independence, showing the populace that reformist organizations could not even achieve their own reformist goals.

The solution both to the quest for democracy and to the agrarian problem, Trotsky continued, lay in the overthrow of British imperialism. However, he stressed that the proletarian party must propose solutions to these major social problems based on the method of class struggle, as opposed to the 'classless' anti-imperialist bloc then being advocated by the Comintern. Trotsky's criticism of the Native Republic thesis lay precisely in the fact that the slogan was premised on a multi-class alliance. Yet, he cautioned, the thesis was not analogous to the call for a white South Africa raised by white labour: 'whereas in the latter there is the case of supporting complete oppression, in the former, there is the case of taking the first steps towards liberation'. In the sense that revolution entailed the political awakening of the black majority, the overthrow of racist social relations and a political role for blacks proportionate to their numbers, the new state would for all practical purposes be a black republic. In this respect, any social revolution in South Africa, Trotsky stressed, would necessarily have 'a *national* character'.[36]

While Trotsky stressed principles and methods of struggle, the subsequent concerns of the International Secretariat were more explicitly programmatic. The International Secretariat's chief concern was the tendency of the young South

African Trotskyist movement to fragment. This tendency, it believed, would weaken attempts to build a working-class base. The International Secretariat unanimously condemned the Workers' Party's break from the Lenin Club as politically premature but, nonetheless, counselled the minority faction 'to preserve the unity of our ranks in South Africa, not to split over differences on the proposals of a party which is yet to be created, and to seek a solution of the conflicts in the ranks of the organization itself'.[37]

The International Secretariat argued that since South Africa's young Trotskyist movement had not yet developed a working-class base, a socialist league was more appropriate than a party, which presumed an organization with working-class support. It emphasized that parties could not exist merely by proclamation, but had to be built up over time through theoretical and practical work. It advised both Trotskyist groups to strengthen their organizations through coordinated activities as a step towards forming a party. It suggested establishing a joint action committee, creating an internal discussion bulletin, enlarging the *Spark* to include articles of interest to rural and urban blacks in Bantu languages, and maintaining regular contact with the international Left Opposition. After several months of joint work, the International Secretariat continued, the South African Trotskyists would be in a position to prepare for a party conference and to develop a common programme of action.[38]

The response of South African Trotskyists

Trotsky's letter, published as a pamphlet by the Workers' Party, had a significant political impact on the way that Trotskyists conceived the national question. Initially, the Workers' Party feared that Trotsky's stress on national self-determination followed the Soviet model too closely. Although the CPSA had put the Native Republic thesis on the back burner during the early part of the New Line period, the debate over the thesis had been revived in late 1931 following Molly Wolton's return from the Lenin School. Instead of calling for a single Independent Native Republic, a revised version of the thesis called for a federation of independent Native republics. This, of course, conflicted with the ANC's aim of transcending tribal divisions. But in the early 1930s, the South African government was trying to wrest control of Bechuanaland, Swaziland and Basutoland from Britain, and in that context, the call for a federation of independent Native republics of the Sotho, Tswana, Swazi, Zulu and Xhosa peoples had a certain logic. Sidney Bunting, for instance, was very impressed with the official Soviet position on multinational societies and around 1934 addressed the Lenin Club on the prospects of a continental federation of autonomous African states. But to Trotskyists – and subsequently to most Communists – such a slogan could only reinforce the national fragmentation fostered by the South African government and impede the building of a united anti-imperialist socialist movement.[39]

Over the next decade Trotsky's letter provoked intense discussion within both Trotskyist groups in Cape Town, and they used it as a basis for re-evaluating the relationship of the land and national struggles to the class struggle. From the late 1930s, all Trotskyist groups placed increasing emphasis on building a national movement for black democratic rights, seeing that as a starting point for building a socialist movement. First, they saw the national movement as a means of mobilizing the black majority around transitional demands that could form the basis for a permanent revolution. Accordingly, the Workers' Party changed its original slogan 'Land to the Natives' to 'Land and Liberty', reflecting the close interrelationship of the land and political struggles. And, while the CLSA had downplayed the role of the black rural majority, its successor, the Fourth International Organisation of South Africa, acknowledged the significance of the land question for social mobilization. A decade after Trotsky's letter, M. N. Averbach, who was then in the Fourth International Organisation, explained that the struggle for democratic rights, especially property rights, could be a turning point leading to a permanent revolution in that implementing the right to own land necessarily entailed the expropriation of large landholdings.[40]

Second, both Trotskyist groups continued to think that white workers were strategically necessary for a socialist struggle because of their position in the urban industrial workforce. But white workers could only be pulled from their alliance with capital to join black workers when they believed the latter to be strong enough to challenge the bourgeoisie. In this sense, as well, building a movement for black democratic rights was seen as a prelude to building a socialist movement. Averbach, for instance, wrote that 'it is absolutely essential that the great bulk of the South African population ... non-Europeans ... become an active, forward-striving, political movement, an independent force to reckon with. Only then will a real possibility be given to the White worker to help materialise socialism on a sound basis'.[41]

Trotsky's influence could also, arguably, be seen in the Ten Point Programme, a list of minimum democratic demands put forward in 1943 by the Non-European Unity Movement, in which the Workers' Party played a influential behind-the-scenes role. Whereas the early Workers' Party had seen the land question as the key to the political revolution, the Ten Point Programme presumed the political question, specifically the franchise (point 1), to be the key to the land question (point 7).[42] However, in its wording and conceptualization, the Ten Point Programme was very closely modelled on the nine-point democratic programme outlined by G. Plekhanov – the father of Russian Marxism – in the 'Second Draft Programme of the Russian Social-Democrats'.[43]

Despite Trotsky's theoretical influence on these local groups, at the practical level neither Trotskyist faction systematically followed the International Secretariat's recommendations for unity. Aside from their short-lived united-front activity in the late 1930s, Trotskyist organizations tended to work independently of each other despite parallel activities, such as organizing in African locations and in trade unions and running discussion clubs. Despite periodic unity talks, their relations were frequently antagonistic.[44]

Unity efforts

The Workers' Party and the CLSA made a few tentative stabs at unity talks. One inspiration for this was the need for united action against Italy's invasion of Abyssinia (now Ethiopia) in October 1935, following the failure of the League of Nations and international diplomacy to resolve the crisis. The invasion sparked massive protests in South Africa, where many Africans, Roux wrote, 'realised for the first time that there existed in Africa an independent country where the black man was master and had his own king. They were inspired by the idea of black men defending their country against white aggressors.'[45]

The International Secretariat saw the Abyssinian struggle as an opportunity for South African Trotskyists to strengthen their movement by uniting in a common struggle against both British and Italian intervention in Africa. It was imperative, argued the International Secretariat, that socialists took an unambiguous stance against foreign intervention in Africa in order to demonstrate '*that in addition to the white oppressors there also exist white revolutionaries who proclaim the right of every people to severe [sic] their ties to the imperialists*'. Socialists must make clear '*that the white oppressor has no business in Africa*'.[46]

The international campaign to support Abyssinia emphasized two types of sanctions against Italy: League of Nations-endorsed economic sanctions designed to prevent Italy from receiving specified war-related goods, and worker sanctions, in which workers withdrew their own labour to hinder Italy's war efforts.[47] The strategies were not mutually exclusive. But Trotskyists saw worker sanctions as a means of encouraging working-class independence and vigorously counterposed them to the League of Nations sanctions, which, they claimed, the CPSA and the Labour Party were endorsing.[48] By controlling the use of their own labour, they believed, black workers would become conscious of their class power. In October 1935 the CLSA informed the International Secretariat that

> We have put forward the slogan 'BOYCOTT FASCIST ITALY' and it is meeting with some success among the working class. ... Our last two open air meetings broke all records. Last week, over a thousand workers listened to our views on the Italian–Abyssinian war, and this week nearly two thousand workers were present.[49]

When Italian agents in South Africa tried to organize the shipment of food supplies for their troops in East Africa, the CLSA's organ, *Workers' Voice*, cried out: 'THE WORKERS MUST REFUSE TO HANDLE FOOD DESTINED FOR THE ITALIAN TROOPS. DEMONSTRATE AGAINST ITALIAN AGRESSION [sic] AGAINST ABYSSINIA!'[50] This was echoed by the *Spark*, which posed the choices as: 'INDEPENDENT WORKING-CLASS POLICY *OR* COLLABORATION WITH THE RULING CLASS', and called on workers to continue their protests.[51]

Black workers were doing just that. From June to August 1935 dockworkers in Durban and Cape Town refused to load goods on to Italian ships. Communists,

Trotskyists and a broad range of democratic forces gave their enthusiastic support to this action. In Cape Town, the League against Fascism and War organized a meeting attended by twenty-three organizations, including the Cape Fabian Society and the *Gezerd*. In September a Friends of Abyssinia committee was launched, in which William Thibedi, back in the CPSA, was involved. Massive demonstrations against the invasion continued into 1936.[52]

Socialist groups attracted popular interest and reaped huge propaganda gains from their support for and coverage of the Abyssinian struggle. Blacks were hungry for news of the war. Sales of the Communist Party organ, *Umsebenzi*, shot up to 7000 a week; the *African Defender*, a monthly paper established by the CPSA front organization *Ikaka labaSebenzi* sold out at 10,000 an issue. But Italian troops entered Addis Ababa in mid-1936, and by the year's end resistance had fallen apart. Once news of the defeat reached South Africa, popular interest in the Abyssinian struggle waned.[53]

While left-wing newspapers captured popular imagination, they were often merely echoing what workers were already doing. When blacks lost hope about the possibility of ousting the Italians, socialist groups had no practical alternatives to keep their interest. So, despite the popular appeal of their position on Abyssinia, Trotskyists were unable to translate their temporary propagandistic success into organizational gains or to build organizational unity. In January and February 1936 the minute CLSA wrote to the Workers' Party, appealing for unity talks and for joint action around the Italian–Abyssinian conflict and against the government's Native Bills curtailing African political rights. The entreaties fell on unsympathetic ears: the Workers' Party scorned the CLSA as social democratic.[54] Eventually, the CLSA collapsed and the Lenin Club disbanded itself in September 1936; a number of the remaining members, including its chairperson, Goolam Gool, joined the Spartacus Club.[55]

Indeed, the inability to build unity around this issue was the scourge of the left. In 1935 three Communists, John Gomas, Moses Kotane and Eddie Roux 'sent an urgent telegram to Moscow stating that the sectarian leadership was splitting the Party just when the Italian attack on Ethiopia made unity more than ever essential'. Like Trotskyists, Communists were still experiencing their own organizational problems, indicated by continual policy swings and expulsions.[56]

Propaganda and trade union work

In Cape Town, the Workers' Party's practical work was largely propagandistic, due both to its tiny numbers and the age and occupational profile of its own members. The group's secrecy and reticence undoubtedly limited its ability to expand its numbers. In its short public life it diligently published the *Spark*, which circulated in the rural areas of the Cape Province and became popular amongst Fort Hare students, despite some attempts by the college authorities to suppress it.[57] Isaac Tabata and Jane Gool organized in Langa Location. The lively Spartacus Club attracted a number of African members but in contrast to the crowds attracted by the Lenin Club's open-air meetings, the indoor Spartacus Club meetings generally appealed to a smaller audience. As Roux recalled, 'most of the "intellectuals," university people and so on, went to the Spartacist [sic] Club, while the others who wanted to hold street-corner meetings stayed with the Lenin Club'.[58]

The Spartacists produced a number of didactic musical plays performed to small audiences at Oddfellows Hall in Loop Street, in Cape Town's city centre. One play, entitled *The Spark*, was performed in November 1937 to commemmorate the October 1917 revolution in Russia. Its first act was set in 1913, after the passing of the Natives Land Act, and it told the plight of a young African couple, Lukosi and Anna, after their decision to move to the city.[59]

The Workers' Party's efforts to reach factoryworkers were also largely propagandistic. This contrasted with the work of a handful of Cape Town Communists like Ray Alexander. Communists were responsible for a spate of industrial trade union organization from the late 1930s in the Western Cape and Natal, reflecting the post-depression and wartime expansion of secondary industry that pulled in blacks and whites, including Afrikaner women. Sometimes black and white were in the same unions; in other cases Communists organized parallel black and white sections, unable to bypass the strict colour bars of many unions. This was a period characterized by the impressive growth of black trade unions.[60]

Prompted both by the large proportion of Coloured workers in Cape Town, for whom Afrikaans was the mother tongue, and by the rapid movement of newly-proletarianized Afrikaners into factory work in the 1930s, the Cape Town Workers' Party began publishing propaganda in Afrikaans. In 1937 it produced an Afrikaans translation of *The Communist Manifesto*, commemorating the ninetieth anniversary of its writing, with a preface by Trotsky.[61] As Clare Goodlatte and Paul Koston explained to the International Secretariat, 'revolutionary literature is not yet to be found in the Afrikaans language ... so that this effort will open up a whole new field of propaganda for Marxism and the Fourth International'.[62] And to Trotsky, Goodlatte idealistically wrote:

> We have hope of the revolutionary movement developing among the factory workers, of whom the Afrikaans-speaking are the most numerous. As yet we are too few to make much progress; but, if the movement can once gain a footing in the factories, even this land of oppression and repression will yet produce a worthy section of the Fourth International.[63]

The Workers' Party tried to organize other branches but only one, in Johannesburg, managed even a tenuous footing. In contrast to the Cape Town group's propagandistic orientation, the tiny Johannesburg branch made more attempts at industrial organization, reflecting the relatively greater strength of trade unionism on the Rand. Fanny Klenerman, who became a Trotskyist after her expulsion from the CPSA, commented on the difficulties of setting up the Johannesburg branch: 'We did not attract large crowds to join us. ... there had never been a large

Comm. Party, so when a group was set up in opposition to the Communists, people were not politically aware enough to understand the issues and differences between us & the Communists.'[64]

Two of the first members of the Johannesburg branch were Ralph Lee and Dr Murray Gow Purdy from the Bolshevist Leninist League. In its first year the group went through personal conflicts, expulsions and resignations that were reminiscent of the CPSA's internal turmoils.[65] A leading African organizer, C. B. I. Dladla, joined in 1936, after being expelled from the CPSA. The Johannesburg branch wrote to the International Secretariat about the particularly arduous process of building a social-ist movement in South Africa. In the West, it pointed out, the working class had already been exposed to political ideas and discourse through the normal workings of democratic political systems. But in South Africa, the low level of mass education made socialist propaganda work a difficult and time-consuming task. Their senti-ments echoed the frustrations evidenced by Bunting a decade earlier:

> With agonising slowness we have added to our circles one by one and this has meant direct personal propaganda. Where in other countries a kind of clear-ing has been effected by the liberal bourgeoisie, by reformists, by Stalinists, we are in this country faced to a large extent by virgin jungle. Those who have already had some grounding in political theory make up altogether only a tiny handful – among natives only a few intellectuals have the necessary grasp of the language to be reached by our written propaganda and these few are subjected to an ideological bombardment from the churches, the Chamber of Mines, the bourgeois nigrophiles and the African nationalists, not to mention the privileges which Imperialism is enabled by its incredible super profits to dole out to submissive native leaders.[66]

Like its Cape Town counterpart, the tiny Johannesburg branch was predomi-nantly middle class in social composition. 'One was a doctor educated in S. Africa', recalled Fanny Klenerman. 'A few students belonged, & one or two pro-fessional people'. But, she added, '[w]e had very few contacts with working people, & therefore could not influence them'.[67] The Johannesburg group estab-lished a local Spartacus Club that held social and educational activities and daily lunch-hour lectures, and it also tried to reach African mineworkers. Max Gordon, who became the leading trade unionist on the Rand in the 1935–40 period, arrived in Johannesburg in 1935 and began organizing mine clerks into a General Workers' Union as a prelude to relaunching the African Mine Workers' Union that Thibedi had built. Heaton Lee, a former Communist and a mine surveyor, sold the *Spark* on the mines. In 1936 the Johannesburg branch began publishing *Umlilo Mollo (Flame)*, on which Ralph Lee and C. B. I. Dladla worked. This was geared to an African audience and contained a number of letters from minework-ers and metal workers. However, it ceased after a few months due to lack of funds.[68]

Eventually the Johannesburg branch attracted a few African workers. 'We did get some worker members', Fanny Klenerman noted, 'some of which [sic] were miners; they came to our public meetings (we were not permitted to go into the workers' compounds)'.[69] The attendance of even a few black mineworkers was seen as a great coup by the Johannesburg branch. As it explained to the International Secretariat: 'The main task that confronts the proletarian party ... is the organising of the totally unorganised native miners. ... The native miners union, given revolutionary leadership, is the battering ram that will smasch [sic] down British Imperialism in South Africa.'[70]

But the Johannesburg group's work was not sustained. In part this reflected objective difficulties. As the group had recognized, organization of black mineworkers proved to be a daunting task. In 1935 and 1936 Thibedi was back organizing mineworkers for the CPSA. But in November 1937 Gana Makabeni and C. B. I. Dladla confided to the visiting African-American scholar Ralph Bunche that almost no organizing was being done in the mining compounds, where African workers were housed, because of the difficulty organizers had in gaining entry. Indeed, Makabeni argued that Africans should be organized first in the reserves.[71] The view was echoed by the Workers' Party: 'The native miners. ... are almost out of reach of propaganda, not only through ideological difficulties (language, illiteracy, political inexperience and backwardness) but also through physical difficulties – they are virtually imprisoned in the "compounds" under police guard most of the time they are above ground'. Yet the group also saw in these conditions the potential for rapid social mobilization:

> [T]he intense concentration of numbers ensures the rapid spread of militant revolutionary doctrines once they are introduced. The experience of past movements (the African National Congress, the I.C.U.) has demonstrated that a revolutionary platform propagated by a determined band of agitators finds enthusiastic support among the miners. ... There are the first signs now of a revolutionary upsurge among the native workers (isolated spontaneous strikes, an increased confidence to the trade revival and the diminishing of unemployment).[72]

Moreover, political activists faced real harassment from the authorities that interrupted their work. Dladla was detained for agitational work around the Vereeniging case where, in September 1937, Africans had attacked police who were raiding the township. A number of Africans were wounded in the battle, 450 arrested and eleven finally convicted. An official inquiry later found that police mistreatment had contributed to the original uprising.[73] Ralph Bunche described a scene at Western Native Township near Johannesburg where

> a young comrade was speaking in defense of Dhladhla [sic] who is in jail for contempt of course [sic] because of public comments on the Vereeniging case which is still in court. A small, diffident group stood by, while a stern looking, rain-coated European C. I. D. man stood a few feet away and was the most alert listener.[74]

But the sporadic nature of the group's work was not due to objective difficulties alone. The organization's internal dynamics also played a role. A few members, such as Ralph Lee and Millie Kahn, were involved in trade union work. But the Workers' Party was far from wholehearted in its support for Max Gordon's systematic shop-floor organizing. He withdrew from the group in September 1935 because of its continuous internal wranglings.[75]

In the late 1930s, the most significant trade union work on the Rand was not that of organizations but of individuals – the Trotskyist Max Gordon and the former Communist Gana Makabeni. Both revived and rebuilt the black trade union movement, which had been decimated by the CPSA's New Line and its expulsions of leading trade unionists. In addition to Gordon's efforts to resuscitate the African Mine Workers' Union, he revived the Laundry Workers' Union and reorganized or launched a number of other unions. In 1938 Gordon formed the Joint Committee of African Trade Unions, a federation that began with affiliates from the African laundry, commercial, baking and printing industries. Gordon's approach was to attract workers by winning higher wages but to avoid the high-risk tactic of strikes. He made representations to the Wage Board and won cases for underpayment and wrongful dismissal. In this he had assistance from A. Lynn Saffery of the Institute of Race Relations and William Ballinger of the Society of the Friends of Africa. This had been founded in 1934 by Winifred Holtby, with members in Britain and South Africa; Julius Lewin was secretary. The Friends of Africa concerned itself with the working conditions and remuneration of black workers and professionals and pressed for the recognition of black trade unions and for the abolition of the industrial colour bar, the pass laws and the poll tax and for improved access to education. It also sought to draw attention to the conditions of rural blacks. Although relations between the Friends of Africa and both the CPSA and the Trotskyists were strained, Ballinger worked with Eddie Roux on a number of occasions in the 1930s and, similarly, Gordon had no compunction about drawing on Ballinger's trade union experience.[76]

The use of the Wage Board had pitfalls, as Baruch Hirson has pointed out, in that the unions could only obtain wage increases at the government's behest. Once wages were pegged, the unions inevitably lost members.[77] Nonetheless, Gordon felt that by gaining small reforms at the start, he would be able to put the unions on a stable basis. The strategy bore fruit: his Joint Committee rapidly expanded. He also organized meetings for unemployed workers, arranged legal and medical assistance for workers and ran a night school that offered literacy, maths, bookkeeping, and history, at which Fanny Klenerman taught. The young writer Peter Abrahams, who knew Gordon, believed that 'his determined refusals to turn his unions into part of the Left faction fight made him unpopular with the majority of his comrades. The African workers, on the other hand, trusted him.' Indeed, his closest professional contacts were Ballinger and Saffery.[78]

Gordon's cautious organizing style was in marked contrast both to the CPSA's earlier New Line agitational style and to that of his fellow Trotskyists. Ralph Lee's venture into trade union work was indicative of the dominant Workers' Party approach to trade union work. In January 1937 Lee and a few other Workers' Party members organized the African Metal Trades Union, of which Lee became secretary. This went on strike almost immediately when the workers' employer, SCAW Works, refused to recognize it. The workers' were ill-prepared for the strike, which was not successful; most of the strikers lost their jobs. The expenses engendered by the strike hit the tiny Workers' Party hard: they had to vacate their 'relatively spacious premises at 90 President Street, and ... move into a small room in Fox Street'. Indicative of the Workers' Party's fragile state, a few months after the strike, in mid-1937, a number of white members involved with the strike emigrated to Britain.[79] Even in 1938, a year after the African Metal Trades Union disaster, the few remaining members rejected Gordon's approach to trade unionism. Their trade union work would 'not be done in the style of Gordon', wrote Max Sapire, the Workers' Party's secretary. In Sapire's view, Gordon was a bureaucrat who had lost control of his bureaucracy.[80]

Despite some creative first steps, the Workers' Party's internal wranglings and small numbers precluded it from sustained practical activity. Its difficulties in continuing the practical work of members like Gordon and Dladla, as well as the failure to establish a joint programme of action with other Trotskyist groups, impeded its ability to build a socialist cadre in the locations and at places of work. Around 1939 another transitory Trotskyist group, the Socialist Workers League, appeared in Johannesburg. Despite its strident criticism of both the Workers' Party and the CPSA, its own theoretical position was quite close to both.[81]

By mid-1939 the small public face of the Workers' Party was veiled. Its views on the need for underground activity had been one of its main contentions with the CLSA, which believed that open political work continued to be possible in South Africa. Trotsky, too, emphasized the need to continue open political work as long as possible, although suggesting that a legal organization be complemented by an illegal apparatus that could carry on underground work, if necessary. In actuality, he argued, socialists working in mass organizations like trade unions often had to operate semi-legally in the sense that such work had to be done with extreme caution in order to bypass the trade union bureaucracy, whose interests lay solely in reformist, rather than revolutionary, work.[82] The Workers' Party was not convinced. In June 1939, fearing that South Africa was on the verge of fascism, it ceased publishing the *Spark* and went underground, its members never again speaking openly of socialism. Nonetheless, its influence on black intellectuals, especially in Cape Town, would continue through its relationship with a radical discussion club called the New Era Fellowship and, later, through its involvement with the All African Convention and the Non-European Unity Movement.[83]

Conclusion

The organizational fragmentation of the early Trotskyist movement reflected the harsh social and political conditions of the day, which made any effort at socialist organizing a tortuous task. But the actions of these tiny Trotskyist groups formed a pattern typical of the broader South African socialist movement: short bursts of intense activity followed by withdrawal. Typically, the withdrawal could take two forms. Some members simply retired from politics. But white Trotskyists had another option, which was not available to blacks – that of leaving South Africa. A number of white Trotskyists emigrated to Britain and became involved in Trotskyist groups there.[84]

Those Trotskyists who continued to engage in political activity resisted coming to terms with the problems of political and organizational unity. They elevated theoretical disputes that had no immediate practical implications for South Africa to a programmatic significance, and used these disputes as a pretext for organizational splits or for refusing to participate in joint campaigns. In this respect, the South African Trotskyists mirrored the Comintern obsession with dogma. Moreover, in terms of theory, black workers saw little to distinguish the Trotskyists from the Communists; they were more interested in practical assistance from socialist organizations. The view of Naboth Mokgatle, a Pretoria trade unionist, was probably not atypical. He recalled that Ralph Lee and Millie Kahn tried to set up a branch in Pretoria but that they gave up after several weeks. Mokgatle was attracted to the CPSA, not because he perceived any ideological difference between the two groups, but because the CPSA had set up a night school in Pretoria that functioned successfully for several months until it lost its premises.[85]

Although the 1930s had opened with some evidence of diversity amongst socialists outside of the CPSA, by the end of the decade, the socialist movement had bifurcated around the two poles of the Third and Fourth Internationals. Numerous individuals entered the CPSA and the Trotskyist groups in the 1930s, only to be expelled or to withdraw. In the absence of any other left tradition, the harsh political landscape offered no shelter to individuals outside the organizations upholding those orthodoxies. Perhaps the paradox of Sidney Bunting's death in May 1936 encapsulated the situation. Bunting's expulsion from the CPSA had precipitated the breakdown in his health that led to his death. Nonetheless, he remained a 'true believer' to the last. He believed that the problems that devastated the CPSA and that led to his expulsion in 1931 were caused by a few misguided if not malevolent individuals, rather than by the Comintern's insistence on obedience to orthodoxy. 'In spite of the way he was treated', wrote Eddie Roux shortly after Bunting's death, 'Bunting's loyalty to the Party remained unswerving. ... He would have no truck with the Trotskyists. He believed that time would prove the correctness of his views'.[86] By the close of the 1930s, the socialist movement was split into two tendencies both of which believed that they had found the one true path to socialism and that time would prove them right.

Notes

1.   Leon Trotsky, 'The Permanent Revolution', [1930] in Leon Trotsky, *The Permanent Revolution and Results and Prospects*, London: New Park, 1962, 1–157; Leon Trotsky, 'Preface to the 1930 French edition' and 'The Draft Programme of the Communist

International – A Criticism of Fundamentals', in Trotsky, *The Third International After Lenin*, xi–xvi and 1–175, esp. 3–56.

2. This chapter is based in part on my article, 'Events were breaking above their heads: Socialism in South Africa, 1921–1950', *Social Dynamics*, 17, 1, June 1991, 49–77 and my introduction to *South Africa's Radical Tradition*, vol. 1, 23–7. Background on the early Trotskyist movement is drawn from an interview with Charlie van Gelderen by Baruch Hirson and Brian Willan, 1974, School of Oriental and African Studies, University of London, tape 837; and interviews with Baruch Hirson, London, March 1987; Kenny Jordaan, Harare, December 1987; Solly Herwitz, Cape Town, March 1988; Herman van Gelderen, Cape Town, September 1989; and Charles van Gelderen, Cottenham, Cambridge, July 1997. See, *inter alia*, Franz J. T. Lee, *Der Einfluss des Marxismus auf die Nationalen Befreiungsbewegungen in Sudafrika*, Frankfurt am Main: Selbstverlag, 1971; Franz J. T. Lee, *Sudafrika vor der Revolution?*, Frankfurt am Main: Fischer Taschenbuch Verlag, 1973; A. J. Southall, 'Marxist Theory in South Africa until 1940', M. A., University of York, 1978; Baruch Hirson, 'The Trotskyist Groups in South Africa', Baruch Hirson, 'The Trotskyists and the Trade Unions', Baruch Hirson, 'Profiles of Some South African Trotskyists', and Ian Hunter, 'Raff Lee and the Pioneer Trotskyists of Johannesburg', all in *Revolutionary History*, 4, 4, Spring 1993, 25–56, 84–92, 93–7 and 57–83, respectively.

3. C. F. Glass, 'The Labour Movement in South Africa', *Militant*, March 29, 1930, 5 and 'The Durban "Raid" in South Africa', *Militant*, April 12, 1930, 5. Manuel Lopes, 'A Tribute from a South African Militant', *Militant*, June 7, 1930, 4. See also Hirson, 'Death of a Revolutionary'; and Simons and Simons, *Class and Colour*, 325–6.

4. Interview with Charlie van Gelderen; Ballinger to Holtby, 21 November 1930, Holtby Collection, folder 4.12, item 21.

5. According to Professor Valentin Gorodnov, Institute of Universal History, Russian Academy of Sciences, Moscow, Johannes Beyers worked variously in a printing house, transport firm and tobacco factory and as a waiter. He joined the CPSA around 1933, helped organize unemployed workers, and studied at the KUTVU in Moscow in 1934. According to Charlie van Gelderen, Beyers was disillusioned by his experience in the Soviet Union, and after his return to South Africa in late 1934, he joined the CLSA. In the mid-1930s he worked as a printer and editor on the *Workers' Voice*.

6. Interviews with Charlie van Gelderen and with Lilian Dubb. Quotes from Charlie van Gelderen. On Gina Medem see 'God or Baal?' and 'Soviet Government "Out to Kill Religion"', *The South African Jewish Chronicle*, 7 October 1932, 665 and 672 respectively; Irena Klepfisz, *'Di mames, dos loshn/*The mothers, the language: Feminism, *Yidishkayt* and the Politics of Memory', *Bridges*, 4, 1, Winter/Spring 1994, 12–47, esp. 27–23. My thanks to Lilian Dubb for this material.

7. Letter from Dennis, 16 November 1932, 8, RTsKhIDNI, 495.64.120.

8. Baruch Hirson, '*Spark* and the "Red Nun"', *Searchlight South Africa*, 1, 2, February 1989, 65–78, esp. 74.

9. Interview with Charlie Van Gelderen by Hirson and Willan; Southall, 'Marxist Theory in South Africa', 34.

10. Peter Abrahams, *Tell Freedom: Memories of Africa*, London: Faber & Faber, 1954, 273.

11. Everett, 'Gool', 2–3. Interview with Minnie Gool Friedrichs, Cape Town, July 1999.

12. Quotes from Hirson, '*Spark* and the "Red Nun"', 73, and Letter from Clare Goodlatte to John Chapman, September 6, 1934, 4, item 45, Clare Goodlatte Papers, MSB.618, 1 (5), South African Reference Library, Cape Town.

13. Lenin Club, *Workers of South Africa Awake!*, 4, British Library.
14. Over the years, this was attended by Ray Alexander, Jack Simons, Bill Andrews, Jack Cope, Sam Kahn, Johnny Gomas, Jimmy La Guma, Abdul Gool, Cissie Gool and Oscar Mpetha, amongst others. Everett, 'Gool', 10; Interview with Jack and Ray Simons.
15. Lenin Club, *Workers of South Africa Awake!*. See also Southall, 'Marxist Theory in South Africa', 33–34.
16. Ballinger to Julius Lewin, 14 February 1935, Holtby Collection, file 4.12, item 58.
17. Interview with Charlie Van Gelderen by Hirson and Willan. In 1997 Van Gelderen maintained that tensions between English and Yiddish speakers lay behind the split. See also Hirson, '*Spark* and the "Red Nun"', 75–6. On the French turn see Leon Trotsky, 'A Program of Action for France', June 1934, 21–32; 'The League Faced with a Turn', June 1934, 33–38; and 'The League Faced with a Decisive Turn', June 1934, 39–44, all in *Writings of Leon Trotsky, 1934–35*, New York: Pathfinder Press, 1974.
18. The main figures in Burlak's group were Paul Koston, Clare Goodlatte, D. Schrire, I.B. Tabata and Jane Gool. Charlie van Gelderen argues that when Burlak's group first broke from the Lenin Club, they comprised a minority of the Club's members. However, the Workers' Party very soon attracted the majority of Lenin Club members. Workers' Party of South Africa Papers, AG2722, A (History), Historical Papers Library, University of the Witwatersrand.
19. Interview with Charlie van Gelderen by Hirson and Willan; Minutes of International Secretariat of the International Communist League (B.L.), 7 May 1935; 'The Lenin Club', *Workers' Voice*, 1, 3, October 1935, 9. The main individuals in Averbach's faction included Joe Pick, Charlie and Herman van Gelderen, Bernard Hertzberg, Harry and David Lunn, Billy Duncan, Joe Urdang, Rose Schur and Goolam Gool.
20. Fanny Klenerman, 'The Bookshop', unpublished memoirs.
21. Letter from [Eugene?] Dennis to comrades, 22 October 1932, RTsKhIDNI, 495.64.79. The group was originally called the Communist Party of Africa. By August 1932 it had changed its name to the Communist League of Africa (Left Opposition). Little is known about the members. One member, Rapalana J. Tjekele was probably the Jacob Tjelele who had been elected to the CPSA's Central Executive in 1927. Alphies Maliba was no doubt Alpheus Maliba who later joined the CPSA. Frans (or France) Mopu and Lucas Malop (or Malupi) were associated with Makabeni's attempt to organize an internal faction in the CPSA in 1932.
22. Letter from T. W. Thibedi to Communist League of America, 26 April 1932, in Drew, ed., *South Africa's Radical Tradition*, vol. 1, 124–5, 125.
23. Letter from T. W. Thibedi to Leon Trotsky, 10 August 1932 and Letter from Leon Trotsky to T. W. Thibedi, 4 September 1932, both in Drew, ed., *South Africa's Radical Tradition*, vol. 1, 129–31.
24. Leon Trotsky, 'Closer to the Proletarians of the "Colored" Races', June 13, 1932, in Drew, ed., *South Africa's Radical Tradition*, vol. 1, 127–8, 128. See also Baruch Hirson, 'Trotsky and Black Nationalism', in Terry Brotherstone and Paul Dukes, eds, *The Trotsky Reappraisal*, Edinburgh: Edinburgh University, 1992, 177–90.
25. 'International Communist League formed in South Africa', *International Bulletin of the International Communist League*, New Series, 2, September 1934, in Drew, ed., *South Africa's Radical Tradition*, vol. 1, 133–4.
26. For overviews of the differences between the two groups see Lenin Club, *Draft Thesis: The Native Question* (Majority) [1934] and Lenin Club, *Draft Thesis: Introduction* (Minority) [1934], both in Drew, ed., *South Africa's Radical Tradition*, vol. 1, 134–40 and 141–44;

'We Smash this Bogey', *Workers' Voice*, 1, 3, October 1935, 9; and 'A Preliminary Discussion on the Native Question', *Workers' Voice*, 1, 6, February 1936, 6–8.

27. Interview with Neville Alexander, Cape Town, July 1987. Rosa Luxemburg, *The Accumulation of Capital*, New York and London: Monthly Review, 1968, 411–16.

28. Lenin Club, *Draft Thesis: The Native Question*, 139. Emphasis in the original.

29. Department of Economics, Natal University College, 'The National Income' and van der Horst, 'Labour'.

30. Lewis Wade, 'Smash the Colour Bar!' and Shop Steward, 'The Trend of Events in the Trade Union Movement', both in *Workers' Voice*, 1, 5, January 1936.

31. 'A Preliminary Discussion on the Native Question', 8.

32. 'We Smash this Bogey'. My emphasis.

33. The minutes of the International Secretariat of the International Communist League (B.-L.), 7 May 1935 acknowledge receipt of theses from both Trotskyist factions in Cape Town.

34. 'Remarks of Comrade Dubois', Internal Bulletin of the International Communist League (B-L), no. 2, May 1935, in Drew, ed., *South Africa's Radical Tradition*, vol. 1, 152–3.

35. International Secretariat of the International Communist League, (B-L), Minutes of meeting, 23 April 1935, in Drew, ed., *South Africa's Radical Tradition*, vol. 1, 151–2.

36. Leon Trotsky, *Remarks on the Draft Theses of the Workers' Party of South Africa*, 20 April 1935, in Drew, ed., *South Africa's Radical Tradition*, vol. 1, 146–51, quotes 148 and 147. Although the People's Front was formally adopted at the Comintern's Seventh Congress in August 1935, the policy was already developing in many Communist Parties by the time of Trotsky's letter.

37. International Secretariat of the International Communist League, (B-L), Minutes of meeting, 23 April 1935, 152.

38. Letter from the International Secretariat of the International Communist League (B-L) to Communist League of South Africa and Workers' Party of South Africa, 24 July 1935, in Drew, ed., *South Africa's Radical Tradition*, vol. 1, 154–6. See also V. I. Lenin, 'What is to be Done?', in Christman, ed., *Essential Works of Lenin*, 53–175, esp. 69.

39. Interviews with R. O. Dudley, Cape Town, April 1988 and Charlie van Gelderen. The letter of the Workers Party of South Africa of 20th June, 1935, to Comrade L. D. Trotsky, Workers' Party of South Africa Papers, AG2722, D3, Historical Papers Library, University of the Witwatersrand.

40. A. Mon [M. N. Averbach], 'A Comment on Trotsky's Letter to S.A.', *Workers' Voice*, 1, 3, July 1945 in Drew, ed., *South Africa's Radical Tradition*, vol. 2, 297–304.

41. A. Mon [M. N. Averbach], 'The Colour Bar and the National Struggle for Full Democratic Rights', *Workers' Voice*, 1, 2, November 1944, in Drew, ed., *South Africa's Radical Tradition*, vol. 1, 321–6, 324.

42. Hosea Jaffe has argued that Trotsky's influence on the Ten Point Programme is seen in the accent on the national question, namely, full voting rights and equality; in the stress on the relationship between the national and land questions; and in the linking of British imperialism and Afrikaner capitalism, as opposed to the early CLSA argument that the Afrikaner peasantry and aspiring bourgeoisie could be a progressive, anti-imperialist force. Interview with Hosea Jaffe, London, February 1987. See also Leon Trotsky, 'Le probleme national et les taches du parti proletarien', in *Leon Trotsky Oeuvres Janvier 1935 – Juin 1935*, intro. by Pierre Broué and Michel Dreyfus, Paris: Institut Leon Trotsky/Etudes et Documentation Internationales, 1979, 242–52, n. 18.

43. Interview with Alexander; G. Plekhanov, 'Second Draft Programme of the Russian Social-Democrats' [1887], *Selected Philosophical Works*, vol. 1, London: Lawrence &

Wishart, 1961, 406–10.

44. On Trotskyists' attacks on each other (and on Communists), see, *inter alia*, 'We Smash this Bogey' and the Workers' Party's apology for 'the making and publishing of certain false and defamatory matter … against the honour and integrity of the members of the General Council of the National Liberation League', *Spark*, 5, 5, May 1939, 4.

45. Roux, *Time Longer than Rope*, 302.

46. Letter from International Secretariat, International Communist League (B-L) to the Workers' Party of South Africa and the Communist League of South Africa, 12 October 1935, in Drew, ed., *South Africa's Radical Tradition*, vol. 1, 157. Emphasis in the original.

47. On Italy's invasion of Ethiopia and the sanctions campaign see Alberto Sbacchi, *Ethiopia under Mussolini: Fascism and the Colonial Experience*, London: Zed, 1985 and Basil Davidson, *Let Freedom Come: Africa in Modern History*, Boston and Toronto: Little Brown, 1978, 181. League of Nations sanctions depended upon the support of member nations. But Sbacchi, p. 230, notes that 'sanctions were limited, slow to work, and only partially supported. The United States never joined the boycott. In the short run, stock-piling and strict regulation of the economy allowed Italy to absorb these irritations without damage to the African campaign. Mussolini played on British and French fears in his threat of a European war should sanctions be extended to oil.'

48. Within the Comintern, the issue of worker sanctions became controversial. See C. L. R. James, *World Revolution 1917–1936: The Rise and Fall of the Communist International*, London: Martin Secker & Warburg, 1937, 387–9. According to James, then a Trotskyist, in August 1935 the Comintern came out for League of Nations sanctions at the IFTU Congress in Brussels and sidelined the issue of worker sanctions at its Seventh Congress, even before internal Ethiopian resistance had ended. In South Africa, the League Against Fascism and War supported League of Nations sanctions. *Umsebenzi* continued to endorse dockworker protests. See 'Refuse to Ship Goods to Abyssinia! Defend the Last Independent Native State in Africa from the Attacks of Italian Imperialism! An Appeal to the Harbour Workers of South Africa', *Umsebenzi*, June 22, 1935, and 'Native and Coloured Workers' Anti-war Strike – Refuse to Load Italian Ships at Durban and Cape Town,' *Umsebenzi*, September 7, 1935, both in Bunting, ed., *South African Communists Speak*, 123–4 and 124–5.

49. Extract of a letter of 24 October 1935 from the COMMUNIST LEAGUE OF SOUTH AFRICA, *Press Service of the International Secretariat, International Communist League (B-L)*, 15 November 1935 in Drew, ed., *South Africa's Radical Tradition*, vol. 1, 157–8; For the CLSA's critique of the CPSA position, see 'United Front with God', *Workers' Voice*, 1, 3, October 1935, 6–7.

50. 'The Drive Towards War', *Workers' Voice*, 1, 2, September 1935.

51. 'To the Workers of South Africa', *Spark*, 1, 8, November 1935.

52. 'HANDS OFF ABYSSINIA!' and '"The Friends of Abyssinia": New Organisation to be Formed', both in *Umsebenzi*, 21 September 1935, 1 and 2 respectively; 'Meetings', *Umsebenzi*, 16 November 1935, 2.

53. Roux, *Time Longer than Rope*, 302–3; Cope, *Comrade Bill*, 328; Simons and Simons, *Class and Colour*, 474.

54. Letter from the Communist League of South Africa to the Workers' Party of South Africa, 13 January 1936; Letter from the Communist League of South Africa to the Workers' Party of South Africa, 18 February 1936; Letter from the Workers' Party of South Africa to N. J. Barclay, 21 February 1936, all in Drew, ed., *South Africa's Radical Tradition*, vol. 1, 158–61.

55. Letter from the Workers' Party of South Africa, Cape Branch, to the International Secretariat, 10 October 1936, Workers' Party of South Africa Papers, Mayibuye Centre Historical Papers Archive, University of the Western Cape.

56. Roux and Roux, *Rebel Pity*, 146; Simons and Simons, *Class and Colour*, 475–7.

57. Minutes of the meeting of the Workers' Party of South Africa, Cape Town Branch, held at 99 Hatfield St. on Monday, 18 May, 1936, beginning at 6 p.m., Workers' Party of South Africa Papers; Letter from *Spark* to M. S. Njisane, Flagstaff, 15 September 1938 in Drew, ed., *South Africa's Radical Tradition*, vol. 1, 178–9.

58. Roux, *Time Longer than Rope*, 312.

59. *Spartacus Club October Revolution Celebrations*, in Drew, ed., *South Africa's Radical Tradition*, vol. 1, 174–6; *Spartacus Club May Day Celebrations 1938*, Workers' Party of South Africa Papers.

60. Roux, *Time Longer than Rope*, 329–31; Callinicos, *Working Life*, 155.

61. Trotsky's preface, 'Ninety Years of the Communist Manifesto', is translated and published (except the last paragraph) in Isaac Deutscher, ed., *The Age of Permanent Revolution: A Trotsky Anthology*, New York: Dell, 1964, 285–95. A copy of the Workers' Party pamphlet is in the CPSA Collection, Hoover Institution Archives, Stanford. There is no information as to how many pamphlets were actually produced or how widely they were distributed. The Workers' Party had also hoped to translate the Manifesto into Xhosa and Zulu, but this was never accomplished, according to R. O. Dudley, due to the difficulties of translating the vocabulary and concepts.

62. Letter from Workers' Party of South Africa to the International Secretariat of the International Communist League (B-L), 11 April 1936, in Drew, ed., *South Africa's Radical Tradition*, vol. 1, 165.

63. Letter from C. R. Goodlatte to Leon Trotsky, 4 January 1938, Trotsky Archives, item 1585, Houghton Library, Harvard University; see also Minutes of the meeting of the WPSA, Cape Town Branch, held at 99 Hatfield St. on Monday, 18 May 1936.

64. Fanny Klenerman, 'The South African Workers Party', unpublished memoirs.

65. Conflicts developed between Purdy and Lee; Purdy was expelled in June 1935. In August 1935 Lee dissolved the minute group and reconstituted it with a few different individuals. Others resigned. Hunter, 'Raff Lee', 70–72.

66. 'Afrique du Sud', *Service d'Information et de Presse de la L.C.I. (B.L.)*, no. 4, 20 July 1936, 27.

67. Klenerman, 'Political Groups', unpublished memoirs.

68. Hirson, *Yours for the Union*, 41–5; Klenerman, 'Max Gordon and the S. A. Worker's Party', unpublished memoirs.

69. Klenerman, 'The South African Workers Party', unpublished memoirs.

70. 'Afrique du Sud', 27–28.

71. Bunche Collection, box 65. Ralph Bunche was a political science professor at Howard University in the 1930s and a winner of the 1950 Nobel Peace Prize for his work on behalf of the United Nations. In late 1937 he spent three months in South Africa as part of a broader research trip funded by the Social Science Research Council. His travel notes are in the Ralph Bunche Collection, Special Collections Department, University Research Library, University of California, Los Angeles. Bunche's South African notes are also in Robert R. Edgar, ed., *An African American in South Africa: The Travel Notes of Ralph J. Bunche: 28 September 1937 – 1 January 1938*, Athens, OH: Ohio University and Johannesburg: Witwatersrand University, 1992; see 1–42 for background on Bunche.

72. 'Afrique du Sud', 27–28.

73. Simons and Simons, *Class and Colour*, 498–9.
74. Bunche Collection, box 65.
75. Hunter, 'Raff Lee', 72.
76. Wickens, *Industrial and Commercial Workers' Union*, 185–6; Brittain, *Testament of Friendship*, 252; circular letter from Ballinger and Roux, 28 March 1934, Holtby Collection, file 4.12, item 52.
77. Hirson, *Yours for the Union*, 42–9.
78. Abrahams, *Tell Freedom*, 258. See also Roux, *Time Longer than Rope*, 326–34; Mark Stein, 'Max Gordon and African Trade Unionism on the Witwatersrand, 1935–1940', in Eddie Webster, ed., *Essays in Southern African Labour History*, Johannesburg: Ravan, 1978, 143–57; Klenerman, 'Max Gordon', unpublished memoirs.
79. 'Letter from the Workers' Party of South Africa, Johannesburg, to the Cape Town branch, 26 August 1937', in Drew, ed., *South Africa's Radical Tradition*, vol. 1, 173–4, quote 173. The members who went to Europe included included Ralph Lee, Heaton Lee, Millie Kahn and Richard Freislich. Interview with Millie Haston, London, May 1991.
80. 'Letter from the Workers' Party of South Africa, Johannesburg, to Cape Town comrades, 2 November 1938', in Drew, ed., *South Africa's Radical Tradition*, vol. 1, 180.
81. The Socialist Workers' League saw the Workers' Party as black nationalist and the CPSA as white chauvinist. But its own programme echoed views held by the CPSA's right wing in mid-1936: 'Our road can only lie in the steady and patient organisation in parallel lines of both sections of the population, drawing them ever closer as objective conditions make this possible, and in the steady spread amongst *both* sections of our revolutionary propaganda and agitation on the basis of the class struggle.' It justified this proposal on the grounds that 'we are compelled to compromise in our tactics of approach [to white workers] in order that we may at least get a hearing, that we may be able to put our point of view'. See *Statement of Policy and Programme of Work for South Africa and Rules and Regulations of the Socialist Workers League submitted for joint discussion*, [1939?], Trotsky Archives, item 16596.
82. Trotsky, *Remarks on the Draft Theses*, 151. Interestingly, the Workers' Party did not include these concluding remarks when it published Trotsky's letter. The CLSA scorned the Workers' Party's position on illegal organization in 'We Smash this Bogey'.
83. As the Workers' Party explained: 'The position is clear. From one side comes the war danger, to be followed immediately by martial law; on the other side the Press law makes the existence of a revolutionary organ like the "Spark" impossible as a legal paper. It will have to go the way of the revolutionary press in Tsarist Russia 50 years ago … the period of legal existence in bourgeois democracy is over.' See 'The Workers' Movement Faces a New Road', *Spark*, 5, 6, June 1939, 1–5. See also Roux, *Time Longer than Rope*, 312.
84. Murray Gow Purdy left South Africa in the late 1930s, finally settling in India where he formed a succession of tiny Trotskyist groups. See Charles Wesley Ervin, 'Trotskyism in India, Part One: Origins through World War Two (1934–45)', *Revolutionary History*, 1, 4, Winter 1988–89, 22–34. Ted Grant left South Africa in 1934; he later became a leader in the Militant Tendency which worked inside the British Labour Party until its proscription in the mid-1980s. The influx of South African Trotskyists to Britain in mentioned in Sam Bornstein and Al Richardson, *The War and the International: A History of the Trotskyist Movement in Britain 1937–1949*, London: Socialist Platform, 1986, 2–3.
85. Naboth Mokgatle, *The Autobiography of an Unknown South African*, Parklands: A. D. Donker, 1971, 192–7.
86. E. R. Roux, 'S. P. Bunting', *Forward*, 28 May 1936, 5.

Chapter 8

Inquisition and recantation

In the future it seems we shall have one right.
When all other freedom is taken away,
The right to get drunk on a Saturday night.
And lie in the gutter till break of day.

The Congress is broken and I.C.U. dead
And Bunting deported across the foam
And everyone who's the least bit red
Is spending his time in a 'government home;'

Tho you've taken our vote in the Cape, and tho
with tear gas bombs you're collecting your fines
It will thrill dear old liberty doubtless to know
We still may get drunk on South African wines![1]

Eddie Roux's ironic lyrics signalled the state of affairs for South African blacks in the mid-1930s. May 1933 saw the election of a coalition government formed by the National and South African Parties and led by General Hertzog as Prime Minister and Jan Smuts as deputy; in December 1934 the two parties merged to form the United South African National Party. The Fusion Government, as it was known, came face to face with the effects of the Great Depression. This had hit South Africa at full force when speculation over whether it would follow Britain off the gold standard precipitated a flight of capital. In May 1935 the Fusion Government tabled two bills in Parliament: the Representation of Natives Bill and the Native Trust and Land Bill. Known as the Hertzog Bills, the first bill curtailed the Cape African franchise and called for the creation of a Natives Representative Council (NRC) with solely advisory status on so-called Native issues, while the second reaffirmed the restricting of African landholding rights to scheduled areas.[2]

The government's erosion of African rights ignited black political activity while Italy's invasion of Abyssinia in October 1935 turned black attention to international affairs and to the threat of fascism in an African context. That year saw the emergence of the first long-term alliance of the black petty bourgeoisie, working-class and rural masses in South African history, one which attempted to cut across the sectional divisions imposed by the state. Proportionately, the black petty bourgeoisie was tiny. Its meagre ranks included a few small shop owners, merchant traders, struggling artisans and teachers, in which Coloureds and Indians predominated. Whites dominated virtually all professions, aside from teaching and religion, and in 1936 less than one per cent of all medical practitioners, advocates, attorneys, dentists, chemists, architects and engineers were black.[3]

Nonetheless, the black petty bourgeoisie's relative access to education and to a limited franchise in the Cape had hitherto given it predominance in black political organizations. Now its movement towards the working class reflected both the loss of its relative privileges and the growing strength of urban black workers, which manifested itself in militant collective protest. Neither the ANC nor the ICU could lead this movement. The ANC was virtually defunct under the conservative leadership of Pixley ka Izaka Seme, and the ICU was in a state of decay and fragmentation, despite some localized support in Natal.[4] Hence, the movement was expressed through the formation of new organizations like the All African Convention, the National Liberation League and the Non-European United Front. The absence of a black bourgeoisie in the 1930s meant that these cross-class organizations turned largely on the relationship between petty bourgeoisie and proletariat. Socialists hoped that these new organizations could provide the basis for an anti-imperialist movement under working-class leadership.

Alongside the emergent black mass movement, urban and rural whites struggled against unemployment and poverty as the depression swept rural Afrikaners off the farms and into the cities. Small-scale Afrikaner farmers lost their land and took up factory work, or sent family members – often daughters – to town to stave off complete proletarianization. In towns, they came into direct competition with black workers, who were also streaming in from the reserves. Afrikaner women and African men were the newest members of the urban industrial workforce. But the urban white working class was also economically ravaged in the 1930s. In 1932 the Carnegie Commission published the findings of its study of poor whites – a joint project financed by the Carnegie Corporation of New York, the South African government and the Dutch Reformed Church. The government's response was to implement a programme of state-led job creation for whites. Afrikaner nationalists and fascists sought to capture this white social base; socialists hoped to counteract this. Communist policy aimed to unite white workers and poor peasants with the black democratic movement into a broad anti-fascist People's Front.

In this aim, the CPSA reflected the influence of the Comintern's People's Front policy. This response to the advances of fascism in Europe was implemented against the backdrop of the rising use of political terror within the Soviet Union.[5] The Nazi seizure of power in 1933 was a disaster for the Comintern. Its New Line tactics were ineffectual at halting this reactionary onslaught and, indeed, were seen by some as facilitating it. In February 1934 French Communist tactics began to shift when French Socialist and Communist workers formed a united front against fascism. This turn was encouraged by George Dimitrov, a Bulgarian Communist who served as the Comintern's secretary from 1934 to 1943. Dimitrov envisioned the People's Front as a national movement to break the class alliance of peasants, workers and finance capital that, in his view, underpinned fascism. The People's Front, in turn, rested on the proletarian united front, which sought united action by all workers irrespective of their organizational affiliations. Dimitrov argued that the proletariat must build an alliance with the petty bourgeoisie and peasantry by appealing directly to their class interests, while also aiming to divide poor peasants and shopkeepers from rich peasants and businessmen. He even suggested that Communists penetrate fascist organizations in order to draw away the peasants and workers.[6] The CPSA tried to implement the People's Front policy in South Africa; however, its own distinctive movement away from the New Line policies, which was accompanied by vituperous wrangling, reflected specifically South African dynamics and preceded the Comintern's adoption of the People's Front policy.

The CPSA in the 1930s

In the mid-1930s the CPSA was in no position to take advantage of the resurgence of black political activity. Although it had begun to recover from the nadir of the New Line period, when its membership had dropped to about sixty, in 1933 it claimed only about 150 members located mainly in Johannesburg and Cape Town, the Durban branch having all but vanished. '*Shortage of forces is the* main obstacle in our way of development towards mass work', complained a member of the CPSA Politburo in December 1933.[7] In terms of numerical strength, the gap between Communists and Trotskyists was probably smaller at that point than at any subsequent time. By contrast, the CPGB's low point of November 1930 had seen its membership reduced to 2555 but by November 1932 this had climbed to 5600; yet that was tiny both relative to Britain's large proletariat and by European standards.[8]

The CPSA's Fourth Plenum in February 1933 had seemed comradely in tone, despite frank criticisms of those comrades deemed to be 'passive' or 'inactive'. Its goal of building the CPSA into 'a mass semi-legal party on a national scale' was certainly overambitious given its small numbers and high turnover. But there was broad agreement amongst the more experienced members on the need to develop underground methods, particularly in light of the increasing legal repression facing political activists and of the mass arrests and deportations in Natal. There was also agreement on the need to link the Native Republic slogan to daily struggles. The Party was trying to build *Ikaka labaSebenzi* into a mass organization open to anyone willing to fight for free speech and democratic rights – ironically, this had been Sidney Bunting's vision for the League of African Rights before the Comintern had ordered it disbanded a few years earlier! But the Plenum's ambitions were not realized. Despite the Party's involvement in a number of popular campaigns in 1932 and 1933, it was not able to make organizational gains. By late 1933 there were signs of growing tension within the Party about its failure to grow.[9]

Much of the blame was attributed to the Woltons, whose hasty departure in August 1933 had left the Party in the lurch. Factions coalesced around the problems of how to explain and to overcome the Party's isolation. Ostensibly, the factional divisions revolved around divergent interpretations of two related issues, the nature of the Native Republic and the existence of an African bourgeoisie. The original

1928 thesis had viewed the Native Republic as a stage towards a workers' and peasants' government, although many Communists had tried to downplay the distinction between the stages. By 1934 Lazar Bach was equating the Native Republic with
a workers' and peasants' government on the grounds that the achievement of a
Native Republic depended on an alliance of those two classes. This view identified
an African bourgeoisie that included moneylenders, established traders, and owners
of rental properties, buses or small shops with hired labour who made money out
of African workers. The African bourgeoisie's anti-imperialist interests were overshadowed by their potential to exploit black workers and peasants, indicated by the
fact that no African nationalist organization was currently raising the slogan of a
Native Republic. In fact, the argument ran, black workers and peasants had more
in common with white workers and poor peasants, who also suffered from imperialist exploitation, than with this African bourgeoisie.[10]

The other principal interpretation of the Native Republic thesis was articulated
by Moses Kotane, who had joined the CPSA in 1929 and become a full-time Party
functionary in early 1931, working as a compositor on *Umsebenzi*. Later that year
he was sent to study at the Lenin School in Moscow, along with Albert Nzula.
Kotane finished his studies in late 1932 and arrived back in South Africa in early
1933. He was shocked at the Party's parlous state. Along with like-minded individuals such as Eddie Roux, Johnny Gomas and Josiah Ngedlane, Kotane challenged
the CPSA's isolation from popular organizations and emphasized the need for a
broad alliance of blacks. He argued that the black majority should be mobilized on
the basis of democratic demands. For Kotane, a black republic based on an alliance
of workers and peasants would solve the democratic tasks through a democratic revolution even though it could not solve the socialist tasks placed on the historical
agenda by the presence of an industrial proletariat. Even amongst Kotane's supporters, however, there were differing interpretations of the thesis. Johnny Gomas,
for one, felt that 'the line of Katane [sic] is Too right and that of the others TOO
left'.[11] As it turned out, of the various positions outlined by the South African comrades, Kotane's would coincide most closely with the Comintern's People's Front
policy.

Behind the intellectual disputes were personal ambitions that were cultivated
through the suppression of democratic methods. Between 1932 and 1934 power
within the minute CPSA became highly centralized in the Politburo, which simultaneously functioned as the head of allied organizations such as *Ikaka labaSebenzi*
and the remnants of the AFTU.[12] Political education dwindled with the collapse of
the Party's night school in the early 1930s. With the Woltons' departure, Bach
shored up his own base with the support of Louis Joffe, who enjoyed some influence as financial secretary, and he gained the backing of Stephen Tefu and Peter
Ramutla, two Pretoria trade union organizers whom Roux described as 'genuine
workers, rather rough proletarians, not tribalist but location born'.[13] Bach and his
coterie – his opponents maintained – controlled the dissemination of information
to enhance their own power. Several years later, Kotane described 'a sickness that
exists in the CPSA since 1931'. Comintern documents were not circulated but were

'just known to the PB, and sometimes not to the whole PB, but to the Secretariat'. Like Roux, Kotane criticized the relationship between the CPSA and the Jewish Workers' Club, complaining that the latter's members knew more about the Party than did most Communists. 'I know it will be denied, but it is a fact', Kotane insisted. 'People outside the Party know more of what is taking place in the C.P. than Party members.'[14]

On Kotane's return from Moscow in early 1933, the Wolton–Bach leadership had insisted that he go into hiding under an alias in Sophiatown. This left him effectively isolated. However, later that year, the balance of power on the Politburo shifted. The departure of Albert Nzula, John Marks and Edwin Mofutsanyana to study in Moscow and of the Woltons to Britain had depleted the Party's leadership. The tiny number of trained cadre meant that those who had been marginalized were once again needed. Eddie Roux and Kotane were reinstated to the Politburo, along with two Cape Town Communists, Johnny Gomas – secretary of the Cape Town District Party Committee – and Josiah Ngedlane. Bach, secretary of the Durban Party Committee, was now in a minority on the Politburo. Kotane also took over as general secretary and as political editor of *Umsebenzi*, working with Roux.[15]

Kotane began steering the CPSA in a more popular direction. In early 1934 *Umsebenzi* began appearing every week. It became more readable, and its circulation increased. That year it ran a series entitled 'What is the Communist Party?' which devoted several articles to the nature of the Native Republic.[16] Kotane came out of hiding and began to travel around the country, becoming more than ever convinced that Bach's interpretation of the Native Republic thesis was leading the CPSA down a dead end. 'There is a potential radical force in the country', he maintained, 'but because of the suspicion of the Natives towards the whites. ... and the lack of forces to carry out revolutionary struggle and propaganda', mass political consciousness could only be developed through an anti-imperialist national liberation movement.[17] Hence, his call in February 1934 to Africanize the Party and for 'a conference of African radicals throughout the country ... to consider the question of a united front'.[18]

However, the internal divisions continued, and the CPSA's own efforts to mediate its factional divisions failed. As in the 1920s, the problems were centred in Johannesburg. On 24 and 27 May and on 2 June 1934 the Johannesburg District held a special meeting on the factional problem. The meeting was marked by the use of political discourse for personal ends. Kotane charged that '[t]he differences in the P.B. are due to mistakes committed in 1931–32 and certain comrades deny that mistakes of a leftist character were made'. In the process of Bolshevization the leaders smashed everything and 'even adopted the ridiculous attitude of wanting physical fights at every meeting, against people who did not agree with them'. That was the root of the present problem, he claimed. Bach's opposition to change reflected 'a fight for position and ... against Native leadership'. Clearly, for Kotane, political education in Moscow was the key factor in the formation of an African leadership. Despite the Party's past claims of having had African leaders, 'they had no understanding but just had black faces'. Only now was it possible to speak of an emerging African leadership, Kotane insisted. 'The C.P.S.A. must develop a Native ideology and outlook.' But the division was not simply one of black versus white. Although Ramutla, for one, held the white comrades responsible for the present disagreements, he 'protest[ed] against any person coming along and saying that the whites are against the Native leadership'. And he resented the fact that 'leading comrades, e.g., Kotane, tell people that I am Bach's puppet'. The meeting ended on an extremely polarized note.[19]

Over the next months Kotane continued to emphasize the differences between the 'Independent Native Republic' and 'Workers' and Peasants' Government'. The first was the appropriate slogan for the anti-imperialist stage, he believed. Bach, Ramutla and Tefu, he maintained, tried to reduce the tasks of the South African working class to proletarian struggles. And he added:

> I categorically declare that there is no Native bourgeoisie in South Africa, but a petty bourgeoisie and that the exploitation of the toiling Native masses by this petty bourgeoisie IS VERY INSIGNIFICANT compared to the exploitation of the Anglo-Boer imperialist bourgeoisie. This petty bourgeoisie in my opinion is more oppressed and exploited than it itself oppresses and exploits.[20]

The dispute remained unresolved. John Marks and Edwin Mofutsanyana returned from their studies in Moscow in August and September 1934. They resumed their seats on the Politburo, shifting the balance of power back to the Bach faction. As Mofutsanyana explained to the ECCI, he and Marks 'found the Party in a sad state'. The Johannesburg branch was now composed overwhelmingly of inactive whites and had only four African functionaries, two in each faction. Although Bach had 'certain left tendencies', his interpretation of the thesis was closer to that of the Comintern, Mofutsanyana believed. Kotane was planning to launch an anti-imperialist organization 'on national-reformist lines', claiming that 'the Natives ... had no confidence in the CP'. This was, Mofutsanyana responded, 'a logical continuation of Buntingism' and echoed Bunting's reformist efforts in the League of African Rights.[21] Early in 1935 the debate spilled over onto the pages of *Umsebenzi*. On 2 February one Party member, the journalist Gilbert Coka, wrote to the paper querying the existence of the African bourgeoisie. Marks swiftly penned a reply to Coka, pointing to 'the Native businessman and trader in every location from Nigel to Randfontein'. Roux and Mofutsanyana entered the fray.[22]

Now, just as the Comintern was moving towards the formal adoption of the People's Front policy, those dominating the CPSA leadership turned the Party in the other direction. Since Kotane's supporters were engaging in fractional activities, Mofutsanyana explained, the Politburo had no recourse but to expel them. In July 1935, Coka was expelled; in September, another spate of expulsions took place. Issy Diamond was suspended for three months for his support 'in converting the Party into a sort of democratic organisation', and Kotane, Ngedlane and Roux were removed from the Poliburo, which now consisted of Bach, Kalk, Marks and Mofutsanyana, the new general secretary. Roux lost control of *Umsebenzi*, and his wife Winifred, secretary of the Friends of the Soviet Union, was subjected to a campaign of isolation by Bach and Joffe. Mofutsanyana, aligned with Bach and his supporters, represented the official CPSA leadership; against them stood Kotane, backed by some of the Johannesburg branch and by Roux and the Cape Town District Party.[23]

The Bach faction called a public meeting at the Jewish Workers' Club to explain the expulsions. Mofutsanyana spoke on behalf of the Politburo, and Roux, for those, including Kotane, who were dubbed 'the opposition'. For the first time, Roux publicly regretted his silent complicity in the earlier vilification and expulsion of Bunting.[24] With the dispute now out in the open, both factions turned to the Comintern.

The Comintern and the South African Commission

Cables and letters flew back and forth between Moscow, Johannesburg and Cape Town. On 14 September Kotane, Roux and Gomas – the opposition – cabled Moscow asking it to intervene immediately to resolve the factional disputes. Three days later the Politburo sent a cable accusing the opposition of splitting the Party. A third cable was sent to A. Z. Zusmanovich at the KUTVU with details of the expulsions. On 20 September ten members of the opposition sent an open letter to the ECCI and all CPSA members. Gomas penned two letters on 16 and 26 September. On 23 September Moscow demanded that the expulsions cease and that two leaders from each faction come to Moscow. Indeed, the Comintern had been calling Bach and Kotane to Moscow for some time.

Kotane had not initially heeded the Comintern's earlier calls, later alleging that he had not seen the official request, but he had eventually left for Moscow in August. Lazar Bach had gone to Moscow and was sent to the KUTVU where he completed a course. Maurice Richter was deputed to represent the Politburo, even though he was not a member, and he was accompanied by his brother Paul. The Richter brothers were members of the Johannesburg branch of the Party. Both in their twenties and, like Bach, of Latvian origin, they lived in the Orange Free State and were well known in Kroonstad, where Paul was nicknamed 'Pinkie'.[25]

On 15, 17 and 19 March 1936 the Anglo-American Secretariat of the Comintern, under the leadership of French Communist André Marty, held a commission in Moscow to investigate the long-standing problems in the CPSA.[26] In reality, the findings of the South African Commission merely underlined what Marty and his personnel had already decided before the testimony of the South African comrades was given.[27] The aims of the South African Commission were to synchronize the CPSA's policies with those of the Comintern and to obtain the necessary obedience of the South African comrades. Chief amongst Marty's complaints were that the CPSA had not sent any official delegates to the Seventh Congress nor adequately publicized its directives in *Umsebenzi*.[28] The 'scholastic discussion' about the Native Republic and the African bourgeoisie had led to the CPSA's isolation, Marty believed, and to serious political miscalculations. The Party had underestimated the potential of both African and Afrikaner nationalism to align with the working-class struggle and, as a result, had developed hostile relationships with nationalist organizations.[29] Moreover, it was pursuing a sectarian line within the trade union movement. These mistakes, continued Marty, were made by both factions, and were aggravated by A. Z. Zusmanovich and I. I. Potekhin of the KUTVU, who had worked with the South African students and whose writings, it was deemed, promoted a point of view that went against the ECCI's official policy. This factional struggle had shattered Party discipline and hampered practical work. Hence, the necessity of 'a programme of action for the eradication of all elements of the fractional and scholastic discussion' and for new leadership. 'In choosing the leadership of Party organs and, above all, of the Central Committee of the Party', Marty stipulated, 'it is necessary to nominate comrades who have been indisputably connected with the country, who have been tested in working with the masses and who have shown … that they have definitely adopted the line of the VII Congress'.

In order to ensure the development of an adequately-trained cadre, Marty proposed that six to ten CPSA members be sent to study at the KUTVU. These would include four or five Africans, one or two Afrikaaners, one or two English-speakers and one Indian.[30]

The Commission began with a discussion of South African conditions and of the CPSA's factional differences. Moses Kotane complained that he had been kept isolated in 1933–34 and had been general secretary in name only. He emphasized that it was necessary to mobilize Africans on the basis of a broad anti-imperialist movement, as their needs went beyond trade union organization. Given the difficulties of building a movement in racially-divided conditions, Kotane indicated that organizing parallel black and white movements might be a way forward:

> By developing a parallel movement, when taking into consideration the prejudices that exist, we will be able to develop a wider movement on both fronts. … We should create a tie between them through the European section which should support the demands put by the Natives. In the trade union front, there is no question about unity. I stand for a parallel movement, where we cannot get the Natives in.[31]

Richter spoke next, claiming that 'a great deal is the fault of the opposition'. But whatever the outcome of the debate on the Native Republic thesis, he stated, the Comintern must provide clear theoretical guidance on any slogan adopted and 'there must not be a loophole for anybody to interpret it in any other way'.[32] Lazar Bach, however, adopted a more conciliatory approach, conceding that the CPSA had not understood the significance of the Seventh Congress resolutions and therefore had not popularized them. He believed that a rapprochement between the two factions was possible.[33]

But for Kotane, the theoretical differences masked the real issue, which concerned practical work. 'The differences', he argued, 'came from the general work and policy of the work among the workers, and also the organisations.' Bodies such as the *Ikaka labaSebenzi* and the Friends of the Soviet Union were meant to be mass organizations. Instead, they were dominated by Communists and became 'duplicate Communist Parties'.[34]

Josie Mpama was also present at the South African Commission. Mpama, a domestic worker who had first demonstrated her organizing skills in Potchefstroom, had been admitted to study at the KUTVU and was determined to go, against the wishes of her husband, Edwin Mofutsanyana. However, she had had difficulties getting a passport, and Tilly First, who had been given a holiday to Yalta in recognition of her husband's financial contributions to the CPSA, allegedly helped her obtain a passport, allowing her to travel as a servant. The two women arrived in Moscow in late 1934 or early 1935. Mpama took up her studies at the KUTVU and attended the Seventh Congress. She was subsequently asked to attend the Commission.[35]

Mpama did not come out clearly for either faction. On the one hand, she was critical of the opposition – particularly Roux, of whom she was scathing and who, she maintained, should not have a leading position in the Party. Yet, she criticized the leadership for allowing the opposition to use *Umsebenzi*, and confirmed that Kotane had been kept isolated and that the Politburo had not communicated with the branches. 'As a whole', she stated, 'our South African Party had a wrong line.' She bemoaned the lack of political education, especially for African members. Aside from Saturday evening classes for functionaries, the only other political education had been occasional study circles led by Richter during Wolton's period of leadership. She also pointed to the pitfalls of organizing on a purely territorial basis, as opposed to organizing in the workplace; local struggles, she believed, tended to remain localized, and this impeded the Party's growth. 'We have two or three members in a group and the groups do not increase. One comes today and leaves and another comes tomorrow', she noted. 'We do not get the workers where they work. Any trouble that arises in one location the other location is not interested in.'[36]

On 15 March the Comintern officials began their evaluation of the CPSA. Despite its Moscow-based perspective and limited knowledge of South African political conditions – it overestimated the significance of the ANC, for example – the very fact that black South African politics were reviving gave the Comintern perspective credibility. Robert Naumann, a German Communist who in the 1930s was the main advisor to the Anglo-American Secretariat on South Africa, pointed to what he and the other Comintern officials saw as the crux of the problem. 'Have we a Party in South Africa? No, we have not', he baldly began. 'Political activity in the country is increasing'; the ANC, ICU and trade union organizations were growing, he claimed.

But only one factor does not exist, and that is the Party. Why? Because you are isolated. ... you are fighting, discussing about future problems ... about the growing over of the democratic dictatorship of the workers and peasants to Soviet Power. That, you are discussing, but the immediate question of struggle today, you do not see.

Naumann pinpointed four key issues. Firstly, none of the South African comrades had as yet shown any self-criticism. Secondly, the Party was not involved in trade union work, aside from a few individuals. Thirdly, the Party did have cadre: Naumann referred to Issy Wolfson and Johnny Gomas as examples of committed and effective mass workers, noting that neither, significantly, was on the Central Committee. Lastly, Naumann argued for the need to penetrate the Afrikaner national movement to contest fascism and propagandize against British imperialism.[37]

At the concluding session of 19 March, Comrade Stepanov continued the Comintern's assessment, arguing that the CPSA had become infected by national politics – 'the attempt to utilise one nationality against the other' – and that this had fuelled the factional struggle. To counteract this, Stepanov continued, the Party needed new leaders:

I think that the present leaders – I do not say 'leadership' because there is no united leadership – are politically bankrupt. That is the mildest way of saying it. They have brought the Party to an abyss. ... it is necessary to give the present leading comrades a rest. ... We want them to remain in the movement, of course, but this will depend on them, and upon their behaviour.[38]

Now came the litany of *mea culpas*. Bach began, stating that when he and Kotane were called to Moscow, he came prepared for theoretical arguments about the African bourgeoisie and the Native Republic thesis. However, his studies at the KUTVU, his observations at the Seventh Congress and his participation on the South African Commission

helped me to see that, in spite of the work I have done, there were still some remnants of the old attitude to some comrades on a number of questions that has [sic] developed as a result of this struggle. This, the comrades pointed out in their speeches; they have helped me to see all this – their criticism, their fight amongst themselves, etc., are of considerable assistance in overcoming all this.[39]

Richter, likewise, conceded that the Party had followed a sectarian line but disputed the allegation that the leadership was all white. He thought that the problem of factionalism could only be resolved in practical work. 'I think I would be dishonest now if I said that I have regained all faith in the opposition by the decisions of this Commission', he admitted. 'I have not.'[40]

Josie Mpama criticized her own passivity and failure to contest the practice of the present Party leadership. 'I just sat down and did not attempt to force the comrades to carry out the Party line', she began.

[W]hen I saw that the PB has a line and the District Committee does not know it, I came to the conclusion that it was not my business, but I realise now I was wrong. But I promise, when I go back, I shall help show the comrades their mistakes and help them come up to our political level and struggle against imperialism.[41]

And finally, came Kotane's turn. Firstly, contrary to Richter's claim of black leadership, Kotane still maintained that the black Politburo members were not autonomous agents. 'You have people who do what they are told, but actually there are European people who … give the leadership from the outside.' Secondly, he disagreed with Richter about the opposition:

They (the opposition) have carried out the line of the C.I. wrongly, but they carried it out the way they understood. There are people like Gomas; some people say he is in the opposition; when something goes wrong with him, they say he is in the opposition; but when he is right, they say he is their man. But people like that worked and have been in the movement for years and they suffered.

Lastly, showing the proper degree of humility, he agreed to carry out the Comintern's decisions but pleaded, 'let me be out of the leadership; let me do some work. … it is only then that I can show my sincerity to the Party'.[42]

Marty summarized the Commission's conclusions. In regards to the dissension over the Native Republic thesis, the CPSA had forgotten that the main point of the thesis was its emphasis on daily demands to mobilize Africans; the Native Repubic slogan only came at the very end of the thesis. Instead of mobilizing around daily demands, the CPSA had engaged in scholastic debate on the Native Republic. In regards to the question of the African bourgeoisie, Marty quoted the Comintern resolution of 19 October 1928: 'The Negro bourgeoisie as a class does not exist, if we except the Negroes engaged in trade and a stratum of the Negro intellectuals who do not play any important role in the economy and political life of the country.' Furthermore, the May 1930 Presidium of the ECCI stated: '[t]he Native bourgeoisie exists only in its embryonic form'. Why debate for years what is clear, asked Marty?

He then outlined the proposals that the South African Commission intended to submit to the ECCI Secretariat: firstly, that the CPSA cease the factional struggle and expel those who sought to continue it; secondly, that it develop a programme of action based on the demands of Africans and of all workers, black and white; thirdly, that it concentrate on the trade union movement and on African rights; fourthly, that the Party leadership should be composed of loyal activists; and fifthly that *Umsebenzi*'s editorial board be reconstituted and that *Umsebenzi* be used to campaign for a paper to represent a united trade union movement. Once those goals were achieved, Marty went on, the CPSA should call a national conference to consolidate its results and discuss the possibility of a monthly organ. 'I think', stated Marty, that if you work on the basis of the programme explained by Comrade Stepanov, with the three main demands: (1) Bread and work for all workers, white, Native, etc.; (2) Land for the Native people, poor whites, etc.; (3) Rights and liberties for all. ... it is possible, on the basis of these demands, to build a big anti-imperialist mass movement. But the backbone is trade union unity – always, always, always.[43]

The Comintern's assessment of the trade union movement and of white labour's political potential rested on an idealized interpretation of South Africa's past – notably the 1922 Rand Revolt. Such a historical idealization was not unique to South Africa. As a means of justifying the People's Front policy, Comintern ideologues emphasized and arguably exaggerated the radical characteristics of nationalist mobilizations in many countries.

Marty interpreted the revolt from within a teleological framework that embued daily experience and struggle – 'life itself' – with a radical potential. He sanitized the racism of the white workers: 'The British were against the natives, but not the workers. ... There was provocation on the 10th and 11th of March, but not by the workers.'[44] For Marty, the Rand Revolt symbolized the potential for South African strikes to transform themselves from purely economic struggles into political mobilizations:

> The big mistake of the white workers was not having been able to draw the Native workers into the strike; they could not find the slogans to get the Native workers into the strike, but it was never against the Natives. ... reality and life give us the slogan of the Independent Native Republic. These workers of the Rand give the solution to us. Their strike began for daily demands, and it finished with a demand against British imperialism, for freedom, for an independent South Africa.

The core of a Communist trade union cadre already existed, Marty emphasized, mentioning both Wolfson and Gomas, 'a mass man' who had sent some 'very good proposals ... for uniting the trade union movement. ... we must help him; he is a leader'.[45] And he questioned whether W. H. Andrews's expulsion from the Party in 1931 had been necessary. After all, Marty pointed out, Andrews was now general secretary of the Trades and Labour Council.[46] Could he not be approached and brought back into the Party? And what about celebrating a Rand Day on 14 March to commemorate the Rand Revolt, as Dingaan's Day was a commemorative day for Africans? Harry Spendiff and Percy Fisher, the Rand Revolt leaders who had died rather than surrender to British imperialism, could be used as symbols to commemorate Rand Day. But, he added: 'The Party must decide this; we cannot decide from here'. Marty reserved his final words for Kotane: whatever the CPSA's decision as to whether or not Kotane would be in the leadership, he must obey.[47]

The People's Front in South Africa

The impact of the Comintern's People's Front policy is directly traceable in the activities of the CPSA. For the Comintern, the struggle against fascism was paramount, and it sought to project this view onto the South African case. Communists in South Africa had often stressed the bifurcated nature of the society – democracy for whites and fascism for blacks.[48] But a report to the Comintern argued that such a position destroyed the possibility of unity: 'The difference must be pointed out: fascism would not allow any democratic rights, would make terrorism and murder constitutional, which is a big difference from ordinary colonial oppression.'[49]

The problems of the People's Front became apparent in its application in South Africa. These were twofold. Firstly, with its tiny numbers, the CPSA had scant resources for building any movement, let alone one as ambitious in scope as the People's Front. The Party did not have its own distinctive or stable base of supporters to bring to a People's Front; moreover, its presence in such fronts often led organizations with substantial memberships to stay away. Secondly, South Africa's racially-divided society posed a serious obstacle to the development of either a proletarian united front or a broader People's Front. The proletarian united front was meant to be colour blind. In this respect, it represented a continuation of the Party's unsuccessful attempts to organize black and white unemployed workers during the depression. Those efforts had demonstrated the futility of organizing joint black–white political action in such a racially unequal society. Moreover, the conception of a single People's Front that could incorporate both a proletarian united front and a national liberation front broke down in practice into two movements that developed along racial lines: one, the white anti-fascist movement to protect the existing democratic rights of white South Africans; the other, the movement to gain democratic rights for blacks, represented by the All African Convention, in which, aside from a few radicals, whites were virtually absent.

The CPSA, like its Trotskyist counterparts, hoped that poor Afrikaners would realise their mutual interests with black workers, and that both would struggle together against the common enemy of fascism.[50] The CPSA's concern with the growth of fascism, both in Europe and in South Africa, pre-dated the People's Front policy. South Africa had its own home-grown fascists: the anti-Semitic Greyshirts, founded in 1933 by Louis Weichart. Shortly thereafter, in March 1934, a diverse group of leftists formed the League against Fascism and War, chiefly through the efforts of Alec Wanless of the Natal branch of the Labour Party. The CPSA supported the endeavour, seeing it as an arena from which to attract white workers. Although the Trades and Labour Council refused to affiliate, the League against Fascism and War nonetheless attracted an array of trade unionists, including Bill Andrews and the Cornelius sisters, Johanna and Hester.[51] The anti-fascist movement grew: February 1935 saw the launch of an Anti-Fascist League in Cape Town; the speakers at its inauguration included Advocate Silke; Sam Kahn, who had joined the CPSA in 1930, while studying law at the University of Cape Town; Mr

G. Botha; Dr Abdul Gool and his wife Zainunnissa 'Cissie' Gool, the youngest daughter of Dr Abdullah Abdurahman.[52]

Communists were also active in the Friends of the Soviet Union. The Johannesburg branch met on Sunday evenings in the Trades Hall and made special efforts to attract Afrikaner workers. In January 1935 the CPSA began publishing a monthly called *Die Arbeider en Arme Boer* (*Worker and Poor Peasant*) in order to attract poor whites. *Umsebenzi* published and endorsed the decisions of the Seventh Congress, even if its coverage was not enough to satisfy the Comintern, calling in September 1935 for 'the forming of a broad people's united front against imperialism, fascism and war'.[53] It also covered Dimitrov's report to the Seventh Comintern Congress. Naboth Mokgatle, for one, refers to the singular impact that Dimitrov's speech had on his own political development; although he did not join the Party until 1941, he became a sympathizer in the mid-1930s, impressed with the Party's anti-fascist stance.[54]

1936 saw a marked increase in the Comintern's efforts to monitor its South African affiliate. In late 1935 the Comintern had asked the CPGB to assist the CPSA in overcoming its internal problems. The British Communist George Hardy sailed to South Africa to represent the Comintern, and spent most of 1936 there. He already had considerable experience as a Comintern agent. In 1926 Hardy, who was married, had an affair with another British Communist, who was herself the wife of a leading member of the British Young Communist League. The woman became pregnant and, fearing a scandal, the CPGB contacted Moscow 'with the recommendation that work be found for Hardy in some other part of the world (China if possible)', particularly as Hardy had expressed concern that the CPGB intended to 'maroon him in Moscow'. The CPGB made it clear that it did not want Hardy's work to be in any way connected with their own organization.[55] Ultimately, it was decided to send him abroad as a Comintern representative, and he visited five countries over a number of years. In South Africa, his mission was to help the CPSA overcome its factional strife, 'isolat[e] … the Trotskyite elements', and promote the policies of the Seventh Congress.[56]

Under Hardy's guidance, new procedures were implemented in 1936 to streamline the CPSA's operations. Nonetheless, it continued to operate in a top-down authoritarian manner, a practice that had begun in the New Line period. A panel commission was responsible for selecting the Central Committee; its criteria for selection and its report were kept secret. It was also a male-dominated Party with very few women members; female leaders were frowned upon. When Ray Alexander suggested that a woman be included on the Central Committee and proposed Josie Mpama, Willie Kalk replied that the panel commission had considered the option but did not think it necessary at present.[57]

Hardy made contact with Bill Andrews in Cape Town, and in Johannesburg he worked closely with Edwin Mofutsanyana, who was then the CPSA's general secretary, and Issy Wolfson, the Party's treasurer. Wolfson was one of two recently-recruited whites who had become prominent in the CPSA since Bach's departure. Wolfson was a first-generation South African, born in the Transvaal in 1906. Since joining the Party in 1934, he had risen rapidly in its ranks, both because of his influential roles in the textile and tailoring unions and on the National Executive of the Trades and Labour Council and because of his oratorial skills; his work had caught André Marty's eye.[58] Together, Wolfson and Kalk were the Party's leading activists in the white labour movement. The other significant white newcomer was Hyman Basner, a Latvian-born and American-educated attorney who had joined the CPSA in 1933, having provided legal services for *Ikaka labaSebenzi* since Bunting's expulsion in 1931. Prior to that, he had worked with Charlotte Maxeke who, as the 'Prisoner's Friend', provided a legal aid service. Maxeke was antipathetic to Communism, however, and their friendship dimmed once Basner joined the Party.[59]

Seeing the organization of whites as pivotal to the struggle against fascism, Hardy pushed for even more attention to their concerns. In April 1936 the CPSA held a plenum, in which it sketched out further efforts to entice white workers into a broad multi-class organization. A Farmer-Labour Party had recently split off from the Labour Party, led by Advocate F. A. W. Lucas. Reports of this new group had attracted the attention of Comintern officials in Moscow; they saw it as evidence of the progressive potential of white workers.[60] The Farmer-Labour Party sought to attract workers and poor farmers, and it endorsed the single-tax system of Henry George; a system of taxation based on land values was its central plank. Following Marty's suggestion, the CPSA sought to promote the new Farmer-Labour Party.[61] This never took off but the idea formed the basis of subsequent attempts at anti-fascist and anti-war fronts organized around the Trades and Labour Council and left-wing Labour groups in these years. The CPSA hoped that these would become the nucleus of a People's Front.

But the considerable difficulties – if not impossibility – of trying to unite black and white in a People's Front led to controversy in the Party; some saw it as a futile exercise.[62] In May 1936, an article by S. B. in *Umsebenzi* argued that proletarian unity in South Africa was possible because poverty was grinding poor whites down towards the level of blacks, while the growth of secondary industries employing both black and white workers was eroding the colour bar. But the People's Front was premature, S. B. added, 'because there is no economic base for the rapproachement of the White bourgeois elements that go to make up such a wider front with the Natives'. Thus, S. B. counselled that the CPSA should concentrate on the proletarian united front. But a reply the following month from a Geo. Robertson argued for a common all-in front, maintaining that there were common interests between whites struggling to preserve their rights and blacks struggling for their rights.[63]

Under Hardy's influence, the CPSA settled on a compromise in which it saw itself as a link between two wings of a broad front of organizations, the black All African Convention and the white People's Front. The CPSA's pamphlet, *Organise a People's Front in South Africa*, published in September 1936, sought to clarify the problem:

> there is only one front of unified labour and its supporters, notwithstanding
> the different political tasks which arise from the varying degrees of oppres-

sion. There are not two fronts as some good comrades would have us believe, and the least effort made to divide the front strengthens the segregationist camp of the enemy.[64]

And a report to the Comintern some months later commented:

The relationship of the A.A.C. to the united front has caused some confusion. There was talk of two united fronts. This had to be fought, as to formulate it this way would never lead to joint activities of natives and Europeans. Therefore, because there are different tasks confronting the natives in developing the National liberation movement upon the basis of an anti-imperialist line, we can only speak of two sectors on the one front which should ultimately be concentrated inside the People's Front of S.A. recently organised.[65]

On 5–6 September 1936 the CPSA held its national conference at the Trades Hall in Johannesburg. At one level, things may have looked auspicious for the Party. A number of its leading figures were highly-placed trade unionists. Wolfson and Kalk were the Party's main activists amongst white workers, and both were on the Trades and Labour Council's National Executive. Other trade unionists at the conference included B. Nikin, William Thibedi, who was secretary of the African Mine Workers' Union in 1936, and who had returned to the Party the year before; Mtini, who represented Railway Workers in Cape Town, and Ray Alexander.[66] But the CPSA had expelled its most experienced activists in 1931, and unlike its British counterpart, it had no significant body of trade unionists who were working their way up the trade union hierarchy from the shop floor. In the Party's efforts to build up its trade union cadre, a number of Afrikaner trade unionists had been given trips to the USSR. Hester Cornelius of the GWU had visited the Soviet Union in 1935 and called it a 'dreamland'. Yet upon her return to South Africa, she wrote to Moscow complaining of Louis Joffe's control of the Party and claiming that the Friends of the Soviet Union was trying to bar her from participating. Hopes that Hester's sister, Johanna Cornelius, might join the CPSA were dashed when she came out in support of the Labour Party.[67] Amongst white trade unionists, broad sympathy for the USSR could coexist with dismissal of the CPSA as a significant political factor. And, although British Communists could count on the occasional support of a few Labour Party politicians for particular policies, in South Africa the colour bar meant that virtually no Labour Party politicians were willing to support Communist campaigns.[68]

The CPSA continued with its efforts to build a People's Front. On 3–5 October it participated in a United Front Conference convened by the Trades and Labour Council and comprising thirty-five organizations, although, notably, the Labour Party had not sent representatives. The conference seemed to be an auspicious step for the CPSA's project. It styled itself the People's Front and took a solidly anti-fascist line. Its main task, it was agreed, was to go out to the platteland and show the poor farmers the emptiness of the Greyshirt–Blackshirt policy and win them over to a real support of democracy. The fascists were already actively propagandising among the Afrikaners, and the farming community which was being broken up and forced into industry had not the experience of Trade Unionism and active work was very necessary among them if fascists were to be prevented from gaining ground.

Yet its focus on whites – especially Afrikaners – meant the neglect of blacks. Archie A. Moore, president of the Trades and Labour Council and chairman of the conference, stressed the need to defend existing rights, essentially a concern of whites. Although Hyman Basner proposed several additions to the conference's draft programme on the Native question, black rights were marginalized.[69]

The Party's increased efforts to attract white workers were also reflected in its paper, *Umsebenzi*. Eddie Roux had been soundly criticized at the South African Commission for his singular views, and he was marginalized over the subsequent months. His speech at Sidney Bunting's funeral in May 1936 occasioned a damning report to the Comintern. He was removed from *Umsebenzi* and isolated within the Party, saved from expulsion only because of his broader popularity; his wife was castigated as a Trotskyist.[70]

With Roux sidelined, Louis Joffe, who had no experience in newspaper production, became the paper's political editor. To attract white readers, in June 1936 *Umsebenzi* was renamed the *South African Worker*, running the slogan 'For a United Working-Class Front Against War and Imperialism'. The new paper curtailed Bantu-language news coverage.[71] A Comintern report argued that it was necessary to change the name

> so as to apply our policy and turn the work towards the Afrikaners which was hindered very much by the Native name and contents. There was some doubt raised as to this change and a little resistance by a number of backward Native comrades. The fact that this was not regarded as necessary, considering Native prejudices among Afrikaners and other whites, indicates how the Party had failed so long to understand South Africa as a whole, carrying on its work mainly among Natives.

Not surprisingly, Roux objected to the name change, a move that the author of the report interpreted as a demagogic attempt to win African supporters. However, the writer went on, it was explained that the Party's aim was to eventually publish two papers, one in African languages and English, and the other in English and Afrikaans, and eventually Roux conceded. White trade unionists like Andrews and Lucas were reported to be very happy about the change.[72]

Hopes for a People's Front able to draw in both black and white faded in 1937. Following Marty's suggestion, in February the CPSA announced plans to commemorate the fifteenth anniversary of the 1922 Rand Revolt.[73] Yet, the difficulty of uniting black and white was seen again in the controversy over the preparations in Johannesburg for May Day in 1937:

> Kalk said that the Labour Party and the Building Union were withdrawing from the [United May Day] Committee because we insisted on Native speakers from both platforms whereas they wanted one platform to have only European speakers. He said that we would have to compromise and not smash up the committee, but in doing so he antagonised Comrade Josie by his manner and this led to a bit of a row.

The committee finally agreed on two platforms, one with all white speakers and one with a combination of black and white.[74] In June the Party appealed to the Labour Party to form a working arrangement for the upcoming municipal elections in October – despite the fact that at the Labour Party's annual conference in January it had failed to repudiate its pro-segregation policy. Not surprisingly, the Labour Party rejected the CPSA's appeal; nonetheless, the CPSA still endorsed the election of Labour candidates.[75]

In practice, the Party's attempts to link black and white labour were far from non-racial: it underestimated the economic, political and social conflicts of interests between the black and white working class that gave white labour a stake in promoting its own interests at the expense of blacks. In the late 1930s, white workers still refused to work in organizations that called for democratic rights for blacks. Tensions in the Party mounted because of its increasingly white orientation, and personal rivalries and factional strife flourished in that atmosphere.

Soviet terror and South African reverberations

Hardy left South Africa in late 1936 or early 1937; his report to the Comintern on the South African situation was greeted with approval by André Marty. Significant problems remained, Hardy wrote. The CPSA was extremely isolated, with a dwindling membership of less than 100, of whom only eight or ten were functionaries. He identified Kotane, Roux and Gomas as factionalists, while Mofutsanaya, in his view, fluctuated between nationalist and leftist attitudes. Moreover, he added, South African Communists were not sufficiently vigilant and aggressive in their fight against Trotskyism. Although Gomas, for instance, had written a critique of Trotskyism for the Party paper, he had failed to denounce or expose any individual Trotskyists. Nonetheless, Hardy optimistically concluded that there was a 50 per cent improvement over last year towards the goal of building a Bolshevik Party, and he proposed that Mofutsanyana, Wolfson and Kalk be selected as the nucleus of a new leadership.[76]

The unfolding terror in the Soviet Union, which reached a peak in 1937, cast a gloomy shadow across the CPSA and widened the cleavage between Communists and Trotskyists. The Great Terror of 1936–38 – 'when literally no one was safe' –

and its accompanying Moscow Show Trials of alleged traitors marked a qualitative increase in the scale of violence from the party purges and 'verification' campaigns that characterized Soviet political life from the late 1920s.[77] The Great Terror ravaged Soviet society and institutions; however, Comintern officials and foreign Communists in the Soviet Union were not spared. Against the backdrop of Japanese and German aggression, Soviet xenophobia and fear of foreign intervention reached a zenith in the late 1930s, accompanied by mass arrests of foreigners, both Communists and non-Communists. Evgeny Varga, a Hungarian Comintern official, wrote to Stalin on 28 March 1938 that 'many foreigners gather up their belongings every evening in expectation of arrest. Many are half mad and incapable of work as a result of constant fear.'[78] And years later Robin Page Arnot, a British Communist in Moscow in 1937, recalled the 'mass hysteria on the part of ordinary people'.[79] The revolution was devouring its own.

Devout Communists in the local affiliates were expected to justify the show trials. On 28 February 1937 the Friends of the Soviet Union sponsored a 'Public Lecture on the Piatakov-Radek Trial (Trotskyist Counter-Revolutionary Criminals Recently Tried in Moscow)' at the Johannesburg Trades Hall. C. B. Tyler was the chair and Advocate George Findlay, one of a small number of Communists in Pretoria, was the speaker. On 4 July Hyman Basner lectured on 'Eliminating Counter-Revolutionaries in the Soviet Union'.[80] But many people saw through the propaganda. Naboth Mokgatle was on the verge of joining the CPSA, but changed his mind when he read about the trials. 'After reading the verdicts', he wrote, 'I remember asking myself, how can I join the party which destroys its cream, the party with no future because its leadership is destroyed?'[81]

Nonetheless, rumours began to circulate about the fate of Lazar Bach and the Richter brothers, fanning the flames of discontent in and around the Party. On 12 July three members of the Politburo, Mofutsanyana, Wolfson and Kalk – the three targeted by Hardy to be the nucleus of the new leadership – reprimanded Joffe for allegedly having warned Bach not to go to the Soviet Union. Evidently, Joffe had recounted his warning to Bach to a Party sympathizer and was deemed to have jeopardized the Party's reputation. In his defence Joffe claimed that he had a nervous condition that made him say things that he did not really mean as they sounded.[82] On 18 July 1937 the Johannesburg *Sunday Express* reported that Bach and the Richter brothers had been sentenced to death, leading, no doubt, to further demoralization. Despite the distress caused by the report, many Communists retained their faith in the Comintern's infallibility.[83] Their fate caught even André Marty by surprise. Following the South African Commission, Marty had recommended that the three men be sent back to Latvia and expelled from the Party. Instead, their Latvian nationality had marked them as likely victims of the terror.[84]

The CPSA continued to be rent by internal squabbles fuelled by personal rivalries and vendettas. The problem was particularly acute in the head office. The League against Fascism and War was damaged by sectarian battles. In June 1936 Solly Sachs of the GWU had written to the League castigating Joffe's control of the organization and accusing him of financial mismanagement. Joffe was accused of diverting the League's funds for use in the CPSA's own anti-fascist work. Although later cleared of dishonesty, he was found slack and incompetent with the finances.[85] Likewise, reeling from internecine battles, in the mid-1930s the Johannesburg branch of the Friends of the Soviet Union split along racial lines.[86]

Johannesburg Communists distrusted each other and did not hesitate to speak badly of one another to outsiders. When Basner went to Europe in 1937 he told Marty that Roux was a 'typical chauvinist intellectual more interested in the national movement than in the Party ... very emotional'; that Gomas and Kotane were nationalists; that the latter, while 'a clever man with a just understanding' could not work within the Party; and that Marks was 'an enemy of the working class. He made open provocations.'[87] Wolfson told the CPGB that Kotane, Gomas and Roux were elements 'to keep a careful eye on'; he insinuated that Kalk was lazy and gave the Party a bad image.[88] When Ralph Bunche was conducting his interviews in Johannesburg, former Communist Josiah Grey spoke of the ' financial corruption, intellectual dishonesty and stuffy bureaucracy of recent Party leaders here' and added that 'all the best men have been lost to the Party.' While disparaging of Mofutsanyana and Gaur Radebe, Grey remained an ardent admirer of Kotane.[89]

When Kotane had returned from Moscow in August 1936, he had undoubtedly hoped to stabilize the Party under his own leadership, given that his political vision dovetailed most closely with the Comintern's Seventh Congress resolutions. He was certainly prepared to follow the Comintern's mandates. At a Politburo meeting on 24 August, Kotane had pledged to 'liquidate fractionalism', announcing that '[a]ll those who are prepared to carry out the line as laid down must be rallied, and those who hesitate to agree must be thrown out'.[90]

Although Kotane was elected district party officer of the Johannesburg office, over the next year he felt himself increasingly stifled by the sectarian local atmosphere and alienated by the CPSA's policy. He thought the Party was paying too much attention to industrial workers and not enough to rural and farmworkers. By early 1937 he had decided to move to Cape Town, and when he informed the head office, Wolfson reported to the CPGB that '[w]e were compelled to take disciplinary action against him and he was romoved [sic] from the Central Committee of our Party'.

With Kotane's departure for Cape Town in February 1937, Josie Mpama took over as Johannesburg district party officer. She continued to encounter sexism. Wolfson's report to the CPGB described her as 'the wife of the leading comrade of the Party', and, he added:

I feel she is not the right person in that job. That in the job of D.P.O. Johannesburg we want a really first class man and if we can get a good comrade to take up that position we will be able to improve our work tremendously. I feel that comrade Josie Mofatsayana [sic] has not made all of the job that she could have. She has domestic duties which interfere with her political activities, and that means she is not able to devote the time.[91]

Membership continued to dwindle, with one report claiming that at the nadir membership had dropped to fifty but that there had subsequently been an influx of new members.[92] A small number of stalwarts still managed to do some practical work, mainly of an educational and propagandistic nature and generally in collaboration with other leftists and anti-fascists. In Britain, a broad-based left organization known as the Left Book Club was formed by the left-wing Jewish publisher Victor Gollancz. South African leftists followed the example. Left Book Club branches were formed in the major cities in the late 1930s. In Johannesburg Fanny Klenerman's bookshop, Vanguard Books, sold Left Book Club books and was a focal point for local leftists. While Pretoria had no CPSA branch, it did have a Left Book Club where Franz Boshoff, George Findlay and Sam Woolf lectured, and a second-hand shop run by a Mr van Leer in Paul Kruger Street supplied Left Book Club books. On intermittent occasions the CPSA was able to organize its own educational activities. For a few months in 1935 Johannesburg Communists managed to set up night classes to teach reading and writing to African students; these eventually succumbed to police intimidation.[93] In the late 1930s they opened a People's Bookshop in the Trades Hall. Louis Joffe organized a youth movement and conducted sporadic study classes. In Cape Town, local Communists set up the October Club as a counter to Trotskyist discussion groups – although Comintern reports mistakenly dubbed the October Club as Trotskyist!

Nonetheless, the Party's tiny numbers in each centre precluded significant practical work. In Cape Town the only activity was 'the publication of a few pamphlets and meetings held on Sunday evenings'.

> The only centre where there is some independent Party activity is at V. where the Party holds meetings. … We hold meetings from time to time in the Transvaal. We hold meetings in the locations … but … our work amongst the european [sic] workers as a whole is very much in the background. … Likewise in Pretoria where we have a good number of Party comrades, no independent Party activity.[94]

Cape Town was seen, both by the head office in Johannesburg and by the Comintern, as a centre of factionalism. Comintern officials saw events in faraway South Africa through lenses coloured by the terrorism in the Soviet Union, of which they, themselves, were a direct target. Thus, they saw Kotane's move to Cape Town in ominous terms: now, it believed, the three former oppositionists, Roux, Kotane and Gomas were together. Comintern reports also noted with concern the actions of Eli Weinberg and Ray Alexander, 'who have been in the background of the factional struggle'.[95] Kotane and Roux began republishing *Umvikele-Thebe/African Defender*, a publication of *Ikaka labaSebenzi*. The paper had been quite successful at the time of Italy's invasion of Abyssinia but sales fell flat once it became clear the Italians were winning.[96] A letter from Naumann to Marty of 4 May 1937 complained of the reappearance of the *African Defender* after a gap of eight months and speculated that Kotane was reviving the factional struggle following his move to

Cape Town. The *African Defender*, he noted, contained nothing about African defence but instead promoted a Gandhist approach. Marty seemingly accepted Naumann's view without question: on 7 May he informed Dimitrov of the revival of factionalism in Cape Town. Once again, the Comintern looked to the CPGB for help with the South African comrades. Marty advised Dimitrov that if some South African comrades were not already on their way to England, a British Communist should be sent to South Africa. Furthermore, it was proposed that the CPGB send a comrade to assist in the education of South Africans studying in Moscow.[97]

The situation in Durban was dire. Pauline Podbrey recalled the despair and collapse of her father, a Lithuanian immigrant and a former Bundist, when reports of the Moscow Show Trials reached South Africa. When she asked him where to find the Durban Communist Party office, he retorted: 'There isn't one. ... The Party is dead'.[98] For all practical purposes that was true. Wolfson reported to the CPGB that 'during the last year [1937] the party has not been able to hold a single independent Party meeting. ... The Party has an office in Durban but does not carry on active political work as a Communist Party. You cannot say that the Party exists in Durban.'[99]

The fewer the members, the more racial tensions escalated. In September 1937 African Communists in Durban complained that the whites were acting like bosses. Mofutsanyana went down to Durban to sort the problem out, counselling the Africans to act more independently and the whites to show more understanding of the barriers facing Africans.[100] The Party's continuing concessions to white chauvinism demoralized many members. In October 1937, Party members Eddie Roux, Sam Kahn, Harry Snitcher and Edwin Mofutsanyana all confided to Ralph Bunche that the Party's overemphasis on whites had led to the neglect of blacks, a view iterated by Basner to Comintern officials in Europe.[101]

However, the CPSA could point to one achievement. Through the efforts of the CPGB, the Comintern's efforts to recruit Andrews back into Party finally succeeded. In October 1937 Harry Pollitt reported that the CPGB had been 'trying to get this comrade to resume his membership of the Party, and if possible we would like him to become the Chairman as this would give us a very good standing'.[102] In November 1937 Andrews visited Moscow for the commemoration of the twentieth anniversary of the revolution, his first visit since he had served on the Comintern in 1923. There, on 29 November, he met with Naumann and several British Communists – Jimmy Shields, who had lived in South Africa in the 1920s, Robin Page Arnot and his wife Olive, and Arthur Horner – at the Lux Hotel. 'The task', reported Naumann, 'was to get the opinion of Comrade Andrews about the C.P. of S.A. and, if possible, to influence him to join the Party'.[103] The international efforts dovetailed with local sentiments: the Politburo minutes of 12 July 1936 had proposed inviting Andrews back into the Party. Andrews rejoined the CPSA on May Day 1938 and subsequently became chair of its Central Committee.[104]

The nadir of 1938

In 1938, a series of accumulated events led to the Party's virtual collapse in Johannesburg. Firstly, in March 1938 the Party organ ceased publication, after twenty-three years of continuous publication, first as the *International*, then as *Umsebenzi* and as the *South African Worker*, allegedly because of lack of funds.[105] Behind this financial issue, though, lay the destructive combination of the Comintern's misguided intervention and the long-term problems in the head office in Johannesburg. From 1936, the two Party members most experienced in newspaper production, Roux and Kotane, were no longer involved with the paper.[106] Lacking adequate management, the paper finally collapsed.

Secondly, long-term tensions between Issy Wolfson and Willie Kalk, the two Communist members of the Trades and Labour Council's Executive Committee, and Solly Sachs finally boiled over in 1938. A former Communist, Sachs had long caused controversy in the CPSA. Regional tensions between the Johannesburg and Cape Town branches over Solly Sachs were apparent: Basner, for instance, reported that the Cape Town branch had given Sachs 'a certain amount of support'.[107] The 1938 dispute centred around the GWU's attempts to negotiate a comprehensive wage agreement for workers in Port Elizabeth and King Williamstown. Disagreements erupted between the GWU and the secretary of the Trades and Labour Council over negotiations, leading to Sach's suspension from the National Executive Committee of the Trades and Labour Council. Sachs took legal action against his suspension and was reinstated. Nonetheless, tensions between Sachs and the majority of the Trades and Labour Council executive remained high. Fearing a split between the GWU and the Trades and Labour Council, the CPSA Politburo resolved that Wolfson and Kalk attempt a reconciliation between Sachs and the NEC. However, they failed to do so, evidently due to their personal antagonisms with Sachs. In essence, the affair meant that the CPSA's two leading white trade unionists, on whom it had pinned its hopes for building a People's Front, were at odds with the majority of the Party.[108]

The CPSA's third leading white figure, Hyman Basner, fell from grace late in the year because of his critical views on the crisis in Czechoslovakia. During the Munich crisis of September 1938 the British Prime Minister Chamberlain conceded to terms stipulated by Hitler that led to the dismemberment of Czechoslovakia and to its disappearance as an independent state in March 1939. Basner was alleged to have introduced Trotskyist views on the Czechoslovakian crisis and to have slandered the Comintern and some of its leading parties. Basner's 'defection' was a major blow to the Johannesburg branch. He was alleged to have done the Party 'irreparable harm'. He was removed from the Central Committee and banned from holding any leading position on any Party organ or committee; the Party resolved to campaign to expose his negative role in all its branches. Basner resigned from the CPSA in 1939, following the Soviet invasion of Finland.[109]

The breakdown of the Johannesburg branch was so extreme that at the Party's annual conference from 29 December 1938 to 1 January 1939, Mofutsanyana proposed the division of the Party into black and white sections with the Executive Committee acting as a connecting link. He argued that in actual fact the CPSA already operated in such a manner and that, despite its official pronouncements, the Party had betrayed the national liberation struggle. A double standard operated, he pointed out. Funds were found for a white paper but not for a black paper; Party meetings were continual 'dog fights' about European politics and Comintern directives that ignored African needs and alienated African members.[110] Radebe supported the proposal, claiming most African members felt that those dominating Party meetings were 'talking Greek', while whites who found themselves sitting next to their 'kitchen boys' never came back. But Moses Kotane vehemently opposed the proposal on the grounds that it would be a capitulation to the government's divide and rule tactic, and Mofutsanyana's suggestion was rejected.[111] Kotane put forward a proposal on behalf of Cape Town District Party Committee that Party headquarters be temporarily moved to Cape Town until the next conference. The motion carried six to five with two abstentions. The Central Committee agreed on the need to strengthen the district party committees; to form local organizations in residential areas, in trade union groups and in factory groups, as warranted; and to raise funds for a new Party organ. It also resolved to continue campaigning against Trotskyism and against petty bourgeois influence.[112]

Despite the Comintern's suspicions about the Cape Town branch, it was, ironically, in Cape Town that things would begin to look up. Although Cape Town reportedly had only twenty-eight members in 1937, by early 1939 it counted forty-two members, most of whom were trade unionists.[113] It now had a core of committed activists who were able to work together. These included Moses Kotane, who had joined the Cape Town District Party Committee and who became chair of the local ANC; Eli Weinberg; Ray Alexander; Jack Simons, who had returned in 1937 with a doctorate from the London School of Economics to take up a lectureship at the University of Cape Town; Jimmy La Guma; Cissie Gool; Johnny Gomas and L. T. Leepile, the Party's national assistant organiser. A new Politburo was elected, the composition of which reflected the shift of power to Cape Town. A new tripartite secretariat was formed of Kotane, Simons and Andrews; Kotane became general secretary, a post he retained for the remainder of his life.[114] Cape Town also had a new, national paper, the *Guardian*, that was broadly anti-fascist and sympathetic to Communist viewpoints. This had been launched in February 1937, spearheaded by a small group of left-wing activists linked to the local Left Book Club, and edited by the journalist Betty Radford.[115] The CPSA headquarters remained in Cape Town until the Party's dissolution in 1950.

The Comintern continued to try to influence the CPSA, chiefly through the visits of South African Communists to Europe. Influenced by Hardy's reading of the South African situation, in August 1937, the CPGB had proposed that the CPSA have three secretaries, 'one Native, one Afrikander and one European', in order to surmount 'the political difficulties which arise from the fact that a Native is General Secretary of the Party'.[116] In December 1937 some Comintern officials were still prioritizing the white anti-fascist struggle and were critical of views that sought to put the national struggle at centre stage. 'When the commission in London put forward a line, that the Europeans are the main force to defeat fascism in S.A.', wrote one official, 'Comrade Basner is of the opinion that only the Natives can defeat fascism.'[117]

However, even then, views within the Comintern on the South African section were shifting. The relationship between the CPGB and the Comintern was now somewhat strained. Harry Pollitt pointed out to the Comintern in November 1937 that the CPGB had never asked for the responsibility of guiding the South African comrades but had accepted the remit placed upon it by the Comintern. He now asked that the Comintern take over this responsibility.[118] At least one Comintern official now began to take a more critical stance towards Hardy's analysis and influence, arguing that he had pushed the Party too far towards white labour at the expense of black. Hardy, it was alleged 'a soutenu vigoureusement des propositions écartant complètement les indigènes de la prochaine campagne pour les élections législatifs. ... L'attitude de HARDY a été particulièrement mauvaise; c'est lui qui a le plus contribué par ses soi-disant connaissances de l'Afrique du Sud à orienter la discussion dans un sens erroné'. Hardy, the report concluded, had tried to push a 'white' line in the CPSA and had negatively influenced Wolfson and another visiting British Communist, Peter Kerrigan, in the same direction. Thus, the author of the report opposed Pollitt's suggestion of sending Hardy back to South Africa.[119]

Following the move of CPSA headquarters to Cape Town, which disrupted the lines of communication between Johannesburg and Moscow, and the outbreak of world war in Europe, Comintern intervention and influence in South Africa began to taper off. By 1940 Naumann was reporting that the Comintern had received very little material from South Africa and that its information was gleaned from reports in the the *Guardian* and the bourgeois press.[120]

Conclusion

The CPSA's adoption of the People's Front policy converged with Moses Kotane's attempt to embrace a more flexible and less sectarian approach to the national liberation struggle. Nonetheless, the endorsement of the People's Front did not mean Kotane's automatic political ascendancy within the Party. Internecine struggles intertwined with personal rivalries continued through the 1930s and led to the virtual collapse of the Party in 1938. Moreover, while the People's Front had some credibility in societies with traditions of liberalism and toleration, in racially-polarized South Africa, the policy proved unable to reconcile the conflicting interests of black and white labour. As white labour strove to protect its privileged status *vis-à-vis* black labour, refusing to support demands for racial equality, practical efforts to unite black and white workers invariably led to concessions to white racism and the compromise of the struggle for black democratic rights. This, in turn, increased racial tensions within the Party.

Comintern intervention in the 1930s had a repeatedly negative impact on the CPSA's development. The numerically tiny Party with its fluctuating membership had scant resources to withstand – let alone contest – this external authority. Unlike the CPGB, the CPSA lacked a body of 'trade union Communists' who had worked their way up the trade union hierarchy from the shop floor and, while 'rendering unto Stalin what was Stalin's', nonetheless were constrained from complete obesiance to Moscow's orders by the pressure of their trade union membership.[121] Paradoxically, the efforts to entice Bill Andrews back into the CPSA represented a tacit admission both by the Comintern and the local Party of the need for this type of cadre. Finally, South African Communists suffered from an inferiority complex, seeing themselves as theoretically backward and unsophisticated compared to their European and Soviet counterparts. The only real protection that the CPSA had from the Comintern was distance. The shift of the CPSA's headquarters away from Johannesburg and the outbreak of war accentuated that factor and provided an opportunity for South African Communists to reassess their situation.

Notes

1. Poem by Eddie Roux on the South African tot system, Ralph Bunche Collection, box 64.
2. Karis and Carter, eds, *From Protest to Challenge*, vol. 2, 3–5.
3. In 1936, 0.3 per cent of all Africans were engaged in commerce and finance, compared to 6.6 per cent of Coloured men, 1.0 per cent of Coloured women, 27.3 per cent of Indian men and 19.4 per cent of Indian women. Van der Horst, 'Labour', 113 and 122–3.
4. Lodge, *Black Politics*, 9–11.
5. McDermott and Agnew, *The Comintern*, 120–57, esp. 142ff for explanations of the Great Terror and its impact on the Comintern.
6. George Dimitrov, 'The Fascist Offensive and the Tasks of the Communist International in the Struggle of the Working Class Against Fascism: Main Report delivered at the Seventh World Congress of the Communist International, August 2, 1935', in George Dimitrov, *Against Fascism and War*, New York: International Publishers, 1986, 1–94, esp. 26, 34–6, 48.
7. Letter from J. W. Macauley, December 6, 1933, RTsKhIDNI, 495.64.126; Roux, *Time Longer than Rope*, 269.
8. Pelling, *The British Communist Party*, 192.
9. Minutes of the Fourth Plenum of the Communist Party (South Africa), 6–11 February, 1933, 14, 33–6, 38, RTsKhIDNI, 495.64.129.
10. *What is the Native Independent Republic?*, [1934], in Drew, ed., *South Africa's Radical Tradition*, vol. 1, 196–211, esp. 205–6 and 209–11; Legassick, 'Class and Nationalism in South African Protest', 51–2.
11. Letter from Gonas [sic] to Rayna, 12 November 1934, and John Gomas, IS *A NATIVE REPUBLIC* IDENTICAL WITH A *WORKERS AND PEASANTS* GOVERNMENT, both in RTsKhIDNI, 495.64.133.
12. Bunting, *Kotane*, 46, 61, 68.
13. Roux and Roux, *Rebel Pity*, 129; 142–4; Simons and Simons, *Class and Colour*, 459.
14. Both quotes Moses Kotane, South Africa Commission, 13 March 1936, 6, RTsKhIDNI, 495.14.20a.

15. Bunting, *Kotane*, 63–4; Roux, *Bunting*, 170; Roux, *Rebel Pity*, 136.

16. Roux, *Bunting*, 170; 'What is the Communist Party? A South African Native Republic, Lesson 3: The Native Republic 1', *Umsebenzi*, 24 February 1934 and 'What is the Communist Party? Lesson 4: What Will be Done in the Bantu Republic', *Umsebenzi*, 17 March 1934, both in Drew, ed., *South Africa's Radical Tradition*, vol. 1, 213–15.

17. Moses M. Kotane, WHY THE SUGGESTION FOR A NON-EUROPEAN RADICAL CONFERENCE, n.d., RTsKhIDNI, 495.64.137.

18. Bunting, *Kotane*, 68; 'Letter calling for Africanisation in the Party from Moses M. Kotane in Cradock to Johannesburg District Party Committee dated February 23, 1934', in Bunting, ed., *South African Communists Speak*, 120–22.

19. Report of Special Meeting, Johannesburg Branch, C.P.S.A., held on Thursday, 24th May, Sunday, 27th May and Sunday, 2nd June 1934, 1, 3, 29, RTsKhIDNI, 495.64.137. On the personalized nature of the political differences see also Letter from M. Basch, J. Flior and P. Voronoff to the Political Bureau, Communist Party of S. Africa, 13 April 1934; Letter from L. Bach to P.B., C.P.S.A., 9 July 1934; and Letter from Hilda Saks to the Political Bureau, C.P.S.A., 13 April 1934, all in RTsKhIDNI, 495.64.135.

20. M. Kotane, *The Slogan 'Independent Native Republic'*, Johannesburg, 31/10/34. Kotane's paper was sent to Moscow and subsequently read by Marty who wrote in February 1936: 'a very important letter, about which I never had been informed'. Both in RTsKhIDNI, 495.14.342.

21. Edwin Mofutsanyana, REPORT TO E.C.C.I., 25 September 1935, quotes 1, 2, 1, RTsKhIDNI, 495.64.149. See also John Marks, SITUATION AS WE FOUND IT, n.d., RTsKhIDNI, 495.64.133.

22. 'Native Bourgeoisie as a Class', *Umsebenzi*, 16 February 1935; see, *inter alia*, E. R. Roux, 'The Native Exploiters: A Reply to "A.Z."', *Umsebenzi*, 20 April 1935; E. T. Mofutsanyana, 'The Native Exploiters in South Africa', *Umsebenzi*, 27 April 1935, all in Drew, ed., *South Africa's Radical Tradition*, vol. 1, 219–20, 222–4, quote 219; Bunting, *Kotane*, 71–3.

23. Mofutsanyana, REPORT TO E.C.C.I., 3. The four people expelled were Hilda Saks, Anna Spilkin, B. Levenberg and A. Kagan.

24. Roux and Roux, *Rebel Pity*, 144–5; Bunting, *Kotane*, 73; Simons and Simons, *Class and Colour*, 477, 664, n. 35.

25. 'Information on the Factional Struggle in the Communist Party of South Africa, 11/3/36', RTsKhIDNI, 495.14.347; Letter from E. R. Roux *et al.* to the ECCI and all members of the CPSA, 20 September 1935, RTsKhIDNI, 495.64.140.

26. Brian Bunting is incorrect when he states, in *Kotane*, 74, that 'at the end of the second session the commission adjourned without reaching any conclusion on the main issue, and never reassembled'. He repeats the error in his annotated edition of Roux, *Bunting*, at 191, n. 48.

27. 'Report from R. K. Nauman', 2/1/36, RTsKhIDNI, 495.14.347; 'Proposal: A draft resolution from the secretariat of the Central Committee of the Communist International concerning the internal situation within the Communist Party of South Africa (from secretary comrade Marty)', 5 March 1936, RTsKhIDNI, 495.14.342. My thanks to Dennis Pennington for translating this document from the Russian.

28. Opening statement of André Marty, South Africa Commission, 13 March 1936, RTsKhIDNI, 495.14.20a.

29. Marty and other Comintern officials believed that the Purified National Party, which

under the leadership of D. F. Malan had broken with the Fusion Government, had radical anti-imperialist potential.

30. 'Proposal: A draft resolution from the secretariat of the Central Committee of the Communist International', RTsKhIDNI, 495.14.342.

31. Kotane, South African Commission, 13 March 1936, 12–13, RTsKhIDNI, 495.14.20a.

32. Richter, South African Commission, 13 March 1936, 17, RTsKhIDNI, 495.14.20a.

33. Eugene [Lazar Bach], South Africa Commission, 13 March 1936, 1, RTsKhIDNI, 495.14.20a.

34. Eugene [Lazar Bach], South Africa Commission, 15 March 1936, 29, RTsKhIDNI, 495.14.20a.

35. Edgar, interview with Mofutsanyana, 19; Gillian Slovo, *Every Secret Thing*, 274–6.

36. Henderson [Josie Mpama], South African Commission, 13 March 1936, 2–3, RTsKhIDNI, 495.14.20a.

37. Naumann, South Africa Commission, 15 March 1936, quote 1 and 2, 4, 10–11, 15–16, RTsKhIDNI, 495.20.14a.

38. Stepanov, South Africa Commission, 19 March 1936, 9, 22–23, RTsKhIDNI, 495.14.20a.

39. Eugene, South Africa Commission, 19 March 1936, 3, RTsKhIDNI, 495.14.20a.

40. Richter, South Africa Commission, 19 March 1936, 7, RTsKhIDNI, 495.14.20a.

41. Henderson, South Africa Commission, 19 March 1936, 7, RTsKhIDNI, 495.14.20a.

42. Kotane, South Africa Commission, 19 March 1936, 2, 5, 7 respectively, RTsKhIDNI, 495.14.20a.

43. 'Concluding speech of Comrade Marty', South Africa Commission, 19 March 1936, 3 and 15a, RTsKhIDNI, 495.20.14a.

44. Naumann, South Africa Commission, March 15, 1936, 14, RTsKhIDNI, 495.14.20a.

45. 'Concluding speech of Comrade Marty', 20 and 16 respectively, RTsKhIDNI, 495.20.14a.

46. The Trades and Labour Council was the successor of the Trades Union Congress. It was founded in October 1930 in Cape Town at a conference of the Trades Union Congress and the Cape Federation of Labour Unions, although the latter refused to join. The Trades and Labour Council was a response to the increasing numbers of industrial workers, as opposed to craft workers, in the labour market. It allowed the affiliation of black trade unions, although the actual number of black members was very small. Although it called for non-racial unions and demanded the abolition of racial labour laws, its practice failed to keep pace with its rhetoric. However, progressive trade unionists were able to advance their positions within it.

47. 'Concluding speech of Comrade Marty', 21–23, quote 21, RTsKhIDNI, 495.20.14a.

48. Simons and Simons, *Class and Colour*, 473.

49. 'Report on the South African Situation', 4 November [?] 1937, 11, RTsKhIDNI, 495.14.354; also in 495.20.662.

50. Trotskyists concurred that economic adversity would help to radicalize white workers. See 'The Poor Whites', *Spark*, 5, 6, June 1939, 8.

51. Simons and Simons, *Class and Colour*, 471.

52. Everett, 'Gool', 9.

53. Bunting, *Kotane*, 76.

54. Mokgatle, *Autobiography*, 197, 233–5.

55. Letter from Albert Inkpin for Political Bureau of CPGB to A. Losovsky, Profintern, 16

December 1926, RTsKhIDNI, 534.7.32; Letter from George Hardy to the Political Bureau of the C.P.G.B., 5 October 1928, RTsKhIDNI, 495.100.514.

56. George Hardy, *Those Stormy Years: Memoirs of the Fight for Freedom in Five Countries*, London: Lawrence & Wishart, 1956, 228–36, quote 236. Hardy and his lover divorced their spouses and married.

57. See RTsKhIDNI, 495.14.343, most of which concerns documentation about the CPSA's Sixth National Conference. The members of the Central Committee in September 1936 included: E. Mofutsanyana, I. Wolfson, W. Kalk, M. Kotane, J. W. Emmerich, E. Weinberg, L. T. Leepile, H. Basner, M. Diamond, Naidoo and J. Gomas. The panel commission originally included Leepile, Basner and Kalk (chair); Gomas, Kotane and Ray Alexander were added. The CPSA also established a political commission, which included Kotane, Mofutsanyana, Basner and Thomas.

58. Simons and Simons, *Class and Colour*, 479.

59. Basner, *Am I an African?*, 23–30, 47–52, 55.

60. Naumann, South Africa Commission, 15 March 1936, 1, RTsKhIDNI, 495.14.20a.

61. 'Communist Party of South Africa Plenum Held from 5th to 8th April 1936', *Umsebenzi*, 16 May 1936, in Drew, ed., *South Africa's Radical Tradition*, vol. 1, 239–40.

62. Simons and Simons, *Class and Colour*, 477–81; Southall, 'Marxist Theory', 67–70.

63. S. B., 'Unite Against Reaction and Oppression: United Front Against National Oppression and Fascism', *Umsebenzi*, 23 May 1936 and 'The United Front in South Africa: A Reply to S.B.', *South African Worker*, 13 June 1936, both in Drew, ed., *South Africa's Radical Tradition*, vol. 1, 240–44. Robertson's reply seems to have carried some authority: it was followed by a line which read: 'The correspondence on this subject is now closed'.

64. Communist Party of South Africa, *Organise a People's Front in South Africa*, Johannesburg, September 1936, 17.

65. 'Report on the South African Situation', 15, RTsKhIDNI, 495.14.354. See also Bunting, *Kotane*, 78.

66. RTsKhIDNI, 495.14.343; Simons, *Class and Colour*, 479, 513. On Thibedi see *South African Worker*, 21 November 1936.

67. Letter from Hester Cornelius to Comrade Salda, 17 January 1936, RTsKhIDNI, 495.14.346; 'On the Situation of the Communist Party of South Africa', 4/4/38, 20, RTsKhIDNI, 495.20.666.

68. Kevin Morgan, 'Harry Pollitt, the British Communist Party and International Communism', unpublished paper, 1997.

69. 'Towards the People's Front – Conference Against Fascism and War', report in *The South African Worker*, October 16, 1936, in Bunting, ed., *South African Communists Speak*, 128–30, quote 130.

70. Eddie Roux, Willie Kalk, C. B. Tyler and Gana Makabeni all spoke at the funeral. E. R. Roux, 'S. P. Bunting', *Forward*, 29 May 1936, 5; 'Meeting of Secretariat on South African Question, Hardy (Report), 17 March 1937, 12, RTsKhIDNI, 495.20.664.

71. Simons and Simons, *Class and Colour*, 471, 479; Bunting, *Kotane*, 78–9; Bunting, ed., *South African Communists Speak*, 125.

72. 'The Inner Party Situation in South Africa', 7 February 1937, 10–11, RTsKhIDNI, 495.14.352.

73. '15th Anniversary of 1922 Rand Strike: Communist Party Calls Mass Demonstration to Commemorate', *South African Worker*, in Drew, ed., *South Africa's Radical Tradition*, vol. 1, 251–2.

74. Letter to 'Dear Comrade', 23 April 1937, RTsKhIDNI, 495.14.351. The writer credits himself and Edwin Mofutsanyana for achieving the compromise. On May Day 1937 in Cape Town see *May Day … Day of Labour Solidarity: Manifesto of the United May Day Committee*, Cape Town: Communist Party of South Africa, Simons Collection, Pamphlet Collection, P225.

75. 'Johannesburg Municipal Elections: Communist Party asks Labour Party for Working Arrangement', *South African Worker*, 12 June 1937, in Drew, ed., *South Africa's Radical Tradition*, vol. 1, 269–70; Simons and Simons, *Class and Colour*, 481–2.

76. 'The Inner Party Situation', RTsKhIDNI, 495.14.352; 'Meeting of Secretariat on South African Question, Hardy (Report)' and 'Meeting of Secretariat on South African Question, Marty (sub-report)' 17 March 1937, RTsKhIDNI, 495.20.664.

77. McDermott and Agnew, *The Comintern*, 144. Steven Rosefielde, 'Documented Homicides and Excess Deaths: New Insights into the Scale of Killing in the USSR during the 1930s', *Communist and Post-Communist Studies*, 30, 3, 1997, 321–31, states that estimates on the number of deaths caused by collectivization, famine, the terror, execution or forced labour in the Soviet Union during the 1930s range from 2 to 10 million.

78. Letter from E. Varga to J. V. Stalin, 28 March 1938 in McDermott and Agnew, *Comintern*, 244–6, quote 246; see also 142–57. The authors indicate that problems of evidence and methodology make it difficult to assess the numbers of those killed as a result of the terror, and there is still much debate about the explanation for the terror. Illegal Communist Parties were more vulnerable and suffered more casualties than their legal counterparts. Particular nationalities, such as the Poles, suffered disproportionately.

79. John Saville, 'Obituary: Robin Page Arnot', *Society for the Study of Labour History Bulletin*, 51, 3, November 1986, 3–5, quote 5.

80. South African Friends of the Soviet Union, Johannesburg branch, flyers, RTsKhIDNI, 495.14.359; 'Execution of Counter-Revolutionaries: A Reply to Attack of "Friend of Soviet Union" (!) in "Forward"' and 'Proletarian Justice for Trotskyist Terrorists', both in *South African Worker*, 5 September 1936, 1 and 2, respectively.

81. Mokgatle, *Autobiography*, 211.

82. Minutes of Politburo of the CPSA, Johannesburg, 12 July 1937, RTsKhIDNI, 495.14.350. At the same meeting the trio also discussed the expulsion of John Marks, which had taken place in June 1937 (see *South African Worker*, 26 June 1937). Marks felt that there had been a campaign against him. He claimed that he had been mysteriously removed from the leadership while visiting Durban in 1935. He stated that it had become clear to him after Tilly First's return from the USSR that Adler, Bach and Zusmanovich were hostile to him, and he had noticed that even Joffe and Mofutsanyana had changed their manner to him. Mofutsanyana also noted that he and Marks had heard rumours that one of them was an informer and that it was believed to be Marks. Edgar, interview with Mofutsanyana, 31. See also Simons and Simons, *Class and Colour*, 482. Marks was readmitted a few years later.

83. The CPSA claimed that the *Sunday Express* reports were false and had been planted by Cape Town Trotskyists. See '"Sunday Express" Lies Again: Scare Story from Trotskyists', *South African Worker*, 1 August 1937, 2. Ray Adler Harmel had lived with Lazar Bach before he went to Moscow. Much later, she heard that he had been accused of Trotskyism and had died while imprisoned. She was anguished but her reaction reveals the seemingly unshakeable faith many Communists had in the Comintern: 'I said once

at the group to which I belonged that if that was the decision of the Comintern I would have to accept it but that never, never had I heard Lazar express Trotskyist views. I couldn't argue with the Comintern. I wasn't there.' Harmel, *Ray's Story*, 41.

84. On 21 August 1937 Marty wrote to Dimitrov about the three men and enclosed typed copies of articles from the *Sunday Express*. He professed no knowledge of how they had come to be sentenced to death. 'After the South African Commission in March 1936, I proposed that these people should be sent out of Russia to their own country, Latvia, expelled from the Party, and that we shall see what they were able to do by their own work. When I returned here on February 28, I was informed that they were expelled from the Party, but I did not know anything about it. ... I have not understood why it was necessary to give such publicity to such little people as Bach and the two Richters. I would like to know your proposals how to help the party answer this campaign.' Letter from André Marty to Dimitrov, 21 August 1937, RTsKhIDNI, 495.14.351. See McDermott and Agnew, *Comintern*, 148–9, regarding the murder of Latvians and other nationalities during the Great Terror.

85. 'The Inner Party Situation', RTsKhIDNI, 495.14.352.

86. Hymie Basner Tapes, Reel 2, School of Oriental and African Studies, University of London.

87. 'Report on Meeting in Paris on October 28', 16 November 1937, RTsKHIDNI, 495.14.354.

88. 'Report to Brother Party in Great Britain', n.d., [October 1937?, date-stamped with Russian stamp 15 March 1938], 41, 46, RTsKhIDNI, 495.14.355.

89. Edgar, ed., *An African-American*, 246.

90. Minutes of CPSA Politburo meeting of 24 August 1936, 2, RTsKhIDNI, 495.14.344. The meeting was attended by Kotane, Mofutsanyana, Gomas, Wolfson, Kalk, Radebe, Fleet and Nikin.

91. 'Report to Brother Party', 41, 46–7, RTsKhIDNI, 495.14.355.

92. 'Report to Brother Party', 42, RTsKhIDNI, 495.14.355.

93. Mokgatle, *Autobiography*, 194–9.

94. 'Report to Brother Party', 44, 52, RTsKhIDNI, 495.14.355.

95. 'On the Situation of the Communist Party of South Africa', 2/12/37, 13, RTsKhIDNI, 495.14.352. See also 'On the Situation of the Communist Party of South Africa', 4/4/38, 20, Comintern RTsKhIDNI, 495.20.666.

96. Roux and Roux, *Rebel Pity*, 141–2; 'Notes of the month', *Umvikele-Thebe/African Defender*, 9, June 1937, in Drew, ed., *South Africa's Radical Tradition*, vol. 1, 267–8.

97. RTsKhIDNI, 495.14.352. 'Draft Resolution for the Secretariat on the line of the Communist Party of the Union of South Africa', 14/3/37, RTsKhIDNI, 495.20.662.

98. Podbrey, *White Girl*, 29.

99. 'Report to Brother Party'. The 'Inner Party Situation', 7/2/37, reported sixteen members in Durban.

100. Statement of Comrade Basner, 5 November 1937, [presented to CPGB 7 March 1938], RTsKhIDNI, 495.14.355.

101. Bunche Collection, boxes 64 and 65; Simons and Simons, *Class and Colour*, 478–80.

102. Harry Pollitt to Comrade [name cut out] 20 October 1937, RTsKhIDNI, 495.14.355.

103. 'On the meeting with Comrade Bill Andrews (South Africa), 3/12/37 (translation of statement of Comrade Naumann)', 1, RTsKhIDNI, 495.14.352.

104. CPSA Politburo Meeting minutes, 12 July 1936, RTsKhIDNI, 495.14.344. Cope, *Comrade Bill*, 330–31.

105. Bunting, *Kotane*, 90; Bunting, ed., *South African Communists Speak*, 133.

106. A tripartite editorial commission was set up, comprising Thomas, Mofutsanaya and Basner. Sixth National Conference of the CPSA, 5–6 September 1936, RTsKhIDNI, 495.14.343. Louis Joffe became political editor. In 1937 the editorial board was expanded and consisted of Mofutsanyana, Kalk, Wolfson, Thomas and Radebe; in practice, though, planning was left to one or two comrades. Report by Comrade Wolfson to CPGB (continued), n.d., [October 1937?], 1–2, RTsKhIDNI, 495.14.355.

107. Minutes of Central Committee of CPSA, 31 December 1937–3 January 1938, Johannesburg, RTsKhIDNI, 495.14.355. See also W. K., 'Mr. Sachs Appeals to Capitalist Court' *South African Worker*, 27 November 1937, 2.

108. Eli Weinberg, Report to Colonial Committee, London, 21 February 1939, RTsKhIDNI, 495.14.360a; 'Resolution of the Political Bureau of the Communist Party of S. Africa', Simons Collection, South African Communist Party, 6.6.1.

109. Resolution on Comrade Basner in Resolutions of Central Committee of CPSA, 29 December 1938–2 January 1939, 5, RTsKhIDNI, 495.14.358. Basner, *Am I an African?*, 97–8.

110. Mofutsanyana, 'Report on the Struggle of Africans', Simons Collection, South African Communist Party, 6.6.1. In his interview with Bob Edgar, 35, Mofutsanyana claimed that no one in the Party had ever argued for black and white sections. The CPSA was not the only socialist group to experience these problems. The ephemeral Socialist Workers League believed in the parallel organization of blacks and whites. See *Statement of Policy*, 4. Similarly, according to I. B. Tabata, during the war the underground Workers' Party briefly met in racially-divided groups as a means of bypassing the problems of travelling to and meeting in residentially segregated areas, but this policy was quickly abandoned. Interview with I. B. Tabata and Jane Gool, Harare, December 1987.

111. 'Minutes of Meeting of C.P.S.A. held in Johannesburg, December 29, 1938 to January 1, 1939', Simons Collection, South African Communist Party, 6.6.1, 2–5; Bunting, *Kotane*, 91; Simons and Simons, *Class and Colour*, 484–5; Basner, *Am I an African?*, 96.

112. 'Statement of Cape Town DPC on Party Organisation' and 'Minutes of Meeting of C.P.S.A. held in Johannesburg, December 29, 1938 to January 1, 1939, 42, both in Simons Collection, South African Communist Party, 6.6.1.

113. 'Inner Party Situation', 7/II/37. In February 1939 the CPSA's membership was reported at 200, including 100–120 members in Johannesburg; 42 in Cape Town, 30 in Durban and various other individuals. Cape Town members included 11 Africans, 4 Afrikaners, 7 Jews, 2 South Africans and 18 Coloured. Report of Colonial Committee, 21 February 1939, RTsKhIDNI, 495.14.360a.

114. Bunting, *Kotane*, 84–7, 91–2, 96; Cope, *Comrade Bill*, 329. See also Report to Colonial Committee, London, 21 February 1939, 5, RTsKhIDNI, 495.14.360a. The Politburo comprised Moses Kotane, Jack Simons, Bill Andrews, Cissie Gool, Sam Kahn and Ray Alexander.

115. Radford moved to South Africa from England in 1931 and worked on the *Cape Times*. She and her husband, the medical doctor George Sacks, were sympathetic to the CPSA and joined it in 1941. The *Cape Guardian* was launched in February. In June it was renamed the *Guardian*. See Les Switzer, 'Socialism and the Resistance Movement: the Life and Times of the Guardian, 1937–1952', in Switzer, ed., *South Africa's Alternative Press*, 266–307, esp. 274.

116. R. Naumann, 'Proposals by the English Comrades on the South African Question', 29 August 1937, RTsKhIDNI, 495.14.352.

117. 'On the Situation of the Communist Party of South Africa', 2/12/37, 12, RTsKhIDNI, 495.14.352.
118. Typed note from Harry Pollitt to Comrade [name cut out], 1/11/37, RTsKhIDNI, 495.14.355.
119. 'Attitude du P.C.G.B. à l'occasion de la question S.A.', 6/11/37, RTsKhIDNI, 495.14.355. But another report, 'On the Situation of the Communist Party of South Africa', 4/4/38, 21, stated that Hardy should have returned to South Africa.
120. R. Naumann, 'Some Notes on South Africa', March 4, 1940, RTsKhIDNI, 495.14.360a.
121. Morgan, 'Harry Pollitt', 3.

Chapter 9

Illusory visions: black unity and left unity in the 1930s

In the political ferment of the late 1930s, Johnny Gomas and Goolam Gool epitomized two archetypal socialists – the former a Communist, the latter a Trotskyist. Both men 'were bitterly opposed to racialism', wrote Peter Abrahams, himself a struggling young writer who roamed in left circles, 'and both were sincere and honest in their strivings for non-European emancipation. And each was all that was untruthworthy to the other. Labels had conquered the men.'[1] While South African socialists had been a discordant bunch since the movement's first years, Soviet terror and the demonization of Trotskyism dashed hopes of unity on the left in the late 1930s. But if unity of the left was revealed as a utopian dream, how much more difficult the goal of uniting all black South Africans in a movement for democracy.

The movement for black unity that developed in the mid-1930s and that straddled both class and sectional divisions had socioeconomic roots and political motivations. The socio-economic underpinnings lay in the impact of capitalist development on those classified as African, Indian and Coloured. Although their histories had begun in different parts of the world, the conditions of South African blacks were slowly and spasmodically ground together through the processes of proletarianization, urbanization and industrialization. This process had the deepest roots in the Western Cape, from the conquest of the Khoisan and the importation and subsequent emancipation of a slave population from Indonesia, India, Madagascar and the East Africa coast. To Ralph Bunche, comparing the urbanized proletarians of the Western Cape with Africans in the reserves, '[i]t would appear that the vast majority of the colored population live in dire poverty and squalor'. Indeed, he argued,

> economically they are worse off than the natives, who living at their kraals, on the locations and reserves, are at least more certain of getting sufficient food. The colored group is completely at the mercy of the white, because it must work for the white in order to get food. The natives, on the other hand, need work for whites, only to be able to pay poll taxes. The colored group has no economic foundations at all – it is suspended – between white and black.[2]

The African population was still predominantly rural in the 1930s. Compared to the obvious proletarianization of the Coloured population, the nature and extent of African proletarianization was masked by remnants of labour-tenancy on white farms and by the reserves system, which gave the appearance of ensuring most Africans a minimum access to the means of subsistence, while restricting the development of a peasantry. In 1936, roughly 57 per cent of all Africans were based in the reserves. But even in the 1920s, the ability of the reserves to ensure African subsistence was illusory, particularly in the Cape. Africans were increasingly proletarianized, the men forced to sell their labour-power through the migrant-labour system. African women formed the majority in the reserves, and although they were the least urbanized group of the population, by the late 1930s they were moving into towns at an increasing rate, a reaction to the deteriorating conditions of the reserves.[3]

The political basis of black unity in South Africa lay in the common lack of democratic rights. The enfranchisement of white women in 1930 reduced the significance of the black vote in the Cape and accentuated the gap between black and white. Government proposals to eliminate the Cape African franchise in 1936 and to include all Africans through indirect representation under the NRC lessened legal differences among Africans. It was only a matter of time before the government began chipping away at the few political rights of Coloureds. This was signalled by the abortive attempt, in the late 1930s, to introduce the Stuttaford Bills to enforce segregation in public and residential areas and by the subsequent efforts in the 1940s to institutionalize the Coloured Affairs Council and Coloured Affairs Department. Similarly, a series of laws in the 1930s and 1940s segregated and restricted the property rights of South Africans of Indian descent, who fell under the jurisdiction of the Commissioner for Immigration and Asiatic Affairs and the Minister for the Interior.[4]

The All African Convention (AAC), the National Liberation League (NLL) and the Non-European United Front (NEUF), all formed in the late 1930s, reflected these social and political developments. Since the late nineteenth century, the black petty bourgeoisie had organized for democratic rights within organizations that followed the sectional framework of the South African polity. The ANC catered in its early years to the interests of chiefs and the minute African elite; when the ICU broke up, the ANC 'failed to co-ordinate or revive the remnants of what could have been its trade union wing'.[5] Similarly, the APO represented the interests of the Coloured petty bourgeoisie, while the Transvaal British Indian Association (later the Transvaal Indian Congress) and the South African Indian Congress, founded in 1919, were dominated by the Indian merchant class. But by the 1930s the struggle for political incorporation using established methods like petitions and deputations had come to a dead end, unable to achieve even minimal reforms.[6]

Dr Abdullah Abdurahman of the APO had already launched a Non-European Conference in Kimberley in 1927, concerned about the impact of the discriminatory legislation passed by the Pact Government. This brought together the ANC, the ICU and a host of other black organizations and met in 1930, 1931 and 1934.

But the leaders of the Non-European Conference, including Dr Abdurahman, Dr Xuma of the ANC and Professor D. D. T. Jabavu, were concerned to achieve their ends through compromise, and they were unsuccessful at abating the onslaught of racist legislation.[7] Confronted with this assault under the Fusion Government, a tiny stratum of black radicals began to organize across sectional lines, forming alliances based on the idea of Non-European unity.

The attacks on black rights occurred alongside a simultaneous attempt by the government to strengthen sectional divisions. In the 1930s and 1940s, political seg-regation into separate African, Coloured and Indian structures reinforced social res-idential and occupational segregation. There was, in this period, an extremely high correlation of occupation and colour: whites performed professional, supervisory and skilled work, and Africans unskilled labour. Coloureds and Indians were an intermediary strata: most were unskilled workers, but some performed skilled, semi-skilled and artisanal work, especially in the Western Cape and Natal.[8] In popular consciousness, these sectional divisions were very much a reality, and the movement for black unity was initiated and led by a tiny radical minority seeking to break down this consciousness.

Initially, urban and rural poor flocked to these black united fronts, and their overwhelming predominance made these organizations a base that socialists, both Communists and Trotskyists, hoped to influence. As with the groundswell of sup-port for Abyssinia against Italy's invasion, the initial enthusiasm for these black united fronts indicated the speed with which black South Africans could be mobi-lized when an issue captured them. Nonetheless, as the 1930s came to a close, these organizations showed themselves unable to sustain the initial popular momentum that had inspired them. As Eddie Roux pointed out, against the backdrop of the ANC's and ICU's decimation, in terms of effective organization the delegates to the AAC 'represented very little but themselves. Most of them had no idea of stirring up the countryside. In vain the communists and other radicals pleaded for militant action. ... They were cold-shouldered into silence. The "big guns" of the Convention were all for negotiation and moderation.' The efforts of socialists to convene mass meetings came to nought, Roux continued. 'An Afrikaner paper pro-claimed in newspaper placards: "*Naturelle bly stil*" (Natives remain quiet). It was only too true; the masses did not act.'[9]

Calling an All African Convention

In 1935 Africans of all political stripes drew together and, building upon the tradi-tion of the first Non-European Conference eight years earlier, sought to form a united front – much as Moses Kotane had proposed in 1934 – to fight the Representation of Natives Bill and the Native Trust and Land Bill. In May 1935, when a joint select committee tabled the two bills in Parliament, Reverend Z. R. Mahabane, a former president of the ANC, called for a national convention, and on 15–18 December Pixley ka Izaka Seme, the conservative president of the ANC, and

Professor D. D. T. Jabavu, oldest son of John Tengo Jabavu, convened the first national conference of the AAC in Bloemfontein.[10]

The left gave its enthusiastic support. Socialist groups adamantly rejected the government's proposed legislation, particularly the attempt to abolish the African franchise and replace it with the Natives Representative Council. The CPSA scathingly described the NRC as 'a mere puppet council, with no real powers or authority', and it called upon black organizations and white workers to 'protest against this new fascist measure'.[11] The CPSA hoped to draw a diverse range of organizations into a People's Front, and in October 1935 it urged blacks to

> put away the difference of the ways toward national liberation. All of us have one common cause, requiring the unity of our efforts. ... The fight against national oppression and exploitation, the fight for the immediate, most nec-essary needs of the people – that is the basis for the united action of all the Native organisations, irrespective of their political differences. That is why we greet warmly the proposal to call a joint convention.[12]

From its inception the AAC embodied a variety of class and regional interests. Of the approximately 400 delegates attending the first conference, 200 were from the Cape, 100 from the Transvaal, 70 from the Orange Free State, 30 from Natal, 10 from Basutoland and one from Swaziland.[13] Formed to fight the curtailment of the African franchise in the Cape, Convention's base was strongest where it repre-sented those people directly affected by the proposed legislation. It was weakest in Natal, where the ICU was still viable. Significantly, the only major African leader to support the Hertzog Bills was John Dube, leader of the Natal ANC, who argued that the measures would increase the amount of land available to Africans.[14] Reverend Abner M'Timkulu, a prominent member of the Natal ANC and one of the Natal delegates to the AAC, tried to explain Natal's distinctive position to Ralph Bunche. His remarks indicate the degree to which the uneven political and eco-nomic development across the country presented material barriers to black unity and to the development of a national consciousness. Bunche recounted that accord-ing to Reverend M'Timkulu:

> Natal has not supported the African Convention because of feeling that the Convention is attempting to usurp the position of existing organizations, such as the I.C.U., which is still strong and active in Natal. He points out that the Convention developed around the Cape franchise question and the Native Rep. Bills, and that Zulus are not interested in the franchise because it is foreign to their experience; their thinking is entirely in terms of *land* and *more land* – they think that if they can get more land their problems will be solved. But they aren't interested in buying any land – they think it must be *given* to them – because they say the land belonged to their fathers and they wish it to be given back to them.[15]

The momentum for forming the AAC was supported by white liberals from the Institute of Race Relations and the Joint Councils of Europeans and Natives, and the black petty bourgeoisie who frequented these groups had a longer and stronger history of class conscious organization than did the black working class in that decade.[16] The social and class divisions among those facing common colour discrimination were apparent at Convention's inaugural meeting in December 1935, when it resolved 'that a civilisation test, such as was contemplated at the National Convention in 1909–1910, is equitable; but that the criterion of race or colour, which is implied in these Bills, is contrary to democratic government'.[17]

Nonetheless, in its unanimous opposition to the Hertzog Bills, the AAC began on a non-conciliatory note, and there were suggestions of a militant strategy. Gilbert Coka, who since his expulsion from the CPSA in July 1935, had begun editing the *African Liberator*, called the government's proposal for African representation 'a sop' and added that '[i]t was the duty of the chiefs, if they wished to do their people good, to organise and struggle to secure the franchise for the Native people'. John Marks urged that '[a]n active policy should be adopted by the Natives, who should refuse to pay taxes until their rights were recognised'. Johnny Gomas argued that '[s]uccess could only be obtained on the basis of the mass organisation of the people', and his resolution that the delegates form local committees to organize protests was met with unanimous approval. Goolam Gool stated that '[t]he Cape delegates were not present to discuss the Native Bills, but to reject them *in toto*', and he exhorted the AAC to 'lay the foundations of a national liberation movement to fight against all the repressive laws of South Africa'.[18]

Women delegates to the AAC saw the resurgence of political activity as an opportune moment to strengthen their own organization. The events of the 1930s placed particular pressure on black women activists. There was little common meeting ground for black and white women in that decade: while the majority of African women still resided in the reserves, Afrikaner women were rapidly moving to the towns and taking up factory work.[19] The 1930 enfranchisement of white women along with the government's first restriction on the movement of African women into towns the same year accentuated the gap between black and white women and signalled the government's commitment to restricting the rights of African women along with those of their men. The Bantu Women's League attended the first AAC conference – it was the only women's organization invited – and its president, Charlotte Maxeke, was introduced by A. B. Xuma as 'the mother of African freedom in this country'.[20] Maxeke had become 'a household name in the Transvaal' because of her legal aid work and her activism on social and educational issues.[21] But the Bantu Women's League was a weak body, and the women delegates to the AAC decided that it was time to establish a new organization that would subsume the Bantu Women's League. Two years earlier, a group of women at Kimberley had laid the groundwork for a National Council of African Women. This would parallel the white National Council of Women, an organization concerned with community welfare and other social issues that had been founded in 1909 as the South African branch of an international women's network. Now, the women at the AAC resolved 'that the time has come for the establishment of an African Council of Women on lines similar to those of the national councils of other races, in order that we may be able to do our share in the advancement of our race'. The Convention endorsed the National Council of African Women, recommending that branches be formed around the country.[22] The first meeting of the AAC showed a broad unity amongst its delegates. At this stage, before the passage of the Hertzog Bills, differences over strategies and tactics were not yet a divisive issue for the participants.

The interregnum

In April and May 1936 the Hertzog Bills became law. Cape Africans lost the qualified franchise and were placed on a separate voting roll that allowed them to elect three white members to the House of Assembly (for the Western Cape, Eastern Cape and the Transkei) and two whites to the Provincial Council. These had no voting rights on financial or constitutional matters. Africans as a whole could vote in indirect elections for four white senators (one for both the Transvaal and Orange Free State, one for Natal and two for the Cape) and for twelve African representatives. The new purely-advisory NRC was to consist of seven white administrators from the Department of Native Affairs and sixteen Africans, twelve of whom were elected and four of whom were government appointments. NRC councillors would receive a handsome stipend of £120 per year.[23]

Now the problems posed by the lack of a common strategy to fight these laws became more acute. Over the next eighteen months two issues became increasingly contentious for the AAC. The first was the question of how to contest the new laws and, specifically, the question of whether or not to boycott the NRC. The second concerned the nature and longevity of the AAC as an organization and its relationship with the ANC.

When the AAC held its second conference at Bloemfontein on 29 June – 2 July 1936, it was still undecided as to how to protest against the new laws. The African-American anthropologist Eslanda Goode Robeson, wife of the internationally renowned Paul Robeson, was touring South Africa in 1936, *en route* to Uganda. She attended the second conference and was impressed: 'The delegates were serious, able, aware. While they were reasonable, they were determined to find some way to improve their situation. The discussions were informative, and the suggestions practical and constructive.' She also met with the women delegates and 'discussed diet, child welfare and women's organizations in other parts of the world', promising to send further information about these issues.[24]

Despite Eslanda Goode Robeson's idealized view of the AAC, conflicting political strategies and tactics were apparent at that conference. Hyman Basner, for one, was scathing about the influence of liberal whites connected with the Joint Councils and about the pecuniary motivations of Africans who decided to stand in the NRC elections, even though he opposed the idea of a boycott.[25] Even though there was no African bourgeoisie, a tiny, but influential, aspirant bourgeois stratum, eager to develop black business, actively promoted its own class interests in all its political activities. Selby Msimang penned a pamphlet around this time called *The Crisis*, which called for 'a complete segregation on a fifty-fifty basis to enable us to establish our own State and government wherein to exercise our political, economic and social independence'.[26] However, the separatist refrain remained a minority viewpoint amongst black political activists, both those supporting the aspirant bourgeoisie and those supporting workers and peasants.

The class interests of the petty bourgeoisie and of an aspirant bourgeoisie were encapsulated in D. D. T. Jabavu's presidential address, in which he expounded a policy of economic nationalism:

> We should burst our way into the vocations that create wealth among our communities. ... Business and Commerce must be stressed and much propaganda carried out to further them. Let us learn how to support our own traders, however humble they may be, out of a patriotic spirit of African nationalism. ... we could multiply the number of our humble shoemakers, tailors, grocers, taximen, bus contractors, butchers, farmers, cooperative stores, adopting a scheme of self-upliftment to counter the Government's anti-Black and repressive 'Civilised Labour' policy.[27]

More to the point, leading figures in the ANC and the AAC began to argue in earnest for participation in the NRC. R. V. Selope Thema, editor of *Bantu World*, was using his paper to promote the NRC, and he announced his own candidacy at the Convention.[28] Professor Jabavu, likewise, came out strongly against the boycott, calling it a 'policy of retaliative reprisals and bottled revenge' that, he claimed, could only succeed with complete unity, and counterposing it to the other extreme of unconditional acceptance of the new laws. He proposed instead '[t]o evolve an intermediary policy of using what can be used and fighting against all that we do not want'.[29]

By contrast, the AAC's small but articulate left wing called for the boycott of all racial institutions. They were not the first to broach the boycott tactic: the Western Cape ANC had suggested a boycott of racial elections at the Second Non-European Conference in 1930.[30] Radicals in the AAC saw the boycott of the NRC as a means to resist the government's systematic exclusion of blacks from national political institutions and their segregation into powerless advisory bodies.

But the majority of the delegates agreed with Jabavu and accepted the somewhat ambiguous resolutions submitted by the AAC's Executive Committee. While deferring to white fears of social integration, they called for political equality, noting that the AAC

> re-affirms its conviction that the only way in which the interests of the various races which constitute the South African population can be safeguarded is by the adoption of a policy of political identity. Such a policy will ensure the ultimate creation of a South African State in which, while the various groups may develop on different lines socially and culturally they will be bound together by the pursuit of common political objectives.

To achieve this end, the Executive was empowered 'to explore all effective avenues of action'.[31]

Over the next eighteen months it became clear that conservative tendencies had the momentum. The ANC took the decision to support the NRC first, nominating its own candidates at its 1936 conference. Although the AAC had not yet taken a decisive stand on the NRC, between June 1936 and December 1937 many of the AAC's leaders decided on their own to participate in it. In the June 1937 indirect elections for the twelve African seats in the newly-established NRC, half were won by members of the AAC executive: R. V. Selope Thema, Thomas M. Mapikela, Reverend John Dube, Max Jabavu, R. H. Godlo and C. K. Sakwe.[32] Within two years of its formation an organization that had originated as the mouthpiece of all Africans, with a mandate to reject the NRC, became the mouthpiece of NRC representatives.

Moreover, liberal whites also saw the new machinery as a platform from which to call for change. The first election for the white Native Representatives took place in November 1937, and a number of liberals won seats: Edgar Brookes and J. D. Rheinallt Jones to the Senate, and Donald Molteno and Margaret Hodgson Ballinger – a liberal 'from Scottish radical stock' – to the House of Assembly. Margaret Ballinger shared her husband William's criticism of the Joint Councils and of the Institute of Race Relations, which was set up, she complained, 'so that anybody who might have really independent views on the direction of native policy and the means to be pursued in respect of it was not included'.[33] Marriage in 1934 had ended her career as a history lecturer at the University of the Witwatersrand – married women were not allowed to serve on staff, and her husband's politics did not help matters. The Ballingers then worked for the Friends of Africa and tried to launch a cooperative movement in South Africa, enthusiastic about 'the social and spiritual value of cooperatives as a training ground for people denied other outlets'.[34] But the Ballingers also saw the new political machinery as a means to 'keep the election door open for natives'. Margaret Ballinger ran for election at the suggestion of Reverend James Calata and the Cape ANC, her campaign financed by the Friends of Africa and by several women's groups who wished to contest the belief that a woman could not win the election.[35]

Socialists, however, still agitated for a more radical approach in the interim between the AAC's second and third national conferences. But Communists and Trotskyists became increasingly polarized as the CPSA reversed its position and decided to endorse the NRC. Although most Communists had emphatically rejected the proposals for the NRC, Hyman Basner had condemned the boycott call from the beginning. But Basner on his own could never have effected a change in the Party's policy.[36] The People's Front policy, which advocated the use of all available political platforms, lay behind the Party's switch. By September 1936 the CPSA was arguing that, whatever the government's intentions, the NRC had 'opened a great avenue for Protest and Propaganda against all reactionary and detrimental legislation and for demands of social and economic freedom of the Native masses'. The Party stressed the need to 'make use of these opportunities'. It urged Africans to support the elections for the NRC and to vote in their local advisory board elections for 'the best men; men who have proved themselves; men you can trust' rather than the government's 'Good Boys'.[37] Following the rush by African elites to contest seats in the NRC, the CPSA, in turn, put forward its own candidates: Edwin Mofutsanyana for the NRC, to represent the urban areas of the Transvaal and Orange Free State, and Hyman Basner for Senate, focusing on the rural areas. In a parallel move, it asked the Labour Party for a working arrangement to support each other's candidates in the October 1937 all-white municipal elections.[38]

The CPSA's decision to contest the NRC elections did not go unchallenged within the Party. Privately, some Communists continued to oppose participation in racist institutions.[39] However, at least some of the pressure on Communists to support participation came from the Comintern; George Hardy, the Comintern's representative in South Africa in 1936, had vehemently opposed the boycott. A report to the Comintern stated that prior to the AAC's conference of 29 June – 2 July 1937, 'some of our comrades became subjective [sic] to the Trotskyite approach of boycotting the Representation Council' and indicated the rationale for participating in the NRC elections:

> [T]here are some possibilities for utilizing this machinery for the purposes of electing anti-imperialist candidates, and during this process raising the political level around a policy demanding full democratic rights. ... This can be carried out in every area by the A.A.C. and around which a mass basis can be organised and developed into a national liberation movement.[40]

For Trotskyists, by contrast, the AAC presented an opportunity to promote the working class independence that Trotsky had discussed in his 1935 letter to South Africa and that they thought was undermined by the People's Front.[41] In the late 1930s, the black population was composed overwhelmingly of a working class and a migrant labour force whose income was supplemented by subsistence farming. This class structure suggested the possibility that these black united fronts could approximate to the revolutionary alliance of workers and peasants that formed the basis of the Russian revolution. Trotskyists believed the AAC had the potential to embody this type of alliance. Because of the coincidence of class and colour, Trotskyists saw non-collaboration with the government's racial institutions as a means to fight class collaboration and promote working-class independence. The boycott tactic came to be viewed as part of a broader non-collaborationist approach to the state's intensified efforts to co-opt black leadership into government-created racial political structures. By confronting state authority, which in South Africa assumed a racial form, the non-collaborationist response raised the possibility that the working class could establish its own institutions and challenge the state through dual power.[42]

C. B. I. Dladla, for instance, had broken with the CPSA because of his disagreement with the Comintern's policies and its repeated interventions in the local Party.[43] Dladla became an organizer for the Johannesburg branch of the Workers'

Party, which he represented at the regional conference of the Transvaal section of the AAC in October 1936. Criticizing the AAC's failure to formulate a clear programme and set of goals, he called for a boycott of the NRC and urged the AAC to establish 'a separate independent Parliament, a council of delegates elected on the basis of universal adult suffrage'. He proposed that a campaign be launched to teach 'the masses of voteless, rightless Africans the necessity for a constituent Assembly to express their needs, their national unity, their revolt against their present slave status'. The Union Parliament was a mock parliament representing only a small minority of the population, and he called on Africans 'to transform this mockery into a real Parliament by the creation of a body of their fellow citizens elected by ballot and given mandates to speak on behalf of the masses of the people'. However, this resolution was rejected, leaving the Workers' Party to criticize those Communists who 'defended the [AAC] "leaders" against the criticism that had been justly levelled against them of failing to produce any programme whatsoever and so leading the Convention to inevitable collapse'.[44]

By 1937 many socialists were aware that the AAC had been hijacked by a leadership that eschewed militancy for petitionary methods and ended up participating in government structures. Yet they were uncertain and divided as to how to stop it. Some socialists, like Dladla and Gana Makabeni, were disillusioned early about the possibility of working in the AAC. When Ralph Bunche met them in November 1937, Makabeni informed Bunche that he was not going to either of the AAC's or ANC's forthcoming conferences. The latter, he said, was 'an attempt to revive a dead organization', and he argued that the best strategy at that time was to organize black workers into trade unions. He 'emphasized the corruption of educated native leader[s] – mentioning Seme, Kdale [sic], etc.'. Bunche reported that Dladla

> says there are no real revolutionaries in South Africa. ... He is bitterly critical of African leadership – says men like Jabavu (a 'white minion') and Seme ('a crook') are hopeless. Says left wing faction in African Convention tried to get the Native Representation Act boycotted. ... But Jabavu, et al said this was a big step toward solution of the native problem and supported the scheme. ... [Makabeni and Dladla] said the corrupt and conservative leaders 'pack' the conventions of native organizations and make it impossible for progressives to do anything.[45]

The AAC's third national conference

December 1937 saw four meetings of significance for black politics: the inaugural meeting of the NRC in Pretoria; and the third national conference of the AAC, the twenty-fifth anniversary or silver jubilee of the ANC, and the first national conference of the National Council of African Women, all in Bloemfontein. The paternalistic tone of the NRC's formal launch merely underscored what radicals had already predicted. The opening session saw the white members of the NRC sitting on a platform, while the black members looked up at them from tables below. D. L. Smit, Secretary for Native Affairs, presided; his strategy, thought Ralph Bunche, a shrewd observer at all the December meetings, was to divide the councillors on provincial lines. While Margaret Ballinger painted a far more positive picture of the NRC's first day, even she noted that the white officials were 'agreeably surprised' at the 'moderate tone' of the African councillors.[46] The NRC's inaugural meeting was a far cry from the ferment that had inspired the first AAC two years earlier.

The about-face represented by participation in the NRC was reflected in the AAC, whose political direction was even more cemented by its third national meeting. Three NRC members, Selope Thema, Mapikela, and Max Jabavu, were elected to the new executive. While the AAC still claimed to oppose all forms of segregation, it nonetheless endorsed the NRC, noting that all candidates elected under the 1936 Representation of Natives Act were 'recognised as the accepted mouthpiece of Africans'. They were, accordingly, expected to attend the AAC at Bloemfontein 'for the purpose of ascertaining ... African views on various questions, securing a mandate for expressing African views on matters arising ... and of giving an account of their stewardship'.[47]

Another significant presence at the meeting, and at the ANC's silver jubilee that followed, was the active participation of six white delegates who represented Africans in the NRC.[48] Their role, thought Ralph Bunche, was 'a dangerous one – they are now counselling extreme moderation among the natives so as not to offend the Afrikaners and thus make their task more difficult in Parliament.' One of the white senators, Bunche reported, a businessman named Karl Malcomess, 'says he wants natives for next few months "*to be moderate,*" to keep natives question from being injected into the coming election. Councels [sic]: "have patience." Says nat. rep. (Europ.) task is to *educate* white people.'

And when Selby Msimang described the slavelike conditions of farm labour and proposed that the AAC organize a Farm Labourers Association, Bunche noted, Senator Malcomess 'suggest[ed] that convention *withold action* on Msimang's report until Government Farm Labour Committee issues its report and then European reps. of natives and native councillors should be called in conference on the recommendations in the report'.

The motion to withold action was voted on and carried almost unanimously. '*Tactics of delay*', Bunche underlined, '*European influence strong.*' Interestingly, the local African Communists were far less critical of white influence. Edwin Mofutsanyana, who had a seat in the NRC, meekly suggested that Convention appeal to white NRC members to seek repeal of the repressive labour laws. Moses Kotane added his defense of the white Native Representatives, arguing that 'Convention has found a scapegoat today in the European reps. of the natives upon whom all burdens are being placed'.[49]

Although Coloured organizations such as the APO had been attending the AAC since its inception, the question of whether or not to mention other Non-European groups in the AAC's draft constitution was still contentious. Just as a strand of Coloured chauvinism, intertwined with the interests of a Coloured middle class, infected the predominantly Coloured organizations of the Western Cape, so a strand of African nationalism sought to make the AAC an exclusively African organization. Thus, when Goolam Gool moved that Coloured and Indian organizations be included in the AAC's draft constitution, the motion was opposed by both Max Jabavu and by Edwin Mofutsanyana. White liberals tried to keep the AAC an African-only body through financial pressure, reinforcing the sentiments of African nationalism. Bunche noted that

> [i]n answer to a question as to whether the Bantu Welfare Trust contribution is for natives only, Rheinold Jones [sic] sayd [sic] 'yes,'; thus implication is that A.A.C. is for natives only if it accepts the contribution and this was clearly defined by one speaker. Motion carried to leave the provision as it stands – a grave mistake and a victory for bigoted, black chauvinism which plays directly into the hands of the divisive policy of the government. There was very vigorous discussion and much wrangling over this issue.

Nonetheless, supporters of Gool's motion succeeded in their aim to include a constitutional clause allowing organizations from all Non-European groups the right to affiliate to the AAC.[50]

Indicative of the bourgeois class aspirations of some of the leadership were the numerous calls to stimulate African business through capital investment and traders' associations. While Max Jabavu declared that 'affluence wins respect', Margaret Ballinger argued that segregation could actually enhance the development of African trading interests.

Bunche commented on the lack of democracy at the conference, describing Professor Jabavu as 'a regular dictator, telling people on the floor to "sit down", etc'. He noted '[a] surprising amount of *levity* in the Convention. Jabavu always leads the laughter.' At one point Goolam Gool 'suggested that time is ripe for another pass-bearing campaign and it met only with unreserved mirth throughout the audience'. Political manipulation was rife: when the AAC's leadership finally endorsed the NRC, Goolam Gool was removed from the Central Executive for his opposition. Gool contended that had AAC leaders brought the issue of participation in the NRC to the Convention floor at its previous conference, it would have been rejected.[51]

By 1937 the organizational rivalry between the AAC and ANC had come to the fore, despite their common aims and their overlapping leadership. Although many top ANC figures occupied high posts in the AAC, Pixley ka Izaka Seme was far from receptive to the AAC, despite his neglect of the ANC, and he opposed the move to make it permanent. The tension between the ANC and AAC had an organizational and a regional basis. In essence, the ANC, a unitary body based on individual membership, feared being swallowed and overshadowed by Convention's federal structure.[52] Resentment of the AAC was especially keen in the Transvaal, even though three out of the five members of the AAC's Transvaal executive were ANC members. In November 1936 the Transvaal ANC resolved that that the AAC was not 'the national organisation to which all other African organisations should affiliate' and decided to boycott it.[53] In July 1937 Selope Thema and R. G. Baloyi, the Transvaal representatives to the NRC, convened a Conference of African Leaders that established a coordinating committee to revive the ANC. Several Transvaal-based Communists – John Marks, Edwin Mofutsanyana, who was also Transvaal Province secretary of the AAC, Gaur Radebe and Hyman Basner – were part of this initiative. Nonetheless, the Communists' concern at this stage was to build the ANC as a constituent of the AAC, not as a rival. 'Unity, in theory, has long been achieved', wrote the *South African Worker*, 'but no work has been done to mobilise and rally the masses around the All-African Convention. Without the revival of defunct organisations, such unity does not count. It is only when there are organisations affiliated to the All-African Convention that such unity will have a meaning.'[54]

The competition between the ANC and AAC crystallized in the debate at the AAC's December 1937 conference over how often Convention should meet. Bunche observed that 'Convention seems to degeneate [sic] toward the end of the afternoon session of the third day – especially when the question of whether the Convention is to meet annually, biennially, or every three, four, or five years'.[55] Moses Kotane interpreted the decision to convene the AAC every three years as a compromise with the ANC members and Professor Jabavu, who had all sought to bury Convention by having it meet only every five years. Yet, by ensuring that Convention met only once every three years and that it endorsed the NRC, ANC leaders effectively restricted its potential to mobilize the African people.

In this political climate, leftists faced a daunting task: it was virtually impossible to promote a radical agenda at the conference. Writing to his comrade Johnny Gomas on 14 December, Kotane mentioned the poor coordination and noted that the

agenda is atrocious, full of ommissions [sic] and badly arranged. The leaders are scared out of their wits. The Presidential Address ... mentioned nothing about the activities of the Executive since the last meeting of the Convention and this item appears no where in the Agenda. The Western Province dele[ga]tion made a stink about this, but they were overruled. There is very little enthusiasm here.[56]

Despite its internal disagreements, the left tried to caucus. Thirty people, of whom five were women, attended the left-wing 'Rump Parliament' of the AAC, which met on the evening of the first day, after the regular session had been adjourned, and criticized Convention's inactivity among the masses. The comments of Jimmy La Guma, who attended the left-wing caucus, echoed those of Dladla. Bunche wrote that La Guma,

says there seems to be some undercover sabotage going on at the Convention – evidenced in the attitudes expressed by men such as Alex Jabavu on the question of other non-European groups than native, the fight of some to put off the next meeting of the Convention for five years, etc. This he attributes to the Nat. Rep. Councillors and the European Nat. Reps., who fear that the Convention will develop into a native mass organization and get out of hand.

Edwin Mofutsanyana reiterated the need for Convention to take a more active approach to mobilizing the masses:

[T]here will never be any change through a Convention that merely meets peri- odically 'to pass pious resolutions'. The only solution must be the organization of the masses of people. The Convention is known to the people and is their only hope, but it must be organized beyond its present skeletal form. There must be branches in every locality which will deal with the day to day activities of the people.[57]

Nonetheless, three days later, on 17 December, Kotane had adopted a more san- guine approach to Convention's problems. He confided to Gomas:

I am not disappointed with the Convention at all. Be it what it may it has come to stay. It now has eleven affiliated and officially registered organisations, and many more give the impression that they are going to affiliate soon. 'Revolutionaries' may be disappointed but those who have a little knowledge of Africans and African affairs and attitude have ground to be optimistic. ... You will unmistakably see or notice that the Convention is moving towards the right. However, not too bad. There is, in it, a strong tendency and willingness to organ- ise.[58]

As the Convention turned to the right, its mass support dwindled. Bunche noted that 'the radicals ... take view that convention, by accepting the Native Representatives Act, instead of boycotting the elections, has destroyed public inter- est in the Convention. They point out that the attendance at the Convention is now meager (about 100) and attribute it to public disgust at the Convention's compro- mises.' Jabavu himself, Bunche continued, noted that the AAC 'has steadily lost ground in public support: there were 700 [sic] present at the first Convention, 400 at the second, and only 100 at this one'.[59]

Despite the decision to revive the ANC, its own silver jubilee conference, which began on 16 December, was a parlous affair. Most of the delegates blamed Seme for the lack of organization. Its programme, noted Bunche, was 'entirely devoid of any serious considerations, but devoted to social celebration of the Silver Jubilee. ... The Congress shows a complete lack of organization or preparation – a ridiculous waste of time.'

Thomas Mapikela tried desperately at the last minute to round up a few speak- ers, finally enticing Selope Thema, amongst others. Thema offered a religious para- ble to explain Africa's lack of industrial development: that God, angered at the

laziness of Africans, had 'sent white men down to make use of the valuable mineral resources' in Africa. Incensed, both Ralph Bunche and Jack Simons finally con-
sented to speak in order to counter Thema's words.

It was not an auspicious start: by the second day no more than fifty people were
in attendance. Mofutsanyana, who represented the AAC, appealed for unity, while
Mapikela, angered at his dismal failure the previous day to get the AAC's vice-pres-
idency, attacked Convention. 'The lone woman speaker', wrote Bunche, 'criticized
the Congress on the extreme attention to festivities.'[60] The silver jubilee was such a
dire affair that by comparison, Kotane concluded on 18 December, '[t]he
Convention was a moral success though theorists might be holding a different view
on this. It put the Congress, with its "Jubilee publicity stunts," in the shade.'[61]

The conference of the National Council of African Women followed the ANC's
silver jubilee. This was attended by about forty or fifty women, predominantly
teachers and nurses, the two professions open to tiny numbers of African women.
Charlotte Maxeke was elected as president, and Minah Soga as general secretary.
While the tone of the conference was certainly far more serious than that of the
ANC's Silver Jubilee, tensions over strategy were apparent. The main issues confronting the women were those of building an effective national body from the various branches and of the organization's relationship to the AAC and to its white
counterpart, the National Council of Women. From the left, Josie Mpama, a
staunch proponent of autonomous women's organization, criticized the leaders of
the National Council of African Women for having already 'buried' the organization. There were already signs of undue white influence. Margaret Ballinger, Edith
Rheinallt Jones and Nellie Marquard were asked to act as advisors, opening the way
for outside influence by the Joint Councils movement. By 1940, Minah Soga was
complaining to Edith Rheinallt Jones that many Africans perceived the National
Council of African Women to be run by whites.[62] The problems facing the organization of black women at this stage echoed those seen at the AAC's and ANC's previous conferences.

The establishment of the NRC had a profound effect on black politics, as it positioned established African leadership firmly within parameters established by the
government. The close of the decade saw an ebb in mass-based political activity as
African political leaders turned to the NRC in a futile attempt to influence the government, while the AAC, with its triennial meetings, lost momentum. Over the
next few years this parlous state of affairs catalysed a generational shift in black politics that would have ramifications for both the AAC and the ANC.

The illusive quest for unity on the left

If the AAC indicated the difficulties of a united front and of joint activity between
the aspirant black bourgeoisie and the left, the trajectories of the National Liberation
League and the Non-European United Front posed the problem of unity even within
the tiny left. Despite their auspicious beginnings, the NLL and NEUF lost steam in

the face of intra-left leadership struggles; then, by default, they drifted towards moderation.[63]

The NLL was officially launched in Cape Town on 1 December 1935 by Jimmy La Guma, Johnny Gomas and Cisse Gool.[64] The NLL's anti-imperialist stance, its emphasis on predominantly black leadership and its call for militant action bore the stamp of the Brussels League Against Imperialism conference that La Guma had attended in 1927 and of the Native Republic thesis that he had enthusiastically promoted in the late 1920s. Undoubtedly some of its radical leaders hoped that it would function as a left-wing pole within the AAC.

The League quickly attracted a working-class base. The occupations listed in its membership roster include a large number of labourers, hawkers, garment, laundry and various other factory workers, tailors, bricklayers and housewives, as well as teachers and municipal employees; its affiliates comprised community groups, trade unions and political organizations throughout the Western Cape. A year later it counted about 2000 members and had branches in Pretoria and Port Elizabeth.[65]

The founding of the NLL brought to the fore another political leader: the charismatic beauty Cissie Gool. Raised in the heady political and intellectual environment of her father's – Dr Abdullah Abdurahman's – home, Cissie Gool became an ardent and articulate political activist. In 1919 she married Dr Abdul Gool, elder brother of Goolam Gool. Her older sister, Dr Waradia Abdurahman, became a medical doctor, and in 1933 Cissie Gool became the first black South African woman to obtain an MA in Psychology from the University of Cape Town. Cissie Gool's public political career was inaugurated by the political controversy surrounding the 1930 enfranchisement of white women. The APO convened a mass meeting on the issue at which Cissie Gool spoke; she captured the crowd and led it on a demonstration to Parliament. Around this time she met and became good friends with Johnny Gomas. Subsequently, together with Gomas and other progressives, she became involved in the anti-fascist movement and, motivated by a belief in the need for a united movement against the government's threats to black rights, in the NLL and the NEUF.[66]

Peter Abrahams gave an eyewitness account of the NLL's early popularity under Cissie Gool, 'champion of the miserably poor' and, increasingly, her father's political rival:

> Her organization, the National Liberation League, was thrustful and young. Coloureds from all walks of life flocked to it. ... [The APO], once the most famous Coloured body in the Cape, was little more than a name. It had never been popular with the mass of the ordinary Coloured people. But they had followed its lead at election times because there had been no other lead. Now, all were for the Liberation League.[67]

The League's intention was to organize blacks on the basis of their local needs and link these with broad democratic demands like the abolition of the colour bar, poll taxes and pass laws. The organizers were concerned to attract members of all

Non-European groups: a manuscript by Moses Kotane in the NLL papers entitled *How to work among urban Africans* argued that the once-mighty ICU and ANC had declined due to their failure to develop local structures like trade union branches and residents' associations with which to begin fighting for immediate demands.[68] Likewise, there was a perception of the need to organize women. On 12 December 1935 Dr Waradia Abdurahman convened the first meeting of a Women's Bureau; nine members were included on its initial membership list. Its main aim was to attract women to build up the NLL and to engage in fund-raising activities, although there was recognition of the plight of unorganized working women – notably domestic workers. Jimmy La Guma was concerned to recruit women, and he lectured at the NLL's Sunday evening lecture series on 'Our Women and the Liberatory Movement'.[69] In August 1938 Cissie Gool organized a Non-European Women's Suffrage League. This, however, proved to be ephemeral: once Africans were removed from the common voting roll in the Cape, the issue of female suffrage appealed only to the small stratum of Coloured women who would have qualified for the franchise had it not been for their sex.[70]

The internal politics of the NLL are murky, reflecting obscure permutations of the Communist–Trotskyist antagonism, intertwined with personal jealousies and rivalries and articulated in terms of colour. Cissie Gool was the NLL's first president, and Jimmy La Guma, its general secretary. Yet in September 1937 she was relieved of her office and suspended from NLL political activities. On 15 November La Guma appealed for her reinstatement and on the 26th she was reinstated to the General Council.[71]

Goolam Gool and his faction assumed direction of the NLL. This faction, whose views are found in the *Liberator*, a monthly that ran from March to September 1937, believed that Cissie Gool's pragmatic tactics were a dilution of the League's original principles. The group promoted political education. In addition to NLL's lecture series, in 1937 Goolam Gool launched the New Era Fellowship, a radical discussion and debating society that met for several decades at the Stakesby Lewis Hostel and in the Fidelity Hall on the edge of District Six.[72] The New Era Fellowship's speakers included progressive university lecturers; local intellectuals, such as Peter Abrahams and Dora Taylor, who lectured on literature; and political activists and foreign visitors. The diverse array of socialists who attended often used the occasions to score points against their political opponents.

The NLL was also involved in trade union organization. In 1937 and 1938 it established several trade unions, chiefly through the efforts of La Guma and Gomas; the NLL's secretary, Hawa Ahmed – Halima Gool, wife of Goolam Gool – organized a Laundry Workers' Union. But the Goolam Gool faction appears to have had trouble maintaining the NLL's initial level of mass support, indicated by a marked decline in branch representation at its April 1938 annual conference. Goolam Gool attributed this decline to a lack of popular understanding, which, he maintained, indicated the need for political education. Gomas, by contrast, blamed the academic approach of the intellectual leadership and their failure to 'get down to the workers and do some spade work'.[73]

By April 1938 factional tensions came to a head when a group of seven or eight walked out of the NLL's annual conference. The ostensible reason for their departure was disagreements over the colour composition of the NLL's leadership, and specifically a proposal put forward by La Guma on behalf of a section of the Cape Town branch that '[t]hat whilst Europeans could be members of the organisation they would not be allowed to hold any official position'. As the NLL's governing regulations stipulated that its leadership should be 'predominantly non-European', La Guma's resolution lost. He, along with Goolam Gool, who had by then joined the Workers' Party, and their supporters left the conference. They were expelled after failing to explain their actions to the General Council but were later reinstated.[74]

However, this dispute took place while the planning for the NEUF was going on. This was formally inaugurated on 18 April 1938 to contest the proposed Stuttaford Bills. Apparently, La Guma had initially been proposed as secretary of the NEUF but declined. Subsequently the NLL's General Council instructed Goolam Gool, its representative on the NEUF, to propose a joint secretariat of La Guma, Kotane and Pilsania; two of the three were Communists, and Goolam Gool evidently failed do this. Subsequently, Cissie Gool was unanimously elected president of the NEUF; La Guma was elected as acting organising secretary, and Harry Snitcher and Johnny Gomas, as senior officials.[75]

While La Guma, himself, felt very strongly about the principle of black leadership of black organizations, the tensions about leadership also reflected the perception of Trotskyists that the CPSA was trying to outmanoeuvre them and assume direction of the NLL and NEUF. The *Spark*, for instance, continually railed at the 'People's Frontists', regardless of the actual threat posed by the tiny, strife-torn CPSA. Presumably the Trotskyists saw Cissie Gool's politics in this light. Cissie Gool was briefly a member of the short-lived South African Socialist Party, which was formed by the Labour MP Duncan Burnside in early 1937 after the Labour Party reaffirmed segregation and refused to join the People's Front. But in the late 1930s she left her husband to live with the Communist lawyer Sam Kahn, and subsequently she joined the CPSA, becoming a Politburo member in 1939.[76]

Despite the animosity amongst the NLL's leadership, the League played a notable role in the struggle against the government's move to eliminate Coloured rights through the establishment of the NEUF. In the late 1930s black radicals were increasingly aware that despite their differential status as Coloureds, Indians and Africans, they all shared a common lack of democratic rights and were all victims of the government's respective attempts to cut back their limited rights even further. What had been done first to the Africans, was now extended to the Coloureds and Indians. Hence, the formation of the NEUF.

Nonetheless, while NLL leaders were bent on building Non-European unity, their own organization did not escape the effects of sectional and class divisions on the political consciousness and aspirations of its members. Ralph Bunche, who observed little contact between Coloureds and Africans outside radical circles, noted that many NLL members were 'still thinking in terms of special status for colored, many now hope for development of non-European business as a way out, are emphasizing the stronger economic position of the American Negro. ... Too high-brow and above the masses.'[77]

Abrahams captured the double-standard of Coloured–African political relations. When the AAC was formed in 1935, he wrote, '[o]ne or two of the more far-sighted of their leaders had called on the Coloureds for joint action and had warned that the Coloured vote would go, after the African vote'. But this warning went unheeded. 'A miserably small handful of Coloureds, chief among them Goolam Gool, had shown interest and tried to work with the Africans. The rest had been indifferent.'

A few years later, the government, having successfully struck at African rights, now attempted to remove Coloureds from the common voting rolls. With the significant exception of the Transvaal ANC, African organizations were generally sympathetic to the NEUF's efforts to woo them. 'Perhaps this was largely due to the part [Goolam] Gool had played in their struggle', Abrahams speculated. 'And quite a surprising number of lesser African organizations came into the United Front.'[78]

In the late 1930s Coloureds were still likely to be mobilized on the basis of 'Coloured rights' rather than black unity and practical support for Africans. Nonetheless, the success of the NEUF in affiliating African groups indicates that neither it nor the NLL can be dismissively stereotyped as 'Coloured'. In a parallel manner, these years saw a political struggle amongst Indians over whether to engage in sectional – Indian only – or joint political struggle. The NEUF maintained that '[t]he reply of the non-Europeans to the Government should not be a separatist and isolated sectional struggle by only a part of the Indian people'. Instead, 'all the oppressed races should combine in joint and simultaneous action'.[79]

The NEUF's first major Western Cape campaign culminated in late March 1939 when 20,000 people marched on Parliament against moves to implement residential segregation. 'Of all nights that was Cissy's night', as she led the demonstration towards Parliament.[80] Although the struggle against residential segregation was of primary concern to the petty-bourgeois Coloured elite, who as homeowners had the most to lose from attempts to move them, Abrahams's account suggests that the issue struck an emotive chord amongst working-class people as well. Anti-segregation protests took place around the Cape, and '[d]elegates poured into Cape Town from all corners of the province, and from farther afield. The streets of District Six seethed. The office of the Liberation League was crowded. Throughout the day a conference was held. ... Delegates made fiery speeches.'

The problem facing socialists was what practical steps to take to retain popular interest once the initial groundswell had receded. In Abrahams' account,

> [t]he monster demonstration was a seven-day sensation throughout the country. ... Some papers revived talk about the 'Black Peril'. There were a number of court cases. Questions were asked in Parliament. The proposed bill was postponed. For many days police vans haunted District Six. Whites did not come near it. Coloureds did not venture far from it. In the end, excitement died down. The League seemed to have exhausted itself in that one giant effort.[81]

The potential strength of the crowd was convincing enough to temporarily make the government back down. In that immediate sense, the NEUF was a success, and contrary to Abraham's perception, the NLL and NEUF reaped organizational gains through the new affiliates that sprung up around the country.[82]

In the afterglow of the demonstration, Cissie Gool was re-elected president of the NLL at its annual conference in April.[83] Political tensions were still rife amongst the leading figures. At a meeting of the NLL's Political Bureau in January, there had been criticisms of liberals who were allegedly diluting the League's anti-imperialist programme. La Guma proposed that an anti-imperialist resolution be submitted to the NEUF's Committee of Action. This was passed with only one dissenting vote: Cissie Gool 'felt that the programme of the League should not be forced just now. She felt that this was premature.'[84] In early March, the Committee of Action had met over an article in that month's issue of the *Spark* that criticized the NEUF's leadership. Isaac Tabata, Jane Gool and Halima Gool defended the piece; Gomas, La Guma, Kahn, and Bill Andrews, amongst others, attacked it. In May, just a month before it ceased publication and the Workers' Party went underground, the *Spark* issued an apology.[85]

Soon after Cissie Gool's re-election, reports of a split in the NLL appeared in the local press, and Jimmy La Guma, Goolam Gool, Halima Gool and A. Brown were expelled; the matter culminated in legal proceedings that favoured the NLL. According to La Guma, the fight concerned the colour composition of leadership; he and his supporters still sought to bar whites from holding office in the NLL. La Guma evidently wanted to 'repudiate' Cissie Gool and her mainly white supporters on the NLL's General Council – Sam Kahn, Booker Lakey, Watlington and Lance Morley-Turner, on the grounds that the conference had been improperly constituted.[86] Behind the issue of colour was the fact that these whites – Communists and non-Communists alike – were perceived to be dampening the potential for militancy. Despite its partiality, the *Spark*'s commentary illustrates how political factions could manoeuvre behind organizational procedures:

> The oldest and most active members of the league left the conference in protest and disgust because the manoeuvres of the People's Frontists, who packed the hall with delegates from 'branches' formed on the very eve of the conference, were too much for them. The victory of the People's Frontists leaves them with the shell of the League but without the body, for its main force, the Cape Town branch, is definitely against them.[87]

But the CPSA's local organ, the *Party Organiser*, presented a different point of view:

> Those who ... are splitting and weakening the movement, defend their action on the ground that some people in the United Front have a record of betrayal of non-European interests. ... The people have no confidence in the workers. They do not believe that it is possible for the workers to unite with other sections and still keep before them the ultimate objectives of the working

class. ... That is why the Trotskyists and others like them go over to the side of the enemy.[88]

From then on, Cissie Gool was at the helm of both the NLL and NEUF. Increasingly, the organizations fell under the shadow of local government electoral politics in Cape Town. In 1938 Harry Snitcher had contested the local City Council elections on a Socialist Party ticket, backed by the NLL. He lost, but in September Cissie Gool was elected to the City Council to represent Ward Seven (which included District Six). Although the NLL's Langa branch, for one, was still involved in local campaigns in 1941, Cissie Gool devoted more and more of her time to the needs of her Coloured constituency. Despite the NLL's radical rhetoric, by 1942 it was approximating the moderate APO in its practice, using the Cape Town City Council to campaign for local issues.[89] By that time Trotskyists were looking elsewhere for an organizational base.

There is no doubt that by the end of the decade Communists assumed a greater influence in the NEUF. In 1939 the NEUF's Committee of Action included Bill Andrews as treasurer, Moses Kotane as secretary, and Jimmy La Guma and W. H. October as trustees. In April 1939 two Communists, Dr Yusuf Dadoo and H. A. Naidoo, were elected to the NEUF's National Council, representing Johannesburg and Durban respectively. In the Transvaal Dadoo led the NEUF on vigorous campaigns against the war, and he played a key role in introducing the strategy and tactics of passive resistance to the NEUF. By 1941 Communists were clearly dominating the NEUF's political direction: when the CPSA began supporting the war following Nazi Germany's invasion of the Soviet Union in June 1941, the NEUF reversed its anti-war position. Through the remainder of the war, the NLL and NEUF lost vitality, no doubt in part a reflection of the CPSA's moderate wartime policy.[90]

Conclusion

In the late 1930s the black petty bourgeoisie was seeking the support of a militant and increasingly organized working class. The prospect of such an alliance raised the question of the political relationship of these classes. Although few in number, some members of the petty bourgeoisie were pursuing policies geared to the development of a black bourgeoisie. In seeking to make the AAC an African-only body or to use the NLL to promote Coloured rights and interests, their actions reinforced racial categories and sectional divisions. Socialists, who sought to influence popular organizations, were divided in their response to the question of political alliances. Communists and Trotskyists endeavoured to promote working-class interests – through a People's Front, in the case of the CPSA, or within black united fronts.

Both types of alliances foundered on their own contradictions, eventually losing popular support. The alliance based on proletarian status, or working-class unity, neglected the socioeconomic and political differentials within the working class that precluded white support for black democratic rights. The alliances based on colour, or black unity, succumbed to the contradictory class aspirations of their constituents. Within the the ANC and the AAC the rival collaborationist and non-collaborationist tendencies could not in practice be reconciled in a single movement. As black leaders began to participate in the state's racial structures or collaborate with government policy their constituencies lost interest.

Although many of the socialists who participated in the launch of the AAC anticipated the withdrawal of the masses as Convention lost its potential for militancy, their own organizational rivalry impeded them from building a sustained relationship with black working-class groups, as the experiences of the NLL and NEUF showed. By the close of the 1930s, none of the black united-front organizations were actively involved in working-class struggles in a sustained fashion. The AAC, the NLL, and the NEUF tended to degenerate into resolution-making bodies or to focus on electoral politics. Although South African Communist historiography has explained the limitations of these organizations as examples of united fronts 'organised from the top, and not from below', their history was far more complex.[91] Black workers, seeking political direction, had rallied behind the black united fronts until it became clear that acknowledged black leaders accepted the state's racial framework instead of offering alternative political guidance. Then, in the early 1940s, many workers turned instead to direct protest over their daily needs of housing, transport and wages.

Notes

1. Abrahams, *Tell Freedom*, 276.
2. Bunche Collection, box 64.
3. Macmillan, *Africa Emergent*, 122–6; Edward Roux, 'Land and Agriculture in the Native Reserves', in Hellmann, ed., *Handbook on Race Relations*, 171–90, 175; Walker, *Women and Resistance*, 41.
4. Maurice Webb, 'Indian Land Legislation', in Hellman, ed., *Handbook on Race Relations*, 206–13; Swan, 'Ideology in Organised Indian Politics'.
5. Walshe, *The Rise of African Nationalism*, 254.
6. Tom Lodge, *Black Politics in South Africa since 1945*, London and New York: Longman, 1983, 1–3; Roux, *Time Longer than Rope*, 53–77; Swan, 'Ideology in Organised Indian Politics', 192.
7. Lewis, *Between the Wire and the Wall*, 141–9.
8. Edgar H. Brookes, 'Government and Administration', and van der Horst, 'Labour', both in Hellman, ed., *Handbook on Race Relations*, 27–40 and 109–57 respectively.
9. Roux, *Time Longer than Rope*, 289.
10. Karis and Carter, eds, *From Protest to Challenge*, vol. 2, 4 and 13.
11. 'Fight the New Fascist Bill – Defend the Cape Native Franchise', *Umsebenzi*, May 18, 1935, in Bunting, ed., *South African Communists Speak*, 122–3.
12. 'For a United Front of the People Against Imperialism', *Umsebenzi*, October 26, 1935, in Bunting, ed., *South African Communists Speak*, 125–7, quote 126–7.
13. 'The All African Convention Proceedings and Resolutions of the AAC, December

15–18, 1935', Karis and Carter, eds, *From Protest to Challenge*, vol. 2, 40; 'Resolutions passed by National Convention on Anti-Native Bills', *Umsebenzi*, 11 January 1936, 1.

14. Karis and Carter, eds, *From Protest to Challenge*, vol. 4, 26 and Basner, *Am I an African?*, 64.

15. Bunche Collection, box 64, emphasis in the original.

16. Lewis, *Between the Wire and the Wall*, 159.

17. 'The All African Convention Proceedings and Resolutions', 33.

18. 'The All African Convention Proceedings and Resolutions', Karis and Carter, eds, *From Protest to Challenge*, vol. 2, quotes 44, 46, 34 and 45, respectively; see also 7.

19. Jonathan Hyslop, 'White working-class women and the invention of apartheid: "Purified" Afrikaner Nationalist agitation for legislation against "mixed" marriages, 1934–9', *Journal of African History*, 36, 1995, 57–81, 62. Hyslop notes that despite the rapid urbanization of African women in the 1930s, in 1936 there were 196,000 white women on the Rand, compared to 107,000 African women.

20. 'The All African Convention Proceedings and Resolutions', 43.

21. Ellen Kuzwayo, *Call Me Woman*, London: Women's Press, 1985, 102.

22. 'The All African Convention Proceedings and Resolutions', 39; Walker, *Women and Resistance*, 34–5, 41–2.

23. The 'electoral colleges' for election of the four white senators and the twelve African representatives consisted of African members of location advisory boards in the urban areas, and members of district councils, chiefs and headmen in the rural areas. Roux, *Time Longer than Rope*, 291–5; Simons and Simons, *Class and Colour*, 495; Basner, *Am I an African?*, 70, 215, n.5; and Margaret Ballinger, *From Union to Apartheid: A Trek to Isolation*, Folkstone: Bailey Bros & Swinfen, 1969, 27–8.

24. Eslanda Goode Robeson, *African Journey*, London: Victor Gollancz, 1946, 66.

25. Basner, *Am I an African?*, 67ff.

26. '"The Challenge" and "The Alternative." Extracts from pamphlet, *The Crisis*, by Selby Msimang', Karis and Carter, eds, *From Protest to Challenge*, vol. 2, 57–61, quote 59, and 9–10.

27. 'Presidential Address' by Professor D. D. T. Jabavu, AAC, June 29, 1936, Karis and Carter, eds, *From Protest to Challenge*, vol. 2, 52.

28. Basner, *Am I an African?*, 70–1.

29. 'Presidential Address' by Professor D. D. T. Jabavu, quotes 51 and 52 respectively.

30. Lewis, *Between the Wire and the Wall*, 110.

31. 'Proceedings and Resolutions of the AAC, June 29–July 2, 1936', Karis and Carter, eds, *From Protest to Challenge*, vol. 2, 54–5.

32. Walshe, *Rise of African Nationalism*, 255; Karis and Carter, eds, *From Protest to Challenge*, vol. 2, 11.

33. Ballinger, *From Union to Apartheid*, 37, 44; Margaret Hodgson to Holtby, 12 October 1932, Holtby Collection, file 4.13, item 4.

34. Hodgson to Holtby, 21 August 1934, Holtby Collection, file 4.13, item 14; Ballinger to Holtby, 27 April 1932 and Ballinger to Lewin, 14 February 1935, Holtby Collection, file 4.12, items 35, 58; W. G. Ballinger, 'Native Co-operation in South Africa' and *Ballinger on Co-operatives*, 5 October 1933, Holtby Collection, file 4.5, items 19, 31.

35. Edgar, ed., *An African-American*, 261; Ballinger, *From Union to Apartheid*, 47–52; Brittain, *Testament of Friendship*, 255–7.

36. Basner, *Am I an African?*, 63–4 and 214, n. 4.

37. 'Advisory Board Elections: Communist Party calls on Location Residents to support All-African Convention for Better Conditions', *South African Worker*, 26 September 1936, in Drew, *South Africa's Radical Tradition*, vol. 1, 246–8, quotes 248 and 247 respectively.

38. Basner, *Am I an African?*, 78–9; 'Johannesburg Municipal Elections: Communist Party asks Labour Party for Working Arrangement', *South African Worker*, in Drew, ed., *South Africa's Radical Tradition*, vol. 1, 269–70.

39. Joe Slovo refers to the existence of a pro-boycott lobby within the CPSA in *Unfinished Autobiography*, 40.

40. 'Report on the South African Situation', 4 November [?] 1937, 12 and 13, RTsKhIDNI, 495.14.354; also in 495.20.662. Simons and Simons, *Class and Colour*, 496.

41. Trotsky, *Remarks on the Draft Theses of the Workers' Party*.

42. Neville Alexander, 'Aspects of Non-Collaboration in the Western Cape 1943–1963', *Social Dynamics*, 12, 1, 1986, 1–14. See also I. B. Tabata, *The Boycott as Weapon of Struggle*, [1952], Durban: APDUSA, excerpted in Drew, ed., *South Africa's Radical Tradition*, vol. 2, 182–8.

43. 'C. B. I. Joins Workers' Party', *Umlilo Mollo/Flame*, 1, 1, September 1936, in Drew, ed., *South Africa's Radical Tradition*, vol. 1, 245–6.

44. 'The All African Convention', *Umlilo Mollo/Flame*, 1, 2, October 1936, in Drew, ed., *South Africa's Radical Tradition*, vol. 1, 248–9, 249.

45. Bunche Collection, box 65.

46. Edgar, *An African-American*, 31–2, 229–37; Ballinger, *From Union to Apartheid*, 146–7.

47. 'Policy of the AAC.' Statement issued by the Executive Committee of the AAC, December 1937, in Karis and Carter, eds, *From Protest to Challenge*, vol. 2, 61–64, quote 63–64, and 8–11.

48. Karis and Carter, eds, *From Protest to Challenge*, vol. 2, 11.

49. Bunche Collection, box 64, emphasis in the original.

50. Bunche Collection, box 64; Edgar, ed., *An African-American*, 266.

51. Bunche Collection, box 64.

52. E. T. M., 'All African National Convention is Approaching', *Umsebenzi*, 6 June 1936, 1; E. T. Mofutsanyana, 'Editorial: We Want Unity of Action', *South African Worker*, 13 June 1936, 2.

53. Quoted in Bunting, *Kotane*, 80.

54. 'All-African Convention Forthcoming Conference', *South African Worker*, 13 November 1937 in Drew, ed., *South Africa's Radical Tradition*, vol. 1, 276. See also 'African Leaders Conference in Johannesburg', *South African Worker*, 1 August 1937, 1; 'African National Congress to be Revived: Leaders' Co-ordinating Committee's Work', *South African Worker*, 4 September 1937 in Drew, ed., *South Africa's Radical Tradition*, vol. 1, 270–71; 'Revival of the ANC – The Co-ordinating Committee and Unity, *South African Worker*, 6 November 1937 in Bunting, ed., *South African Communists Speak*, 311–12; Bunting, *Kotane*, 81.

55. Bunche Collection, box 64.

56. 'Letters from Moses Kotane to John Gomas, 14, 17, 18 and 23 December 1937', in Drew, ed., *South Africa's Radical Tradition*, vol. 1, 277–9, 277.

57. Bunche Collection, box 64.

58. 'Letters from Moses Kotane', 277–8.

59. Bunche Collection, box 64. There were, in fact, about 400 delegates at the AAC's

December 1935 conference.

60. Edgar, ed., *An African-American*, quotes 275 and 274.

61. 'Letters from Moses Kotane', 278.

62. Walker, *Women and Resistance*, 35–6; Josie Mpama, 'African Women must be Organised: We are prepared to move', *South African Worker*, 26 June 1937, 4; Edgar, ed., *An African-American*, 277–8. Kuzwayo, *Call me woman*, 101–3, recounts her personal observations of the first national meeting of the National Council of African Women.

63. For other discussions of the NLL and NEUF see Mary Simons, 'Organised Coloured Political Movements', in Hendrik W. van der Merwe and C. J. Groenewald, eds, *Occupational and Social Change among Coloured People in South Africa*, Cape Town: Juta, 1976, 202–37; Everett, 'Gool', 7–75; Maurice Hommel, *Capricorn Blues: the Struggle for Human Rights in South Africa*, Toronto: Culturama, 1981, 65–71; Lewis, *Between the Wire and the Wall*, 179–206; and La Guma, *Jimmy La Guma*, 58–70.

64. Everett, 'Gool', 10.

65. Edgar, ed., *An African-American*, 264; John Gomas, 'Organisational Activities at Port Elizabeth: National Liberation Branch Formed', *South African Worker*, 18 July 1936, 3.

66. Everett, 'Gool', 7–9.

67. Abrahams, *Tell Freedom*, 274–5.

68. *How to Work Among Urban Africans*, in Drew, ed., *South Africa's Radical Tradition*, vol. 1, 281–4.

69. Minute Book, the NLL of S. A., Women's Bureau, Record Book 3, box 4, Abdurahman Family Papers, Manuscripts and Archives Department, University of Cape Town Libraries; Lewis, *Between the Wire and the Wall*, 180–81. La Guma's lecture was advertized in *Liberator*, 1, 5, September 1937.

70. Walker, *Women and Resistance*, 54; Hawa H. Ahmed (Halima Gool), *Address Delivered at Inaugural Meeting of the Non-European Women's Suffrage League*, in Drew, ed., *South Africa's Radical Tradition*, vol. 1, 285–95.

71. 'The National Liberation League of South Africa, 1935–1941', folder A3, Dr Waradia Abdurahman Papers, Manuscripts and Archives Department, University of Cape Town Libraries.

72. Rosemary Neale, interview with R. O. Dudley, Cape Town, 13 July 1994.

73. Minutes of the Second Congress of the National Liberation League, 17 April 1938, folder 1, box 4, Abdurahman Family Papers; Lewis, *Between the Wire and the Wall*, 187.

74. *Programme of the National Liberation League of S.A. as Revised and Adopted at First Congress*, in Drew, ed., *South Africa's Radical Tradition*, vol. 1, 253–61, 258.

75. National Liberation League of South Africa, *Honesty is the Best Policy* (c. 1938), in Drew, ed., *South Africa's Radical Tradition*, vol. 1, 280–81. Everett, 'Gool', 27.

76. Cissie Gool was the subject of vituperative public condemnation in the 1930s concerning both her politics and her personal relationships. See Everett, 'Gool', 16–17, 31.

77. Bunche Collection, box 64.

78. Abrahams, *Tell Freedom*, 279; Simons and Simons, *Class and Colour*, 504.

79. Non-European United Front of South Africa, *Statement of Passive Resistance Movement*, in Drew, *South Africa's Radical Tradition*, vol. 1, 299–300, quotes 300.

80. Quoted in Everett, 'Gool', 40a.

81. Abrahams, *Tell Freedom*, quotes 280, 282–3 respectively; see also Everett, 'Gool', 38–40a.

82. Lewis, *Between the Wire and the Wall*, 194.

83. Everett, 'Gool', 35–6.
84. Second Meeting of Political Bureau, 23/1/39, Record Book 1, 1937–1940, 14, box 4, Abdurahman Family Papers.
85. *Spark*, 5, 3, March 1939 and 5, 5, May 1939, 3.
86. Everett, 'Gool', 41–2; *Spark*, 5, 5, May 1939, 3; Lewis, *Between the Wire and the Wall*, 195. Hommel, *Capricorn Blues*, 69 offers a different interpretation of this split.
87. *Spark*, 5, 5, May 1939, 3.
88. *Party Organiser*, official organ of the Cape District Communist Party, no. 3, [March 1939?], 1–2, box 7, folder 1, Abdurahman Family Papers.
89. Everett, 'Gool', 22–60; Lewis, *Between the Wire and the Wall*, 204–6.
90. Swan, 'Ideology in Organised Indian Politics', 200–202; Simons, 'Organised Coloured Political Movements', 223; *Statement of Dr. Y. M. Dadoo, Secretary, Non-European United Front (Transvaal), before the Court, 6 September 1940*, in Drew, ed., *South Africa's Radical Tradition*, vol. 1, 335–9; 'Arms for Non-Europeans.' Flyer issued by the Non-European United Front of South Africa, March 18, 1942 and 'Non-European Peoples' Manifesto.' Adopted at Non-European Conference Convened by the Non-European United Front, June 28, 1942, both in Karis and Carter, eds, *From Protest to Challenge*, vol. 2, 389–91; Roux, *Time Longer than Rope*, 357–8.
91. Bunting, *Kotane*, 94.

Chapter 10

'Wars and rumours of wars': socialists confront the Second World War

Abyssinia's fight against Fascist Italy's invasion in October 1935 captured the hopes of politically-engaged black South Africans but these were dashed with Abyssinia's defeat. When war broke out in Europe in 1939, many of the black South Africans who followed international politics were broadly sympathetic to the struggle against fascism. But they were not prepared to fight for democracy in another continent while they lacked democratic rights at home. Most blacks, in fact, were indifferent to the war. The South African Parliament itself was deeply divided in its response to the outbreak of hostilities in Europe in September 1939; ultimately, South Africa's declaration of war against Germany, supported by a thin parliamentary majority, reflected its position within the British Empire. The white electorate was sharply divided in its sympathies and antipathies. The government needed the compliance of black South Africans in order to develop the war economy.[1]

The war years spurred rapid industrial development and urbanization, especially on the Witwatersrand, which became the most volatile centre of black working-class activity. Moreover, African women's rate of urbanization surpassed that of African men, indicating the non-viability of subsistence production in the reserves and turning the urban African population into a more stable settled one.[2] This pattern of urbanization was reflected in the composition of the industrial workforce. African workers were a growing presence in primary and secondary industry. The increasing proportion of Africans in private manufacturing from the 1930s was paralleled by the decline of whites, many of whom first moved into state enterprises and later left for the war. Against this backdrop, Smuts's famous 1942 'retreat from segregation' speech and the relaxation of pass-law enforcement were seen as signalling the possibility of political liberalization.

Controversies of war

The accord over domestic issues that white politicians had sustained through most of the 1930s was financed by South Africa's departure from the gold standard. The resulting rise in gold prices facilitated the country's recovery from the depression.

Between 1931 and 1940 income generated by the mining industry almost tripled, and this meant additional tax revenues for the state coffers. The government budget surpluses between 1933 and 1937 were used to reduce foreign debt and to spur domestic industrial development. Secondary industry, at first linked to the mining industry but increasingly diversified, grew substantially in the 1930s. The Iron and Steel Corporation (ISCOR) established by the Pact Government in 1927 became a key component in state-led industrialization. The country's growth led to a substantial increase in foreign investment, much of which went into the gold-mining industry. The 1930s saw a rise in the white standard of living and a significant reduction of the poor white problem. Blacks did not share in the benefits of this growth.

But the Fusion Government collapsed when its two leaders, Prime Minister Barry Hertzog and Jan Smuts, failed to agree over the war. Smuts, recalling Germany's role in the First World War, was acutely sensitive to South Africa's responsibilities within the British Empire and supported the British position. Hertzog, sympathetic to the ethos of Nazism, put forward a motion for neutrality in Parliament. This was defeated, Smuts replaced Hertzog as Prime Minister and led a coalition of the United and Labour Parties. Although Hertzog rejoined the *Herenigde* (Reunited) National Party a year later, as the *Herenigde* National Party moved to the right, he was subsequently forced out and D. F. Malan took over its leadership. White politics, still very much divided along regional and ethnic lines, was pulled to the right by the rise of proto-fascist movements such as the pro-Nazi *Ossewabrandwag* (Ox-wagon Sentinel), the *Handhawersbond* (Defence League) and Oswald Pirow's 'New Order' movement.

Despite this dissent, the government's war drive went ahead. At the ANC's annual conference in December 1939 delegates resolved '[t]hat unless and until the Government grants the African full democratic and citizenship rights, the African National Congress is not prepared to advise the Africans to participate in the present war, in any capacity'.[3] Six months later, however, this position softened, as the National Executive Committees of the ANC and AAC expressed their loyalty to the British Empire and, pleading for participation in the war effort on an equal basis, called upon the South African government 'to take immediate and adequate steps for the guidance, organisation, discipline, and protection of the people against any emergency that might arise out of, and as a result of the present conflict'.[4] South Africa sent a volunteer army of about 300,000 to fight in North Africa and Europe; about one-quarter of these were black: members of the Native Military Corps, the Cape Coloured Corps and the Indian and Malay Corps. But they were restricted to non-combatant roles and subjected to all the varieties of racial discrimination that they experienced at home.[5]

Socialists and world war, 1939–41

The relationship of socialists to the war was complex. In a dramatic foreign policy about-face, the Soviet Union signed a Non-Aggression Pact with Nazi Germany in

August 1939. Soon thereafter, on 7 September, Stalin and Dimitrov met to discuss the future tasks of the Comintern's national sections. Stalin put forward his new reading of the war as a struggle amongst capitalist states for the re-carving of the world. In that context, he argued, 'the division of capitalist countries into fascist and democratic has lost its former sense', and he insisted that the People's Front slogan be dropped. The destruction of Poland, he added, 'would mean one less bourgeois fascist state'. He proposed that the ECCI Secretariat denounce the war and repudiate all support for it. Stalin's arguments were encapsulated in the Comintern's '"Short Thesis" on the Second World War' of 9 September. This new thesis, significantly, was not based on an analysis of the needs of the national sections but rather grew from Stalin's concern to pacify Hitler. Thus, the Comintern's ready endorsement of the Soviet about-turn signalled the culmination of its subordination to Soviet foreign policy interests as determined by Stalin.[6]

Although the national affiliates, predictably, fell in line, the psychological confusion that the new policy caused and the manner of implementation varied from one affiliate to another, depending on the national context. In the CPGB, for example, the policy led to a bitter and well-documented dispute amongst the leadership. Until early October the CPGB's Central Committee publicly maintained the need to 'struggle on two fronts' – both against the Nazi regime in Germany and against the Chamberlain Government in Britain – that is, to 'resist fascism whether it comes from abroad or at home'. But after the publication of the 'Short Thesis', two camps polarized. The pro-Comintern position won the majority support of the Central Committee, leading to a change in the Party's leadership. Although the CPGB's initial response to the war was that it was an anti-fascist struggle, the need to preserve Party unity, combined with the identification of the USSR with socialism and the need to believe in the legitimacy of the Comintern, led it to support the new line.[7]

The Nazi–Soviet Non-Aggression Pact certainly confused many Communist sympathizers in South Africa. Harold Baldry, an academic who wrote on foreign affairs for the *Guardian* under the pen-name 'Vigilator', and who joined the Party in 1941, produced tortuous speculations in the September and October 1939 issues about the durability of the Pact and the nature of the war.[8] But Naboth Mokgatle reacted decisively when, on the brink of the joining the Party, he heard about the Pact: 'Fascism joining hands with Communism, enemies becoming friends: "No," I said, "not for me"'.[9]

Although there is no direct evidence that South African Communists were as deeply shocked and divided by the Non-Aggression Pact and the Comintern's volte-face on the war as were some of the leaders of the CPGB, there were, nonetheless, signs of confusion within the South African affiliate. The CPSA had relatively close ties with its British counterpart in the late 1930s, both through George Hardy, the British Comintern representative in South Africa, and through reciprocal visits of South African and British Communists to each other's countries. Moreover, a number of new, young members, who would become leading Party figures in the 1940s and 1950s, had lived in England and had contact with the CPGB. Michael Harmel, for instance, had been sent to London in 1938 by his father after completing an MA in Economics at Rhodes University in the hopes that this would cool his radicalism. Instead, he hawked the left-wing *Daily Worker* on street corners, and on his return to South Africa in 1939, he joined the CPSA.[10] In the 1930s English-born Hilda Watts lived both in England, where she had been in the Young Communist League, and in South Africa. Eventually she settled in South Africa.[11] Jack Simons had returned from studying in London in October 1937. He had gone to London in September 1932 and joined the CPGB shortly thereafter. In 1934 Simons had been chair of the student Marxist Society at LSE and had sold the *Student Vanguard*, organ of the CPGB's national student association, suffering a temporary expulsion from the LSE for his political activities.[12] He presumably maintained contacts with CPGB members. Thus, through these individual connections, the CPSA might have picked up some of the tensions in the CPGB.

Both South African Communists and Trotskyists had been actively involved in the local anti-fascist movement throughout the 1930s and were supporters of the anti-fascist struggles in Europe. In June 1939, following the start of negotiations between Britain and the Soviet Union, Communists in Johannesburg began to think that Britain was going to stand up to Nazi Germany and argued, accordingly, that the CPSA should support the South African government's National Registration drive as a statement against fascism. But members of the Cape Town branch took a different view. A Party pamphlet entitled *Must We Fight?*, which was published in Cape Town in June 1939 and reflected the position of Jack Simons, answered the question with a 'YES! For Our Rights'. It argued that support for registration was tantamount to support for the United Party government. Instead, it said, '[t]he fight against Fascism must start in our own country' and then, echoing the CPGB, went on to advocate a '"struggle on two fronts"':

> At home, the expulsion of Nazi agents, a definite declaration not to hand South-West Africa to the Nazis, and a campaign for the exposure of Fascism to the people. Abroad, a clearly stated determination to resist Fascist violence with armed force. These are the only ways to peace.[13]

Once the Nazi–Soviet Non-Aggression Pact was signed, 'the Party was asked to be cautious in its attitude to the war that was ahead'.[14] When war was declared, its members held conflicting views, and a few leaders of the National Liberation League enlisted. Similarly, editorials in the *Guardian* argued, with some wavering, for conditional support.[15] The initial response of the CPSA's Cape Town-based Central Committee was that it was

> a struggle between rival imperialisms for raw materials, markets, capitalist domination and the power to exploit colonial peoples in Africa and Asia. ... The capitalists of Britain and France are waging a war in their own interests and not to improve the position of the workers in Britain and France. ... But the people of Britain and France are fighting in this war because they wish to destroy capitalism in its most brutal and aggressive form – Fascism. ... in the interests of humanity it is essential that Nazism be destroyed.[16]

Fascism, then, was seen as the greater evil; but South Africans had to fight first and foremost against its local manifestation in their own country. However, the Cape Town and Johannesburg branches did not see eye to eye. The Cape Town branch was more unambiguously opposed to the war. Yet, Cape Town Communists also saw themselves in a dilemma because of what they believed to be South Africa's distinctive situation: the only strong and organized anti-war movement in the country was on the far right. How then, to be critical of the war, while not appearing to support the far right? As Jack Simons argued,

> at the moment the struggle was in South Africa against the Nazis. This undoubtedly weakened the line of struggle against the war, since it meant a passive acceptance of the Smuts Government and its war policy. But the dilemma – support Smuts and the war *or* oppose the war and support the pro-Nazi, anti-Trade Union, anti-colour Nationalists – could not be avoided by other means than the policy adopted: oppose the war and resist the Nationalists.[17]

The Johannesburg branch, by contrast, initially supported the war. Advocate George Findlay, for one, stated that the Party's attitude 'to the war was one of whole-hearted co-operation with all the forces opposing Fascist aggression', arguing that it was necessary to strike capitalism at its weakest point. Others, such as Issy Wolfson, argued for conditional support for the war.[18] In Durban, where the Party had been all but wiped out, parallel debates took place amongst leftists of various hues at Sunday-night meetings of the Left Book Club that revived in 1939.[19] The arguments in the CPSA reflected two broad positions about the war found amongst European leftists. One position, which looked back to the dreadful experience of the First World War, argued that it was reasonable to support the war only if it could be fought under a democratic and progressive agenda. The other argued more bluntly that fascism was a distinctive threat that had to be fought. Most Johannesburg Communists believed that the Party should give conditional support to the war while demanding the replacement of the Smuts Government by a more progressive government. This echoed arguments made in Britain about the possibility of a pro-war coalition government – a prospect that was realized in May 1940. But in the South African context, it was a naive supposition. The only real threat to the Smuts Government came from the right. The changing views of the Johannesburg branch are seen in the pages of *'Nkululeko (Freedom)*, a mimeographed newsletter that the Johannesburg Party District Committee began publishing in 1939, spearheaded by Edwin Mofutsanyana, Michael Harmel and Michael Diphuko, a teacher who had just joined the Party that year. The September 1939 issue of *'Nkululeko* argued:

> There is a sharp division between fascist countries which have brought about the war by their policy of aggression, and democratic countries in which the people can hope for progress only if they resist aggression and fascism, both inside their countries and outside them.[20]

Two months later, following the turn of the CPGB, *'Nkululeko* had changed its view of the war, seeing it as a war of competing oppressor countries – imperialist Britain versus Nazi Germany. 'The British working class', it wrote,

> is demanding peace, and is demanding that a government of people should be formed in England in place of the present government of the rich. *We in South Africa support the British working people in these demands.* We declare that this is an unjust war in which we have no interest except our desire to end it.[21]

By the Party's March 1940 conference the Cape Town and Johannesburg branches were in clear agreement that the war was an intra-imperialist one. Jack Simons effectively acknowledged the CPGB's influence on the local Party, indicating the CPGB's new line had helped the Party to clarify its own anti-war stance. Now, the main problem facing the Party was how to propagate its anti-war line without strengthening the Nationalists.[22] Most Communists still believed that it was vital to get support from Afrikaner workers and thought that the new line would facilitate this. Sam Kahn, for instance, naively believed that most Afrikaners were anti-imperialist rather than pro-Nazi, arguing, 'if it is possible for Hitler to co-operate with Russia, so it must affect the people here whose sympathies were with Hitler. We will be able to get more readily the ear of the Afrikaners to the line of the C.P.'[23] That was an untenable argument under the circumstances. To Johnny Gomas, the issue was clear-cut: 'How can we be interested in fighting Nazism thousands of miles away, while in reality we have a similar monster devouring *us here* daily?. ... If Non-Europeans must fight, let them fight for their own democratic rights.'[24] But for other blacks, the issue was far more ambiguous. As Edwin Mofutsanyana conceded, the Party's anti-war stance had confused Africans, some of whom mistook the Party's opposition to the war for support of Hitler.[25]

The March 1940 conference was a turning point for the Party in several respects. The problem of the location of its headquarters loomed large, as did its dismal trade union record. The headquarters remained in Cape Town, even though the delegates concurred that ultimately they should be returned to the industrial centre of the Rand. Despite pressure from their British counterpart, the delegates were nonetheless emphatic that the headquarters remain in Cape Town until Johannesburg was able to build up an organizational machinery and a cadre. Moreover, Jack Simons raised the question of organizational structure, arguing that a separate Central Committee was not necessary in South Africa and that the Central Committee and Politburo be merged. 'Let the conference say who are to be the five or six men who are going to control things for the next period', he argued. 'Never mind if this is a breach of practice.' Despite Issy Wolfson's caution that some members of the Central Committee might be disappointed to find themselves removed, Simons's proposal was accepted, and six members of the Cape Town branch were selected to function as a combined Central Committee and Politburo.[26] It would not be the last time that a CPSA conference took a decision of magnitude without consulting its membership. Finally, the conference resolved to reverse its poor track record in the trade union field. As Willie Kalk moaned, 'the Trotskyists in Johannesburg can call a meeting of 10,000 Africans, but the Party can't. ... The Trotskyists have succeeded because they had one man [Max Gordon] with considerable influence.' This was a situation that the Party was not prepared to leave unchallenged.[27]

Opposing the war

For almost two years Communists and Trotskyists were united in their opposition to the war; however, this shared stance did not in any way lessen their mutual suspicions of each other. The local Trotskyist groups, the Fourth International Club in Cape Town and the Socialist Workers' League in Johannesburg, had already declared their opposition to the impending war, in August 1939. They published their views in an ephemeral bilingual paper called *Socialist Action/Sosialistiese Aksie*. The war could not be characterized as a struggle between democratic and fascist countries, they argued, because the so-called democratic countries were imperialist powers supporting repressive regimes.[28] Their own outlook was influenced by the formation of the Fourth International in 1938. Anticipating that the intra-imperialist conflict would precipitate a post-war collapse of capitalism, Trotskyists hoped, idealistically, that the Fourth International would attract mass support and provide new revolutionary leadership capable of counteracting the reformist policies of Stalinism. The Trotskyist trade unionist Max Gordon announced his opposition to the war – 'I am anti-Nazi and anti-imperialist' – at the annual conference of the Trades and Labour Council in 1940, but he proceeded to condemn the CPSA's anti-war stance as opportunistic.[29]

The leadership of the NLL and the NEUF also came out against the war. A number of radical Indians, such as the Communists D. A. Seedat and Dr Yusuf Dadoo campaigned against the war, influenced by the anti-war stance of anti-colonial leaders in India. In Natal, a group of radicals had set up a Liberal Study Group in the late 1930s. Amongst its virtually all-male regulars were M. D. Naicker, H. A. Naidoo and D. A. Seedat, as well as Peter Abrahams, who had recently left Cape Town and was planning to emigrate, and Wilson Cele. At one meeting, several people decided to form a 'nationalist bloc' within the Natal Indian Association. Although the nationalist bloc was expelled from the Natal Indian Association, its members went on to campaign against the war and for democratic rights and were prosecuted under the War Measures Act. Sedaat was jailed in April 1941 on a charge of subversion. In the Transvaal, Dadoo led the NEUF on vigorous anti-war campaigns, and in July 1940 he was charged under the war emergency regulations for publishing a leaflet that argued: 'Don't support this war: where the rich get richer and the poor get killed'. Dadoo was jailed several times over the next year.[30]

In their overt opposition to the war left-wing activists risked internment and thus jeopardized the very organizations that they had been working to build up. By contrast, British Communist trade unionists were very careful not to let their Party's opposition to the war threaten their trade union positions. In South Africa, opponents of the war – both Nazi sympathisers and socialists – were subjected to vituperous condemnation and severe repression by the government. On the one side, the government faced right-wing threats ranging from street skirmishes and bombings to an aborted insurrection and a plot to depose the government. The more serious episodes led to the internment of several hundred people. On the other side, the government faced the far less significant threat of socialist anti-war propaganda. Leftists who opposed the war were branded as 'Communazis'. Several leading left-wing trade unionists and activists were interned for periods of between nine and fifteen months. These included a number of Communists, such as Arnold Latti, a Port Elizabeth trade unionist, and the Joffe brothers, Max and Louis. Also interned were the trade unionist Fritz Fellner, husband of Johanna Cornelius; the veteran socialist J. E. Brown; E. J. Burford, a trade unionist and Labour Party member who had only recently arrived from England and who believed in the organization of both black and white workers; and Max Gordon. As arguably the leading trade union organizer on the Witwatersrand, Gordon's internment reverberated in the growing trade union movement.[31]

The CPSA's influence in trade unions on the Rand had dwindled during the 1930s as a result of its New Line policies and the expulsion of its most experienced organizers. The black trade union movement had been damaged by the Party's internecine battles, and the rebuilding of the trade unions involved a number of Trotskyists – most notably Max Gordon. He also trained several black trade unionists, the most significant of whom was Daniel Koza, who had qualified as a teacher at the Diocesan Training College in Grace Dieu near Pietersburg before turning his hand to trade union work.[32]

Gordon had formed the Joint Committee of African Trade Unions in 1938. This reorganized the following year; David Gosani, a former member of the defunct Johannesburg Workers' Party, became chair; Gordon, secretary; and Koza, assistant secretary. That year its membership was estimated at 15,700. By 1940 it was the largest trade union group on the Witwatersrand, claiming to represent twenty-one unions with approximately 23,000 to 26,000 members. The other leading trade union federation was the Non-European Trades Union Coordinating Committee, led by Gana Makabeni, an ardent believer in black leadership of black unions.[33]

Gordon was arrested in May 1940 and interned in the Ganspan Internment Camp. Not until 20 December 1940 did he learn the allegations behind his internment. These were: 1) that he had organized African trade unions for personal financial gain; 2) that he had agitated amongst Africans to create unrest and hostility between them and their employers and that he had organized a troublesome laundry strike in 1936; 3) that he used the trade unions to propagate his Communist views; 4) that he attempted to incite racial hostility by issuing an inflammatory leaflet that called for a meeting about an illegal strike of black mineworkers at Nkana, Northern Rhodesia and by organizing the meeting; and 5) that the study classes that he organized were used as a means to indoctrinate African workers with Communist ideas – as 'a very welknown communist woman was one of the teachers'.[34] Significantly, none of the reasons given for his incarceration concerned the war.

The 'welknown communist woman' was, ironically, the Trotskyist Fanny Klenerman, owner of Vanguard Books, who, spurred by her concern for Gordon, helped to organize and became secretary of the Committee for the Relief of Anti-Nazi Internees in early 1941. This aimed to assist anti-Nazi and anti-fascist internees by providing comforts, financial aid and literature; transporting family members for visits; providing assistance to released internees and appealing to improve conditions in the camps. Klenerman's Trotskyist views did not inhibit support from an eclectic array of white progressives, including Johanna Cornelius, Fritz Fellner, Solly Sachs and Betty Radford of the *Guardian*.[35] Despite the efforts of this Committee and of the Civil Liberties Association, only after the CPSA shifted its stance on the war in June 1941 was there any appreciable amelioration in the situation of left-wing internees.

Communists in support of war

Almost immediately after Germany's invasion of the Soviet Union on 22 June 1941 the CPSA joined the war effort, arguing that defence of the Soviet Union gave the war a progressive character and was a precondition for the defeat of fascism.[36] The Comintern had revived the People's Front, and following its lead the CPSA developed a much more elastic conception of the social classes that were potentially anti-fascist and that now included some elements of the bourgeoisie. Although the CPSA's decision to support the war effort eased the pressure from the government, the impact on black sympathizers was ambivalent. Communist speakers were heckled at meetings in Johannesburg and Natal by people in the audience demanding why they should be asked to support Smuts now, when previously the Party had vilified him. It was not an easy about-face to make, as Joe Slovo, still too young to join the Party, conceded. 'In line with Communist Parties everywhere our Central Committee had changed its stance on the war after the Nazi attack on the Soviet Union', he recalled.

> But this somersault was more difficult for us than for most parties. How did you tell a black man to make his peace with Smuts — the butcher of Bulhoek and the Bondelswarts? To the average member of the rightless and voteless majority, the regime's exhortation to 'save civilisation and democracy' must have sounded like a cruel parody.[37]

The decision to support the war created stress within the Party. Moses Kotane, for one, had difficulty accepting the new stance on the war. As Jack Simons recalled, '[w]e were under pressure from Johannesburg to throw ourselves completely into the war effort without any holds barred, even to the extent of damping down strikes'. Michael Harmel and Edwin Mofutsanyana came down to Cape Town from Johannesburg 'in order to press this on us', Simons added. 'And Moses [Kotane] opposed it, very strongly, and this is one of the reasons why the CC was unable to declare it.' Nevertheless, Party activists ultimately reconciled their differences in support of the new policy.[38]

In contrast, Trotskyists remained adamantly opposed to the war and to the government's war efforts.[39] Their anti-war views sometimes struck a chord in mass organizations or, at least, coincided with other anti-war expressions. Despite the predominance of Communists in the national offices of the NEUF, for example, its regional branches did not simply toe the line. At the annual meeting of the Port Elizabeth branch of the NEUF in 1942, a motion put forward by Communists to support the war was rejected. Instead, the meeting unanimously opposed the establishment of a second front in Europe and declared that blacks 'must refuse any compromise from the Government. The Government should demonstrate its sincerity in advance'.[40]

The CPSA's policy reversal meant that it now found itself allied with the government that it had hitherto attacked in its comparison of racial oppression in South Africa with fascism in Europe. Its pro-war position meant an endorsement of the government's domestic war policies that set the Party on a distinctly accommodationist path. The Party gained a dual dividend from its new stance. Its anti-war position had alienated white labour support. Now, like other Communist Parties, it was able to benefit from the pro-war nationalism of sections of the white working class and petty bourgeoisie. Between 1941 and 1943 the CPSA's national membership increased to over 1300. This was nowhere near the growth reported by the CPGB; its reported membership in December 1941 was 22,738, and by December 1943 this had climbed to 55,138. Nevertheless, the CPSA gained in confidence from its growing numbers.[41]

Throughout the war, the CPSA directed itself to the white electorate. In addition, the Party was no longer at odds with the leaderships of the AAC and ANC over the war, even if most members of these organizations were apathetic about a struggle against fascism in Europe while their own democratic demands remained unmet. Moreover, despite the seeming contradiction between the CPSA's new stance and the increasing militancy of blacks, by the war's end the Party was the strongest socialist organization and had regained some influence in the black trade union movement.

What did the CPSA's pro-war stance mean in practical terms? The Soviet Union's entry into the war led to the disappearance of anti-Soviet propaganda from official channels and a warming of relations between the Soviet and South African governments. State repression of Communists eased measurably after June 1941. The Joffes were released from the internment camp in September 1941, and while Communists were still subjected to arrest, appeals to the Minister of Justice, Dr Colin Steyn, generally resulted in their release. The new situation meant that a number of individuals who had been covert Party members now came out. In Durban, where the CPSA had been all but extinguished by severe and unremitting repression, Communists were able to act openly and began publishing the *Call*.[42]

The CPSA continued to call for repeal of the pass laws but now combined this with appeals to support the war. It launched a 'Defend South Africa' campaign and called for the right of blacks to bear arms to defend their country, taking as its point of departure Smuts's declaration in Parliament that '[b]efore the Japanese take this country I will see to it that every Coloured man and every Native who can be armed will be armed'. Communists were still harassed, however: Kotane was arrested in November 1942 for demanding that enlisted blacks should have the right to bear arms.[43]

The 'Defend South Africa' campaign was particularly successful in enabling the CPSA to attract white recruits. Whites who had hitherto been sympathizers now felt able to join the Party because of its support for the war. Many of them 'in this heady, pro-Soviet period, were enthusiastic, albeit short-lived, Party supporters', observed the young Communist Pauline Podbrey.[44] The weekly circulation of the *Guardian* soared from about 12,000 in 1940 to over 42,000 in 1943. In the late 1930s Party activists had helped form a South African Youth League. This organized along sectional lines, with recruitment into European, Coloured and African sections. But the organizers were mainly in contact with white youth, and the African section in Sophiatown was neglected. In 1940 the South African Youth League had begun publishing *Ware Republikein* (*True Republican*) to reach Afrikaner workers.[45] The Party now turned its efforts more squarely to the white electorate, running nine candidates in the 1943 general elections. Although none of the candidates was successful – together they polled about 7000 votes – the results nonetheless indicated that the Party had made some advances amongst the white electorate. The Party was more successful in local elections. In 1943 Betty Radford and Sam Kahn were elected to the Cape Town City Council, and Archie Muller to the East London Council. In 1944 Hilda Watts won a City Council seat in the Johannesburg suburb of Hillbrow. The CPSA's concern to attract whites inevitably led it to downplay the issue of social equality. While acknowledging the common interests of all workers, it was equivocal on the issue of social integration.[46] Nonetheless, the CPSA's black membership grew, and it gained a number of notable black recruits in the early 1940s: Naboth Mokgatle, for one, a shopworker and union organizer, joined immediately following the Party's decision to support the war.[47]

Although participation in the local advisory board elections was controversial and was rejected by many blacks, the CPSA nonetheless contested the elections, in line with its support of the NRC. The Party hoped that participation would help it to achieve visibility at the local level. In late 1942 all six Communist candidates in the East London Advisory Board elections were successful. In December 1943 three Communists won seats on the Advisory Board in Orlando, near Johannesburg, and a year later, in December 1944, Communists won all the seats in the Langa Advisory Board elections, outside Cape Town.[48]

The Party's decision to support the war led to improved relations with the ANC, which was now slowly beginning to revive. The ANC's paper, *Abantu Batho*, had folded after many years. The ANC now began to publicize its views in the *Guardian* and in the official Party organs, *Inkululeko* (the newly anglicized form of '*Nkululeko*) and *Freedom*, a monthly journal of the Cape Town branch that began publication in August 1939. A number of Communists took up leading positions in the ANC, including Moses Kotane, John Marks, Dan Tloome, David Bopape and Gaur Radebe. There was certainly much tension in the ANC about the presence of Communists – Xuma, for one, was far from pleased. Nonetheless, a still weak ANC needed activists, even if they were Communists. As one indicator of the ANC's tolerance towards its Communist members, in 1943 it appointed Kotane, Marks and Mofutsanyana to its committee to draft a bill of rights entitled *Africans' Claims in*

South Africa. This was modelled on the Atlantic Charter, a charter of rights for the post-war era that had been drawn up in August 1941 by British Prime Minister Winston Churchill and American President F. D. Roosevelt.[49]

International developments – local reverberations

Two events in the international Communist movement in the early 1940s had repercussions in the CPSA and in other national affiliates. The first was the dissolution of the Comintern, a decision now recognized to be Stalin's. On 15 May 1943 the ECCI announced that

> the organisation for uniting the workers chosen by the First Congress of the Comintern ... has more and more been outgrown by the movement's development and the increasing complexity of its problems in separate countries. It has even become a hindrance to the further strengthening of the national working class parties.

Moreover, the world war had ' further sharpened the differences in the situation in various countries', especially between the Allied and the Axis powers. In short, implied the ECCI, the national sections needed more autonomy to fight fascism.[50]

In terms of practical politics, the Comintern had effectively been an appendage of the Soviet Union since its about-face on the war in September 1939. After the Soviet Union entered the war, Stalin informed Dimitrov that the Comintern's role was to defend the Soviet Union and defeat fascism – not to propagate revolution. By 1943 the Comintern was no longer necessary for Soviet security. The Red Army had defeated Nazi Germany in the Battle of Stalingrad. Under pressure from the United States to dissolve the Comintern, Stalin apparently saw the dissolution as a means to strengthen his relations with the Allied powers.[51]

What impact did the Comintern's dissolution have on the national affiliates? For many Communists the decision was unexpected. Yet within four weeks, thirty-one of the Comintern's sixty-five affiliates, including the CPSA, had endorsed the resolution. The CPSA argued that the decision was 'inspired by a desire to bring about the maximum degree of unity between the United Nations in the struggle against Hitler and his allies'.[52] Nonetheless, most Communists still saw the Soviet Union as the centre of world revolution, and their faith in Soviet orthodoxy and authority remained unshaken. Despite the formal dissolution of the executive bodies of the Comintern, much of its organizational framework was maintained under the direction of Dimitrov and other former Comintern officials. Arguably, Soviet influence on the national parties became more direct.[53] However, the war had already disrupted the previous link between the Comintern and its South African affiliate. As the war progressed, the strategic concerns of the Soviet leadership became ever more focused on the military battle for survival, and South African affairs were of little immediate significance.

By late 1943, the relationship between the Allied powers had certainly warmed. In December 1943, the big three – Stalin, Roosevelt and Churchill – met in Teheran where they agreed to work together to make an enduring post-war peace. The Teheran meeting had a profound impact on Communist politics in the United States, which would echo back to South Africa. Earl Browder, leader of the American Communist Party, saw the Teheran meeting as 'history's greatest turning point', signifying both that the Western powers had finally accepted the Soviet Union as a legitimate state and that the Soviet Union had agreed not to promote socialism in Western Europe. In short, he maintained, 'capitalism and socialism have begun to find the way to peaceful coexistence and collaboration in the same world'. To fight for socialism in the United States would only divide the nation and weaken progressive forces. Browder proposed that the American Communist Party dissolve and that Communists regroup as a Communist Political Association, which would be 'one of many "democratic and progressive groupings which operate ... through the two-party system"' and which would align with broader forces.[54]

Browder's arguments won the support of the majority of his comrades. His views dovetailed with those of a generation of Communists who were tired of sectarian politics and state repression and who craved acceptability. The principal opponent to this move was William Z. Foster, a worker and syndicalist radical turned Communist, who had led the American Communist Party during a period of growth but had become marginalized in the 1930s. Indicative of the role that Moscow still played a year after the Comintern's dissolution, a copy of Foster's objections was cabled to Dimitrov, who advised Foster to withdraw his opposition to Browder. Foster complied; the American Communist Party was briefly disbanded and replaced by the Communist Political Association.[55] 'Browderism', as it became known, caused quite a stir in the CPSA. Although most South African Communists opposed the policy, a substantial minority were sympathetic to Browder's argument, believing that the post-war era would see the end of class conflict – an omen that many in the CPSA would be unprepared for the repression the Party would face at the war's end.[56]

Conclusion

South Africa's decision to enter the Second World War led to increases in industrial growth and in the movement of black people from rural areas to cities. In relative terms, the first few years of the war were ones of cautious optimism about the prospects of political liberalization for blacks. The impact of the war on the left was more ambivalent. Despite the animosity between Communists and Trotskyists in the late 1930s, those were the years when their limited efforts at cooperation, notably in the NLL and NEUF, reached a modest peak. While their common opposition to the war positioned them both against the government, this did not provide a basis for left unity. With the assassination of Leon Trotsky in August 1940, followed by the CPSA's decision to support the war in 1941, the schism between Communists and

Trotskyists became even more pronounced. Communists gained a new legitimacy while Trotskyists remained marginalized. This schism meant that socialist responses both to the wartime popular protest movements and to the mounting political repression in the last years of the war would be divided and inevitably diminished.

Notes

1. For a discussion of black attitudes towards the war see Baruch Hirson, 'Not Pro-war, and not Anti-war: Just Indifferent. South African Blacks in the Second World War', *Critique*, 20–21, 1987, 39–56. See also Tom Lodge, 'Class Conflict, Communal Struggle and Patriotic Unity: the Communist Party of South African during the Second World War', Paper presented to the African Studies Seminar, African Studies Institute, University of the Witwatersrand, 7 October 1985; and Patrick J. Furlong, 'The Bonds of War: the African National Congress, the Communist Party of South Africa and the Threat of "Fascism"', *South African Historical Journal*, 36, May 1997, 68–87.

2. Between 1936 and 1946 African urbanization increased by 48.81 per cent, white by 32.25 per cent, Coloured by 26.61 per cent, and Indian by 27.28 per cent. H. Sonnabend, 'Population', and Ellen Hellmann, 'Urban Areas', both in Hellmann, ed., *Handbook on Race Relations*, 4–26 and 229–74 respectively, esp. 23 and 239.

3. 'Resolutions of the ANC Annual Conference, December 15–18, 1939', Karis and Carter, eds, *From Protest to Challenge*, vol. 2, 154–5, quote 155.

4. 'Resolution on the War. Adopted by the National Executive Committees of the AAC and the ANC, July 7, 1940', Karis and Carter, eds, *From Protest to Challenge*, vol. 2, 339–40, quote 340.

5. Hirson, *Yours for the Union*, 77–8.

6. McDermott and Agnew, *The Comintern*, quote 193, 198.

7. McDermott and Agnew, *The Comintern*, 194–5.

8. Bunting, *Kotane*, 98; Hirson, *Yours for the Union*, 79; Switzer, 'Socialism and the Resistance Movement', 293.

9. Mokgatle, *Autobiography*, 212.

10. Harmel, *Ray's Story*, 42; Elizabeth Ceiriog Jones, '*Inkululeko*: Organ of the Communist Party of South Africa, 1939–1950', in Switzer, ed., *South Africa's Alternative Press*, 344; Edgar, interview with Mofutsanyana, 37–8.

11. Joshua N. Lazerson, *Against the Tide: Whites in the Struggle Against Apartheid*, Boulder, San Franciso and Oxford: Westview and Bellville: Mayibuye, 1994, 37–8.

12. John Saville, unpublished memoirs, 27–31, n.d. Edgar, interview with Mofutsanyana, 37. Brian Bunting, interview with Jack Simons, tape 1, 1, c. November 1973, Brian Bunting Collection 8.4.1, Mayibuye Centre Historical Papers Archive, University of the Western Cape.

13. *Must We Fight?*, Cape Town: CPSA, n.d. [June 1939], quotes 1, 15, 16. See also 'Extracts from "The War and South Africa" by J. Morkel [Jack Simons], report delivered at a conference of the Communist Party held on March 23 and 24, 1940', in Bunting, ed., *South African Communists Speak*, 147–50, esp. 149 for a discussion of various Communist positions advocated in 1939.

14. 'Extracts from "The War and South Africa" by J. Morkel', 149.

15. NLL officials Lance Morley-Turner and Booker Lakey enlisted, as did Jimmy La Guma. Simons and Simons, *Class and Colour*, 531–2; Bunting, *Kotane*, 98–9.

16. Quoted in Bunting, ed., *South African Communists Speak*, 136.

17. 'Extracts from "The War and South Africa"', 150; emphasis in the original.

18. Quoted in Bunting, *Kotane*, 97.

19. Podbrey, *White Girl*, 55.

20. *'Nkululeko*, September 1939, 1, quoted in Hirson, *Yours for the Union*, 79.

21. Editorial 'Money for War', *'Nkululeko*, 15 November 1939, in Bunting, ed., *South African Communists Speak*, 137; emphasis in original.

22. 'Extracts from "The War and South Africa"', 150. See also 'Minutes of Conference of the Communist Party of South Africa, held at Cape Town, on 23rd and 24th March 1940', Karis and Carter microfilm collection, Reel 3A, 2:CC1:32. By contrast Cope, *Comrade Bill*, 331–4, glosses over the CPSA's internal ambiguities about the war.

23. 'Minutes of Conference of the Communist Party of South Africa, held at Cape Town, on 23rd and 24th March 1940', 39. See also Hirson, *Yours for the Union*, 80.

24. '"The War and Segregation" by J. Gomas, published in *Freedom*, organ of the Communist Party, June 1940' in Bunting, ed., *South African Communists Speak*, 150–52, quote 151–2.

25. Edgar interview with Mofutsanyana, 38.

26. 'Minutes of Conference of the Communist Party of South Africa, held at Cape Town, on 23rd and 24th March 1940', 54–5. The combined Central Committee/Politburo consisted of Bill Andrews, Jack Simons, Moses Kotane, Johnny Gomas, Ray Alexander and Sam Kahn.

27. 'Minutes of Conference of the Communist Party of South Africa, held at Cape Town, on 23rd and 24th March 1940', 65.

28. 'Manifesto Against Imperialist War', *Socialist Action*, August 1939, in Drew, ed., *South Africa's Radical Tradition*, vol. 1, 332–4.

29. Quoted in Hirson, *Yours for the Union*, 78.

30. The nationalist bloc included, amongst others, Dr G. M. Naicker and several Communists: C. I. Amra, H. A. Naidoo and D. A. Seedat. Roux, *Time Longer than Rope*, 308–9; Simons and Simons, 531–2; Bunting, *Kotane*, 105; Podbrey, *White Girl*, 58; *Statement of Dr Y. M. Dadoo*.

31. Roux, *Time Longer than Rope*, 328–9; Simons and Simons, *Class and Colour*, 533; Cope, *Comrade Bill*, 332; Hirson, *Yours for the Union*, 82–3; Berger, *Threads of Solidarity*, 159 and 328, n. 28.

32. Hirson, *Yours for the Union*, 94–5; Abrahams, *Tell Freedom*, 224, 258. Brian Bunting interview with Simons, tape 1, 1.

33. Roux, *Time Longer than Rope*, 326–34; Simons and Simons, *Class and Colour*, 511; Hirson, *Yours for the Union*, 43–4.

34. 'Letter from Max Gordon to Fanny Klenerman, 21 December 1940', in Drew, ed., *South Africa's Radical Tradition*, vol. 1, 339–40; Stein, 'Max Gordon', 152–3.

35. The Committee sought assistance from Senator Edgar Brooks, Margaret Ballinger, Donald Molteno, Senator Rheinallt Jones and Lynn Saffery. Gana Makabeni and A. Thipe made statements indicating that they, not Gordon, had produced the leaflet and organized the meeting for the Nkana strike. Koza was also involved with the initiative. Committee for the Relief of Anti-Nazi Internees, 19 March, 1941 and Letter from Betty [Radford] to Fanny [Klenerman], 26 March 1941, both A2031/C1.1, Klenerman Papers; Constitution, Committee for the Relief of Anti-Nazi Internees; Internment of Max Gordon, Statements by A. Thipe and G. Makabeni; both A2031/C2, Klenerman Papers.

36. '"All Support for the Soviet Union", statement by the Central Committee of the Communist Party of South Africa, published in *The Guardian*, June 26, 1941', in Bunting,

ed., *South African Communists Speak*, 162–5; H. Morkel, [Jack Simons], 'Why We Must Support the Government in the War Against Fascism', *Freedom-Vryheid*, 9, April 1942, 1–3.

37. Slovo, *Unfinished Autobiography*, 28; Bunting, *Kotane*, 107–8.

38. Brian Bunting, interview with Simons, tape 2, 9.

39. See, for instance, 'The Programme of the 4th International in South Africa', *Workers Voice*, 1 July [1943?] in Drew, ed., *South Africa's Radical Tradition*, vol. 1, 352–4.

40. Quoted in Bunting, *Kotane*, 108. Roux, *Time Longer than Rope*, 313 credits the position to the intervention of a Trotskyist.

41. Callinicos, *A Place in the City*, 63; Pelling, *The British Communist Party*, 192.

42. Roux, *Time Longer than Rope*, 310–11; Bunting, *Kotane*, 113–4; Lodge, 'Class Conflict', 2 and 5*ff*; and Iain Edwards, 'Recollections: the Communist Party and Worker Militancy in Durban, early 1940', *South African Labour Bulletin*, 11, 4, February–March 1986, 65–84, 67–8.

43. Bunting, *Kotane*, 109–12, quote 109. Brian Bunting, interview with Simons, tape 2, transcript p. 9. Simons credits Kotane with shaping the CPSA's wartime policy calling for the arming and equal treatment of enlisted black men.

44. Podbrey, *White Girl*, 98.

45. *Report on a) The Building of a Youth Movement. b) The Work for Peace*, n.d. [1938/39], annexure 9, 4–6, and CPSA Conference, March 1940, Simons Collection, South African Communist Party, 6.6.1.

46. Lodge, 'Class Conflict', 6–7; Hirson, *Yours for the Union*, 12; Lazerson, *Against the Tide*, 34–7.

47. Callinicos, *A Place in the City*, 45, 49, 63–7; Luli Callinicos, 'The Communist Party During the War Years', *South African Labour Bulletin*, 15, 3, 101–5.

48. Bunting, *Kotane*, 114–15.

49. Black activists argued that as a wartime ally of the anti-fascist Allies, South Africa had a moral obligation to apply the Atlantic Charter's human rights agenda to its own affairs. '*Africans' Claims in South Africa*, Including "the Atlantic Charter from the Standpoint of Africans with the Union of South Africa" and "Bill of Rights," Adopted by the ANC Annual Conference', in Karis and Carter, eds, *From Protest to Challenge*, vol. 2, 209–23; Bunting, *Kotane*, 117.

50. 'Dissolution of the Comintern – resolution passed by the Presidium of the Executive Committee of the Communist International on May 15, 1943', in Bunting, ed., *South African Communists Speak*, 177–80, 178; McDermott and Agnew, *The Comintern*, 205.

51. McDermott and Agnew, *The Comintern*, 204–7; Edward P. Johanningsmeier, *Forging American Communism: The Life of William Z. Foster*, Princeton: Princeton University, 1994, 294.

52. 'Dissolution of the Comintern – Statement issued by the Central Committee of the Communist Party of South Africa, June 3, 1943', in Bunting, ed., *South African Communists Speaks*, 180.

53. McDermott and Agnew, *The Comintern*, 205–11.

54. Johanningsmeier, *Forging American Communism*, 295–6.

55. Johanningsmeier, *Forging American Communism*, 300–301.

56. Tom Lodge, 'Political Organisations in Pretoria's African Townships, 1940–1963', in Bozzoli, ed., *Class, Community and Conflict*, 401–17, 404–6; Hirson, *Yours for the Union*, 85, 92, n.18, 111, 197; George Findlay, *Browderism*, April 1944 and George Findlay Diary, 1944, both in Findlay Papers, A1199, Historical Papers Library, University of the Witwatersrand.

Chapter 11

'Not in word, but in power': socialists and black protest during the war

Hopes of political liberalization for black South Africans dimmed in 1943. Preparations for the general election in May 1943 unleashed a backlash against the temporary relaxation of segregationist and racist policies as the competition between the United Party and the Nationalists intensified. The small number of liberals who styled themselves as friends of the 'Natives' – notably Margaret Ballinger in the House of Assembly and Edgar Brookes in the Senate – found themselves increasingly sidelined. In 1943 the government rescinded its suspension of influx control and renewed its assaults on the remaining political rights of Coloureds and Indians. This inspired a resurgence of black political activity. Concurrently, a host of grass-roots mobilizations over transportation and living and working conditions erupted. In response, a new and radicalized generation of political leaders sought either to revitalize existing organizations such as the ANC and the AAC or to establish new organizations. Previous appeals to the white government and attempts by both blacks and whites to reform the political system from within had failed. The continued disenfranchisement of black people and the mounting political repression led to debates about methods of struggle. The left's response to this popular militancy was ambiguous. The CPSA's support for the war effort led it to take a top-down approach to popular struggles, inevitably leading it to suppress popular militancy. By contrast, Trotskyists remained marginalized by their opposition to the war, despite their enthusiasm for working-class militancy.

Socialist rivalries and black politics

The resurgence of black protest offered opportunities for socialists to interact with and influence these movements. But the schism on the left, which had widened since the late 1930s, reinforced organizational rivalries in the broader liberation movement. The CPSA had been unsuccessful at obtaining leadership posts in the AAC: it had failed to get any representatives on the National Executive, and only one Communist, Edwin Mofutsanyana, had been elected to a Provincial Committee.[1] Now, under Kotane's leadership, the Party tried to strengthen its relationship with the ANC. Certainly, the Communists hoped to gain more influence in the ANC than they had achieved in the AAC; in this they were successful. Because of the rivalry that existed between the leadership of the ANC – particularly the Transvaal leaders – and the predominantly Cape-based AAC, the CPSA's concern to work with the ANC inevitably meant that it began to distance itself from the AAC. In an analogous manner Trotskyists in the now underground Cape Town Workers' Party were rethinking their role in the AAC. Several Workers' Party members, notably Isaac Tabata, Jane Gool, Goolam Gool and S. A. Jayiya, hoped to revive the AAC as a potential African parliament that would incorporate pre-existing African organizations.

The ANC's eventual prominence was far from assured in 1940. Its estimated membership that year was 1000. At that year's annual conference A. B. Xuma was elected president-general by a majority of one; he declared the reorganization of Congress as his first goal. Although the ANC was in a stronger position than it had been in 1937 and 1938, it was still functioning in a top-down manner: its leaders debated policy but did not launch any mass activity. C. S. Ramohanoe, general secretary of the Transvaal branch of the ANC, blamed the members, claiming that they attended conferences 'to criticise the officials. … But they do nothing between conferences, about establishing and working in branches in their own localities to further the work of the organisation.'[2]

ANC officials were still opposed to the continuation of the AAC, and even the AAC's own leaders seemed to stall on the publicizing of their 1941 annual conference.[3] At the December 1941 conference Tabata and Goolam Gool launched an avalanche of criticism against Convention's old guard. Gool blamed the inadequacies of the NEUF on the AAC's reformist leaders and their association with liberals in the Joint Councils, churches and welfare societies. The renewal of the NEUF, he argued, depended on the revival of the AAC under new leadership. Tabata presented a vision of a revived AAC. He still hoped that it could become an umbrella body to which all African organizations could affiliate. While acknowledging its failure to achieve any tangible results in its first six years, he blamed this on the leaders, who 'were afraid of its becoming a mass organisation. They advocated no branches, a Federal constitution, meetings every three years', Tabata complained. 'And when Convention adopted a resolution that didn't suit the leaders, it was simply brushed aside … or conveniently buried in the archives by the secretaries.' Moreover, he added, as popular support for the AAC had dwindled, the ANC's leadership had intensified their campaign against it, '[s]o that today we can hear them openly shouting: "Away with Convention!"'.

Although Tabata had been a prime mover for the boycott of the NRC back in 1935, he now conceded the impracticability of the boycott as long as black leaders worked in the NRC:

> If you cannot agree to the idea of the boycott of the elections (and such a boycott today would be less effective than five years ago) at least do something to enhance the prestige of the Convention and show unmistakable African unity to the oppressors. Let Convention agree on the nominations, if nominations there must be.

Yet, his own assessment of the ANC was mechanical and just as coloured by political rivalry as was the ANC's appraisal of Convention. 'I am convinced that it can never become a national organisation, able to replace Convention', Tabata asserted, as 'an organisation which has once proved bankrupt, cannot hope to flourish again and win the confidence of the people. ... Congress belongs to the past. Convention is a national organisation of all parties and stands for the future!' This would prove to be a false prophecy indeed.[4]

Tabata's ideas for the AAC had been carefully thought out in the Workers' Party, which now met only as a secret discussion group. Its leading figures also organized and frequented the New Era Fellowship, a public discussion club that met in District Six in Cape Town. Tabata and his comrades in the Workers' Party used the New Era Fellowship as a testing ground for their ideas and as a recruiting ground for potential members of their inner circle.[5] They began to promote their views in the *Trek*, a bilingual English–Afrikaans magazine that dealt with politics and the arts and that styled itself, somewhat incongruously, as 'The Family Magazine for all South Africans'. Its pages included an eclectic range of radical writers. Eddie Roux, for instance, published a series of articles on the liberation movement in *Trek* that were later incorporated into his book *Time Longer than Rope*. In 1941 Dora Taylor produced a series on poverty and another on democracy, which included a piece entitled 'Education for Democracy – First Stage', a theme endorsed by Cape Town Trotskyists, who were strong advocates of political education as a means of political mobilization.[6]

The following year, 1942, an exchange in the *Trek* provided a glimmer of Tabata's ambitions for the AAC. A Mr D. Robinson wrote an open letter 'To a Non-European Intellectual' in which he speculated on black views of the war and argued that winning the war and ensuring post-war prosperity was only possible through the removal of all racial discrimination. '[T]o achieve this end', he wrote, 'it is more necessary for you yourself to work than for the sympathetic and progressive Europeans.' Black South Africans, he argued, needed a representative political organization to express their views in order to make an impact on political policy. 'Perhaps', Robinson speculated, 'the All African Convention could be made into such an organisation' if it were to include the Indians and Coloureds. Then, it could 'achieve the very useful object of canalising and crystallising non-European thought in the country'.[7]

Robinson's letter provoked a rapid rejoinder from 'A Few Non-Europeans' writing 'On Behalf of the Non-European' – undoubtedly representing the views of Tabata and his comrades. Stating their aim to be 'nothing less than *full democratic rights*', they supported the revitalization of the AAC. 'Liberals want to give us promises and the Communist Party arms', they noted, but this was not enough. 'When we have full citizenship rights we will wax as poetic about the democratic idea as the most fulsome Liberal and we will defend it as well as any Soviet man or woman defends the U.S.S.R.'[8] But a response from a 'Non-European Non-Intellectual' demanded to know why all Coloureds – let alone all blacks – should unite in a single political organization when they did not necessarily share common political views. 'We have been thinking too much in terms of "the group" instead of thinking in terms of "the individual". We have disregarded *the man*, and emphasised *the race.*' What did Non-Europeans want? Non-European Non-Intellectual's reply was: 'opportunity, opportunity, opportunity'.[9] The idea of a mass organization encompassing all blacks was not without its critics.

Building Non-European unity

Political developments in the Western Cape were jolted by the government's announcement in February 1943 of plans to establish a Cape Coloured Permanent Commission (later renamed the Coloured Affairs Council) and a Coloured section of the Department of the Interior. This initiative was part of the government's scheme to erode Coloured voting rights – following its curtailment of African rights in the late 1930s. In response, the New Era Fellowship held a series of meetings and launched the Anti-Coloured Affairs Department (Anti-CAD) movement to protest against the government's measures. The initiative was led by Ben Kies, a member of the Workers' Party and a prominent activist in the Teachers' League of South Africa, an organization of Coloured teachers.[10] The Anti-CAD, which was enormously popular in the mid-1940s, was a federal body that argued for full democratic rights for all the oppressed people, called for the boycott of all racial institutions and made overtures to other black organizations to build Non-European unity.

A number of individuals from the Workers' Party assumed leading positions in the Anti-CAD, and they aimed to influence this mass mobilization through the dissemination of ideas. At the first National Anti-CAD conference in May 1943 Ben Kies expounded the thesis that teachers could play a vanguard role in the liberation struggle by educating and leading the people 'along the right road', and he argued for a united front of all Non-European organizations as a means of contesting the government's divide and rule strategy.[11]

The call for Non-European unity had a stronger appeal in the Cape, particularly the Western Cape, than in the Transvaal, where African nationalism exerted greater influence. But Non-European unity also had a resonance amongst Indian radicals in Natal. In April the South African Indian Congress gave notice of its intent to call for support of this goal at its June conference and to press for the establishment of an organization of all Non-Europeans.[12] In June 1943 the Western Province of the AAC – Tabata's branch – issued a leaflet entitled *Calling All Africans* that argued that 'the different Non-European groups have now realised the need for unity – unity not only within their respective groups, but of all Non-European groups. The present conditions demand such unity.' December 1943 saw the first conference of the Non-European Unity Movement (NEUM).[13]

The conference delegates adopted a list of minimum democratic demands known as the Ten Point Programme. This had been drawn up by the Workers' Party, and it bore the imprint of the nine-point democratic programme formulated by Plekhanov in his 'Second Draft Programme of the Russian Social-Democrats'. This had been written in 1887 and first published, in Geneva, in 1888. There is no doubt that the socialists in the Workers' Party felt an affinity with Plekhanov's approach and saw reflections of their own country in the conditions that he described – notably, the oppressive state, the large and politically backward peasantry and the mobile industrial proletariat. Plekhanov argued that in countries where the working class was 'oppressed by a double yoke' of a 'rising capitalism' combined with an 'obsolescent patriarchal economy', socialists had to develop a strategy that aimed at 'transitional stages'. Political absolutism was a barrier to the development of a socialist party, Plekhanov maintained. Thus, the primary task of socialists living under such regimes was to overthrow absolutism and to implement a democratic constitution. The parallels with the South African case were compelling. Where the architects of the Ten Point Programme went beyond Plekhanov and strove to incorporate the Trotskyist idea of permanent revolution, was in their emphasis that the Ten Point Programme was a minimum programme. Believing that the ten points could not be achieved within a capitalist framework, they hoped that these democratic demands could serve as a transitional programme to socialism. Yet in stipulating that adherence to the programme was a precondition for affiliation to the NEUM, they adopted a formalistic approach to political organizing that ultimately left them marginalized.[14]

The NEUM was set up as a federal body that hoped to attract a wide range of popular organizations. While the AAC and Anti-CAD accepted the Ten Point Programme and affiliated to the NEUM, it was not able to draw in the South African Indian Congress, which, under the conservative leadership of A. I. Kajee, indicated that it would only cooperate on 'specific questions'. Kajee had already accepted the idea of a qualified communal franchise and thus felt unable to support the Ten Point Programme's call for universal franchise. Indian radicals from Natal formed an Anti-Segregation Council in response to government efforts to restrict Indian rights. Some of these attended the Third Unity Conference of January 1945; however, even after they ousted Kajee from the leadership of the Natal Indian Congress that October they did not affiliate to the NEUM. Of the forty-six new officials of the Natal Indian Congress, twelve were Communists. A similar radical takeover occurred in the Transvaal Indian Congress, where Yusuf Dadoo was elected president. Certainly, this strong Communist presence amongst Indian radicals predisposed the South African Indian Congress to align with the ANC rather than affiliate to the NEUM.

But there was also a concern that the NEUM was too rigid in its approach to unity. Indians had been hit by a series of discriminatory laws. In the 1930s the government restricted Indian occupancy of land in the Transvaal; in 1943 the Pegging Act prohibited the transfer of property between whites and Indians in Durban, closing off the main avenue of investment still available to Indians. The 1946 Asiatic Land Tenure and Indian Representation Act, popularly known as the Ghetto Act, extended the Pegging Act throughout Natal and the Transvaal and introduced an Indian communal franchise.[15] Indian leaders responded by launching a passive resistance movement. This was supported in the Cape through the launching of a Passive Resistance Council, chaired by Cissie Gool and endorsed by the CPSA. But the NEUM leadership derided the campaign as sectional, a stance that further alienated many Indian activists and that was criticized by Trotskyists outside the NEUM, despite their own criticisms of the campaign. The alliance between the South African Indian Congress and the ANC was strengthened in March 1947 by the 'Joint Declaration of Cooperation' signed by Drs Xuma, Naicker and Dadoo. Known as the Doctors' Pact, this pledged practical Non-European cooperation in pursuit of democratic rights – but not on terms dictated by the NEUM.[16]

Revitalizing African nationalism

On the Rand, urban blacks were disillusioned with the inactivity of both the AAC and the ANC and concentrated on specific grievances rather than broad programmes, protesting about their living and working conditions through bus boycotts, squatters' movements and strikes. These mass protest movements inspired younger and ambitious political leaders, as they challenged the older established leadership. In some cases, these activists hoped to revitalize existing organizations; in others, they took new political initiatives – indicating that many activists were not willing to concede the entire political terrain to established organizations. Non-European Non-Intellectual's suggestion that black South Africans needed a diverse range of political organizations to represent their interests briefly became a reality.

The drive to reform and reinvigorate the ANC and to inspire it towards greater mass activity came from a group of relatively young professional men, in their mid-twenties to early thirties, who became the founders of the Congress Youth League. The direct impetus for the formation of the Congress Youth League was Self Mampuru's bid for the presidency of the Transvaal ANC in mid-1943. To this end, Mampuru sought the support of other younger members, although many were alienated by his willingness to work with whites – he had been a protégé of William Ballinger and had studied at the Co-operative College in Manchester, England between 1937 and 1939. But by August, Mampuru had lost interest in the ANC. The group succeeded in getting Xuma's support, and at its December 1943 conference the ANC resolved to form both a youth league and a women's league and offered full membership rights to women. The inaugural meeting of the Congress Youth League was held in April 1944 at the Bantu Men's Social Centre in Johannesburg. Guided intellectually by Anton Lembede, its concern was to build a spirit of African nationalism as a basis for mass mobilization. It hoped to push the ANC towards greater involvement in mass action, especially through the use of boycotts, strikes and civil disobedience. In the late 1940s the Congress Youth League would become a significant player in the ANC's internal politics.[17]

Grass-roots struggles and new political ventures

That there was some political space for new organizations was signalled by the number of grass-roots initiatives in the 1940s that blossomed despite limited support from the ANC or the CPSA. One such initiative was the Alexandra bus boy-cott of August 1943, which catalysed the formation of the African Democratic Party.[18] Alexandra, a relatively long-established black township, then had a popula-tion of about 50,000. It was distinctive as one of the few black townships where Africans and Coloureds had freehold rights. Transport was a problematic issue for the residents, both because of its relatively high cost and because of the township's distance from Johannesburg; by 1943 the township had experienced a number of bus boycotts. Although a few blacks had owned buses, including ANC treasurer-general and businessman Richard Baloyi, by 1943 repeated fare increases had driven them out of business, and all the buses were owned by whites. The CPSA had some presence in Alexandra but by 1943 this had faded considerably. A branch of the South African Youth League organized by Max Joffe had collapsed after his intern-ment, and Gaur Radebe, a local Communist who had clashed with Baloyi over busi-ness interests, had recently been expelled from the Party.

In August 1943 an increase in the bus fare to Johannesburg precipitated a nine-day boycott. Locals formed an Emergency Transport Committee, which was chaired by Hyman Basner. The rapidity of the organization and the massive support for the boycott succeeded in blocking the fare increase and led to the appointment of a commission of enquiry. For the ANC's Xuma, this was a 'great victory'.[19] But the ANC's passivity during the boycott prompted the launch of the African Democratic Party in September. Its backers were an eclectic group: Self Mampuru; Paul Mosaka of the NRC; Dan Koza, the trade unionist; J. J. Lesolang, president of the Transvaal African Teachers' Association; Lilian Tshabalala of the local Women's Brigade; Hyman Basner and Lillian and Vincent Swart. This new group adopted a social democratic programme and promised more activity than the ANC.[20]

The following year, in November 1944, a fare increase prompted another bus boycott. From the outset, the state and the police played a far more aggressive and intimidatory role than in the previous strike. A Workers' Transport Action Committee was formed, and, compared to the previous strike, political organiza-tions were more directly involved: the Alexandra Workers' Union, the Women's Brigade, the African Democratic Party and the CPSA all took part. A compromise resolution after seven weeks aggravated tensions between different political factions, and the coalition that had formed the basis of the African Democratic Party splin-tered. Koza left the African Democratic Party during the strike and joined the Fourth Internationalists. Lilian Tshabalala and the Swarts joined the newly-consti-tuted Workers' International League, another Trotskyist group. Radebe returned to the CPSA and the ANC. Basner castigated those who left the African Democratic Party as wreckers, while the Workers' International League accused the African Democratic Party of betraying the struggle. Following the second boycott, the African Democratic Party's hope of challenging the ANC was seriously dented.[21]

The squatters' movements that began in the mid-1940s in the black townships around Johannesburg were also testimony to the reticence of both the ANC and the CPSA in the face of certain types of mass struggles. The region had been flooded with people coming in from the reserves in search of jobs, and this urban movement had been intensified by the temporary relaxation of influx controls to supply the labour needs of the war industries. This rapid influx of people led to massive home-lessness and to the mushrooming of shanty towns around the black townships. In 1944 the problem became particularly acute in Orlando, a recently built 'model' African township to which the inhabitants of Prospect township had been trans-ferred *en masse* in 1937. In April 1944 thousands of people left the overcrowded township and built a shanty town 'of sticks, sacking, old tins, and maize stalks' on nearby municipal ground.[22] Knowing that they were trespassing, and expecting to be evicted, they took as their slogan, '*Sofazonke!*' ('We shall all die!'). James Mpanza, a member of the Orlando Advisory Board, became their leader. Mpanza initially approached both the CPSA and the African Democratic Party for assistance. While the CPSA claimed that shanty towns were not a solution to the housing crisis, Basner began negotiating with the squatters and the local authorities. The Congress Youth League also showed some interest in helping the squatters. In 1946 the CPSA still opposed the shanty towns on the grounds that it was irresponsible to allow people to occupy them in the winter. Only in early 1947 did the Johannesburg District Committee modify its stance. By then, however, it was too late for the Party to offer any real practical help; six months later the squatter camps were moved to the new township of Moroka and their leaders were deported. Despite Basner's assistance, by the end of the squatters' movement the African Democratic Party was virtually moribund and could no longer contemplate challenging the ANC, despite the latter's obvious limitations.[23]

A number of white leftists, based mainly in the Transvaal and Natal, were also seeking an alternative space outside the established white political parties and the organizations of the Third and Fourth Internationals. Some, such as Ben Weinbren and Alec Wanless, hoped to reform the Labour Party from within. They believed that the support of white workers and the broader white electorate were necessary for the establishment of socialism. Once white workers were no longer economical-ly vulnerable, their argument went, racism would fade away. A group of about fifty formed the Progressive Labour Group as a faction within the Labour Party. In May 1943 Solly Sachs, leader of the Garment Workers' Union, launched the Independent Labour Party to contest the general election on a socialist platform. Sachs believed in the progressive potential of white workers. Most members of the Garment Workers' Union supported the Labour Party or the United Party and were being pursued by the National Party; hoping to translate his success as a trade unionist into political success, Sachs sought to attract them to the Independent Labour Party. But the new group proved a non-starter – faring even worse in the 1943 election than the CPSA. In September 1943 the Independent Labour Party merged with the Progressive Labour Group to form the Socialist Party, led by Johanna Cornelius and Anna Scheepers of the Garment Workers' Union. Despite verbal opposition to racism and fascism, membership of the Socialist Party was restricted to whites. This, too, was an abortive effort; white labour, on its own, could not provide a social base for democratic – let alone socialist – politics.[24] In 1946 the Socialist Party changed its position on the colour bar and united with the remnants of the African Democratic Party but this revamped Socialist Party also proved to be a non-starter, and the attempted alliance floundered.[25]

On the Rand, in particular, the failure of these new political ventures left the field open to the ANC, whatever its limitations. Despite the efforts of Communists to strengthen the Party's relationship with the ANC, that relationship remained ambivalent, although its influence on the ANC was greatest in the Transvaal, where a number of Communists, notably Marks, Mofutsanyana and Gaur Radebe, gained high positions. Although few in numbers, these Communists were visible and active. Their presence generated tensions within the Congress Youth League; nonetheless, both the Communists and the Congress Youth Leaguers put pressure on the ANC for greater activity. Certainly, there were instances of cooperation between the ANC and the CPSA, such as the Anti-Pass Campaign that the CPSA launched in November 1943 following the government's decision to tighten influx control. Led by Xuma, Dadoo and Bopape, local anti-pass committees were set up to raise signatures for a million-signature petition to be presented to the government. Although presented as a high point of CPSA-ANC cooperation in South African Communist historiography, the campaign was conducted in a desultory manner and proceeded in fits and starts, with *Inkululeko* reporting in March 1945 that 'the local committees have gone to sleep'.[26] Xuma, embarrassed by the Communist presence, even refused to lead the delegation presenting the anti-pass petition to Parliament in June 1945.[27] But developments in the trade union movement swept up both the CPSA and the ANC in the latter years of the war. It was through their joint activities in the trade union movement, and particularly through their involvement in the African Mine Workers' Strike of 1946, that the relationship of the Party and the ANC would be enhanced.

Trade unions and the war

The increasing severity with which the state attacked black workers seeking moderate improvements in their working conditions was a gloomy harbinger of the ever more vicious policies to be pursued by the National Party after its electoral victory of 1948. In this context, although a striking number of socialists held leading positions in trade union organizations, the stark inability of Communists and Trotskyists to work cooperatively depleted the trade union movement's meagre resources. The harsh repression facing socialists working in the trade union movement, both during and immediately after the war, signalled the fate of the left as the Cold War hit South Africa.

The detention of Max Gordon was symbolic. Because of Gordon's pivotal role in rebuilding the black trade union movement and running the Joint Committee of African Trade Unions, his detention from May 1940 until June 1941 was inevitably disruptive. Despite the political charges against Gordon, he himself thought that the authorities 'were not concerned about my doing any political work but objected to the Trade Unions as such'.[28] And, as Fanny Klenerman observed, the resulting disorder in the Joint Committee of African Trade Unions was 'no doubt ... a very desirable state of affairs in the eyes of certain Government elements'.[29] At a meeting between representatives from the Institute of Race Relations and the Joint Committee to discuss Gordon's replacement, the insinuation that only a white person could effectively handle the position and the suggestion that Lynn Saffery of the Institute of Race Relations take over the post understandably angered Koza and other trade unionists in the Joint Committee. Most of them concurred on the need for black leadership, and David Gosani was elected as secretary. However, over the next few months, the Joint Committee of African Trade Unions lost members and splintered, some of its unions remaining with Koza and others aligning with Makabeni or with the CPSA.[30]

In the 1940s, much of the agitation in the black trade union movement concerned the Industrial Conciliation Act. Passed in 1924, this had introduced a system of collective bargaining between employers and employees and had given trade unions their long-sought goal of legal protection – but at a price. While the legislation facilitated the growth of white trade unions, the left criticized it as class collaborationist. The legislation was fundamentally racist. Using an extremely restrictive definition of 'employee', it excluded from its coverage workers in the agricultural, domestic and government sectors, as well as pass-bearing Africans. African women did not carry passes, and in 1944 the Supreme Court ruled that they could therefore be considered as employees. Thus, from 1944 African women could join registered unions, while African men were excluded. Registered craft and industrial unions could include white, Coloured and Indian workers and, from 1944, African women. Some registered unions restricted their membership to whites only; these tended to be linked with parastatals such as ISCOR, the South African Railways and the Posts and Telegraphs.[31]

Unions within the conciliation system were organized into several different federations, and the question of affiliation proved contentious for the left. Although affiliation to the Trades and Labour Council was open to trade unions on a nonracial basis, in practice few black unions affiliated and those that did, claimed representation on a basis that was smaller than their actual numbers. In 1937, the Trades and Labour Council had thirty-eight affiliates; by 1941 it had forty-six. Eight of these were African or mixed in composition but they represented only 400 out of 21,500 affiliated members. Thus, as Roux noted, black membership of the Trades and Labour Council was 'little more than a token of that body's theoretical break with the colour bar'. However, Roux added, its willingness to cooperate with black unions had increased through the 1930s. Hence, in the 1940s many Communists, especially those in the Western Cape, argued that black trade unions should affiliate to the Trades and Labour Council. However, trade unionists such as Makabeni favoured an autonomous federation of black trade unions.[32]

The pressing need to contest the exclusion of African men under the Industrial Conciliation Act made unity of the black trade union movement imperative. The Institute of Race Relations helped to facilitate unity talks. In November 1941 preliminary talks took place between several leading trade unionists on the Rand:

Gordon, who had been released in June, and A. Thipe, Gana Makabeni and W. A. R. Mokoena. Later that month trade unionists held an All-in Conference of All African and Coloured Trade Unions that established a new Transvaal-based federation called the Council of Non-European Trade Unions (CNETU). This incorporated the trade union federations established by Gordon, Koza and Makabeni. Makabeni became president; M. Philips, vice-president; David Gosani, secretary; and B. Nikin, assistant secretary. Naboth Mokgatle became secretary of CNETU's Pretoria branch. There, the Friends of Africa had been organizing trade unions in opposition to the CPSA through the efforts of Ethel Binyon; these remained outside the CNETU.

This new unity effort took place against the backdrop of a strike wave centred in Johannesburg and Durban in 1941 and 1942 that boosted the growth of the black trade union movement. The state's initial response was to contain the strikes by granting concessions. But the experiences of African coalworkers, organized by Koza's African Commercial and Distributive Workers Union, illustrated the growing difficulty of gaining concessions from the state. A strike by these workers in May 1941 led to a Wage Board settlement that granted wage increases and prohibited the future use of convict labour as scabs. But in 1943, a similar effort failed: the government deemed wage increases to be inflationary, and wages were pegged nationally.

An armed attack on municipal workers in Marabastad in December 1942 inaugurated an increase in state repression and the use of troops to quell strikers. That same month the government passed War Measure 145, which prohibited strikes by Africans and provided for compulsory arbitration of labour disputes, using arbitrators appointed by the Minister of Labour. In August 1944 War Measure 1425 prohibited meetings of more than twenty people on 'proclaimed land'. Its principal objective was to prevent the organization of mineworkers; it also impeded other organizing efforts.[33] The use of law to curtail the rights of black workers underscored the government's use of force and highlighted the increasingly narrow space for any form of working-class organization.

Socialists and trade union work

Despite its diminished trade union role on the Rand in the late 1930s, the CPSA threw itself with vigour into trade union work in the region in 1940, capitalizing on years of organizing by non-Communist trade unionists, such as Makabeni, Gordon and Koza. The CPSA's support for the national war drive after June 1941 did not mean a decline in its trade union activity. The Party's new-found legitimacy, once it came out in support of the war, provided scope for further involvement. Although it tried to curb strikes, the CPSA nonetheless recognized the legitimacy of black working-class demands. Thus, when it opposed War Measure 145, it did so on the grounds that better pay and recognition of African trade unions would be a more effective means of preventing strikes. However, neither the Party's efforts to restrain illegal protest activity nor War Measure 145 failed to stop the wave of organized and spontaneous strikes.[34]

In the Cape the CPSA was likewise able to build upon the prior work of other left-wing trade unionists. Although the Cape was less industrialized than the Rand, in 1936 Solly Sachs had given the Cape trade union movement a shot in the arm when he attempted to gain national status for the Garment Workers' Union. The ensuing struggle between competing unions helped to reinvigorate trade union activity in the Cape. In Cape Town, a number of notable activists, such as Ray Alexander, Johnny Gomas, Jimmy La Guma and Eli Weinberg, organized trade unions in the 1930s. Ray Alexander was the local CPSA's pre-eminent organizer, establishing about a dozen new unions, most of whose members were black. In 1936 she helped found the Non-European Railway and Harbour Workers Union, which grew rapidly, claiming more than 20,000 members in 1943. In 1941 she formed the Food and Canning Workers' Union, with branches throughout the Cape.[35] A similar pattern took place in Port Elizabeth, a leading industrial centre of the Eastern Cape. The Institute of Race Relations sent Max Gordon to Port Elizabeth in January 1942 where he formed seven unions. But the Minister of Labour halted this work, and within a few months Gordon retired from trade union work. Subsequently, A. Z. Tshiwula, a protégé of the Friends of Africa, began the first sustained trade union work there since the collapse of the ICU. In 1943 he set up the first union of African railway workers in Port Elizabeth. Once again, Communists succeeded in taking over the leadership of the unions Gordon had organized and in eroding Tshiwula's influence amongst railway workers.[36]

In Natal, the virtual non-existence of the CPSA had precluded Communist involvement in the trade unions during most of the 1930s. However, in 1937 a strike of 400 African and Indian workers at the Falkirk plant erupted in protest at the retrenchment of sixteen members of the Natal Iron and Steel Workers' Union. This brought to the fore two Communist trade unionists, H. A. Naidoo and George Ponnen. The industrial stimulus provided by the war provided scope for a small but eclectic group of activists who were drawn into the organization of African and Indian workers.[37]

Despite the notable achievements of individual Trotskyist trade unionists in the late 1930s, this tendency did not benefit from the CPSA's accommodationist stance. In 1939 Cape Town Trotskyists regrouped as the Fourth International Club and later formed the Fourth International Organisation of South Africa, under the intellectual leadership of M. N. Averbach and Arthur Davids. With the exception of Hosea Jaffe, who organized electrical workers and briefly edited the *Militant Worker*, most of the Trotskyists in the Fourth International Organisation were still concerned with propaganda and education rather than trade union work. According to Kenny Jordaan the group made a few half-hearted attempts to organize domestic workers and waiters. But its main contribution was the production of a journal called *Workers' Voice*, which published some original and extremely interesting theoretical articles on South African politics.[38]

Johannesburg Trotskyists were more oriented towards trade union work, but with the significant exception of Gordon's initiatives, each wave of activity ended in organizational collapse. The tiny Johannesburg Workers' Party, which had derided Gordon's efforts, was succeeded by the ephemeral Socialist Workers' League in 1939. Ralph Lee, the Workers' Party maverick who had sailed to England in 1937, returned in 1940, hoping to organize a local counterpart of the British Workers' International League. At the time, the Cape Town Fourth International Organisation and the Johannesburg Trotskyists were engaged in unity talks. But the talks stalled over disputes about the location of the headquarters and of the paper, fuelled, as always, by personal rivalries. The Workers' International League was formed around 1943–44, its ranks augmented by the African Democratic Party's split in Alexandra, and in 1945 it began publishing *Socialist Action*. Its fluctuating membership included, amongst others, Issie Pinchuk, Baruch Hirson, the Swarts, and a number of trade unionists such as Dick Mfili and John Motau. Although unity talks with the Fourth International Organisation resumed in a desultory fashion, they soon floundered.[39] This organizational fragmentation left the Trotskyist tendency ill-prepared to combat Communism's moderating influence on the black trade union movement.

CNETU and the left

Precisely because of the prominent role that socialists played in the development of the black labour movement, their sectarian battles penetrated trade union organizations. Within a few years of its formation, the CNETU was divided between a Communist-influenced leadership urging moderation and a faction in which the Workers' International League and its trade union allies figured prominently. Essentially, the Communists and Trotskyists saw themselves as competing for influence in CNETU. The federation had scant resources. By late 1943, Naboth Mokgatle noted, 'some of us were lucky to get our wages regularly every month. The motto was sacrifice. Without it there would never have been African trade unions in existence in South Africa.'[40] Thus, the internal wranglings of the socialists took their toll on a federation beset by state harassment and financial difficulties.

To some extent the differences between the CNETU leadership and its Trotskyist critics involved divergent approaches to policy. For one thing, despite advocating better wages and working conditions, the ANC and CPSA tried to promote worker restraint in support of the war effort. This irked Trotskyists and others who were anti-war and supported strike action. Dan Koza, for instance, maintained the right of workers to strike during the war and led his own unions on strikes. Moreover, factional differences emerged over the Industrial Conciliation Act. The CNETU leadership argued that African workers should be recognized under the Industrial Conciliation Act. For many leftists, though, such recognition was seen as likely to produce deradicalization. Solly Sachs, for one, argued that the Industrial Conciliation Act had 'killed' the white unions. Koza, too, was critical of CNETU's ready acceptance of the Industrial Conciliation Act's premises. In December 1943 Koza attended the AAC conference as a delegate of the Fourth International Organisation. There he argued against the separate recognition of African unions under the Native Affairs Department, instead calling for full legal recognition of African trade unions with the right to strike, without the restrictions that the Industrial Conciliation Act imposed even on white workers. Although arguably unrealistic, the demand was adopted by the Workers' International League and its trade union supporters.

Political battles over control of the federation's leadership and direction were evident at CNETU's conference in April 1944. The ANC and the CPSA were vying for control of the federation. *Inkundla ya Bantu* (People's Forum) reported a 'vigorous tug-of-war between Dr Xuma and the communists for trade union support', an allegation denied in *Inkululeko*.[41] Despite their rivalry, the ANC and CPSA were nonetheless united both by their support for the war and by their common antipathy to Trotskyist influence. Hyman Basner addressed the conference, and while critical of the CPSA, he was even more scathing of the Workers' International League, whose members he castigated as 'wreckers at work', the title of his recent pamphlet. Makabeni, too, denounced the Trotskyists as provocateurs. But Makabeni soon 'fell out of favour with [the Communists]' and lost control of the federation, which elected John Marks of the CPSA as its new president.[42]

Tension between trade unionists identified with Communist and Trotskyist tendencies worsened during a strike led by the African Milling Workers' Union in Johannesburg in September 1944. In May the workers' wage agreement had expired and attempts to negotiate an increase and to obtain arbitration assistance failed. A strike broke out, run by an *ad hoc* group within the union known as the 'General Staff'. When the state responded by charging seventeen workers and two trade union officials with public violence, the union's secretary, S. Molefi, asked the Workers' International League to support a general strike call. The League's agreement led to criticism from the CNETU and the Trades and Labour Council. The trade unionists involved with the milling workers' strike reorganized themselves as the Progressive Trade Union group (PTU) and called for the removal of the CNETU leadership. Albert Segwai became the PTU's secretary; Koza joined the PTU and became the *de facto* leader until it fell apart in 1946.[43] Although the Workers' International League was heavily involved with the PTU, there were nonetheless differences in the personnel and in the approaches of the two groups.[44]

At the previous CNETU conference, Koza had proposed an all-in conference of Non-European trade unions to discuss policy on trade union recognition and minimum wage legislation and on the setting up of a national Trade Union Centre. When the CNETU met at Bloemfontein in August 1945 it was rent by internecine battles. Xuma admonished against

> chasing ideological theoretical party rainbows ... [because] it is of less importance to us whether capitalism is smashed or not. It is of greater importance to us that while capitalism exists we must fight and struggle to get our full share and benefit from the system.

The delegates were divided over how to obtain recognition of African trade unions. Makabeni called for recognition of Africans as workers under the Industrial Conciliation Act; Hosea Jaffe of the Fourth International Organisation proposed an addendum, which was agreed, that the anti-strike clause be deleted from the Industrial Conciliation Act and that workers of all occupations have the same rights under it. Koza's proposal for the repeal of the Act and for 'collective bargaining machinery along the lines of the National Labour Relations [Board] of the USA' was defeated.[45]

The proposal that CNETU expand beyond its Transvaal base to become a national body proved controversial as well. Most delegates supported such an option. But Communists were divided amongst themselves over whether to work for a national body of black trade unions or to press for affiliation of black unions to the Trades and Labour Council. The previous year the Trades and Labour Council had endorsed a Workers' Charter that upheld equal rights for all workers, regardless of sex or colour, and that maintained that 'the only solution to our problems lies in South Africa adopting Socialism as our form of government, which will bring emancipation ... from exploitation and oppression'.[46] To Cape Town Communists such as Ray Alexander, the Trades and Labour Council appeared to be receptive to progressive pressure, and affiliation of all unions to the Council would have provided the basis for a united working-class movement. This position was subsequently endorsed by the CPSA at its next conference. Although the resolution to seek national status had majority support at the CNETU conference, it was opposed by the CPSA, and at one stage most of the Cape Town delegates left the meeting. The resolution was referred back to CNETU's executive as the conference closed. On 19 August claiming that CNETU was stalling on the implementation of the all-in conference resolutions, Dan Koza and C. R. Phoffu of the PTU called a meeting to inform workers of the conference resolutions. The CNETU executive then expelled Koza and Phoffu, alleging that they had accused Makabeni of misappropriating funds and that they had held a factional meeting.[47]

These divisions developed in a period of great social stress. The hopes of a post-war liberalization for black South Africans were dashed at the war's end. After peace was declared in Europe in May 1945, the South African government signalled its commitment to racial inequality by proclaiming that black soldiers would receive less benefits than whites. The war with Japan ended in August. At General Smuts' homecoming in September, welcoming blacks were driven away by white military police – eloquent testimony that their contributions to the war effort had been for naught.[48]

Organizing on the mines

Tensions were simultaneously building up in the mining industry. Organizing mineworkers was extremely difficult because of the controlled conditions in which they lived. At the CPSA's March 1940 conference, the Party decided to challenge

Max Gordon's dominance in the industry. Daunting as organizing mineworkers was, Ray Alexander argued, the Party must make the effort. 'It can be done. It must be done', she insisted. 'All obstacles must be overcome by Bolsheviks. ... We have done this in the docks. Now we have an organisation of 12,000 railway and harbour workers led by the Communist Party.'[49] At a meeting of the Transvaal ANC in August 1941, the CPSA's Gaur Radebe and Edwin Mofutsanyana proposed reviving the African Mine Workers' Union (AMWU). In July 1944 the Communist stalwart John Marks was elected president of the union.[50]

Mineworkers' conditions were dire, and they were denied the cost-of-living adjustments that were given to other workers in 1942. The next few years saw many angry meetings and wild-cat strikes. AMWU officials appealed in vain to the Chamber of Mines. Members called for strike action, only to be counselled against this by trade union organizers, who felt that the union was too weak. War Measure 1425 forced the union to hold secret meetings. The government cut mineworkers' meat rations in 1945, leading to further anger and protests. In March 1946 police killed a worker at a food demonstration and wounded forty others. Even after a government-appointed commission recommended a modest wage increase and minor reforms – recommendations that fell far short of the union's demands – the Chamber of Mines adamantly rejected these, claiming that the fixed price of gold precluded wage increases. Yet the wages of white mineworkers rose during the war, even while a shortage of black labour from other Southern African countries led to a decline in productivity.[51]

The African mineworkers' strike erupted on 12 August 1946. Although it lasted only one week, it was the biggest strike of black mineworkers since the 1920 strike. On the following day – at short notice – CNETU called a sympathy strike but heavy police presence prevented a substantial turnout. However, the CPSA organized a mass sympathy demonstration in Cape Town on 18 August with reports of 10,000 in attendance. African mineworkers were subjected to severe physical retaliation. Workers who began a sit-down strike underground were forced up to the surface and into their compounds. The strike was unconditionally defeated without any concessions. Thirteen people were killed and about 1200 were wounded. The defeat devastated the AMWU and led to the widespread demoralization of the mineworkers.[52]

The brutal squashing of the strike reverberated through black trade unions and political organizations and through the socialist movement. It accelerated the decay of the black trade union movement, as one union after the other collapsed. The Workers' International League collapsed shortly after the strike when the majority of its members, demoralized, decided to withdraw from trade union work. The PTU, financially dependent on the Workers' International League, became moribund.[53] The following year, 1947, twenty-two unions withdrew from CNETU, claiming disillusionment with the strike tactic and with Communist leadership.[54] By CNETU's conference on 30 August 1947, political factions in the diminished federation had shifted. Now Koza, Makabeni and several other trade unionists condemned the role of Communists in CNETU. An attempt at an alternative anti-Communist federation foundered; subsequently Makabeni regained control of CNETU's presidency.[55]

Within the ANC, the strike's defeat led to disenchantment with Xuma, who had been lacklustre in his support of the strike. In particular, it aggravated tensions between the Congress Youth League and Xuma, which would reach fruition only in 1949, when Xuma lost the presidency. The defeat also led to the adjournment of the NRC, which was agreed at an Emergency Conference of Africans called by Xuma in October 1946. Pressure on the NRC members to resign *en bloc* had been building up for some time in light of their demonstrable failure to achieve even minimal reforms.[56] Yet this decision was adopted hesitantly and only reaffirmed six months later, in May 1947, after General Smuts had showed himself unwilling to consider or concede any of the NRC's demands. The resignation of the NRC members raised the question of the boycott once again – this would become an issue of growing contention in the late 1940s and 1950s.[57]

Finally, it set the stage for an intensified attack by the state on the left. The CPSA headquarters were ransacked during the strike, and Dannie du Plessis, secretary of the Johannesburg District Party Committee, arrested. On 26 August 1946 fifty-two members of the AMWU, CNETU, ANC and CPSA were charged with conspiracy under the Riotous Assemblies Act and with violating War Measure 145. The main charges were dropped and the defendants were fined. But in November 1946 the government charged the eight members of the CPSA's Central Executive Committee with sedition. Again, the charges were eventually dismissed. But in 1950, the state would act decisively against the left with the Suppression of Communism Act.[58]

Conclusion

During the war, a striking number of the leading organizers and officials of black trade unions were or had been associated with socialist organizations. Although socialists gained leading positions in the black trade union movement – not least because they had formed many of the new unions – this did not mean that their political views were shared by their rank-and-file membership. Nonetheless, despite the CPSA's repeated policy oscillations, its continuing efforts to recruit white labour and its efforts to dampen black working-class militancy during the war, it emerged at the war's end with a tenuous foothold in the black trade union movement. In contrast – with the significant exception of Max Gordon, who was successful precisely because he kept socialist politics out of his union work – the tiny numbers and organizational fragmentation of the Trotskyist movement made sustained practical work virtually impossible. Trotskyists tended, therefore, to concentrate on propaganda. Thus, they were unable to profit from the CPSA's ambiguous and, at times, unenthusiastic response to black workers' protests either at the workplace or in the community. Yet the disintegration of the black trade union movement following the squashing of the African mineworkers' strike led, by 1947, to disenchantment with and a backlash against Communist influence in many unions. With the black trade union movement seriously weakened, and with the shadow of apartheid looming over their heads, socialists, weak and divided, had little alternative but to focus their attention on the national liberation movement.

The rigid bifurcation of the socialist movement penetrated the broader national liberation movement. Communists aligned with the ANC; in 1946 the ANC increased the number of seats on its National Executive, enabling Kotane, Marks and Tloome to win seats without displacing the established leaders.[59] Trotskyists worked behind the scenes in the rival AAC and the NEUM and also gained leading positions in these organizations. As was the case with the left leadership of the trade unions, their socialist views did not, with rare exceptions, filter down to ordinary members. Nonetheless, despite their small numbers, the activism of socialists and their ability to win leading positions enabled them to influence the political outlooks and policies of the national organizations to which they were linked. The socialist movement's internal bifurcation interacted with organizational and personal rivalries within the broader liberation movement, precluding joint cooperation against the apartheid regime. Apartheid – South Africa's own local variant of the Cold War – was launched at a time when black working-class organization had been virtually demolished and the socialist movement was at a very low ebb. It was nonetheless rationalized, both at home and abroad, in terms of the Communist threat.

Notes

1. Walshe, *African Nationalism*, 186.
2. Quoted in Bunting, *Kotane*, 106; Walshe, *African Nationalism*, 389–90.
3. Letter from B. Penza [I. B. Tabata] to Editor, *Umteteli*, August 1941, Unity Movement of South Africa Papers, Manuscripts and Archives Department, University of Cape Town Libraries.
4. 'Address by I. B. Tabata, AAC Conference, December 16, 1941', in Karis and Carter, eds., *From Protest to Challenge*, vol. 2, 340–46, quotes 343–4, 341, 345 and 346, respectively.
5. Sarah Mokone [Victor Wessels], *Majority Rule: Some Notes*, Teachers' League of South Africa: Cape Town, 1982, 20–21; interview with Ali Fataar, Harare, December 1987; Neale interview with Dudley.
6. Eddie Roux's historical articles were published in *Trek* throughout 1944. Dora Taylor, 'Education for Democracy – First Stage', *Trek*, January 16, 1941, 7.
7. D. Robinson, 'To a Non-European Intellectual', *Trek*, July 31, 1942, 9.
8. 'On Behalf of the Non-European', *Trek*, August 14, 1942; see also Mokone, *Majority Rule*, 21.
9. 'D. Robinson and the Non-European Intellectual', *Trek*, August 14, 1942, 20.
10. Karis and Carter, eds, *From Protest to Challenge*, vol. 2, 110; Neale interview with Dudley.
11. B. M. Kies, 'The Background of Segregation', Address delivered to the National Anti-CAD Conference, 29 May 1943 in Drew, ed., *South Africa's Radical Tradition*, vol. 2, 54.
12. Mokone, *Majority Rule*, 30; Karis and Carter, eds, *From Protest to Challenge*, vol. 2, 112–13.

13. *Calling All Africans (For Non-European Unity)*, Issued by All African Covention Western Province Committee, June 1943. For other discussions of the NEUM see Simons, 'Organised Coloured Political Movements'; Hommel, *Capricorn Blues*; Lewis, *Between the Wire and the Wall*, 207–71; and Bill Nasson, 'The Unity Movement: Its Legacy in Historical Consciousness', *Radical History Review*, 46/7, 1990, 189–211.

14. Plekhanov, 'Second Draft Programme', 407; interview with Alexander.

15. Roux, *Time Longer than Rope*, 359–60; George Singh, *The Asiatic Land Tenure and Indian Representation Act of South Africa*, Durban: Council for Human Rights, 1946.

16. Lewis, *Between the Wire and the Wall*, 230; Everett, 'Gool', 76–86; Y. M. Dadoo, 'The Non-European Unity', *Freedom*, 4, 1, February 1945, and Peter Meissenheimer, 'Smuts' Anti-Indian Bill: Economic Sanctions or Non-European Unity', *Workers' Voice*, April 1946, both in Drew, ed., *South Africa's Radical Tradition*, vol. 2, 73–9; 'Joint Declaration of Cooperation.' Statement by Dr A. B. Xumas of the ANC, Dr G. M. Naicker of the Natal Indian Congress, and Dr Y. M. Dadoo of the Transvaal Indian Congress, March 9, 1947, in Karis and Carter, eds, *From Protest to Challenge*, vol. 2, 272–3; see also 114.

17. Karis and Carter, eds, *From Protest to Challenge*, vol. 2, 101–2; Lodge, *Black Politics*, 21–2. On Self Mampuru in Manchester see his academic transcripts at the Co-operative College and *Report of the Seventy-First Annual Co-operative Congress*, edited by R. A. Palmer, Manchester: Co-operative Union, 1939, 73. My thanks to Ruth Millington at the Co-operative College, Loughborough, for sending me copies of this material.

18. On the 1943 boycott see Alf Stadler, 'A Long Way to Walk: Bus Boycotts in Alexandra, 1940–1945', in P. Bonner, ed., *Working Papers in Southern African Studies*, vol. 2, Johannesburg: Ravan, 1981, 228–57; Roux, *Time Longer than Rope*, 317–20; Hirson, *Yours for the Union*, 136–47; Callinicos, *A Place in the City*, 41–4.

19. Quoted in Stadler, 'A Long Way to Walk', 241. The Emergency Transport Committee included, amongst others, Self Mampuru, Paul Mosaka, Gaur Radebe, A. E. P. Fish of the Alexandra Workers' Union, Lilian Tshabalala of the Women's Brigade, and Lillian and Vincent Swart.

20. Manifesto of the African Democratic Party, September 26, 1943, in Karis and Carter, eds, *From Protest to Challenge*, vol. 2, 391–6, also 110–12; Hyman Basner, Interview transcript, item 3, 62–85, Hyman Basner Papers, Institute of Commonwealth Studies, University of London; Hirson, *Revolutions*, 149.

21. Hirson, *Yours for the Union*, 139–45; Roux, *Time Longer than Rope*, 317–20.

22. Roux, *Time Longer than Rope*, 322–3.

23. Hirson, *Yours for the Union*, 148–62; Roux, *Time Longer than Rope*, 322–5; Lodge, *Black Politics*, 22.

24. In 1947 the Garment Workers' Union reaffiliated to the Labour Party. Roux, *Time Longer than Rope*, 361–3; Leslie Witz, 'A Case of Schizophrenia: the Rise and Fall of the Independent Labour Party', in Bozzoli, ed., *Class, Community and Conflict*, 261–91; Hirson, *Yours for the Union*, 142; 'South Africa Forges a New Socialist Movement', *New Leader*, November 20, 1943, 4–5.

25. Hirson, *Revolutions*, 213–14; *South African Socialist Review*, 3, 2, May 1946, item 10, Basner Papers.

26. Quoted in Lodge, 'Class Conflict', 9.

27. Bunting, *Kotane*, 118–19; Roux, *Time Longer than Rope*, 320–22; Walshe, *The Rise of African Nationalism*, 313–4, 361–5.

28. Letter from Max Gordon to Fanny Klenerman, 21 December 1940 in Drew, ed., *South Africa's Radical Tradition*, vol. 1, 339–40, quote 340.

29. Letter from Fanny Klenerman to Senator Edgar Brookes, 11 January 1941, Klenerman Papers, A2031/C1.1.

30. Roux, *Time Longer than Rope*, 328–9; Hirson, *Yours for the Union*, 48, 85–86.

31. Callinicos, *A Place in the City*, 81.

32. Roux, *Time Longer than Rope*, 332.

33. Hirson, *Yours for the Union*, 86–7, 96–7, 111–14.

34. For the CPSA's policies after it joined the war effort see *6 Point Communist Programme* and *Communists in Conference: the 1943/44 National Conference of the Communist Party of South Africa* in Drew, ed., *South Africa's Radical Tradition*, vol. 1, 343–9 and 354–62; 'Extract from statement issued by the Central Committee of the Communist Party on May 25, 1942'; and 'The Strike of African Workers and Compulsory Arbitration', statement by the Central Committee of the Communist Party, December 31, 1942, in Bunting, ed., *South African Communists Speak*, 172–3 and 175–7.

35. Roux, *Time Longer than Rope*, 330; Simons and Simons, *Class and Colour*, 520, 554; Callinicos, *Working Life*, 156.

36. Lodge, *Black Politics*, 50–51; Stein, 'Max Gordon and African Trade Unionism', 155–6.

37. These included, amongst others, Errol Shanley, who ran the Durban office of the Trades and Labour Council assisted by fellow Communist Pauline Podbrey, and Alec Wanless, M. P. Naicker and P. M. Harry. Callinicos, *Working Life*, 155–8; Podbrey, *White Girl*, 71–9. For further discussion of the CPSA's role in the Durban trade union movement see Edwards, 'Recollections', 65–84 and Vishnu Padayachee, Shahid Vawda and Paul Tichmann, 'Trade Unions and the Communist Party in Durban in the 1940's: A Reply to Iain Edwards', *South African Labour Bulletin*, 11, 7, August 1986, 50–66.

38. Interview with Jordaan.

39. The tensions between the two groups had a regional basis, sparked off by disagreements between the balance of local and regional news in their publication, and exacerbated by the difficulties of long-distance communication and personality conflicts. Interviews with Hirson and Jordaan. See '4th International Conference', *Workers' Voice*, 3, 1, 1 February 1944, 5; Letters from B. Hirson to J. Haston, 5 December 1945 and from J. Haston to B. Hirson, 25 December 1946 [sic], both in Jock Haston Papers, Brynmor Jones Library, University of Hull; 'Draft Letter to F.I.O.S.A. adopted by P. B. 3/1/45 for League Discussion' and 'Unity with the Workers' Voice Group', Workers' International League, *Internal Bulletin*, 1, 6, January 1946 and 1, 7, February 1946, 26–30, Karis-Carter Microfilm Collection, 2:DW2:85/1; Hosea Jaffe, 'A Critique of the Workers International League (W.I.L.) JO'BURG', *Internal Bulletin of the Fourth International Organisation of South Africa*, no. 2, October 1945, 4–9 and 2, 1, January 1946, 1–4, both in author's possession; Hirson, *Yours for the Union*, 41, 103–4.

40. Mokgatle, *Autobiography*, 245; see also Hirson, *Yours for the Union*, 114.

41. Hirson, *Yours for the Union*, 101–4 and quote, 115.

42. Roux, *Time Longer than Rope*, 333. According to one report, the elections were chaotic and the conference ended in confusion. See 'The Transvaal Conference of the Non-European Trade Unions', *Inyaniso (The Voice of African Youth)*, May 1945, 1–2, Kenneth Glazier microfilm collection, reel 5.

43. 'Our Programme', *Progressive Trade Union Bulletin*, 1, 1, February 1945, in Drew, ed., *South Africa's Radical Tradition*, vol. 1, 363–8; S. Molifi, statement on the African Milling Workers' Union strike, *Progressive Trade Union Bulletin*, 1, 1, February 1945, 8; Hirson, *Yours for the Union*, 102–3.

44. Some members of the Workers' International League saw PTU officials as bureaucrats.

See Workers' International League, *Internal Bulletin*, 1, 7, February 1946.

45. Both quotes Hirson, *Yours for the Union*, 117.
46. Quoted in Callinicos, *A Place in the City*, 96.
47. Lodge, 'Class Conflict', 14–15; Hirson, *Yours for the Union*, 119; Hirson, *Revolutions*, 196. For a Communist view on affiliation to the Trades and Labour Council see Ray Alexander, 'Trade Unionism in South Africa', *Discussion*, 1, 6, 1952 in Drew, ed., *South Africa's Radical Tradition*, vol. 2, 206–12. The Fourth International Organisation and the Workers' International League were at odds during the conference. For the former's view see 'Editorial: the Bloemfontein Trade Union Conference and the Industrial Conciliation Act', *Militant Worker*, October–November 1945 in Drew, ed., *South Africa's Radical Tradition*, vol. 1, 368–9.
48. Roux, *Time Longer than Rope*, 316–17.
49. 'Minutes of Conference of the Communist Party of South Africa, held at Cape Town, on 23rd and 24th March 1940', quote 59, 67–70.
50. Lodge, *Black Politics*, 19–20; Bunting, *Kotane*, 120; Simons and Simons, *Class and Colour*, 569; Callinicos, *A Place in the City*, 97; 'Organising African Miners', article by Moses Kotane, general secretary of the Communist Party, published in *Freedom-Vryheid*, September 1941, in Bunting, ed., *South African Communists Speak*, 165–8.
51. Callinicos, *A Place in the City*, 97–102; Hirson, *Yours for the Union*, 183–95; Letter from James Majoro, African Mine Workers' Union, to the Hon. The Minister for Labour, W. B. Madeley, Esq., 9 January 1943 and *Critical Situation on the Mines: Africans Resent Ration Cuts*, 18 July 1945, both in Bunting Papers; *The Impending Strike of African Miners: A statement by the African Mineworkers' Union*, 7 August 1946, in Drew, ed., *South Africa's Radical Tradition*, vol. 1, 369–72; South African Communist Party, *A Distant Clap of Thunder: Fortieth Anniversary of the 1946 Mine Strike*, 1986.
52. Callinicos, *A Place in the City*, 103–4; Hirson, *Yours for the Union*, 185–7; W. H. Andrews Diary, 18 and 22 August 1946, W. H. Andrews Collection, 2.1–2.3, Mayibuye Centre Historical Papers Archive. My thanks to Lungisile Ntsebeza for sending me copies of this material. Transvaal Council of Non-European Trade Unions. Strike Committee, *All Workers to Strike 15th August, 1946*, Bunting Papers; *Strike Bulletin*, issued by the African Mine Workers' Union, nos. 3–5, 14–16 August, 1946, Southern African Archives, Borthwick Institute of Historical Research, University of York; South African Communist Party, *A Distant Clap of Thunder*, 10–27.
53. Callinicos, *A Place in the City*, 105–7; Hirson, *Yours for the Union*, 189–92. Ralph Lee withdrew from the Workers' International League in May 1945 and later returned to England; Hirson resigned in December 1945. Letter from Baruch Hirson to Jock Haston, 5 December 1945, Haston Papers.
54. Lodge, *Black Politics*, 20.
55. Walshe, *The Rise of African Nationalism*, 364; Hirson, *Yours for the Union*, 190–92.
56. Tabata, for instance, had evidently asked Paul Mosaka to agitate for *en bloc* resignation. 'They can use as a pretext for resigning', Tabata suggested, 'the passage in [Parliament] of the new Amendment Bill to the Urban Areas Act'. Letter from I. B. Tabata to Tsotsi, Unity Movement of South Africa Papers, 1946.
57. On the NRC's demise see Karis and Carter, eds, *From Protest to Challenge*, vol. 2, 92–98; *Reasons Why the Native Representative Council in the Union of South Africa Adjourned [on August 14, 1946]*. Pamphlet by Professor Z. K. Matthews, published in November 1946, in Karis and Carter, eds, *From Protest to Challenge*, vol. 2, 224–33; and Jordan K. Ngubane, *Should the Natives Representative Council be Abolished?*, Pro and

Con Pamphlet No. 4, Cape Town: African Bookman, 1946. For discussions of the boycott in the Transkei see, for instance, *Inkundla ya Bantu*, 20 February 1947, 27 February 1947, 15 May 1947, 12 June 1947 and 24 July 1947. On differences within the CPSA over the boycott see Brian Bunting, interview with Simons, tape 2, 4–5.

58. Andrews Diary, 16, 19 and 24 August 1946; 4 and 5 October 1946; 21 February, 21 July, 28 August, 10 November and 22 November 1947; Bunting, ed., *South African Communists Speak*, 194; Hirson, *Yours for the Union*, 188–9, *Inkululeko Daily Trial Bulletin*, no. 3, 19 September 1946, Southern African Archives.

59. Walshe, *The Rise of African Nationalism*, 363.

Chapter 12

'Peace; and there was no peace': the Cold War and the suppression of socialism

The end of the Second World War brought a transient peace. By 1947 the wartime Allies were well on their way to becoming implacable enemies. The world war was replaced by a Cold War, a war for hearts and minds, one of ideological battles and localized but virulent military conflicts. The United States emerged as the leading world power and the dominant Western protagonist in the alliance against the Soviet Union. America's enmity against the Soviet Union was a prelude to its own war at home, as the United States government launched an all-out attack on American socialists and their sympathizers. Across much of the globe, the Cold War became a pretext to attack the left.

The South African government fought its own Cold War against its domestic critics. In May 1948 the *Herenigde* (Reunited) National Party won the national elections by a slim parliamentary majority over the United Party.[1] It had fought on a platform of preserving white power. White electoral support for the *Herenigde* National Party not least from the working class had been boosted by fears of the militancy symbolized by the 1946 African mineworkers' strike. Was white labour, having fought in the world war, to be replaced by cheaper black labour? Were white towns to be swamped by blacks flooding in from the impoverished reserves and the slave-like conditions on white farms? Was white purity to be sullied through mixed marriages? A central debate concerned the migrant labour system, and whether it should be maintained so that Africans would effectively be prevented from large-scale permanent settlement in towns or whether a stable urban African proletariat should be allowed to develop. The Fagan Commission, whose recommendations were supported by the United Party, argued for the latter, although it still believed in social and political segregation. The Sauer report, however, argued for the complete separation of black and white and that Africans should develop along their 'own lines' and be permitted in cities on a temporary basis only. Its findings were endorsed by the newly-elected Nationalist Government.

After its marginal electoral victory, the *Herenigde* National Party passed a series of laws that codified separate racial development and suppressed political dissent. In 1950–51 racial classification was tightened through the Population Registration Act, segregation was sharpened through the Group Areas Act and, as with the qualified African franchise years earlier, the Coloured vote was neutralized through the

Separate Registration of Voters' Act. Discriminatory laws targeted the small numbers of black businesses and property owners, and urban Africans and freeholders were resettled in townships. Influx controls, labour bureaux and restrictions on African trade unions curtailed the strength of the urban African working class.[2]

The post-war years also saw increased government intervention in the reserves. The Betterment Proclamation of 1939 had ostensibly aimed to stabilize the economic deterioration of the reserves in order to ensure their viability for a permanent class of migrant labourers. The 1945 Rehabilitation Scheme, implemented after the war, resettled people into newly-constructed villages where afforestation and soil conservation programmes would be implemented. In effect, the Scheme aimed to create reserve-based proletarian settlements for the families of migrant labourers and to impede the development of an urban African working class. The 1951 Bantu Authorities Act empowered tribal authorities to control the black labour supply at the reserve end of the urban–rural nexus. The Act laid the foundations for the future bantustan system. While curtailing popular electoral participation and prohibiting unauthorized public meetings of more than ten, it expanded and consolidated the powers of chiefs, whose legitimacy thereafter declined as they became direct symbols of the oppressive state.[3] The increasing state repression in the reserves catalysed waves of rural protests from the 1940s until the early 1960s.

South African Communist historiography has portrayed the post-war period as one in which the class and the national liberation struggles merged.[4] But it was a merger made when black working-class organizations had reached a low ebb. After the war trade union membership declined drastically and the Council of Non-European Trade Unions fell apart from the pressure of a wave of failed strikes and internal political struggles for control of the federation. With many of their own class organizations demolished, black workers moved towards nationalist leadership for direction. The absence of any socialist tradition outside the destructive rivalry of the Third and Fourth Internationals' local representatives left socialist organizations particularly vulnerable to the Cold War onslaught. The idea and practice of socialism went into eclipse: socialists had not been able to offer a sustained and viable alternative to the broader national liberation organizations, and between 1946 and 1950 socialist groups either collapsed or, subsequently, disbanded to avoid the Suppression of Communism Act of 1950.

The state of the left in post-war South Africa

Within the international Communist movement, the defeat of fascism at the end of the Second World War was seen as a shift in the balance of class forces towards the working class, leading to left electoral advances across much of Western Europe. Nonetheless, with fascism still considered a potential threat, Communist Parties maintained the wartime People's Front policy and advocated broad fronts of progressive, anti-fascist forces. By 1947 and 1948, however, the notion of a broad progressive front that included Communists was no longer seen as viable in most

Western countries as Labour and Social Democratic parties and other ostensibly progressive groups aligned with anti-Communists in the developing Cold War.

The CPSA tried to apply the concept of the post-war People's Front to South Africa but, in the absence of any significant social-democratic or liberal movement, the conditions were far too divergent for the concept to be meaningful. In August–September 1946, as the mineworkers' drama was unfolding, the Party argued that the war's end inaugurated 'a new phase in the class struggle'.[5] It anticipated a period of increasing class conflict that shattered Browder's vision of class collaboration, and it saw its main contribution in terms of extra-parliamentary action, especially, the 'education, organisation and leadership of the dispossessed and unfranchised masses'.[6] In November 1946 the Smuts government charged the CPSA's Central Executive Committee with sedition, stemming from the Party's involvement with the African mineworkers' strike; the government was not able to substantiate the charge and the case was finally dismissed in May 1948.[7] But the newly-elected Nationalist Government made clear its intention to outlaw the CPSA and suppress socialist influence more broadly.

The CPSA still faced its perennial problem of a fluctuating membership. But the demise of the Workers' International League and the failure of the ephemeral united Socialist Party left the CPSA as the only socialist group on the Rand. Thus, in the absence of any alternative, young people who were interested in socialism inevitably turned to the CPSA. Although Communists had organized the left-leaning South African Youth League during the war years, the Young Communist League, itself, had been dormant for many years. In the mid-1940s this was revived. Initially, most of its members were white but in the late 1940s it apparently recruited some African members. It also attracted a number of key figures who would become significant in the 1950s, notably the intellectuals Ruth First and Lionel Forman.[8] There was a certain degree of tension between the CPSA and the Young Communist League, as the parent body sought to control the younger generation. But the CPSA's attempt in 1944 to impose CPSA policy on the Young Communist League was resisted on the grounds that 'it was essential for the Y.C.L. to retain its complete independence' even though Dadoo and other Communists argued that 'there was no real need for complete independence'.[9]

There was significant pressure within the Party against any public criticism either of the CPSA or of the Soviet Union. As a member of the Young Communist League, Lionel Forman, for instance, had dared to publicly challenge the implicit colour bar within the CPSA, which, to commemorate Red Army Day, 'held two celebrations – a big one for the whites in the City Hall and a little one for the non-Europeans in the Gandhi Hall' and which fought 'white elections in colour-bar halls', proclaiming its 'few hundred votes in Hillbrow' but saying nothing of the Party's defeat in the African township of Orlando. The reaction was swift: 'Why don't you just get out and join the Trotskyites?'[10] one Party member asked Forman. And in Cape Town, Pauline Podbrey was 'solemnly reprimanded' at a full meeting of the District Committee for having publicly criticized Soviet policy regarding Soviet women who married Westerners. 'Is it such a crime to give one's honest opinion?', she asked

Moses Kotane, who replied, 'We can differ and argue as much as we like inside the Party ... but once a decision is reached we must all abide by it. That is democratic centralism.' Podbrey acceded, with admiration, to Kotane's authority.[11]

Pressure to conform was also seen in the Party's contempt for socialists who refused to accept the authority of the Soviet Union. The lack of any alternative socialist perspective, especially on the Rand, necessarily gave the Communist view credibility and meant that those seeking an organizational home had to comply. Trotskyism remained a dirty word for Communists. Forman was stunned to learn, when he moved to the more liberal environment of Cape Town, that Communists were working with Trotskyists on the Students' Socialist Party at the University of Cape Town – because '[i]f there was one thing he had learned, it was that to call a man a Trotskyite was the biggest insult possible. They did their dirty work from within the working-class movement.'[12]

Although Cape Town's liberal tradition did, indeed, mean greater tolerance of political diversity than in Johannesburg, its left was nonetheless fragmented. However, the Cape Town CPSA was forced to take Trotskyist influence more seriously. In 1947 tensions between the Fourth International Organisation and the Workers' Party were as rife as ever: the Fourth International Organisation described the latter group as 'a petty-bourgeois tendency which has forfeited all claim to being called socialist internationalists'.[13] In 1948 the Fourth International in Europe held a conference in Paris. Hosea Jaffe represented the Fourth International Organisation of South Africa. Arthur Davids, then studying in Europe, joined him. Evidently the Workers' Party was not represented but sent a document. Jaffe left Paris critical of the Fourth International's stance on imperialism. Back in Cape Town, the Fourth International Organisation of South Africa voted to disband. Jaffe argued that its members devote their energies to the NEUM; apparently he and Willem van Schoor opted to join the Workers' Party. M. N. Averbach and Arthur Davids argued that a Trotskyist programme was premature in South African conditions, and they advocated the formation of a discussion club open to all socialist tendencies. This eventually materialized as the Forum Club, which began publishing its proceedings in 1950. The Forum Club was frequented by former members of the Fourth International Organisation and by a number of local Communists but it was boycotted by the Workers' Party and the NEUM, which increasingly mirrored the CPSA in its intolerance of other left tendencies.[14]

The failure of left united fronts

The failure of the left to build united fronts to contest the government's implementation of apartheid reflected the increasing polarization and fragmentation of the socialist movement, both across the Communist–Trotskyist divide and amongst Trotskyists. These divisions were due not only to political socialization but to the divergent stances adopted on critical issues such as participation in Parliament and in racial structures.

While the CPSA's main strategy, both before and after the 1948 election, was to defeat the *Herenigde* National Party through the formation of the broadest possible front, many Trotskyists claimed to see no difference between the United Party and the *Herenigde* National Party. The Workers' Party and, by extension, the NEUM, scathingly dismissed all the white parties as part of the *Herrenvolk* or master race – a term that arguably deflected from a class analysis and bolstered nationalist sentiments. More fundamental were the opposing positions taken by Communists and Trotskyists over the NRC and other racial political structures. The resignation of the NRC members in May 1947 posed once more the question of the boycott. The NRC's nickname, 'toy telephone', signified the widepread perception that it was unable to provide any real communication between Africans and the white Parliament or to achieve any real reforms, and popular support for its boycott was high.

The Workers' Party saw non-collaboration with racial structures as a fundamental principle of political practice. Non-collaboration meant, argued Tabata, the refusal by the oppressed black population to work the instruments of their own oppression, that is, segregated and inferior political institutions. In the view of the Workers' Party, those quislings who worked within these institutions represented petty-bourgeois rather than working-class interests. Hence, the Workers' Party saw non-collaboration as a means to prevent a multi-class movement from co-optation by petty-bourgeois and aspirant bourgeois interests in a period when overt socialist propaganda carried high risks. As far as Tabata was concerned, the boycott was an active rather than an abstentionist policy in that its success depended on political education and signified the development of political consciousness.[15]

Initially, the CPSA also supported the boycott. 'Let all of us who recognise the Fascist danger co-operate wholeheartedly and without reserve to make the boycott plan a huge success', urged Yusuf Dadoo in June 1947.[16] Communists in the Western Cape concurred. 'The boycott does not represent a "repudiation" of parliament … such as Lenin denounces so vigorously in *Left Wing Communism* – it is regarded by the people as a weapon with which to gain admission to parliament', stated a position paper produced in Cape Town. The question, argued the author, was whether a boycott would be more effective in the fight for democracy than the efforts of the small number of white representatives whom blacks had the right to elect. The author decided in favour of the boycott, which 'raises in the sharpest possible form the issue of a popular franchise and direct non-European representation … [and] exposes the hollowness and deceit of the indirect representation system'. Thus, the writer concluded, 'on the assumption that the boycott will be an active one, having the visible support of the bulk of the non-European people, it will prove the more effective weapon in the struggle for democracy'.[17]

Hardly had the boycott of the NRC been endorsed by the Transvaal branch of the ANC, which called on all advisory boards to adjourn in support, when Paul Mosaka, Hyman Basner and the Ballingers began an anti-boycott movement. Margaret Ballinger had been a Natives' Representative for the Eastern Cape since 1938 and served until 1960; Basner was a Senator for Africans in the Transvaal and

Orange Free State from 1942 to 1948, as William Ballinger would be from 1948 to 1960. By December 1947 ANC leaders began to backtrack from their earlier boycott decision, and in January 1948 Dr Xuma proposed that the previous councillors be returned *en bloc* 'as a second step in our strategy to organise our people for the final stage – the complete boycott of elections'.[18] The retreat from the boycott did not go unchallenged. Nelson Mandela of the Congress Youth League argued that 'the masses of people all through the country are in favour of the boycott' and urged that sufficient time remained to organize a boycott of the upcoming elections.[19] And Gana Makabeni cynically noted that '[t]he people who were so eloquent for the boycott last year are fighting it as eloquently this year. The people are being deliberately misled.'[20]

In a repeat of its shift a decade earlier, the CPSA reversed its position on participation in the NRC, and it began to campaign for 'boycott candidates'.[21] While the CPSA affirmed, in January 1948, that '[t]he NRC cannot achieve any useful purpose, and the African peoples' efforts must be directed towards its abolition', it nonetheless 'resolve[d] to work for the election of a bloc of candidates pledged to repeal of the Act'. It followed a similar line in regards to advisory board elections, resolving 'to support candidates ... who are pledged to work for the abolition of this fraudulent system of deception'.[22] Edwin Mofutsanyana began campaigning for the Transvaal and Orange Free State seat, arguing 'that a total boycott can only be achieved when sufficient organisational work has been done in the country. The people to-day are not ready as one man to abstain from going to the polls.'[23] Despite the CPSA's references to 'boycott candidates', it did not explain how they could actually fight the system of racial structures.

The CPSA's new policy flew in the face of continued support for the boycott. In April 1948, for instance, the Transkei Organised Bodies and Transkeian Voters' Association 'repudiate[d] the authority of the new Native Representative Council to "speak on behalf of the people who have on several occasions declared they do not wish to participate in any elections under the 1936 Act"'. Those members who were contesting seats in the NRC were expelled on the grounds that 'by seeking election to the council they flouted the decision of every meeting held in the Transkei on the boycott question', and Africans were urged 'to intensify the campaign to implement the boycott resolution'.[24]

By January 1950 the CPSA was overtly critical of the manner in which, it claimed, boycotts were being conducted. '[A] refusal to "co-operate" can be effective only when the ruling class *wants, must* have co-operation, as in war' – a position, ironically, which the Party had rejected during much of the war – 'or in order to forestall a revolutionary situation', it added elliptically. 'An obvious, organic weakness in the boycott tactic, therefore, is that the ruling class itself wants to abolish the institutions concerned, the NRC, the Advisory Boards, the African parliamentary franchise.' Instead of forcing the conciliatory members of the NRC and other racial bodies to take a militant line, the CPSA argued, proponents of the boycott promoted political abstentionism.[25] The CPSA was not alone on the left in its criticism of the NEUM's application of the boycott and its practice of non-collaboration.[26] But the CPSA and the ANC undoubtedly deflected some of the anti-boycott sentiment. Despite the widespread disapproval of the NRC, it limped along until November 1950. The government had the final word when the Bantu Authorities Act of 1951 abolished the Council.

The abortive history of the Train Apartheid Resistance Campaign (TARC) illustrates the divergent approaches of Communists and Trotskyists to political mobilization.[27] The *Herenigde* National Party began its tenure with a test case – the extension of train apartheid to the historically liberal Cape peninsula. It was a test not only for the government but also for the left. The TARC was formed in August 1948 to fight the government's plan. The APO, the NEUM, the Teachers' League of South Africa, the Fourth International Organisation, the CPSA and a host of trade unions and other organizations, all declared their opposition to train apartheid, and the campaign snowballed, attracting massive demonstrations. The NEUM had initially hoped to link the issue of train apartheid to the broader democratic struggle under its Ten Point Programme. But unable to rally sufficient support under its own banner, it formed a united front with the other organizations. NEUM representatives formed the majority of the TARC's leadership, while the Communists were a minority.

From the beginning, differences of strategy and tactics began to emerge within the leadership. The divergent approaches foreshadowed both the ANC's Defiance Campaign of 1952, with its use of civil disobedience, and the NEUM's growing reticence to engage in tactical campaigns. The TARC leadership reached agreement that train apartheid be made unworkable by the use of volunteers who would board the trains and flout the discriminatory laws. Given the clear popular enthusiasm, the CPSA argued that small groups of individuals should immediately begin boarding train carriages reserved for whites. The NEUM thought that this was premature and called for intensive organization as a prerequisite for mass action. A compromise to begin the boarding of trains by volunteers when a sufficient number had been enrolled broke down in quarrels over what constituted an adequate number. Although about 400 volunteers had been enrolled, the NEUM felt that thousands would be necessary for a successful campaign and argued that action be delayed until more volunteers could be recruited. With the NEUM representatives insisting that mass action was premature, the Communists dropped out of TARC. While a few individuals from the Fourth International Organisation were privately critical of the NEUM's stalling tactics, this was the 'brief honeymoon' period of Cape Town's Trotskyist groups; hence, the Fourth Internationalists refrained from any public criticism of the NEUM. In essence, argued Kenny Jordaan, the volunteers were put in 'cold storage', and people began to lose interest. Within six months, the movement had fizzled out; several months later, following their acquittal in May 1949 of the charge of incitement, the remaining TARC leadership announced its decision to affiliate to the NEUM.[28]

Although some of the leadership of the ANC and AAC still entertained hopes of uniting the organizations in the interests of broader African unity, black politics became increasingly polarized in two blocs: one, the ANC and the SAIC, supported by the CPSA; the other, the NEUM, including the AAC, the Anti-CAD and other affiliates, in which the Workers' Party played a behind-the-scenes role. The ostensible line of division between these two blocs was the question of the boycott of racial institutions. It is an irony that although the ANC adopted the Congress Youth League's pro-boycott Programme of Action in 1949, that same year unity talks between the ANC and the AAC ground to a halt, allegedly over incompatible positions on the boycott.[29]

The South African left never even formed a united front to challenge the Suppression of Communism Act or the Group Areas and Mixed Marriages Acts. Arthur Davids of the defunct Fourth International Organisation commented at the time that 'the Acts were introduced and are being enforced without any resistance whatsoever. The impression of the invincibility of the State this creates in the minds of the people leaves them more apathetic and indifferent than ever.'[30]

The suppression of socialism

The CPSA was certainly cognizant as early as 1947 that the *Herenigde* National Party intended to ban socialist organizations if it were elected. But there is no evidence that the Party made any attempt to build an underground structure. On the contrary, South African Communists seemed unable to deal, at a pragmatic level, with the likely consequences of their own intellectual perceptions. At one level, the failure to set up an underground structure before its banning was hardly surprising, given the Party's weakness as a legal organization. In a report presented by Moses Kotane to the Party's national conference in January 1949, the Party claimed a total of 2482 members, of whom only 992 were designated as members 'in good financial standing'. The remainder were more than three months in arrears with their dues. The situation was bleakest in the Cape District, which claimed 1042 members, of whom only 270 were up to date with their dues. Other centres fared badly as well. Port Elizabeth claimed 75, of whom 9 were in good standing; Pretoria claimed 133, with 21 in good standing; and Johannesburg 666, with less than half, 324, in good standing.[31] If the legal Party was so organizationally weak, what prospects would Communists have for forming an illegal group? And there is little doubt, as Jack and Ray Simons contend, that the police seizure of the Party's membership lists in 1946 would have made any direct transition to underground status virtually impossible.[32]

But at another level, the explanation for the Party's failure to prepare for its impending illegality was psychological – an intellectual recognition of the probable future could not prepare South African Communists to act according to a reality that they had not yet experienced. In this respect, the CPSA was not unique. In a number of significant cases, European Communist Parties had failed to take steps to set up underground structures, even though they recognized the probability that they would become illegal under fascist regimes. '[T]he experience of the German Communist Party under Nazi rule had shown the difficulty involved in passing from legal to illegal work without a pause', wrote Jack and Ray Simons. The German example 'weighed heavily' upon the South African Communists, they claimed.[33]

Instead, despite its own organizational weakness and the setback that the Durban District suffered following the violent clashes between Zulus and Indians in January 1949, the Party remained ostensibly optimistic about its potential. In July 1949 Kotane emphasized the need to stabilize and to build the Party's membership; to improve morale, efficiency and discipline; and to strengthen the Party's relationships with other progressive organizations. The government's reactionary policies were generating more interest in the CPSA, Kotane claimed, and therefore this should be an auspicious time for the Party to grow – an echo of the optimistic views expressed by Communists in the 1930s who had forecast that economic immiseration would radicalize Afrikaner workers. It was imperative that the Party break up the 'white united front' that the government was building. Kotane suggested that the Party strengthen its organization through the establishment of more factory groups, through a reduction in the size of some of its units and through political education.[34] The Central Committee was still thinking in terms of building a broad mass campaign against the *Herenigde* National Party's policies. The discussion turned on whether, as Brian Bunting argued, the Party should take the lead, or whether, as Fred Carneson maintained, 'while we should work for a united democratic front, we should in the meantime get individual organisations to take action'.[35]

Six months later, in January 1950, the CPSA held what would be its last national conference. There was still no apparent recognition that the Party might face imminent dissolution. Its self-assessment was contradictory. Despite its assertion that '[t]he people are turning to the Party in ever increasing numbers', it now claimed only three 'properly functioning' district organizations – in Johannesburg, Cape Town and Durban.[36] In May the government introduced the Unlawful Organizations Bill. That month the CPSA Central Committee resolved to dissolve the Party in the event of the bill becoming law. Of the seventeen members on the Central Committee, only Bill Andrews, Michael Harmel and, by his own account, Moses Kotane voted against dissolution. The law was finally enacted as the Suppression of Communism Act in June. On 20 June 1950 the Communist MP Sam Kahn publicly announced the Party's immediate dissolution.[37]

The Central Committee took this decision seemingly without forethought and without consultation with the membership. There was, without question, a great deal of disarray and confusion in the minds of the Central Committee members. Edwin Mofutsanyana, for instance, claimed that only after the Unlawful Organizations Bill was introduced did the Central Committee call an emergency meeting to discuss the matter. In his words, 'we rushed to that emergency conference to find discussions running in this line: we must dissolve the Party. That is the fact.' He had presumed that 'the suppression of the Party was going to be like in all other countries', where, Mofutsanyana was under the impression, 'they would declare the Party illegal and it would go underground'. Instead, he remembered Jack Simons saying, 'We are dissolving the Party. We cannot really know how the Party in the future will be formed. What form it will take. What it will be called.' Only subsequently did Mofutsanyana claim to realize that the vote for dissolution had not been a vote to go underground but to 'liquidate' the Party.[38] But Ray Alexander felt that it was necessary for the CPSA to reorganize before embarking on underground work as many members were not at the time prepared to be part of an illegal organization.[39] For many socialists, the threat of further repression led not to greater radicalization but to caution and disillusionment.

Moses Kotane and Isaac Horvitch, the national chairman, visited local branches to announce the decision. Kotane himself felt 'faced with the decision to resign or to carry out the decision'. Although no one contested the decision, many people were apparently stunned and assumed it to be a ploy.[40] Naboth Mokgatle recalled that the Central Committee 'circulated a notice of its intentions to dissolve, asking us to inform all members and to obtain objections and consents' and that his district group had approved the decision. Mokgatle saw it in the context of the illegality that other Communist Parties had faced. 'I was not the only unfortunate one', he wrote. 'I was one of the many ... who had suffered the same fate in Italy, Germany and other lands.'[41]

Counting about 2000 members in 1950, in absolute terms the Party was significantly smaller than at its peak in January 1929, when it had claimed 3000 members. But given the general increase in population since the late 1920s, the CPSA was proportionately far smaller in 1950 than it had been in the late 1920s.[42]

In its own dissolution, the CPSA completed a process that had begun when the tiny Workers' Party went underground in 1939 in anticipation of fascism. One by one, independent socialist groups collapsed as the 1940s drew to a close. Despite the contributions that a relatively small number of people had made to the liberation struggle – most notably in laying the foundations of the black trade union movement – autonomous socialist organization was a weak movement. The membership of these socialist groups was at any one time small, although many more individuals had passed through these organizations and had either lost interest or been disillusioned or victimized by the sectarian politics they encountered. There was, however, no other viable left-wing political home outside the organizations of the Third and Fourth Internationals as the country lacked any other socialist tradition. The merger between socialists and national liberation organizations – both the Workers' Party and the NEUM and the Communist Party and the ANC – occurred not only in the absence of any alternative social-democratic or non-racial labour party but when the socialist movement itself had reached its nadir.

Notes

1. In 1951 the *Herenigde* National Party became the National Party.
2. Lodge, *Black Politics*, 39, 67–8; Brian Bunting, *The Rise of the South African Reich*, Harmondsworth, Middlesex: Penguin, 1969, 131–57.
3. Govan Mbeki, *South Africa: the Peasants' Revolt*, Harmondsworth, Middlesex: Penguin,

1964, 34–42; William Beinart and Colin Bundy, 'State Intervention and Rural Resistance: The Transkei, 1900–1965', in Martin A. Klein, ed., *Peasants in Africa: Historical and Contemporary Perspectives*, Beverly Hills and London: Sage, 1980, 305–6.

4.   Simons and Simons, *Class and Colour*, 10; Dan O'Meara, 'The 1946 African Mine Workers' Strike and the Political Economy of South Africa', *Journal of Commonwealth and Comparative Politics*, 13, 2, July 1975, 167.

5.   'National Front and Class Struggle: Report to the Central Committee of the Communist Party of South Africa', *Freedom*, 5, 4, August-September 1946, in Drew, ed., *South Africa's Radical Tradition*, vol. 1, 373.

6.   'Report on the Relationship of the Party to other Workers' Organisations in South Africa', *Freedom*, 5, 4, August-September 1946, in Drew, ed., *South Africa's Radical Tradition*, vol. 1, 379.

7.   Statement on sedition case issued by the Central Committee of the Communist Party, *The Guardian*, November 28, 1946 in Bunting, ed., *South African Communists Speak*, 194–6.

8.   J. Shulman, 'History of the Y.C.L.', and 'Report on the National Y.C.L. Conference', in *Young Communist League Newsletter*, no. 5, April-May 1945, 1–2 and 13–14 respectively, author's possession; Forman and Odendaal, eds, *Trumpet*, 120–22.

9.   'Report on the National Y.C.L. Conference', 13.

10. Forman and Odendaal, eds, *Trumpet*, 124.

11. Podbrey, *White Girl*, 105.

12. Forman and Odendaal, eds, *Trumpet*, 125.

13. Letter from the Fourth International Organisation of South Africa to [Revolutionary Communist Party?], 6 March 1947, in Drew, ed., *South Africa's Radical Tradition*, vol. 1, 380.

14. Letter from Hosea Jaffe to author, 1 July 1999; Interview with Jordaan. Kenny Jordaan believed that the Paris Conference had called for a rapprochement between the Fourth International Organisation of South Africa and the Workers' Party. However, Hosea Jaffe did not recall any such decision. Averbach emigrated to Israel after the passage of the Suppression of Communism Act.

15. Tabata, *The Boycott as Weapon of Struggle*; Interview with Tabata and Gool.

16. 'Dadoo on the Boycott: "Time for Action"', *Guardian*, 19 June 1947; see also 'Boycott of Advisory Boards', *Guardian*, 4 December 1947.

17. *Towards a Free Democracy – or Back to Serfdom: the Denial of Democracy*, Cape Town, 8/8/47, Simons Collection, South African Communist Party, 6.6.3, quotes 5 and 6.

18. 'New Tactics Proposed for N.R.C. Boycott: Xuma's Address to African Congress', *Guardian*, 18 December 1947.

19. 'Transvaal A.N.C. Rejects Smuts' New Proposals', *Guardian*, 4 December 1947.

20. 'N.R.C. Boycott Campaign to be Intensified', *Guardian*, 18 December 1947.

21. 'Dr. Xuma Ignores A.N.C. Decision on Elections' and 'Scurrilous Attacks on Communist Candidate', both in *Guardian*, 22 January 1948.

22. 'Resolution on 'The Struggle for Democracy' adopted at the national conference of the Communist Party held in Johannesburg on January 2, 3 and 4, 1948', in Bunting, ed., *South African Communists Speak*, 196–7, quotes 196 and 197 respectively.

23. 'Militant Campaign by Communists in N.R.C. Election', *Guardian*, 8 January 1948; 'Call To Voters: Moses Kotane Answers Some Questions,' *Guardian*, 20 May 1948.

24. 'Transkei Voters Maintain Boycott', *Guardian*, 8 April 1948. See Mbeki, *South Africa: the Peasants' Revolt* and Allison Drew, 'Theory and Practice of the Agrarian Question in

South African Socialism, 1928–60', *Journal of Peasant Studies*, 23, 2/3, January–April 1996, 53–92 for discussions of boycott campaigns in the Transkei.

25. 'Nationalism and the Class Struggle', extract from Central Committee report to the National Conference of the Communist Party in Johannesburg on January 6, 7 and 8, 1950, in Bunting, ed., *South African Communists Speak*, 209.

26. See, for example, A. Davids, 'A Critical Analysis of I. B. Tabata's Book – *The All-African Convention*', Cape Town: Forum Club, [1950], 18–20.

27. For three different assessments of the TARC see Sarah Mokone [Victor Wessels], 'The T.A.R.C.', *Majority Rule: Some notes*, chapter 19; 'Short History of Betrayal', *Freedom*, New Series, 1, 5, 1 November 1948; and K. A. Jordaan, 'The T.A.R.C. Debacle', *Discussion*, 1, 1, [June 1950], all in Drew, ed., *South Africa's Radical Tradition*, vol. 2, 81–6 and 97–103 respectively.

28. Interview with Jordaan.

29. Joint Sitting of the Executive Committees of the All-African Convention and the African National Congress, 17 April 1949, in Drew, ed., *South Africa's Radical Tradition*, vol. 2, 87–94.

30. Davids, 'A Critical Analysis of I. B. Tabata's Book', 20.

31. Report of the Central Committee to the National conference to be held in Cape Town on the 8th, 9th and 10th January 1949, signed by Moses M. Kotane, 20, Simons Collection, South African Communist Party, 6.6.2.4.

32. Simons and Simons, *Class and Colour*, 607.

33. Simons and Simons, *Class and Colour*, 607.

34. Moses M. Kotane, Report on Party Organisation. Submitted to the Meeting of the Central Committee of the Communist Party of South Africa held in Cape Town on the 9th & 10th July, 1949, Simons Collection, South African Communist Party, 6.3.

35. Minutes of meeting of the Central Committee of the Communist Party of South Africa held at Library, City Hall, Cape Town, Saturday and Sunday, 9th & 10th July, 1949, Simons Collection, South African Communist Party, 6.3.

36. Bunting, ed., *South African Communists Speak*, 200.

37. Central Committee statement read out in the House of Assembly, Cape Town, on June 20, 1950, by Communist MP Sam Kahn, in Bunting, ed., *South African Communists Speak*, 214–15. Sam Kahn, a white man, was elected under the system of Native Representation to represent the Africans in the Western Cape. For Kotane's position see Sonia Bunting, interview with Kotane, 8.

38. Edgar, interview with Mofutsanyana.

39. Interview with Jack and Ray Simons.

40. Sonia Bunting, interview with Kotane, 8. David Everatt, 'Alliance Politics of a Special Type: the Roots of the ANC/SACP Alliance, 1950–1954', *Journal of Southern African Studies*, 18, 1, March 1991, 19–39, 21–2; Slovo, *Unfinished Biography*, 51; Bunting, *Kotane*, 174.

41. Mokgatle, *Autobiography*, 279.

42. Karis and Carter, eds, *From Protest to Challenge*, 107.

The burden of history and the burden of choice

Before its transition to democracy, South Africa was often compared to Tsarist Russia in terms of revolutionary potential. Superficially, the conditions of South Africa might have looked similar to those of pre-revolutionary Russia. Both countries had vast, semi-literate, semi-proletarianized peasant populations, a small urban proletariat and a migrant labour system that linked urban workers with the rural population and permitted the diffusion of new ideas from town to countryside. In both societies a tiny, privileged elite lived at the expense of a virtually rightless majority. Both had authoritarian regimes and lacked traditions of evolutionary social-democracy or of political liberalism. There, the similarities stopped.

Unlike Russia's revolution of October 1917, capping decades of underground struggle, South Africa's democratic transition has heralded no social revolution and only a very limited reform of capitalism. Day-to-day life has changed very little for the black majority – or for the white minority. The political terrain is still largely defined in terms of black and white. While the 1994 and 1999 elections saw a plethora of tiny political parties, their minute electoral support only underlined both the absence of effective political pluralism in the country and the degree to which sectional divisions structured political options. South Africa still lacks any social-democratic movement or a significant liberal tradition. Socialist ideology, so apparent in the 1980s, has been eclipsed in the 1990s, as the movement has seen organizational decline.

The constraints on building socialism in South Africa have been enormous. The distinctive conditions faced by South African socialists lay in the movement's historical timing and international origins as well as in the extremely racially-divided society in which it emerged. Compared to Russian socialism, which could connect to radical anti-Tsarist agitation extending back to the Decembrist uprising of 1825, or to British socialism, which could trace its antecedents back to the Chartist movement of the 1840s, the South African socialist movement, dating from the first years of the twentieth century, was a late developer. This, of course, reflected the relatively recent and rapid formation of the modern South African political economy and its industrial working class – catalysed by the discovery of diamonds and gold in the late nineteenth century. In Russia, socialism emerged as 'the lifeblood of the intelligentsia' before the formation of an urban working class, and Russian socialists appealed first to the peasantry in the 1870s before turning to the urban proletariat. In Britain, by contrast, home of the world's first industrial revolution, socialism emerged after the development of an urban working class. South Africa's experience differed from both those countries: there, the socialist movement developed along-side a black proletariat.

The racial division of the South African working class proved an immense bar-rier to the development of a socialist movement in either a social-democratic or a revolutionary form. Social democracy in Europe was forged with the strength of an emerging working class and a developing democratic tradition that expanded suffi-ciently to allow an organized and enfranchised or partially enfranchised labour force to form political parties. Those conditions were absent in South Africa for most of this century, where the labour movement was dominated by a racist minority that controlled access to the most skilled work.

The conditions for a social democracy based on the hope of evolutionary change were absent from pre-revolutionary Russia as well. There, it was the most skilled and urbanized workers who, denied the right to form trade unions, began looking to the revolutionary underground for assistance. Russia's pre-revolutionary industrial boom, financed by foreign capital, was facilitated by the comparatively cheap price of Russian, as compared to European, labour. Despite the political repression facing craft workers agitating for improved conditions, the demand for their skills meant that such workers 'roamed from factory to factory', easily able to find work.[1] But this was markedly different from South Africa, where the skilled workers had a vested interest in preventing social change, while those workers who desired change were kept in unskilled work, prevented from permanent settlement in towns and could be readily sent back to the reserves.

The ripples created by the Russian Revolution reached South African shores and made a profound impact on the mentality of local socialists. The overwhelming attrac-tion that the Russian Revolution held for socialists around the world was that it demonstrated that their goal was not merely a utopian dream but a feasible project. The subsequent absence of a successful socialist revolution in any other European country underscored the Soviet achievement and strengthened the increasingly dom-inant view that the Bolsheviks had the right answer. In this respect, the South African socialist movement followed a worldwide pattern, which saw the eclipsing of diverse strands of socialism by the shadow of the Bolshevik Party. In other words, the para-digm for revolutionary socialists that became dominant after the Russian revolution rejected the earlier diversity. However, while this paradigm rejected pre-existing social-democratic traditions, premised on the idea of evolution rather than revolution, it left them largely untouched. Thus, in Britain, where a strong social-democratic move-ment already existed, some of the diverse socialist strands had been able to take root. But in South Africa, the seeds of these diverse socialist strands had not had time to germinate, and they were swept aside. The weakness of any prior socialist tradition made the subsequent South African socialist experience particularly vulnerable to the Soviet paradigm. Moreover, the Soviet paradigm was buttressed in South Africa by successive waves of immigration from Eastern Europe.

Along with the model of a successful revolution, went the prototype of a revo-lutionary embraced by many nineteenth-century Russian radicals and later promoted by the Comintern – one who sacrificed all for the party and 'the struggle'.[2] In South Africa, the virtual absence of any surviving pre-existing socialist tradition meant that there were few alternative models for socialists. Olive Schreiner might arguably have become such a model. But she became obscured in the history of South African socialism very soon after her death. Her marginalization was part of the general decline of an organizationally eclectic, multifaceted socialism, as a centralized form of socialism became hegemonic on the left after the Russian Revolution. This intolerance of diversity within the socialist movement prevented the possibility that feminism could provide a radical dimension to socialism, and it narrowed the space available for women socialists. The model of a Bolshevik who gave unquestioned loyalty to the Party was uncritically adopted by most South African socialists.

But despite the burdens of history and of social structure, South African socialists nonetheless had some scope for manoeuvre. Socialist groups have historically pursued a range of organizational strategies, ranging from the decision to retain organizational autonomy and, generally, to engage in selected activities with other groups; to efforts to forge broader socialist unity; to attempts at building more systematic alliances, premised either on the preservation of autonomy within a broad alliance or the subordination of organizational goals within a broader agenda.[3] South African socialist organizations pursued all these options in various permutations in different decades. Up to 1921, their aim was initially to retain organizational autonomy and then, encouraged by the events of 1917, to promote broader socialist unity. In the 1920s, those groups that had not joined the CPSA faded into oblivion. Given the absence of any social-democratic tradition, the tiny CPSA enjoyed a virtual monopoly on the left.

The possibilities open to Communists were greatest after 1924, when the CPSA's turn to black workers indicated its ability to respond to local conditions, notably the growing significance of black labour. The Party now showed interest in gaining influence in the ICU. Aside from its flirtation with the Labour Party between 1922 and 1924, this was the CPSA's first attempt at alliance politics. But the ICU's expulsion of Communist members signalled the failure of that strategy, and the CPSA turned its hand directly to trade union organization.

The late 1920s presented a juncture, when the growing CPSA subordinated its programme more definitively to the Comintern, thus downplaying the significance of local specificities in favour of an authorized model. The CPSA's geographic distance from the Soviet Union and its lack of political importance to the Comintern, compared to European and Asian Communist Parties, had offered the CPSA some protection from Comintern intervention. Nonetheless, the New Line had a far more destructive impact on social relations inside the CPSA than in some other Communist Parties, such as the CPGB. At the end of the 1920s, the tiny CPSA found itself squeezed between the increasing repression of the South African state, on the one side, and the mounting demands of the Comintern for obedience, on the other. Although all Communists were liable to the threats of harassment and imprisonment, those categorized as Africans bore the brunt of state brutality.

Caught between these two pincers, South African Communists turned on each other. It was virtually inevitable, under such conditions, that South African Communists, believing so intensely in the inviolability and symbolism of the Comintern and lacking other points of reference, would point the finger at each other and that generational and racial tensions would thrive in such an atmosphere.

The New Line inevitably led to schisms in the CPSA as nonconformists left or were expelled, dynamics that local socialists explained and justified in terms of international rather than local politics. Criticisms were couched in highly personalized terms as the failures of individuals to follow Moscow's guidelines. That the alternative to the changes wrought by the Comintern's intervention coalesced under the banner of Trotskyism again reflected both the porosity of the South African movement to international socialist developments and the hegemony of the Bolshevik model on the South African left. The Comintern vilified its opponents as Trotskyists, and Trotskyists they became.

Like the ethical socialist current that flickered on the political landscape in the early twentieth century, the ILP-type socialism that William Ballinger hoped to build in the late 1920s and 1930s could not take root and grow. In part this reflected the decline of the ICU, where Ballinger worked, and his lack of a following, as both outsider and newcomer. More profoundly, it reflected the dominance of Comintern discourse in shaping political attitudes on the left and in framing what local socialists saw as the range of possible political options. Ballinger faced hostility from both Communists and, later, Trotskyists, because of his refusal to support either tendency. The two socialists willing to work with Ballinger – Eddie Roux and Max Gordon – were also the least doctrinaire and the most pragmatic. Otherwise, Balllinger's political allies and sympathizers were liberals.

Two turning points in the late 1920s and early 1930s were critical in establishing the CPSA's future direction. The first was seen in the abortive history of the League of African Rights. Established by Sidney Bunting in early 1929, the League was meant to be a broad-based organization with both democratic and national liberation components. Before the Comintern ordered it to be disbanded, the League was reportedly growing by leaps and bounds – an organization of ordinary people – as opposed to the then tiny ANC, which was dominated by chiefs and other political and economic elites. One can only speculate whether, had the League been allowed to survive, it could have offered the basis for a working-class or social-democratic challenge to the ANC. That possibility was closed off by its dissolution. Ironically, a few years later Moses Kotane tried to build *Ikaka labaSebenzi* on precisely the lines Bunting had envisioned, despite his earlier vociferous criticism of Bunting. By then, however, the CPSA was far too weak, its numbers too diminished, to sustain such an organization.

The second turning point was the decision by Bunting, Makabeni and others in 1932–33 not to rally all the forces of opposition both within and outside the CPSA and to form a new socialist body. There is no doubt that Bunting was in a position to do so, because of the large following that he had amongst Africans in the Party and the respect that he commanded more broadly on the left. Although any new socialist group emerging at that time would undoubtedly have been branded with the stigma of Trotskyism, regardless of whether or not it aligned itself with Trotskyists overseas, the larger numbers that it could have attracted would have made it a force for the CPSA to reckon with. It might have been able to incorporate the CPSA and develop a more critical stance towards Comintern intervention. But this is precisely what Bunting was unable to do. He refused, in the 1930s, to reassess the interpretation of the Comintern that he had formed in 1921.

Instead, opposition to the Comintern and its influence in the CPSA remained regionally and organizationally fragmented. Attempts to merge the various minute Trotskyist groups came to naught, while the demonization of Trotsky and the virulent denunciation of Trotskyism precluded any possibility of broader socialist unity.

Moreover, most South African socialists lacked alternative political identities outside their socialist organizations. It is no accident that the Communist most able to weather the storm of the 1930s was Bill Andrews, and he weathered it because he had built up another identity in the white labour movement. For many decades, the black or non-racial trade union movement was too weak to provide a stable home for many socialists. Precisely because the impetus to organize black workers came from socialists, this made the black trade union movement particularly vulnerable to the destructive impact of socialist in-fighting. Nor was there a strong cooperative movement or women's movement, despite sporadic attempts to build them, in which individual socialists could work independently and establish an alternative political base as a counterweight to a political party. Unlike Britain, where many socialists had established their positions in trade unions, in cooperative societies and in women's organizations, the weakness of those movements in South Africa meant that local socialists had no political home outside political organizations. In other words, aside from the very few who worked in the white labour movement, most South African socialists lacked autonomous social bases and were virtually totally dependent on political organizations for their political identity. This reinforced the centrality of the Comintern and of the struggle between the Third and Fourth Internationals.

The 1930s and the early 1940s were decisive years for the South African left in limiting the possibilities for the future. A series of choices in those years reshaped the political terrain and narrowed political options. The bifurcation of the socialist movement in the 1930s coincided with a crucial debate within the national liberation movement about how to fight the government's curtailment of African rights. The central question was whether or not to boycott the powerless and racist Natives Representative Council. The rigid Communist–Trotskyist divide was reinforced by the CPSA's decision to accept the framework of the Natives Representative Council as a platform for propaganda and the decision of Trotskyists to boycott it. These divergent political stances accentuated the rivalries of the national liberation organizations to which each socialist tendency aligned.

The politics of the Second World War reinforced the division of the left. The CPSA virtually collapsed at several points in the 1930s; its organizational survival was far from inevitable. While the relocation of its headquarters to Cape Town in 1939 helped to stabilize the Party, it was an international event – the Soviet Union's decision to enter the war in 1941 – that enabled the CPSA to gain legitimacy from its support for the war effort and thereby to recover from its previous phase of *de facto* illegality. By contrast, Trotskyists remained social outcasts because of their continued opposition to the war.

In precluding the option of broader unity of the left, the rigid ideological and political bifurcation of the socialist movement necessarily pushed socialists towards the choice of organizational autonomy or the pursuit of alliances. In the 1940s the Cape Town-based Fourth International Organisation of South Africa and the Workers' International League pursued the first option most clearly, although the latter was concerned to develop trade union links. By contrast, the Workers' Party and the Communist Party pursued the alliance strategy. The underground status of the Workers' Party led it to submerge itself completely to the Non-European Unity Movement, where its members worked clandestinely; the Workers' Party offered no distinct programme aside from the NEUM's Ten Point Programme. Similarly, having failed to gain positions of leadership on the AAC's National Executive, the CPSA turned its attention to the ANC and helped to resuscitate it. Through the 1940s the CPSA pursued a policy of tactical alliances with the ANC. As long as the CPSA remained a legal, above-ground organization, it retained a distinctive identity. Only after it reformed as an underground group in the 1950s did it subordinate its strategy to that of the ANC.

By the end of the Second World War, the socialist movement was so rigidly divided that Communists and Trotskyists could not work in joint activities to fight the implementation of apartheid. Autonomous Trotskyist groups collapsed. Although the CPSA's pro-war stance had enabled it to recoup some of the losses of the 1930s, it remained both proportionately and in absolute terms far smaller than at its peak in the late 1920s. It is not surprising, with hindsight, that the CPSA's leadership chose to disband the Party in 1950 and that it was reconstituted in 1953 under a stronger nationalist agenda. In the era of apartheid and Cold War, South African socialism subordinated itself to nationalism.

The fleeting appearance of the Forum Club in the early 1950s was a last attempt to build broader socialist unity, at least amongst intellectuals. This agenda reflected a desire to keep socialist thought alive after the Suppression of Communism Act of 1950 made overt socialist activity illegal. The Forum Club also indicated a concern about the debilitating effects of sectarianism on the left. But thereafter, the subject of socialist unity was scarcely broached for another forty years.

Paradoxically, the 1940s and 1950s were years of socialist intellectual activity, despite the organizational collapse of the movement. Whereas British and Russian socialists had been writing histories of or theorizing their own national experiences for decades, the South Africa left lacked a written intellectual tradition of its own and suffered from an intellectual inferiority complex *vis-à-vis* Europe and Russia. This made it very dependent on imported ideas – particularly, those of the Comintern. Not until the 1940s and 1950s, catalysed largely by Eddie Roux, did

South African socialists begin to write histories of their movement and of political protest in their country – a process interrupted by the blanket of repression that smothered the country in the 1960s.[4]

The unification of South Africa in 1910 had inaugurated an authoritarian state built on colonial conquest and its corollary, an ideology of national and racial supremacy. Outside a narrow spectrum reserved for whites only, the state did not allow political pluralism. Authoritarianism and repression do not produce an environment in which diverse and iconoclastic ideas can flourish. Political authoritarianism bred intolerance, both of differences amongst people and of different ideas. An authoritarian regime that legitimated itself through appeals to national and racial supremacy and that denigrated diversity, left little space for political alternatives. In the absence of social democracy and of any significant liberal tendency, and with only a weak socialist current, nationalism became the dominant and sometimes hegemonic discourse of political opposition during the Cold War. The lack of pluralism lent itself to the development of multiple binary oppositions, the most central of which was a polarization between proponents and opponents of the regime. 'Total oppression', wrote Jack and Ray Simons, 'evoked total resistance.'[5]

The state's Manichean approach to politics was mirrored by and reinforced the growing intolerance of diversity amongst socialists and within the national liberation movement: either with the ANC or against it; either acceptance of the NEUM's Ten Point Programme or condemnation by the movement. Political repression also fostered secrecy and mitigated against the establishment and maintenance of democratic practices. Paradoxically, although socialists reviled the lack of democracy in their own country, they frequently failed to practice it in their own ranks.

The collapse of socialism as an autonomous movement in the first years of apartheid and of the Cold War was not foreordained. Rather, a 'complex set of events conspired to assure this result'.[6] South African socialist history presents itself as a sequence of events in which, at each major turning point, the opportunities for a radical reorientation became fewer. Socialists put their faith in the belief that a model that appeared to them to have succeeded in building socialism in the Soviet Union could work in quite different conditions. By the 1930s socialists saw each other as images projected by another country, the Soviet Union. This created a schism that closed off possibilities of socialist unity and inevitably pushed objectively tiny groups towards strategic alliances with national liberation organizations. Ultimately, as overt socialist activity became virtually impossible, socialist agendas were subordinated to the demands of nationalism. In turn, that choice limited the prospects for the development of class consciousness and of autonomous working-class political organization. Labels truly had conquered the South African left, as the writer Peter Abrahams lamented, recalling the 1930s. In this respect, the South African left mirrored its own society.

Notes

1. Orlando Figes, *A People's Tragedy: The Russian Revolution, 1891–1924*, London: Pimlico, 1996, 120.
2. Figes, *A People's Tragedy*, 130–34.
3. The following discussion draws on David Howell, *British Workers and the Independent Labour Party, 1888–1906*, Manchester: Manchester University and New York: St Martin's, 1983, 389–97.
4. In addition to Roux see, *inter alia*, correspondence from Wilfred Harrison and L. Storman in *South African Socialist Review*, October 1945 and May 1946; Harrison, *Memoirs of a Socialist*; Lionel Forman, *Chapters in the History of the March to Freedom*, New Age, 1959; Forman and Odendaal, eds, *A Trumphet from the Housetops*; Cope, *Comrade Bill*; Mnguni [Hosea Jaffe], *Three Hundred Years*, Cape Town: 1952; Nosipho Majeke [Dora Taylor], *The Role of the Missionaries in Conquest*, Society of Young Africa, 1952.
5. Simons and Simons, *Class and Colour*, 624.
6. Stephen Jay Gould, *Wonderful Life: The Burgess Shale and the Nature of History*, London: Penguin, 1991, 278.

Bibliography

Archival collections

Abdurahman Family Papers, Manuscripts and Archives Department, University of Cape Town Libraries

Dr Waradia Abdurahman Papers, Manuscripts and Archives Department, University of Cape Town Libraries

African Collection (South Africa), Manuscripts and Archives, Yale University Library

African National Congress Papers, Institute of Commonwealth Studies, University of London

W. H. Andrews Collection, Mayibuye Centre Historical Papers Archive, University of the Western Cape

Hyman Basner Papers, Institute of Commonwealth Studies, University of London

Hymie Basner Tapes, School of Oriental and African Studies, University of London

Ralph Bunche Collection, Special Collections Department, University Research Library, University of California, Los Angeles

Brian Bunting Collection, Mayibuye Centre Historical Papers Archive, University of the Western Cape

S. P. Bunting Papers, Historical Papers Library, University of the Witwatersrand

Communist International Archives, *Rossiiskii tsentr khraneniia i izucheniia dokumentov noveishei istorii* (RTsKhIDNI) [Russian Centre for the Conservation and Study of Modern History Records], Moscow

Communist Party of South Africa Collection, Hoover Institution Archives, Stanford

R. K. Cope Papers, Historical Papers Library, University of the Witwatersrand

Findlay Papers, Historical Papers Library, University of the Witwatersrand

Ruth First Collection, Institute of Commonwealth Studies, University of London

Clare Goodlatte Papers, South African Reference Library, Cape Town

Jock Haston Papers, Brynmor Jones Library, University of Hull

Winifred Holtby Collection, Kingston upon Hull Local Studies Library

I. O. Horvitch Papers, Institute of Commonwealth Studies, University of London

Francis Johnson Papers (on microfilm, National Museum of Labour History, Manchester)

Fanny Klenerman Papers, Historical Papers Library, University of the Witwatersrand

Tom Mann Papers, University of Warwick Modern Records Centre

Tom Mann Papers, Working Class Movement Library, Salford

James Middleton Papers, Labour Party Archives, National Museum of Labour History, Manchester

E. R. Roux Papers, Institute of Commonwealth Studies, University of London

Jack Simons Collection, Manuscripts and Archives Department, University of Cape Town Libraries (and on microfilm, University of York)

South Africa. Department of Justice Files, 1914–1928, (on microfilm, School of Oriental and African Studies Library, University of London)

Southern African Archives, Borthwick Institute of Historical Research, University of York

Trotsky Archives, Houghton Library, Harvard University

Unity Movement of South Africa Papers, Manuscripts and Archives Department, University of Cape Town Libraries

Workers' Party of South Africa Papers, Mayibuye Centre Historical Papers Archive, University of the Western Cape

Workers' Party of South Africa Papers, Historical Papers Library, University of the Witwatersrand

Newspapers and periodicals

A.P.O.
Bolshevik
Cape Times
Communist Review
Discussion
Forward
Freedom
Guardian
Illustrated Star: Town and Country Journal
Inkululeko/Freedom
Inkundla ya Bantu/People's Forum
Internal Bulletin of the Fourth International Organisation of South Africa
International
International Press Correspondence
Inyaniso/Voice of African Youth
Justice
Labour Leader
Liberator
Militant
Militant Worker
New Leader
Progressive Trade Union Bulletin
Socialist Action
South African Socialist Review
South African News Weekly Edition
Spark
Torch (1923)
Torch (1940s)
Trek
Umlilo Mollo/Flame
Umsebenzi/South African Worker
Umvikele-Thebe/African Defender
Workers' Dreadnought
Workers' Herald
Workers' Voice (1930s and 1940s)
Workers' International League Internal Bulletin
Young Worker

Interviews by author

Neville Alexander, Cape Town, July 1987
Lilian Dubb, Cape Town, July 1999
R. O. Dudley, Cape Town, April 1988
Ali Fataar, Harare, December 1987
Minnie Gool Friedrichs, Cape Town, July 1999
Millie Haston, London, May 1991
Solly Herwitz, Cape Town, March 1988
Baruch Hirson, London, March 1987
Hosea Jaffe, London, February 1987
Kenny Jordaan, Harare, December 1987
Jack and Ray Simons, Cape Town, October 1994
I. B. Tabata and Jane Gool, Harare, December 1987
Charlie van Gelderen, Cottenham, July 1997
Herman van Gelderen, Cape Town, September 1989

Other interviews

Charlie van Gelderen by Baruch Hirson and Brian Willan, 1974, School of Oriental and African Studies, University of London, tape 837
R. O. Dudley by Rosemary Neale, Cape Town, 13 July 1994
Moses Kotane by Sonia Bunting, October 1972, Brian Bunting Collection, 8.2.2.1, Mayibuye Centre Historical Papers Archive.
Edwin Mofutsanyana by Robert Edgar, Roma, Lesotho, July 1981
Josie Palmer [Mpama] by Julie Wells, Orlando West, 19 and 26 October 1977, Institute of Commonwealth Studies, University of London
Jack Simons by Brian Bunting, c. November 1973, Brian Bunting Collection 8.4.1, Mayibuye Centre Historical Papers Archive

Books and pamphlets

Abrahams, Peter, *Tell Freedom: Memories of Africa*, London: Faber & Faber, 1954.
Andrews, W. H., *Class Struggles in South Africa: Two Lectures Given on South African Trade Unionism*, Cape Town, 1941.
Ballinger, Margaret, *From Union to Apartheid: A Trek to Isolation*, Folkstone: Bailey Bros & Swinfen, 1969.
Ballinger, W. G. and M. L., *The British Protectorates in South Africa. Should they be transferred to the Union?*, [British] Labour Party, International Department, Advisory Committee on Imperial Questions, no. 155, April 1935.
Basner, Miriam, *Am I an African? The Political Memoirs of H. M. Basner*, Johannesburg: Witwatersrand, 1993.
Berger, Iris, *Threads of Solidarity: Women in South African Industry, 1900–1980*, Bloomington and Indianapolis: Indiana University and London: James Currey, 1992.
Bornstein, Sam and Al Richardson, *The War and the International: A History of the Trotskyist Movement in Britain 1937–1949*, London: Socialist Platform, 1986.

Bradford, Helen, *A Taste of Freedom: The ICU in Rural South Africa, 1924–1930*, New Haven and London: Yale, 1987.

Brittain, Vera, *Testament of Friendship: The Story of Winifred Holtby* [1940], London: Virago, 1980.

Bunting, Brian, *The Rise of the South African Reich*, Harmondsworth, Middlesex: Penguin, 1969.

Bunting, Brian, *Moses Kotane: South African Revolutionary*, London: Inkululeko, 1975.

Bunting, Brian, ed., *South African Communists Speak: Documents from the History of the South African Communist Party 1915–1980*, London: Inkululeko, 1981.

Bunting, Brian, ed., *Letters to Rebecca: South African Communist Leader S. P. Bunting to his Wife, 1917–1934*, Bellville: Mayibuye, 1996.

Bunting, S. P., *'Red Revolt': The Rand Strike, January-March, 1922*, CPSA: Johannesburg, 1922.

Callinicos, Luli, *Gold and Workers, 1886–1924*, Johannesburg: Ravan, 1981.

Callinicos, Luli, *Working Life: Factories, Townships, and Popular Culture on the Rand, 1886–1940*, Johannesburg: Ravan, 1987.

Carr, E. H., *The Twilight of Comintern, 1930–1935*, London and Basingstoke: Macmillan, 1982.

Claudin, Fernando, *The Communist Movement: From Comintern to Cominform*, part 1, New York and London: Monthly Review, 1975.

Coleman, Stephen, *Daniel De Leon*, Manchester and New York: Manchester University, 1990.

Cope, R. K., *Comrade Bill: The Life and Times of W. H. Andrews, Workers' Leader*, Cape Town: Stewart, 1944.

Cronwright-Schreiner, S. C., *The Life of Olive Schreiner*, London, T. Fisher Unwin, 1924.

Davids, A., 'A Critical Analysis of I. B. Tabata's Book – *The All-African Convention*', Cape Town: Forum Club, [1950].

Davidson, Basil, *Let Freedom Come: Africa in Modern History*, Boston and Toronto: Little Brown, 1978.

Davies, Robert H., *Capital, State and White Labour in South Africa 1900–1960: An Historical Materialist Analysis of Class Formation and Class Relations*, Brighton, Sussex: Harvester, 1979.

De Leon, Daniel, *Two Pages from Roman History: Plebs Leaders and Labour Leaders; The Warning of the Gracchi*, Edinburgh: Socialist Labour Press, 1908.

Drew, Allison, ed., *South Africa's Radical Tradition: A Documentary History*, vol. 1, Cape Town: Buchu, Mayibuye and University of Cape Town, 1996.

Drew, Allison, ed., *South Africa's Radical Tradition: A Documentary History*, vol. 2, Cape Town: Buchu, Mayibuye and University of Cape Town, 1997.

Dubofsky, Melvyn, *'Big Bill' Haywood*, Manchester: Manchester University, 1987.

Dubow, Saul, *Racial Segregation and the Origins of Apartheid in South Africa, 1919–36*, Basingstoke and London: MacMillan, 1989.

Edgar, Robert R., ed., *An African American in South Africa: The Travel Notes of Ralph J. Bunche: 28 September 1937 – 1 January 1938*, Athens, OH: Ohio University and Johannesburg: Witwatersrand University, 1992.

Figes, Orlando, *A People's Tragedy: The Russian Revolution, 1891–1924*, London: Pimlico, 1996.

Fine, Robert with Dennis Davis, *Beyond Apartheid: Labour and Liberation in South Africa*, London and Concord, MA: Pluto, 1991.

First, Ruth and Ann Scott, *Olive Schreiner: A Biography*, New Brunswick, NJ: Rutgers University, 1990.

Forman, Sadie and André Odendaal, eds, *A Trumpet from the Housetops: the Selected Writings of Lionel Forman*, London: Zed, Athens, OH: Ohio University, and Cape Town: David Philip and Bellville: Mayibuye, 1992.

Forman, Lionel, *Chapters in the History of the March to Freedom*, New Age, 1959.

Gandhi, M. K., *Satyagraha in South Africa*, Ahmedabad 14: Navajivan, 1972.

Ginwala, Frene, *Indian South Africans*, London: Minority Rights Group Report No. 34, 1977.

Gould, Stephen Jay, *Wonderful Life: The Burgess Shale and the Nature of History*, London: Penguin, 1991.

Hardy, George, *Those Stormy Years: Memoirs of the Fight for Freedom in Five Countries*, London: Lawrence & Wishart, 1956.

Harmel, Ray Adler, *Ray's Story*, unpublished memoirs, London, January 1993.

Harrison, Wilfred H., *Memoirs of a Socialist in South Africa 1903–1947*, Cape Town, 1948.

Herd, Norman, *1922: The Revolt on the Rand*, Johannesburg: Blue Crane, 1966.

Hirson, Baruch, *Yours for the Union: Class and Community Struggles in South Africa*, London: Zed and Johannesburg: Witwatersrand University, 1989.

Hirson, Baruch, *Revolutions in My Life*, Johannesburg: Witwatersrand University Press, 1995.

Hirson, Baruch and Gwyn A. Williams, *The Delegate for Africa: David Ivon Jones, 1883–1924*, London: Core, 1995.

Hommel, Maurice, *Capricorn Blues: the Struggle for Human Rights in South Africa*, Toronto: Culturama, 1981.

Howell, David, *British Workers and the Independent Labour Party, 1888–1906*, Manchester: Manchester University and New York: St Martin's, 1983.

James, C. L. R., *World Revolution 1917–1936: The Rise and Fall of the Communist International*, London: Martin Secker & Warburg, 1937.

Jeeves, Alan H., *Migrant Labour in South Africa's Mining Economy: the Struggle for the Gold Mines' Labour Supply, 1890–1920*, Kingston and Montreal: McGill-Queen's University and Johannesburg: Witwatersrand University, 1985.

Johanningsmeier, Edward P., *Forging American Communism: The Life of William Z. Foster*, Princeton: Princeton University, 1994.

Johns, Sheridan, *Raising the Red Flag: The International Socialist League and the Communist Party of South Africa, 1914–1932*, Bellville: Mayibuye, 1995.

Johnstone, Frederick A., *Class, Race and Gold: A Study of Class Relations and Racial Discrimination in South Africa*, London: Routledge & Kegan Paul, 1976.

Kadalie, Clements, *My Life and the ICU: the Autobiography of a Black Trade Unionist in South Africa*, ed. by Stanley Trapido, London: Frank Cass, 1970.

Karis, Thomas and Gwendolen M. Carter, eds, *From Protest to Challenge: A Documentary History of African Politics in South Africa 1882–1964*, vol. 1, Stanford, CA: Hoover Institution, 1972.

Karis, Thomas and Gwendolen M. Carter, eds, *From Protest to Challenge: A Documentary History of African Politics in South Africa 1882–1964*, vol. 2, Stanford, CA: Hoover Institution, 1973.

Karis, Thomas and Gwendolen M. Carter, eds, *From Protest to Challenge: A Documentary History of African Politics in South Africa 1882–1964*, vol. 4, Stanford, CA: Hoover Institution, 1977.

Katz, Elaine N., *A Trade Union Aristocracy: A History of White Workers in the Transvaal and the General Strike of 1913*, Johannesburg: African Studies Institute, University of the

Witwatersrand, 1976.

Keegan, Timothy, *Rural Transformations in Industrializing South Africa: the Southern Highveld to 1914*, Braamfontein: Ravan, 1986, 22;

Kotkin, Stephen, *Magnetic Mountain: Stalinism as a Civilization*, Berkeley, Los Angeles and London: University of California, 1995.

Kuzwayo, Ellen, *Call Me Woman*, London: Women's Press, 1985.

La Guma, Alex, *Jimmy La Guma: A Biography*, ed. by Mohamed Adhikari, Cape Town: Friends of the South African Library, 1997.

Lazerson, Joshua N., *Against the Tide: Whites in the Struggle Against Apartheid*, Boulder, San Franciso and Oxford: Westview and Bellville: Mayibuye, 1994.

Lazitch, Branko in collaboration with Milorad M. Drachkovitch, *Biographical Dictionary of the Comintern: New Revised, and Expanded Edition*, Stanford: Hoover, 1986.

Lee, Franz J. T., *Der Einfluss des Marxismus auf die Nationalen Befreiungsbewegungen in Sudafrika*, Frankfurt am Main: Selbstverlag, 1971.

Lee, Franz J. T., *Sudafrika vor der Revolution?*, Frankfurt am Main: Fischer Taschenbuch Verlag, 1973.

Lerumo, A. [Michael Harmel], *Fifty Fighting Years: The Communist Party of South Africa 1921–1971*, London: Inkululeko, 1971.

Levy, Norman, *The Foundations of the South African Cheap Labour System*, London and Boston: Routledge & Kegan Paul, 1982.

Lewis, Ethelreda, *Wild Deer* [1933], Cape Town: David Philip, 1984.

Lewis, Gavin, *Between the Wire and the Wall: A History of South African 'Coloured' Politics*, Cape Town and Johannesbug: David Philip, 1987.

Lewis, Jon, *Industrialisation and Trade Union Organisation in South Africa, 1924–55*, Cambridge: Cambridge University, 1984.

Lodge, Tom, *Black Politics in South Africa since 1945*, London and New York: Longman, 1983.

Luxemburg, Rosa, *The Accumulation of Capital*, New York and London: Monthly Review, 1968.

Macintyre, Stuart, *A Proletarian Science: Marxism in Britain, 1917–1933*, Cambridge: Cambridge University, 1980.

MacMillan, W. M., *The South African Agrarian Problem and its Historical Development*, Johannesburg: Council of Education, Witwatersrand, 1919.

MacMillan, W. M., *Africa Emergent: A Survey of Social, Political and Economic Trends in British Africa*, Harmondsworth, Middlesex: Penguin, 1949.

Majeke, Nosipho [Dora Taylor], *The Role of the Missionaries in Conquest*, Cape Town: Society of Young Africa, 1952.

Marks, Shula, *The Ambiguities of Dependence in South Africa: Class, Nationalism and the State in Twentieth-century Natal*, Johannesburg: Ravan, 1986.

Martin, Roderick, *Communism and the British Trade Unions 1924–1933*, Oxford: Clarendon Press, 1969.

Marx, Karl, *Capital: A Critique of Political Economy*, vol. 1, edited by Frederick Engels, New York: International, 1967.

Mbeki, Govan, *South Africa: the Peasants' Revolt*, Harmondsworth, Middlesex: Penguin, 1964.

McDermott, Kevin and Jeremy Agnew, *The Comintern: A History of International Communism from Lenin to Stalin*, Basingstoke and London: Macmillan, 1996.

Mnguni [Hosea Jaffe], *Three Hundred Years*, Cape Town: 1952.

Mokgatle, Naboth, *The Autobiography of an Unknown South African*, Parklands: A. D. Donker, 1971.

Mokone, Sarah [Victor Wessels], *Majority Rule: Some Notes*, Cape Town: Teachers' League of South Africa, 1982.

Montefiore, Dora, *From a Victorian to a Modern*, London: E. Archer, 1927.

Musson, Doreen, *Johnny Gomas, Voice of the Working Class: A Political Biography*, Cape Town: Buchu, 1989.

Nasson, Bill, *Abraham Esau's War: A Black South African War in the Cape, 1899–1902*, Cambridge: Cambridge University, 1991.

Ngubane, Jordan K., *Should the Natives Representative Council be Abolished?*, Pro and Con Pamphlet-No. 4, Cape Town: African Bookman, 1946.

Nzula, A. T., I. I. Potekhin and A. Z. Zusmanovich, *Forced Labour in Colonial Africa*, ed. and intro. by Robin Cohen, London: Zed, 1979.

Odendaal, André, *Vukani Bantu! The Beginnings of Black Protest Politics in South Africa to 1912*, Cape Town and Johannesburg: David Philip, 1984.

Pelling, Henry, *The British Communist Party: A Historical Profile*, London: Adam and Charles Black, 1958.

Plaatje, Solomon, *Native Life in South Africa*, ed. by Brian Willan, Burnt Mill, Harlow: Longman, 1987.

Podbrey, Pauline, *White Girl in Search of the Party*, Pietermaritzburg: Hadeda, 1993.

Robeson, Eslanda Goode, *African Journey*, London: Victor Gollancz, 1946.

Roux, Edward, *Time Longer than Rope* [1948], 2nd edition, Wisconsin: University of Wisconsin, 1964.

Roux, Edward, *S. P. Bunting: A Political Biography* [1944], Bellville: Mayibuye, 1993.

Roux, Eddie and Win, *Rebel Pity: The Life of Eddie Roux*, London: Rex Collings, 1970.

Sachs, Bernard, *Multitude of Dreams: A Semi-Autobiographical Study*, Johannesburg: Kayor, 1949.

Saville, John, unpublished memoirs, n.d.

Sbacchi, Alberto, *Ethiopia under Mussolini: Fascism and the Colonial Experience*, London: Zed, 1985.

Seton-Watson, Hugh, *The Russian Empire 1801–1917*, Oxford: Oxford University, 1967

Shimoni, Gideon, *Jews and Zionism: the South African Experience (1910–1967)*, Cape Town: Oxford University, 1980

Simons, Jack and Ray, *Class and Colour in South Africa 1850–1950* [1968], International Defence and Aid Fund for Southern Africa, 1983.

Singh, George, *The Asiatic Land Tenure and Indian Representation Act of South Africa*, Durban: Council for Human Rights, 1946.

Slovo, Gillian, *Every Secret Thing: My Family, My Country*, London: Little, Brown, 1997.

Slovo, Joe, *Slovo: The Unfinished Autobiography*, Randburg: Ravan, 1995 and London: Hodder & Stoughton, 1996.

South African Communist Party, *A Distant Clap of Thunder: Fortieth Anniversary of the 1946 Mine Strike*, 1986.

Tabata, I. B., *The Boycott as Weapon of Struggle*, [1952], Durban: APDUSA.

Through the Red Revolt on the Rand: A Pictorial Review of Events, January, February, March, 1922, compiled from photographs taken by representatives of *The Star*, Johannesburg: Central News Agency, 1922, 1st and 2nd editions.

Trotsky, Leon, 'The Permanent Revolution', [1930] in Leon Trotsky, *The Permanent Revolution and Results and Prospects*, London: New Park, 1962, 1–157.

Trotsky, Leon, *The Third International After Lenin*, London: New Park, 1974.

Trotsky, Leon, *Writings of Leon Trotsky*, 1934–35, New York: Pathfinder Press, 1974.

Trotsky, Leon, *Leon Trotsky Oeuvres Janvier 1935 – Juin 1935*, intro. by Pierre Broué and Michel Dreyfus, Paris: Institut Leon Trotsky/Etudes et Documentation Internationales, 1979.

Tsuzuki, Chushichi, *H. M. Hyndman and British Socialism*, Oxford: Oxford University, 1961.

Tsuzuki, Chushichi, *Tom Mann 1856–1941: The Challenges of Labour*, Oxford: Clarendon Press, 1991.

van der Post, Laurens, *In a Province*, London, The Hogarth Press, 1934.

van Onselen, Charles, *Studies in the Social and Economic History of the Witwatersrand 1886–1914*, vol. 2, Johannesburg: Ravan, 1982.

Walker, Cherryl, *Women and Resistance in South Africa*, London: Onyx, 1982.

Walker, Ivan L. and Ben Weinbren, *2000 Casualties: A History of the Trade Unions and the Labour Movement in the Union of South Africa*, Johannesburg: SATUC, 1961.

Walshe, Peter, *The Rise of African Nationalism in South Africa: the African National Congress, 1912–1952*, London: Hurst & Co., 1970.

Wasserstein, Bernard, *Herbert Samuel: A Political Life*, Oxford: Clarendon, 1992.

Wickens, P. L., *The Industrial and Commercial Workers' Union of Africa*, Cape Town: Oxford University, 1978.

Willan, Brian, *Sol Plaatje: South African Nationalist, 1876–1932*, London, Ibadan, Nairobi: Heinemann, 1984.

Articles and chapters

Adler, Taffy, 'The Class Struggle in Doornfontein: A History of the Johannesburg Jewish Workers' Club, 1928–1950', Paper presented at the African Studies Seminar, University of the Witwatersrand, 23 August 1976.

Alexander, Neville, 'Aspects of Non-Collaboration in the Western Cape 1943–1963', *Social Dynamics*, 12, 1, 1986, 1–14.

Beinart, William and Colin Bundy, 'State Intervention and Rural Resistance: The Transkei, 1900–1965', in Martin A. Klein, ed., *Peasants in Africa: Historical and Contemporary Perspectives*, Beverly Hills and London: Sage, 1980, 270–315.

Bonner, P. L., 'The 1920 Black Mineworkers' Strike: a Preliminary Account', in Belinda Bozzoli, comp., *Labour, Townships and Protest: Studies in the Social History of the Witwatersrand*, Johannesburg: Ravan, 1979, 273–97.

Bonner, Philip, 'The Transvaal Native Congress, 1917–1920: the Radicalisation of the Black Petty Bourgeoisie on the Rand', in Shula Marks and Richard Rathbone, eds, *Industrialisation and Social Change in South Africa*, London: Longman, 1982, 270–313.

Brookes, Edgar H., 'Government and Administration', in Ellen Hellmann, ed., *Handbook on Race Relations in South Africa*, Cape Town, London and New York: Oxford University, 1949, 27–40.

Callinicos, Luli, 'The Communist Party During the War Years', *South African Labour Bulletin*, 15, 3, September 1990, 101–5.

Davenport, T. R. H., 'The Consolidation of a New Society: the Cape Colony', in Monica Wilson and Leonard Thompson, eds, *A History of South Africa to 1870*, London and Canberra: Croom Helm, 1982, 272–333.

Davies, Robert, 'The White Working-Class in South Africa', *New Left Review*, 82, November–December 1973, 40–59.

Davies, Robert, 'Mining Capital, the State and Unskilled White Workers in South Africa,

1901–1913', *Journal of Southern African Studies*, 3, 1, October 1976, 41–69.

Davies, Robert, 'The 1922 Strike on the Rand: White Labor and the Political Economy of South Africa', in Peter Gutkind, R. Cohen and J. Copans, eds, *African Labour History*, Beverly Hills and London: Sage, 1978, 80–108.

Davies, Rob, 'The 1922 Strike and the Political Economy of South Africa', in Belinda Bozzoli, comp., *Labour, Townships and Protest: Studies in the Social History of the Witwatersrand*, Johannesburg: Ravan, 1979, 298–324.

Department of Economics, Natal University College, 'The National Income and the Non-European', in Ellen Hellmann, ed., *Handbook on Race Relations in South Africa*, Cape Town, London and New York: Oxford University, 1949, 306–47.

Dimitrov, George, 'The Fascist Offensive and the Tasks of the Communist International in the Struggle of the Working Class Against Fascism: Main Report delivered at the Seventh World Congress of the Communist International, August 2, 1935', in George Dimitrov, *Against Fascism and War*, New York: International Publishers, 1986, 1–94.

Draper, Hal and Anne G. Lipow, 'Marxist Women versus Bourgeois Feminism', in Ralph Miliband and John Saville, eds, *The Socialist Register 1976*, London: Merlin, 1976, 179–226.

Drew, Allison, 'Events were Breaking above their Heads: Socialism in South Africa, 1921–1950', *Social Dynamics*, 17, 1, June 1991, 49–77.

Drew, Allison, 'Theory and Practice of the Agrarian Question in South African Socialism, 1928–60', *Journal of Peasant Studies*, 23, 2/3, January–April 1996, 53–92.

Edwards, Iain, 'Recollections: the Communist Party and Worker Militancy in Durban, early 1940', *South African Labour Bulletin*, 11, 4, February–March 1986, 65–84.

Elphick, Richard and Hermann Giliomée, 'The Origins and Entrenchment of European Dominance at the Cape, 1652 – c.1840', in Richard Elphick and Hermann Giliomée, eds, *The Shaping of South African Society, 1652–1840*, 2nd edition, Cape Town: Maskew Miller Longman, 1989, 521–66.

Ervin, Charles Wesley, 'Trotskyism in India, Part One: Origins through World War Two (1934–45)', *Revolutionary History*, 1, 4, Winter 1988–89, 22–34.

Everatt, David, 'Alliance Politics of a Special Type: the Roots of the ANC/SACP Alliance, 1950–1954', *Journal of Southern African Studies*, 18, 1, March 1991, 19–39.

Furlong, Patrick J., 'The Bonds of War: the African National Congress, the Communist Party of South Africa and the Threat of "Fascism"', *South African Historical Journal*, 36, May 1997, 68–87.

Hale, Frederick, 'Socialist Agitator, Traitor to the British Empire, or Angel of Peace? James Keir Hardie's Visit to Natal in 1908', *Journal of Natal and Zulu History*, XIV, 1992, 1–18.

Hellman, Ellen, 'Urban Areas', in Ellen Hellmann, ed., *Handbook on Race Relations in South Africa*, Cape Town, London and New York: Oxford University, 1949, 229–74.

Hill, Robert A. and Gregory A. Pirio, '"Africa for the Africans": the Garvey Movement in South Africa, 1920–1940', in Shula Marks and Stanley Trapido, eds, *The Politics of Race, Class and Nationalism in Twentieth-Century South Africa*, London and New York: Longman, 1987, 209–53.

Hirson, Baruch, 'Not Pro-war, and not Anti-war: Just Indifferent. South African Blacks in the Second World War', *Critique*, 20–21, 1987, 39–56.

Hirson, Baruch, 'Death of a Revolutionary: Frank Glass/Li Fu-Jen/John Liang 1901–1988', *Searchlight South Africa*, 1, September 1988, 28–41.

Hirson, Baruch, '*Spark* and the "Red Nun"', *Searchlight South Africa*, 1, 2, February 1989, 65–78.

Hirson, Baruch, 'Bunting vs. Bukharin: the "Native Republic" Slogan', *Searchlight South Africa*, 3, July 1989, 51–65.

Hirson, Baruch, 'The Black Republic Slogan – Part II: the Response of the Trotskyists', *Searchlight South Africa*, 4, February 1990, 44–56.

Hirson, Baruch, 'Trotsky and Black Nationalism', in Terry Brotherstone and Paul Dukes, eds., *The Trotsky Reappraisal*, Edinburgh: Edinburgh University, 1992, 177–90.

Hirson, Baruch, 'Profiles of Some South African Trotskyists', *Revolutionary History*, 4, 4, Spring 1993, 93–7.

Hirson, Baruch, 'The Trotskyist Groups in South Africa', *Revolutionary History*, 4, 4, Spring 1993, 25–56.

Hirson, Baruch, 'The Trotskyists and the Trade Unions', *Revolutionary History*, 4, 4, Spring 1993, 84–92.

Hirson, Baruch, 'The General Strike of 1922', *Searchlight South Africa*, 3, 3, October 1993, 63–94.

Hofmeyr, Willie, 'Rural Popular Organisation Problems: Struggles in the Western Cape, 1929–1930', *Africa Perspective*, 1983, 26–49.

Hunter, Ian, 'Raff Lee and the Pioneer Trotskyists of Johannesburg', *Revolutionary History*, 4, 4, Spring 1993, 57–83.

Hyslop, Jonathan, 'White Working-class Women and the Invention of Apartheid: "Purified" Afrikaner Nationalist Agitation for Legislation against "Mixed" Marriages, 1934–9', *Journal of African History*, 36, 1995, 57–81.

Johns, Sheridan, 'The Comintern, South Africa and the Black Diaspora', *Review of Politics*, 37, 2, 1975, 200–234.

Johns, Sheridan, 'The Birth of the Communist Party of South Africa', *The International Journal of African Historical Studies*, 9, 3, 1976, 371–400.

Johnstone, Frederick , 'The IWA on the Rand', in Belinda Bozzoli, comp., *Labour, Townships and Protest: Studies in the Social History of the Witwatersrand*, Johannesburg: Ravan, 1979, 248–72.

Jones, Elizabeth Ceiriog, 'Inkululeko: Organ of the Communist Party of South Africa, 1939–1950', in Les Switzer, ed., *South Africa's Alternative Press*, Cambridge: Cambridge University, 1997, 331–72.

Jones, David Ivon, 'Communism in South Africa' [Part 2], *Communist Review*, 1, 4, August 1921, 63–71.

Jordaan, K. A., 'The Land Question in South Africa', *Points of View*, 1, 1, October 1959, 3–45.

Kanet, Roger E., 'The Comintern and the "Negro Question": Communist Policy in the United States and Africa, 1921–41', *Survey*, 1973, 19, 4, 86–122.

Kelley, Robin D. G., 'The Religious Odyssey of African Radicals: Notes on the Communist Party of South Africa, 1921–34', *Radical History Review*, 51, 1991, 5–24.

Klepfisz, Irena, '*Di mames, dos loshn*/The mothers, the language: Feminism, *Yidshkayt*, and the Politics of Memory', *Bridges*, 4, 1, Winter/Spring 1994, 12–47.

Krikler, Jeremy, 'William MacMillan and the Working Class', in Hugh MacMillan and Shula Marks, eds., *Africa and Empire: W. M. MacMillan, Historian and Social Critic*, London: University of London, Institute of Commonwealth Studies, 1989, 35–71.

Krikler, Jeremy, 'Women, Violence and the Rand Revolt of 1922', *Journal of Southern African Studies*, 22, 3, September 1996, 349–72.

Krikler, Jeremy, 'The Commandos: The Army of White Labour in South Africa.' *Past and Present*, 163, 1999, 202–44.

Legassick, Martin, 'Class and Nationalism in South African Protest: the South African Communist Party and the "Native Republic," 1928–1934', *Eastern African Studies*, 15, July 1973.

Lenin, V. I., 'What is to be Done?' [1902], in Henry M. Christman, ed., *Essential Works of Lenin*, New York, Toronto, London: Bantam, 1966, 53–175.

Lenin, V. I., 'Imperialism, the Highest Stage of Capitalism' [1916], in Henry M. Christman, ed., *Essential Works of Lenin*, New York, Toronto, London: Bantam, 1966, 177–270.

Lodge, Tom, 'Class Conflict, Communal Struggle and Patriotic Unity: the Communist Party of South African during the Second World War', paper presented to the African Studies Seminar, African Studies Institute, University of the Witwatersrand, 7 October 1985.

Lodge, Tom, 'Political Organisations in Pretoria's African Townships, 1940–1963', in Belinda Bozzoli, ed., *Class, Community and Conflict: South African Perspectives*, Johannesburg: Ravan, 1987, 401–17.

MacMillan, W. M., 'The Truth about the Strike on the Rand', *New Statesman*, 19, 474, 13 May 1922, 145–6.

Mantzaris, E. A., 'The Promise of the Impossible Revolution: The Cape Town Industrial Socialist League, 1918–1921', *Studies in the History of Cape Town*, 4, 1981, 145–73.

Mantzaris, Evangelos A., 'The Indian Tobacco Workers Strike of 1920: A Socio-Historical Investigation', *Journal of Natal and Zulu History*, 6, 1983, 115–25.

Mantzaris, E. A., 'Radical Community: The Yiddish-speaking Branch of the International Socialist League, 1918–1920' in Belinda Bozzoli, ed., *Class, Community and Conflict: South African Perspectives*, Johannesburg: Ravan, 1987, 160–76.

Meer, Fatima, 'Indentured Labour and Group Formations in Apartheid Society', *Race and Class*, 26, 4, 45–60.

Morgan, Kevin, 'Harry Pollitt, the British Communist Party and International Communism', unpublished paper, 1997.

Nasson, Bill, 'The Unity Movement: Its Legacy in Historical Consciousness', *Radical History Review*, 46/7, 1990, 189–211.

Nyawuza, 'The Road to the "Black Republic" in South Africa', *African Communist*, 122, 3rd quarter 1990, 42–50.

Nyawuza, 'Left, Right on the Road to the Black Republic', *African Communist*, 123, 4th quarter 1990, 52–61.

O'Meara, Dan, 'The 1946 African Mine Workers' Strike and the Political Economy of South Africa', *Journal of Commonwealth and Comparative Politics*, 13, 2, July 1975, 146–73.

Padayachee, Vishnu, Shahid Vawda and Paul Tichmann, 'Trade Unions and the Communist Party in Durban in the 1940's: A Reply to Iain Edwards', *South African Labour Bulletin*, 11, 7, August 1986, 50–66.

Philips, John, 'The South African Wobblies: the Origins of Industrial Unions in South Africa', *Ufahamu*, 8, 3, 1978, 122–38.

Plekhanov, G., 'Second Draft Programme of the Russian Social-Democrats' [1887], *Selected Philosophical Works*, vol. 1, London: Lawrence & Wishart, 1961, 406–10.

Robinson, D., 'To a Non-European Intellectual', *Trek*, 31 July 1942, 9.

Rosefielde, Steven, 'Documented Homicides and Excess Deaths: New Insights into the Scale of Killing in the USSR during the 1930s', *Communist and Post-Communist Studies*, 30, 3, 1997, 321–31.

Roux, Edward, '1922 and All That', *Trek*, 11 February 1944, 12.

Roux, Edward, 'Land and Agriculture in the Native Reserves', in Ellen Hellmann, ed., *Handbook on Race Relations in South Africa*, Cape Town, London and New York: Oxford

University, 1949, 171–90.

Rowbotham, Sheila, 'Rebel Networks in the First World War', *Friends of Alice Wheeldon*, London: Pluto, 1986, 5–107.

Sachs, Bernard, 'The City Hall Steps', *South African Personalities and Places*, Johannesburg: Kayor, 1959, 118–21.

Saville, John, 'Obituary: Robin Page Arnot', *Society for the Study of Labour History Bulletin*, 51, 3, November 1986, 3–5.

Simons, Mary, 'Organised Coloured Political Movements', in Hendrik W. van der Merwe and C. J. Groenewald, eds, *Occupational and Social Change among Coloured People in South Africa*, Cape Town: Juta, 1976, 202–37.

Simson, Howard, 'The Myth of the White Working Class in South Africa', *The African Review*, 4, 2, 1974, 189–203.

Sonnabend, H., 'Population', in Ellen Hellmann, ed., *Handbook on Race Relations in South Africa*, Cape Town, London and New York: Oxford University, 1949, 4–26.

Stadler, Alf, 'A Long Way to Walk: Bus Boycotts in Alexandra, 1940–1945', in P. Bonner, ed., *Working Papers in Southern African Studies*, vol. 2, Johannesburg: Ravan, 1981, 228–57.

Stein, Mark, 'Max Gordon and African Trade Unionism on the Witwatersrand, 1935–1940', in Eddie Webster, ed., *Essays in Southern African Labour History*, Johannesburg: Ravan, 1978, 143–57.

Studer, Brigitte and Berthold Unfried, 'At the Beginning of a History: Visions of the Comintern After the Opening of the Archives', *International Review of Social History*, 42, 1997, 419–46.

Swan, Maureen, 'Ideology in Organised Indian Politics, 1891–1948', in Shula Marks and Stanley Trapido, eds, *The Politics of Race, Class and Nationalism in Twentieth-Century South Africa*, London and New York: Longman, 182–208.

Switzer, Les, 'Socialism and the Resistance Movement: the Life and Times of the Guardian, 1937–1952', in Les Switzer, ed., *South Africa's Alternative Press*, Cambridge: Cambridge University, 1997, 266–307.

Taylor, Dora, 'Education for Democracy – First Stage', *Trek*, 16 January 1941, 7.

Thorpe, Andrew, 'Comintern "Control" of the Communist Party of Great Britain, 1920–43', *English Historical Review*, June 1998, 637–62.

Trotsky, Leon, 'Ninety Years of the Communist Manifesto', in Isaac Deutscher, ed., *The Age of Permanent Revolution: A Trotsky Anthology*, New York: Dell, 1964, 285–95.

van der Horst, Sheila T., 'Labour', in Ellen Hellmann, ed., *Handbook on Race Relations in South Africa*, Cape Town, London and New York: Oxford University, 1949, 109–57.

Walker, Cherryl, 'The Women's Suffrage Movement: the Politics of Gender, Race and Class', in Cherryl Walker, ed., *Women and Gender in Southern Africa to 1945*, Cape Town: David Philip and London: James Currey, 1990, 313–45.

Webb, Maurice, 'Indian Land Legislation', in Ellen Hellmann, ed., *Handbook on Race Relations in South Africa*, Cape Town, London and New York: Oxford University, 1949, 206–13.

Wilson, Monica, 'Co-operation and Conflict: the Eastern Cape Frontier', in Monica Wilson and Leonard Thompson, eds, *A History of South Africa to 1870*, London and Canberra: Croom Helm, 1982, 233–71.

Witz, Leslie, 'A Case of Schizophrenia: the Rise and Fall of the Independent Labour Party', in Belinda Bozzoli, ed., *Class, Community and Conflict: South African Perspectives*, Johannesburg: Ravan, 1987, 261–91.

Wolpe, Harold, 'The "White Working Class" in South Africa', *Economy and Society*, 5, 2, 1976, 197–240.

Yeo, Stephen, 'A New Life: the Religion of Socialism in Britain, 1883–1896', *History Workshop*, 4, Autumn 1997, 5–56.

Dissertations and theses

Everatt, David, 'The Politics of Non-racialism: White Opposition to Apartheid, 1945–1960', DPhil, University of Oxford, 1990.

Everett, Elizabeth, 'Zainunnissa (Cissie) Gool, 1897–1963: A Biography', BA Honours, University of Cape Town, October 1978.

Grossman, Jonathan, 'Class Relations and the Policies of the Communist Party of South Africa, 1921–1950', PhD, University of Warwick, 1985.

Hofmeyr, Willie, 'Agricultural Crisis and Rural Organisation in the Cape: 1929–1933', MA, University of Cape Town, 1985.

Mason, David J., 'Race, Class and National Liberation: Some Implications of the Policy Dilemmas of the International Socialist League and the Communist Party of South Africa, 1915–1931', MSc, University of Bristol, 1971.

Ntsebeza, Lungisile, 'Divisions and Unity in Struggle: The ANC, ISL and the CP, 1910–1928', BA Honours, University of Cape Town, January 1988.

Southall, A. J., 'Marxist Theory in South Africa until 1940', MA, University of York, 1978.

Index